QUEER INCLUSIONS, CONTINENTAL DIVISIONS

Public Recognition of Sexual Diversity in Canada
and the United States

No area of public policy and law has seen more change in recent years than that of lesbian, gay, bisexual, and transgender rights. *Queer Inclusions, Continental Divisions* explores the politics of sexual diversity in Canada and the United States by analysing three contentious issues – relationship recognition, parenting, and schooling. Focusing on long-standing debates on these issues in the two countries, the book provides a much-needed comparative study of national policies and practices while paying close attention to regional differences.

David Rayside's examination of developments in the public recognition of sexual minorities is based on extensive quantitative analysis, as well as on a broad survey of media, legal, and social science accounts. Rayside explores the relatively early success in Canada in regard to policy change on relationship recognition and parenting. At the same time, he points to pioneering efforts by American LGBT activists, an impressive number of successful court challenges by American lesbian and gay parents, and reforms in schooling in the United States that, while still modest, are on the whole more substantial than those instituted within Canada.

A timely and informative examination of controversial policy areas, *Queer Inclusions, Continental Divisions* provides a comprehensive record and a reasoned assessment of the progress of sexual diversity issues in North America.

DAVID RAYSIDE is a professor in the Department of Political Science and director of the Mark S. Bonham Centre for Sexual Diversity Studies at the University of Toronto.

DAVID RAYSIDE

# Queer Inclusions, Continental Divisions

## Public Recognition of Sexual Diversity in Canada and the United States

UNIVERSITY OF TORONTO PRESS
Toronto   Buffalo   London

© University of Toronto Press Incorporated 2008
Toronto Buffalo London
Printed in Canada

ISBN 978-0-8020-8945-8 (cloth)
ISBN 978-0-8020-8629-7 (paper)

Printed on acid-free paper

**Library and Archives Canada Cataloguing in Publication**

Rayside, David M. (David Morton), 1947–
    Queer inclusions, continental divisions : public recognition of sexual diversity
in Canada and the United States / David Rayside.

    Includes bibliographical references and index.
    ISBN 978-0-8020-8945-8 (bound).  ISBN 978-0-8020-8629-7 (pbk.)

    1. Gay rights – Canada.   2. Gay rights – United States.   3. Homosexuality
– Political aspects – Canada.   4. Homosexuality – Political aspects – United
States.   I. Title.

HQ73.3.N67R39 2007        306.76'60971        C2007-906326-8

This book has been published with the help of a grant from the Canadian
Federation for the Humanities and Social Sciences, through the Aid to
Scholarly Publications Programme, using funds provided by the Social
Sciences and Humanities Research Council of Canada.

University of Toronto Press acknowledges the financial assistance to its
publishing program of the Canada Council for the Arts and the Ontario Arts
Council.

University of Toronto Press acknowledges the financial support for its
publishing activities of the Government of Canada through the
Book Publishing Industry Development Program (BPIDP).

*dedicated to a remarkable future for the*
*Mark S. Bonham Centre for Sexual Diversity Studies*

# Contents

# Tables and Figures

**Tables**

**Figures**

# Preface

My original intentions for this book were quite different from the final result before you. This was to have been a comparative treatment of developments in British Columbia and the American Northwest (Washington State in particular). The idea was to focus on the stark cross-border differences in the public policy recognition of lesbian and gay relationships through the lens of two regions widely seen to have more in common with one another than with other regions in their own countries. The comparative analysis would allow for the exploration of regional variations in pro-equity activism, organized opposition, and political outcomes within the United States and Canada, and across the forty-ninth parallel.

My interest was piqued by the early recognition of same-sex relationships in BC legislation, especially when in 1995 the province became the first jurisdiction in the world to statutorily recognize gay and lesbian adoption rights, and again when major sections of family law were changed in 1997 to include same-sex couples. In the meantime, there were at best only small steps being taken in the same direction in Washington State. The legislature there had repeatedly baulked at the extension of even basic civil rights protections to gays and lesbians.

Shortly after I launched this project, a 1998 ruling by the Supreme Court of Canada generated heated controversy over gay rights in the province of Alberta, suggesting an expansion of my study to a three-point comparison. But at the end of the 1990s, the public recognition of sexual diversity in Canada was dramatically altered, and change was moving at a steady pace across the United States. These seemed to be powerful shifts in tectonic plates, calling for a broad exploration of developments across the continent, still framed by a comparison of the relative strength of regional and international differences. The task was challenging. At the outset, there were few overviews of the complex developments on the issues that mattered to me in the United States, and fewer in Canada. Some have since been published, but none with quite the broad view I sought or that took in the rich complexities required of a comprehensive analysis of these two countries. The important Canadian case seemed particularly elusive to comparative writers.

My work until now has been largely focused on detailed case studies. I have told stories that I hope have illuminated the entry of sexual diversity issues and activists into the political mainstream. I have done so not because I believe that formal recognition in law and policy is the only important goal of the lesbian/gay/bisexual/trans-gendered (LGBT) movement, but because I believe it is one of several important goals. The story of how some issues and some segments of the activist movement have gained a foothold in that arena, then, is one that I have tried to capture through interviews and close analysis of printed sources.

In this book I have moved away from telling very specific stories, though not entirely. I weave the elements of a broad chronology, but along the way I try to tell a few particular stories. Several come from the early work I completed in BC and Washington State; others from my own observations, media accounts, and published work.

I have been fortunate in my opportunities to participate in the process of securing public recognition of sexual diversity, locally in Toronto, provincially in Ontario, within my home institution (the University of Toronto), and throughout the broader academy. In that sense I write this book as an engaged scholar, but in so doing I also strive for an analytical and critical care that I hope marks my earlier work.

A project such as this incurs extraordinary debts. The original project from which this grew benefited from major funding provided by the Social Sciences and Humanities Research Council of Canada (SSHRC), supplemented by grants from the Department of Political Science and the Faculty of Arts and Science at the University of Toronto. The publication of this book has been assisted by a grant from the Canadian Federation for the Humanities and Social Sciences, through the Aid to Scholarly Publications Program (using funds provided by SSHRC).

The original project entailed confidential interviews with many activists, policy makers, academics, and journalists in BC, Washington

State, and Alberta, all of whom enriched my understanding of American and Canadian politics. My first analytical steps into the American Northwest were assisted by Professor David Olson (of the University of Washington), Bill Lunch and Brent Steel (both of Oregon State University), and Gary Moncrief and Stephanie Witt (both of Boise State University).

The collection of relevant documentation was assisted by Derek Leebosh (of Environics Research in Canada), Michah Rynor (then of the U of T's Department of Public Affairs), Mark Rupp, Stephen Wasby, Ed Nolan and the staff of the Washington State Historical Society Archives, Joan Barton and the staff of the BC Legislative Library, the staff of the Alberta Legislative Library, the City of Edmonton Archives, and the Washington State Legislative Archives, Ken Sherill, and the extraordinary pair of women (Jean Mayberry and the now-deceased Aleta Fenceroy) who for some years ran the LGBT news service 'fenceberry.'

Over the years I have received very able research assistance from Nicole Anastasopoulos, Cheryl Auger, Gina Cosentino, Sebastien Dallaire, Jim Farney, Adrian Guta, Patrick Hossais, Juan Marsiaj, Karen Murray, Julie Simmons, Dagmar Soenneken, Joerg Wittenbrinck, and Ruben Zaiotti, and more recently Cheryl Auger and the inimitable Robbie Morgan. For a variety of assistance on other fronts, I am indebted to Joe Boyle, Piet Defraeye, Terry Farley, Kathy Jenner, Jo Godfrey, Paul Perron, and Mariana Valverde.

Various friends and colleagues have commented on parts of this manuscript, and helped enormously. They include Angela Campbell, Charles Gossett, Mona Greenbaum, Kevin Jennings, Catherine Lugg, Miriam Smith, Steven Solomon, Morgan Vanek, Steve Wasby, Kris Wells, and the much-missed Tim Cook. Several conference papers received useful commentary from a variety of discussants and audience members in Toronto, and at meetings of the Canadian Lesbian and Gay Studies Association and the American Political Science Association.

Virgil Duff was my editor at the University of Toronto Press, and I join the long list of Canadian academics indebted to him for his support in seeing this book through its sometimes-difficult birth process. At an intermediate stage in its preparation, one anonymous American reviewer took great care to provide insightful and constructive criticisms. Closer to the end, three other reviewers also applied critical intelligence in responding to the manuscript, and the final product is stronger for their input. Charles Stuart's perceptive copy editing helped smooth out the prose edges of the manuscript.

For part of the time that I was preparing this book, I was Graduate Director and Associate Chair of the Department of Political Science. I could not have made any progress whatsoever on this book without the administrative assistance of Joan Kallis and Carolynn Branton, the overall support of Rita O'Brien, the department's business officer, and the encouragement of Rob Vipond, the best department chair an academic could hope to have.

For the entire life of this project, I have had the good fortune to form part of the leadership team of the Mark S. Bonham Centre for Sexual Diversity Studies. I owe a debt to the students in the undergraduate program, the community supporters of SDS, and my faculty colleagues. Maureen FitzGerald and Mark Bonham stand out, but the list of essential contributors is long. In my two earlier books, my old friend Judi Stevenson was a crucial editorial contributor. Her work commitments precluded that kind of role in this manuscript, but her support and encouragement were always there.

My dear partner, Gerald Hunt, has been a part of every scholarly project I have undertaken over the last two decades. For better or for ill, he suggested that this time I needed to take a broader view. So if this is deemed a worthy contribution to our understanding of progressive change, he deserves much credit. If it is not, only I am at fault.

QUEER INCLUSIONS, CONTINENTAL DIVISIONS

Public Recognition of Sexual Diversity in Canada
and the United States

# 1 Publicly Recognizing Queer Families

By the middle of the first decade of the twenty-first century, Canadian lesbian and gay couples could marry. In 2003, the first marriages in the world without explicit discriminatory limitations were being performed in the country's three largest provinces.[1] Canada was now 'cool' enough to be featured on the cover of the *Economist*, and it was not because of successful deficit fighting! At the same time, constitutional amendments prohibiting same-sex marriage were sweeping across the United States, most of them with wording that extended far beyond marriage, threatening to bar any public recognition of same-sex family rights.

In both countries, issues related to family and children had become increasingly prominent, moving to the front burner of activist agendas among those seeking public recognition of sexual diversity. The same was true for conservative opponents. American elections from the 1980s on ignited a barrage of anti-gay campaigning, much of it based on a venomous prejudice against homosexuality. Even more intensively from the 2000 election on, the Christian right campaigned for what it claimed to be traditional family values and the protection of children against advocates of the 'gay agenda.' Canadian voters have also faced campaigning against gay rights, and, though not on the scale and apparent effectiveness of its American counterpart, it too has focused on the family and children.

Canada and the United States share a continent, and much more. Their legal systems, social policy legacies, media systems, geographic regions, immigration patterns, economic structures, and popular belief systems have much in common, and visitors from other continents are often struck at the similarities between the two countries. Canadians are more likely to watch American television programs and films, and to work for and buy products from U.S. corporations, than anyone else in the world apart from Americans themselves.

On the question of whether sexual diversity should be publicly recognized, however, the contrasts seem categorical. With regard to debates over family and children, there is growing divergence in law, public policy, and institutional practice between the two countries despite the powerful pressures for cross-border integration and convergence in other areas. This strengthens the view that Canada and the United States retain core differences.

## Pioneering and Take-Off

There is great complexity behind first impressions. On a wide range of family-related issues, we find American local or regional authorities, courts, and private institutions acting as pioneers in responding favourably to activist pressure. American lesbians and gay men were securing parental rights, and school authorities were acknowledging the diversity of their own students, before change was inaugurated anywhere else in the world. What is distinctive about the American case, however, is the continuing power of the opposition to such gains. Even in the most progressive of regions, social conservatism is strong enough to effect reversals of policies that recognize sexual diversity. The changes that occur in the United States, then, are gradual, uneven, and sometimes temporary.

The Canadian story has a beginning similar to the American, with isolated shifts in policy and law at a stage that is early by international standards, though no earlier than those across the border. But in the 1990s the recognition of sexual diversity on issues like relationship recognition and parenting picked up enough speed that we can refer to 'take-off.' We see this in a few other countries, mostly in northern Europe, but nowhere as clearly as in the Canadian case. And while regionalism is a hallmark of Canadian politics, even an obsession, the changes in policy and practice on most family issues are more striking for their cross-regional similarities than their differences.

What the 'take-off' metaphor represents is a short time period during which change to existing patterns of regulating sexual diversity extends rapidly beyond just one or two specific policies or practices, and spreads rapidly across regions. As we will see, the loosening or elimination of official barriers to parenting for Canadian lesbian and gay couples achieved a form of take-off from 1995 to 2001. In the United States positive change was spreading, but very slowly and unevenly across policy areas.

The take-off pattern is not evident in all issue areas. Recognition of sexual diversity in Canada's public school systems may at some point acquire the pattern we find in other areas, but we are a long way from that now. There has been little concerted action to confront bullying and harassment based on sexual diversity or gender deviation, and even less acknowledgment of such difference in the curriculum. No take-off on schooling has occurred in the United States either, not surprisingly, though a considerable amount of change has been effected to recognize sexual difference in that country's educational systems, and the number of student groups taking up these issues – most notably Gay-Straight Alliances – has increased dramatically since the early 1990s.

What explains the contrasting patterns on some issue fronts, and the absence of such contrast on others?

## Explaining Differences

Several sets of factors are influential. Advocates for change work within very different institutional and policy contexts.[2] Legal and constitutional frameworks provide for very different opportunities in Canada and the United States; indeed, some may argue that the contrasting approach of their respective courts towers over other explanations.[3] The dispersion of power in the American system, both across jurisdictional levels and within each government, creates some opportunities for American innovation but also slows radical change. Policy inheritance is also a factor in easing or impeding the recognition of sexual diversity, particularly in the area of family law.[4]

Obviously central to any treatment of cross-border differences is the place of religion in social and political life. Religious belief, and in particular conservative belief, is a more important factor in national politics in the United States than it is in just about any other country in the industrialized world. Dimensions of faith form part of a broader 'political culture' that creates some openings for reformist change, but more impediments. The strength of individualism in the American belief system has contributed in more recent years to heightened anxiety of social disintegration and moral decay. Canadian political culture, no matter how variegated and hard to pin down, is less permeated by religious faith and social anxiety, and seems to be creating more room for diversity in sexuality as well as in other areas. Canada is undoubt-edly subject to more U.S. influence than ever, but belief systems on the issues we confront here display intriguing signs of divergence.[5]

Differences in party systems also create opportunities for Canadian activists that are not as readily available for Americans. The American Republican Party is, for now at least, closely tied to the Christian right, and this helps keep anti-gay rhetoric in the forefront of election cam-paigns. Canadian parties on the right have encountered more diffi-culty combining the anti-state politics of neo-liberalism and moral con-servatism, and most of those preoccupied with the former do not even attempt to give much profile to the politics of abortion and homosex-uality. Canada's social democratic parties – the New Democrats and the Parti Québécois – have also been firm advocates of greater policy inclusiveness for most of the last fifteen years, applying pressure on more centrist parties.

And, finally, these contrasts in outcomes may be explainable by differences in the resources and skills marshalled by activist move-ments. LGBT activists and their allies in the United States are as well resourced and skilful as any, but they face opponents who are much more formidable than those encountered by Canadians, and they operate in a complex institutional context that provides some oppor-tunities but many impediments.

**Chronicling Complexity**

An exploration of why Canada and the United States display the dif-ferences that they do requires first a chronicle of changes in policy and practice within three issue areas closely linked to conceptions of family. One is relationship recognition: which intimate relationships get recognized by the state (through marriage and other mechanisms), employers, and other institutions, and which do not? Parenting is another realm that is encompassed by the notion of family regime. Who is accorded the rights and obligations associated with parenting in the complex web of laws and practices that regulate adoption, child custody, fostering, and assisted reproduction? To what extent are lesbian, gay, bisexual, and transgendered children and adolescents fully accepted, given second-class standing, or rendered invisible? Schooling is a third area in which policy and practice privilege some family forms, reject others, or make less valued forms invisible.

Patterns of change in any of these areas are highly complex, and often incoherent. Public policy is an important part of the process by

which a family regime is maintained, and a crucial ingredient in constituting full 'citizenship' in formal terms and public perception,
defining who belongs to the political community and contributes to it,
and who does not. There are, however, hundreds or even thousands
of statutory provisions defining what counts as family and what
doesn't.

Public policy regulation of family relationships, for example,
includes the following areas:

- *Family law*
  - definition of eligibility for marriage rites and divorce
  - division of property and provision of support after termination
    of relationship
- *Parenting policy*
  - assumptions on who parents are, with accompanying decision-
    making power
  - custody and visitation rights
  - rights to adopt and foster children
  - access to assisted reproduction
  - access to leave for birth or illness of child
  - access to birth control
- *Provisions for death, incapacity, injury, illness of partner*
  - decision making or guardianship in the case of a partner's
    incompetency
  - management of funeral and other affairs in the event of a
    partner's death
  - inheritance rights, with and without will
  - access to state-enforced leaves for partner's illness
  - access to private insurance provisions for partner's accident or
    death
  - right to legal action for injury to partner
- *Social policy and taxation*
  - access to social insurance provisions for spouses, including
    survivor pensions
  - tax measures adjusting benefits and obligations in regard to
    partner's income
- *Criminal and civil law*
  - regulation of conflict of interest and nepotism
  - protections for inter-party communications and testimony in
    court proceedings
  - criminalization of certain sexual practices

- *Immigration*
  - rights of foreign partners to immigrate and obtain work
- *Schooling*
  - policies on harassment and bullying
  - recognition of parental authority in school decisions about children
  - recognition of diverse family forms in counselling and curriculum
  - acceptance of teachers with same-sex partners

Employers also have what amount to family policies in workplace benefit plans that recognize some relationships as legitimate and some children as supportable. In Canada and especially the United States, benefit packages are crucial supplements to welfare systems that are not as comprehensive as most in Europe. Human resource policies, particularly for professionals and managerial staff, will often include recruitment and retention strategies that assume only one form of family. Religious institutions also play a role in defining and legitimizing some family relationships over others, most obviously in the case of marriage. The media play a role in recognizing some family forms and not others, celebrating marriages but not necessarily other forms of union; mentioning significant partners in obituaries but maybe not; portraying affectional moments between heterosexuals and not same-sex couples.

Schools play a crucial role in resisting challenge to established norms around gender and sexuality.[6] The official and 'unofficial' curriculum in both elementary and secondary education may still replicate traditional gender norms, even where there are explicit attempts by teachers and curricular materials to challenge them. The everyday language of school corridors, gymnasia, and surrounding fields may be rife with explicitly homophobic language, with no one called to account. School personnel may still face restrictive expectations about their behaviour both within and beyond the classroom.

Children are in fact central to the public debates over relational issues and schooling. An increasing number of same-sex couples who seek recognition of their relationships have children, and these parents are often at the forefront of debates over school policies. When opposition to the recognition of any form of sexual diversity is being mobilized, the question of what happens to children is regularly placed at centre stage. Throughout most family regimes, children and adolescents are assumed to be heterosexual and clearly differentiated by gender. In most institutional and social settings, if youngsters are thought of as sexual beings at all they are seen through an exclusively heterosexual lens.

Family regimes are buttressed by, and in turn reinforce, public beliefs on what family forms are most estimable and what are least. Public fears about societal instability are easily focused on family issues, and particularly when children's interests are thought to be at stake. Religious conservatives in many countries prey on public prejudice by placing the vulnerable child at the centre of their rhetoric.

Chronicling change is therefore not straightforward, for the issue areas we are taking up are shaped by decisions taken at all levels of government, and by private-sector institutions. Tracking shifts in the regimes that regulate sexual difference requires taking into account the contradictory directions embodied in many such decisions, and the gaps that frequently exist between formal policy and institutional practice. We are not dealing here with simple or smooth transitions in any country or region; we are also facing rapidly shifting terrain.

The concept of 'family regime' should therefore not be allowed to suggest coherence in the patterns privileging some family forms over others. Indeed, we have seen much change in the treatment of heterosexual relationships over the last half century showing just the opposite – changes in some policy areas that contradict tenacious traditionalism in others.[7] In the United States in particular, we also see striking variation from one state to another in the way in which heterosexual and same-sex couples are treated. In using the term 'regime,' we simply acknowledge that the privileging of heterosexuality or monogamy or clear gender demarcation within any country occurs not simply through marriage or adoption law, but through thousands of policies and practices in the public and private sectors. Meaningful change requires shifts across all these areas.

## Does Formal Public Recognition Matter?

For so long, and in so many places, activists demanding visible recognition of sexual diversity worked on the fringe. They were usually excluded from arenas of influence and power, at times consulted but not heard. Social and political marginality ranged widely among and within countries, but the full rights and obligations associated with human dignity and citizenship were elusive even in the most progressive of settings.

Much has changed in the last decade and a half. Voices once silenced are now audible; public policies once unassailable are now changing. Can we talk yet of 'queer inclusion'? The answer depends on our standard for inclusion. For many the phrase contains a contradiction in terms, for the very nature of 'queer' means that it cannot be fully accommodated by existing institutional and normative systems. From such a perspective, the term suggests a radical questioning of the very grounds of civil inclusion, and of the norms about gender and sexual conformity that still hold such powerful sway.

## Critical Perspectives

Not everyone, then, agrees that the recognition of sexual diversity in formal institutional policy is worth seeking, or is effective if attained. This was an implicit theme in gay liberationist writing from the early 1970s, by the likes of Kenneth Plummer and Dennis Altman, which regarded the exercise of state authority in entirely negative terms and rejected all family-centred norms.[8] Michel Foucault and the many theorists influence by him (including Shane Phelan, Mark Blasius, Judith Butler, and Michael Warner) have a similar distrust of state regulatory authority and the constricting or normalizing role of traditional family regimes.[9] They are joined by several writers in critical legal studies (such as Didi Herman, Carl Stychin, Susan Boyd, and Nancy Polikoff) who point to the limitations of seeking change through law.[10]

One strand of this argument is distrustful of any change in family regime that extends state regulation to sexual minorities, arguing that their 'recognition' will contribute to the assimilation of those deemed respectable. Others argue that law and public policy are limited in their reach, operating within traditional heterosexual frameworks, and in any event are unlikely to effect the shifts in public norms or institutional practices needed for genuine inclusion. Prioritizing a politics of recognition, then, shifts a once-radical movement towards a limited set of accommodationist goals.

There are echoes here of debates that have recurrently marked the internal life of all social movements, and of academics writing about them. On one side are those who seek transformation of, and resist acquiescence to, existing social, economic, and political institutions. Writers such as Alain Tourraine and Albert Melucci, in fact, essentially defined social movements as transformative in their objectives and rejecting of existing political processes.[11] Any significant movement towards engagement with existing legal frameworks or political process, then, becomes a shift from the 'essence' of the social movement, and perhaps a betrayal of it. On the other side are those more willing to imagine an accommodation to such institutions, providing that advances in the movement's political agenda can be secured within them. Examples include social movement theorists such as Sydney Tarrow and Doug McAdam, and writers on LGBT activism such as John D'Emilio, Dennis Altman, and Barry Adam.[12]

The first of these views is rooted in philosophical traditions that see oppression and inequality as deeply embedded in existing systems – political, legal, corporate – and the very language we use.[13] Those who make gains within existing institutions and frameworks effect only very limited reform, and inclusion within them retains or sharpens divisions between those previously on the margin who conform to respectable norms and those who do not. Demanding the political recognition of same-sex relations, for example, will import rules and obligations enforced by governments and courts according to criteria that have little or nothing to do with the lives of lesbians, gay men, and other sexual minorities. In addition, the sheer complexity of legislative, administrative, electoral, and judicial processes privileges those with the professional skills to manoeuvre within them, and prioritizes those issues and frameworks that are understandable within them. This can easily expand the play of formal rights claims, and draw activists into an exaggerated belief that the success of such claims will be transformative. Steven Seidman provides an articulate example of this view, and sees a shift in activism towards 'a politic of citizenship aimed at civic inclusion by means of gaining equal rights and normalizing or purifying a gay identity.'[14] He contrasts this with an agenda that seeks to liberate all sexualities from normalizing regulation, and to eliminate the invidious distinction between good and bad versions of homosexuality.

## Marriage and the Privileging of Relationships

No issue so sharpens the critical edge of such views as marriage. This is an institution that is seen not only as irretrievably encumbered with traditional and inequitable baggage, but as specifically oppressive of women and sexual minorities. Seeking marriage rights most clearly embodies what to critics is an assimilative politics of 'letting us in' and undermines the transformative objectives of liberationist or queer politics.[15] When gay conservatives such as Andrew Sullivan support same-sex marriage because of its 'civilizing' influence, marking a shift away from a preoccupation with sexual promiscuity, these more sceptical views are reinforced.[16]

David Bell and Jon Binnie argue that marriage claims implicitly base citizenship status on a marginalization of sexual and affectional relationships that don't fit the model of the family. This marginalization contributes to a model of sexual citizenship that is 'privatized, deradicalized, de-eroticized and CONFINED in all sense of the word: kept in place, policed, limited.'[17] Some writers wonder why the state is involved at all in certifying marriage and urge a thoroughgoing overhaul of the regulatory regime governing the recognition of relationships. Writers such as Brenda Cossman and Bruce Ryder have urged going back to basics to explore the logic (if there is any) that underlies the recognition of 'conjugal' relationships and not others.[18]

Critics of marriage fear that prioritizing it reinforces already existing disparities along gender, race, and class lines. The strategies used to attain such recognition emphasize the safe respectability of those seeking rights, and those who are already privileged will be most strategically placed to take advantage of expanded recognition. Associated with this is the view that a narrow focus on marriage ignores the much larger agenda of the conservative opposition, which campaigns for tighter divorce policies, abstinence-only sex education, greater control over reproductive choices, and welfare cutbacks. By ignoring this range of issues, marriage campaigns risk acquiescing to an increasingly restrictive family regime.

The prioritization of relationship rights is also cited as an unfortunate example of what is widely referred to as identity politics – the kind of activism that treats sexual minorities as if they belong to a discrete and clearly bounded constituency analogous to an ethnic or language group. This is rooted in the argument that categories and boundaries are restrictive in themselves and historically employed to reinforce marginality. Allied to this is the more empirical point that identity politics portrays the constituency of sexual minorities as more uniform than it is, underplaying differences among groups within it, and sidelining those who straddle the boundaries or move across them. This line of argument points to the near invisibility of bisexuality and transgenderism in the campaigning for same-sex relationship recognition.[19]

A good part of this commentary can be extended to other issues under consideration here. There can hardly be an issue area where equity demands are more shaped by existing institutional expectations than parenting. Whether in a courtroom or in the media, same-sex couples and activists strive to look as normal as possible, and insist that their children will grow up 'normal.'[20] In a point that applies far beyond American parenting regimes, Valerie Lehr points to the persistence of frameworks that offend the complexity of the multiple family forms that members of sexual minorities have constructed for themselves.[21] Cheshire Calhoun makes a similar argument, pointing to the persistent legal, political, and social pressures 'preventing new gay and lesbian persons' by making sexual-minority children and youth invisible and reducing the likelihood of temptation or recruitment to homosexuality.[22] Such analytical unease is only reinforced when support being garnered for gay and lesbian parenting claims comes from anti-welfare neo-liberals who see them as reducing the likelihood of children depending on state welfare.

On the schooling front, equity initiatives are often add-ons to a curriculum and administrative system that needs more fundamental change. Programs to counter marginality and harrassment can easily lean more towards punishment than building inclusiveness over the longer term, and in that sense conform to the most traditional of school responses to misbehaviour. Remedies may also target the 'protection' of sexual minorities rather than address the need to challenge traditional constructions of sexuality and gender in the wider school population. And of course any response to sexual diversity that does not take into account the very different place occupied by various racial groups, women and men, the transgendered and bisexuals, different social classes, and those of a range of post-immigrant generations will risk creating a hierarchy of opportunity among students and teachers. As with parenting, campaigning for school recognition often relies on the most respectable of identity politics and on downplaying sexuality itself, in particular among young people.

## Why Formal Recognition Does Matter

This volume is built on the claim that formal public recognition is important, whether of same-sex relationships, of parenting claims by members of sexual minorities, or of the diversity of students and school staff. A number of the critical points raised above provide vital cautionary notes for assessing the limits of gains secured so far. However, recognition by governments, courts, employers, schools,

and religious institutions does matter, and can produce more significant transformation than sceptics generally acknowledge.

Changes in one part of a family regime will sometimes exacerbate
the overall tensions within that regime and build on earlier shifts. The
normative order that forms part of any such system has elements of
instability and periods in which foundational principles can be challenged. As we will see in more detail later on, relationship regimes
have been undergoing significant change over several decades, perhaps more in Canada and the United States than most of Europe, and
in the process they have become more fractured and inconsistent
than ever. Much change has been effected in the ideological under-
pinnings of marriage, reflecting the extent to which it has been the
site of social and political struggle.[23] The same could certainly be
said of parenting regimes, and to some extent of schooling systems.
Campaigning for inclusion within existing political and social institutions, then, often creates significant openings for shifts in dominant norms or practices.

Even if parenting and relationship claims are dressed up in the most
respectable clothing, the way in which they are made predicts little of
the relational and parenting approaches taken by lesbians, gays, bisexuals, and the transgendered. Interviews conducted by Jeffrey Weeks,
Brian Heaphy, and Catherine Donovan show that the relationships
within the British lesbian and gay couples they study vary widely and
are relatively unencumbered by traditional heterosexual norms.[24]
They use the language of 'family' in ways that more often differentiate
their relationships from what they perceive to be heterosexual norms
than to mark their sympathy with and similarity to those norms.

Canadian feminist Shelley Gavigan acknowledges that lesbian
custody cases generally do not radically challenge prevailing definitions, but focus on 'how to resolve or address a situation that lesbians
themselves have created through their relationships.' And here, as she
says, 'the language of assimilation vs. anti-assimilation seems inapt.'[25]
Many parents also challenge traditional gender norms in their everyday living, and armour their children against anti-gay prejudice,
however they present themselves to courts or school authorities. And
in any event, the very fact that they are parents confronts the most
insidiously persistent stereotypes about homosexual predation on
children.

No equity advocate can seriously question the need for change in
schooling. The persistence of rigid gender expectations does immeas-

urable harm to all students, and the cold climate facing teachers, administrators, students, and parents whose sexuality or gender deviate from traditional norms can be brutal. The persistence of wilful blindness to the need for change makes the case for a formal recognition of sexual diversity in educational policy self-evident. Writers who seek transformative change will quite properly see such policy steps as only a beginning, but even those most radically critical of state authority would not deny the importance of at least beginning the process of recognizing sexual diversity in official policy. No matter how tame, policies aimed at making the open expression of difference easier among students and teachers cannot help but challenge prejudice about homosexuality, and assumptions about the exclusive naturalness of heterosexuality.

On the specific question of marriage, Cheshire Calhoun acknowledges that some arguments are framed in ways that normalize homosexuality, wedging it into traditional conceptions of family. But she properly adds that the denial of marriage is an important mechanism for preserving heterosexual domination.[26] The very fact that supporters of 'traditional' marriage describe it as a 'pre-political' and 'foundational' institution makes it an especially powerful instrument for maintaining the invisibility of sexual minorities and characterizing them as unfit to raise children.

## Citizenship

Inescapable issues of citizenship are embedded in the claims for public recognition of sexual minorities in family and school regimes. Theorist Shane Phelan invokes such language to argue that members of sexual minorities are still 'strangers' in the United States.[27] Their exclusion from the military and the denial of their basic rights under the constitution form crucial demarcators of who belongs to and is excluded from the political community. Phelan is profoundly uneasy with political agendas and strategies that simply assimilate some portion of marginalized populations into existing institutional forms, but her argument about the importance of citizenship regimes effectively makes it hard to say that formal public recognition, including that by state institutions, does not matter. Jeffrey Weeks and his colleagues are similarly wary of assimilationist politics, but they recognize the power of claims to citizenship, and to equal rights and inclusion in relationship regimes. 'Citizenship,' as they say, 'is about belonging, and the nexus of rights and responsibilities which entitle the individual to be included within the polity.'[28]

Constructions of citizenship that include some variants of sexual diversity might well treat as unworthy those who fit less respectable templates. But this still creates more room for manoeuvre for those deemed unworthy than a categorical exclusion of all those who are sexually different. Challenges to laws that barred mix-race marriages in the United States were not inherently narrow and assimilationist: they were part of a centuries-long struggle over the core meanings of citizenship that affected all African Americans.[29] In North America and elsewhere, most lesbians, gays, bisexuals, and transgendered people would not argue that formal public recognition – for example, of relationship rights – should supplant all other issues. But they would see such rights as having substantive and symbolic relevance to the overall agenda – part of the fabric of policies and practices that define who is counted as a citizen and who is not.

### The Need for Care

Does such an argument mean that there are no risks in taking up issues of political and legal recognition? Of course not. When claims for recognition emphasize the normalcy of gay life and of same-sex relationships, while underplaying the presence of sexual minority youth, rendering invisible those whose sexual practices or identities cross gender lines, then there is risk. When advocates for change portray themselves in the language of tax-paying consumers, there is a danger of their demands being too isolated from the daily lives of most people whose interests are being represented. The engagement with political and legal processes also has strong assimilative pulls, and an activist movement that has access to the mainstream will have difficulty reflecting the diversity of the constituencies it seeks to represent. The gains they secure, too, will be unevenly distributed across those constituencies.

Some of the openings for the recognition of family forms that embody sexual diversity also come from 'privatizing' shifts in the regimes governing all relationships and families. As Margrit Eichler argues, the creation of formal equality between men and women, and legal entrenchment of norms of individual responsibility, may be used to support a reduced state responsibility for the care of children and for non-conjugal dependent relationships (including those that entail care of elders).[30] As we have seen, the same argument can be used to justify the expansion of relationship and parenting policies to include sexual minorities.[31]

What counters these tendencies to some extent is that campaigns for recognition of family rights and schooling visibility have been broadly based. This is in part because social conservatives have placed these issues at the centre of their agendas, making them stand for the full range of sexuality issues. It is also because the numbers of gay men and especially lesbians who are parents has increased significantly since the 1980s, and for most of them the issues of formal recognition in law or institutional practice are inescapable. And because family-related claims arise in workplaces, in schools, in hospitals and dental offices, in foster homes, and, yes, in court, countless people find themselves on the front lines. Some are willing, and intentionally place themselves there as part of their commitment to a broader activist movement. Others just discover themselves there by accident, and then find support or counsel from those who have gone before.

## What Follows

Each of the following chapters has a story to tell, and within each story there are many smaller stories. The complexity of each of these is intended in part to demonstrate how long the struggle for equity has been, and on how many fronts. It is also designed to construct a time-line showing when pioneering gains were secured, and where. Some of these complex stories will challenge what are becoming prototypical images of Canadian and American political life.

The major story behind chapter 2 is that advocates for change in the United States work in a difficult context in which victory is hard to win and setbacks common. Canadian activists have had to fight hard for change, but, in particular circumstances and at particular times, opportunities have opened widely for them. Chapter 3 then explores the emergence of family and schooling issues onto activist agendas, both for those aiming to expand the recognition of sexual diversity and those opposing it. It points to strong similarities in social movement priorities and strategies, but also to important differences when particular issues like marriage and schooling became high profile. The chapter also highlights the much larger resource base of the American LGBT movement, in comparison to a Canadian movement that is smaller and more episodically organized at all levels. This of course does not predict greater success on the American side, precisely because of the scale of opposition faced by American advocates, and other features of the context in which they work.

Chapters 4 and 5 track the expanding public recognition of lesbian and gay couples. The Canadian story ends up being a surprisingly uniform one across an otherwise high regionalized system, with particularly dizzying acceleration of change from the mid-1990s on. The American story looks at first to be an utterly discouraging one, with one state after another entrenching opposition to same-sex marriage. But it is an infinitely convoluted story with more twists and turns – and overall gains – than is revealed just by the struggle over marriage.

Chapters 6 and 7 focus on parenting issues, which are obviously related to the relationship agenda. Here is a similar pattern on the Canadian side – a surprisingly uniform story, rapidly evolving, across regions. The U.S. parenting story has much similarity with changes in relationship recognition, but with the intriguing twist that the possibilities for lesbian and gay couples to have kids of their own has increased steadily. There is no policy take-off in recognizing the parenting status of both partners, but the spread of recognition may well be greater than for simple couple relationships.

Chapters 8 and 9 examine school systems, and here we see trends that contradict the findings of earlier chapters, especially on the Canadian side. We can find relatively early developments in one urban school board, but additional major steps only in the last few years. Overall, there is a lamentable record in formal policy, let alone implementation. The American story finds surprisingly high levels of activism at a comparatively early stage, not all of it in the progressive regions of the country. We also see real victories more widely across the American landscape than we can find in Canada.

And, finally, chapter 10 places Canada and the United States in a broader comparative context, and tries to explain both early American pioneering on the issues raised in these chapters and the take-off pattern evident not only in Canada but also across several countries in northwestern Europe. No single explanatory factor dominates the analysis of American and Canadian distinctiveness, despite the temptations so evident in the writing on these subjects to attribute cross-national contrasts to individual factors. Understanding change is just as complex as chronicling it.

# 2 Activist Contexts

There is no country in the world where activists have been able to mobilize support for the public recognition of sexual diversity as widely, intensely, or continuously as in the United States. Yet they operate in a context that creates formidable challenges for them, far greater than those faced by their much smaller and more irregularly mobilized counterparts in Canada and in those parts of Europe where most gains have been secured. This fact affects the issue areas – and regions of the country – in which they are most likely to make gains. It also shapes the organizational structures and the strategies they adopt, some of them destined to intensify activist isolation from the constituencies they represent.

The most important features of the contextual landscape shaping movements and their impact in Canada and the United States are the structure of political institutions, legal norms and rights frameworks, the policy legacies traditionally defining what counts as family, the character of religious belief, and the public belief systems about morality in general and sexuality in particular.

These contextual factors vary across localities and regions within any country, and on the face of it regionalism would seem an equally powerful factor in both Canada and the United States. Political decentralization in each country provides the potential for drastic variations in activist opportunities. Regional differences are a defining element of Canadian federalism, and American commentators portray their own nation as divided into large regional blocs, sometimes corresponding to the partisan divisions between 'red' and 'blue' states. Moral values are among those most commonly associated with regional differences.

## Family Regimes and Policy Legacies

Activists seeking recognition of sexual diversity on all fronts come up against a vast array of institutional policies and practices that make up what might be called a family regime. Within a single country, there is usually enough uniformity in patterns of privileging some family forms over others that the term applies at the national level. In public regard and institutional policy across these two countries, the privileging of some family forms over others maintains a hierarchy of family types and conjugal relationships.

- *'Normal' families*: married, heterosexual, with children
- *'Incomplete' families*: married, heterosexual, and childless
- *'Modern' couples*: cohabiting monogamously, with or without children
- *'Inadequate' parents*: single and non-monogamous heterosexuals, with children
- *'Respectable' same-sex couples*: cohabiting monogamously, with or without children
- *'Deviant' homosexuals*: cohabiting non-monogamously, or crossing gender boundaries

Family regimes almost always treat married heterosexual couples, unless proven to be inadequate, as fully entitled to all of the relational and parenting rights and obligations available to couples. A married man is assumed to be the father of a child born to his wife during the life of the marriage, without needing to prove paternity. Married women and men are given entitlements to a range of public and private family benefits, without having to prove anything substantive about their relationship.

Although married heterosexual couples are not required to have children, they are widely viewed as incomplete or even immature if they do not. Married women who do not want children or who do not take primary responsibility in raising them are widely viewed as selfish. Those conjugal couples who choose not to get married are much more socially accepted than they would have been half a century ago, but they are not seen as being committed to one another in the same way that married couples are, and, in the United States especially, they are not accorded the same institutional recognition. Single mothers are regularly disparaged as bad mothers and burdens on state welfare, and as a result they are much more likely to receive critical scrutiny by courts and social agencies.

Same-sex parents are regularly denied full official recognition. They are viewed as offering insufficiently gendered role models for their children or, at their worst, as providing models of corruption and ill health. Gay male couples are even more likely than lesbians to be suspect, since they are assumed to not have the advantage of whatever natural child-rearing instincts are the province of women. Lesbians are no doubt commonly viewed as less naturally inclined towards motherhood than are heterosexual women – less 'feminine' in all respects. But men are more likely to be thought unstable in their relationships, narcissistic in their search for pleasure, and predatory on children.

Still lower in the hierarchy would be relationship or parenting claims from those whose gender identities or sexual relationships deviate from clearly defined and monogamous homosexual relationships. Bisexuals and transgendered people, whatever their relational and sexual behaviour, are considered by their very nature unrecognizable or unpredictable, and therefore suspect, whatever legal protections are extended to them.

Within any of these categories, of course, there are inequalities. The costs associated with parenting exacerbate social inequalities, and privilege middle- and upper-class families in public regard and institutional practice. The pressures associated with economic or ethnic marginality will often result in the right of individuals and couples to parent being questioned by authorities. The impediments facing same-sex couples who wish to parent may well make inequalities along such lines especially pronounced.

Hierarchies are maintained by government policy at all jurisdictional levels, by state agencies with discretion over parenting, schools, employers with 'family' benefits, religious authorities, media outlets, and public belief systems. Throughout, children are thought to be asexual and adolescents are assumed to be heterosexual and clearly differentiated by gender. Transmitting clarity on this front is a crucial function of parents and schools.

Family hierarchies are not fixed – the distance between categories may narrow or widen, and some categories may leapfrog others over time.[1] 'Respectable' lesbian and gay couples with children, for example, may well acquire higher social and political standing than families headed by single parents. Incoherence is also a recurrent feature of the regulatory regimes upholding such hierarchies.

*Changes in the Regulation of Heterosexual Marriage*

The regulation of heterosexual relationships has changed much over the last half century, in some respects narrowing the gap between married and cohabiting couples, and the relationships between women and men within them. Family-like structures, and the norms associated with them, have shifted as a result of long-term changes in the social and economic relationships of women and men, the challenges to traditional family ideology mobilized by late-twentieth-century feminism, and more recently the pressures arising from neo-liberal resurgence.

There is no inevitable coherence in family regime shifts. Changes on some fronts may be contradicted by others, just as the principles underlying some reforms may be at odds with others still embodied in policy and practice. Within a particular policy area, a court in one municipality may make decisions quite out of line with others, and the actual practices of social agencies may not be predictable from either the letter or the prevailing interpretation of the law.

Still, there are some broad trends. Across the liberal democratic world, including both Canada and the United States, marriage has been increasingly regulated as a contract between two individuals who in turn are viewed as independent and equal and are given leeway (within limits) to adjust the terms of their contract and to exit (through divorce) at least some of its terms. This is replacing the treatment of marriage as a 'status' that amalgamates individuals into a single legal entity, surrounded by an elaborately stipulated set of rules and obligations that are very difficult to exit from. In the course of this shift, the state system becomes less of a moral defender and more of a contract enforcer.[2]

The welfare state even in its most generous forms always incorporated assumptions of mutual support within families, and welfare assistance programs were often the first to expand the boundaries of 'family' in order to curtail demands on the public purse (sometimes kicking in at the moment of cohabitation rather than after a delay of a year or two or more). But over the last few decades we have seen greater pressures towards privatization of responsibilities for care and support, and therefore more pressure to recognize family-like obligations.[3]

These shifts have come with some invasiveness, especially in challenging welfare claims, but in other respects they have expanded the notion of privacy rights within the conjugal relationship, at least for heterosexuals.[4] In 1965, the U.S. Supreme Court struck down a Connecticut law barring contraceptive use, and in 1973 the court substantially liberalized access to abortion – all argued in large part on privacy grounds. In 1969, wide-ranging amendments to Canada's criminal code liberalized access both to contraceptives and abortion.

Women's shifting ideas about their public roles, including their occupational futures, alongside their access to more effective birth control, led to crucial changes in reproductive patterns from the 1960s onward. The number of children declined, and the duration of women's childbearing years was reduced. This allowed more women to enter the workforce for the long haul and allowed couples more choice as to how much to prioritize parenting over the length of their relationship. Marriage had never been framed as exclusively about parenting, but these changes allowed a further shift towards seeing marriage as embodying dimensions additional to or instead of parenting.

Laws governing marriage have also moved substantially in the direction of formal equality. Property once held exclusively by men has come to be seen as shared. In the event of relationship breakdown, many jurisdictions start with a presumption that assets are to be equally divided. At the same time, regulatory regimes have been extending the social support obligations that derive from de facto as well as marital relationships. This has certainly not eliminated substantive inequalities between women and men, but it has resulted in some shift in norms against which continued inequality is measured.

In Canada, changes in the legal apparatus governing marriage and marriage-like relationships have been relatively uniform across the country, with a few exceptions in Quebec. The American form of federalism gives states more room for autonomous action in reforming family law, and greater variety persists there than in Canada, even if some reforms adopted relatively early on by individual states (e.g., Nevada in divorce) were able to spread across state borders through the 'full faith and credit' provision in the American constitution that normally obliges states to accept the acts of other states.

*Contrasting Recognition of De Facto Heterosexual Relationships*

In the crucial area of recognizing de facto heterosexual relationships, change has been slower overall in the United States than in Canada, and more uneven. Canada has steadily and significantly expanded the public recognition of such relationships, as much as any country in the industrialized world. This has created vital openings for lesbian and gay couples, who were able to gain most of the substantive rights and obligations associated with marriage by claiming equivalence to de facto heterosexual couples. No U.S. state comes close to the Canadian norm in the recognition of de facto couples, and many states have moved only slightly in according marriage-like rights and obligations to cohabiting couples. This was a major factor in pushing the highly explosive issue of same-sex marriage to the front burner at a comparative early stage.

Kathleen Lahey and Kevin Alderson point out that Canadian policy change was evident soon after the Second World War, when unmarried 'war brides' were given access to veterans' pension benefits.[5] In the 1960s, de facto heterosexual couples were included in federal pension and old age security benefit coverage; in the 1970s, hundreds of federal and provincial laws were changed in the same direction; and in the 1980s and 90s, some rights to property associated with marital status were extended to separating de facto couples.[6] Parental rights and obligations were part of this shift towards the recognition of de facto relationships and of what were read as implied contracts.

In 1995, the Supreme Court of Canada, in determining the eligibility of a cohabiting heterosexual couple for income-loss benefits, could find no rational basis for discriminating against such couples, which further narrowed the gap between marriage and 'common law' relationships (*Miron v. Trudel*).[7] Subsequent court rulings have reinforced that direction.

Quebec has pursued a somewhat different tack, its ability to do so strengthened by its unique retention of a civil code. By the mid-1990s, one in four straight Quebec couples were unmarried, compared to one in ten for the rest of Canada, and by 2003, 59 per cent of registered births in Quebec were to unmarried couples or individuals. But these trends did not translate into the same rights and obligation for de facto couples as prevailed in most other provinces. Among the factors contributing to distinct trajectories was the position taken by many Quebec feminists that the automatic inclusion of de facto couples in the family law provisions of the Civil Code would be too restrictive.[8] Many social policy and taxation statutes (not the Civil Code) were recognizing such couples, and a few provisions in the Civil Code were amended in the early 1990s in the same direction. With such changes, de facto heterosexual couples were given more recognition than they were in most American states. However, until the early twenty-first century that recognition was substantially more contained than in the rest of Canada.

The United States was home to pioneering legal steps recognizing de facto couples.[9] In 1973, California's Supreme Court (in the *Cary* case) applied principles in family law to the division of assets in the case of a separated de facto couple. Three years later, in a case launched against actor Lee Marvin, the same court pulled back somewhat, granting property rights to his unmarried partner but only because of a contract between them. Also at a relatively early stage, in the mid-1970s, Washington State courts moved towards defining the property held by unmarried couples as effectively 'community property.'[10] Since the mid-1980s, appellate courts in Oregon and, surprisingly, Mississippi have at times applied similar principles.[11] Other states are more likely to require that there be an explicit contract between the cohabiting partners than to imply obligations from the marital character of the relationship.

In the absence of such contracts, most U.S. states infer no rights or responsibilities for cohabiting couples even when they have had a child together.[12] Some states have in fact closed what may have become a loophole through which couples who had not been formally married may have been legally recognized. The period of rapid westward expansion in the nineteenth century led to the recognition of what were called 'common law' marriages, recognizing an intent to marry but in isolated contexts where official rites were difficult to secure.[13] The number of states recognizing such marriages, though, significantly declined over the twentieth century, in the face of pressure to restrict the rights and obligations associated with marriage to those who went through official religious or civil procedures. In more recent years, some of the measures enacted by states to 'defend' against same-sex marriage have also included restrictions on recognizing all but properly married heterosexual couples. This is reflected in most workplace benefit plans, which still tend to recognize only married partners of employees.

The reluctance of most American jurisdictions to recognize de facto relationships is in some sense surprising. After all, divorce rates have been comparatively high and climbing, and public policy moves to recognize obligations on the part of separating partners would have found support in the highly visible feminist movement. Such change would also be compatible with the strong neo-liberal pressure to privatize welfare and reduce claims on the public purse.

On the other hand, reform has been slowed by fears about social and moral decay, and a belief that family ties should be buttressed. Catherine Lugg and others have pointed out that preoccupations with stabilizing the family also have a racial component, with African-American families widely portrayed as dysfunctional.[14] The fact that American families are highly prone to breakdown seems to feed nostalgia about traditional family forms, fear of the decline of family values, and opposition to legitimizing anything other than heterosexual marriage.[15] The power of religious conservatism is clearly a factor in resisting moves away from the primacy accorded to an institution with strong religious connotations. Those who advocate reform also face political institutions in which power is highly fragmented, and legislation difficult to enact. And of course there are also cost issues for employers in the public and private sectors. Health-care benefits are often included among employment benefits in Canada, but they are supplementary to state-secured Medicare rather than providing core coverage, and therefore much cheaper to provide than the very costly health insurance required in the United States.

Challenges to the exclusion of sexual minorities from regimes of family recognition, then, operate from very different legal and policy platforms in Canada and the United States, with additional variations from state to state on the American side. The widespread recognition of cohabiting straight couples in Canada helped in some respects to demystify marriage, and to offer claimants a path to substantive recognition that did not invoke marriage itself.

## Rights and Constitutions

The rights framework embodied in Canada's Charter of Rights and Freedoms, enacted and constitutionally entrenched in 1982, amplified opportunities for advocates of public recognition of sexual diversity. The American rights fabric was weaker and more unevenly woven across the states, but even at its best it would not provide the same advantageous platform.

In the United States, litigation has been a prominent social movement strategy for decades. The American constitution has long enshrined the right to free expression, privacy, and equality before the law, though it was only in the second half of the twentieth century that court rulings adopted more 'scrutiny' of discriminatory acts, first on questions of race and then on those of gender. In its 1973 ruling on *Roe v. Wade*, and its earlier decisions on race, the U.S. Supreme Court seemed ready to read the equality and privacy provisions of the Constitution broadly and assertively, increasing the temptation for activists on other fronts to litigate around legislative or popular resistance.

Sexual orientation has only begun to climb the 'scrutiny' ladder established in court interpretations of the fourteenth amendment to the constitution (containing the equal protection guarantee).[16] In fact, the U.S. Supreme Court permitted explicit discrimination based on sexual orientation in a 1995 case arising from a gay contingent's exclusion from Boston's St Patrick's Day parade (*Hurley v. Irish American Gay, Lesbian, and Bisexual Group of Boston*), and in a 2000 case challenging Boy Scout policy explicitly barring homosexuals (*Boy Scouts of America v. Dale*). Additionally, repeated attempts to strike down the military's discriminatory policy directed at lesbians and gays have failed in federal courts.

Claims to a right to privacy have had more success, though the criminalization of homosexual activity in state law was ruled unconstitutional only in the Supreme Court's 2003 ruling on *Lawrence v. Texas*. Indeed, the fact that the Supreme Court had upheld discriminatory sodomy laws in its 1986 ruling on *Bowers v. Hardwick* was to have a major dampening effect on the success of other claims. In those parts of the United States that still had such laws on the books, relational, parenting, and schooling demands were regularly countered with claims that criminal activity should not be legitimized. Even after *Lawrence v. Texas*, not a single state with a sodomy statute that still criminalized homosexual activity has repealed its law. Such laws may not be widely enforceable and would not pass constitutional muster, but their symbolic power has not disappeared.

The Supreme Court's uneven record on sexuality cases has left much room for variations in rights protections across the states. The existence of state constitutions, with their own rights provisions, contributes to that variation, creating formidable barriers to change in some regions but real opportunities in others to pursue claims through state courts. States also have their own criminal codes, increasing their jurisdictional reach over issues related to sexuality, and reinforcing the variation of litigation opportunities across American regions.

In Canada, the 1982 Charter increased the capacity of courts to challenge the acts of governments, and created new opportunities for activists. Gays and lesbians were among those who took most frequent advantage of those openings, and with striking success.[17] Despite operating in a political order more fundamentally decentralized than the American, Canadian activists have faced a much more uniform rights framework. There is a single, federally controlled criminal code, so that when male homosexual activity was largely decriminalized by Parliament in 1969, the change applied across Canada (at a time when only two American states had repealed their sodomy laws).[18] Canada also has a more integrated court system than does the United States, with the federal government responsible for most significant court appointments.

The enactment of the Charter of Rights and Freedoms has reinforced the integration of the legal and rights frameworks in Canada and given lesbian and gay advocates more consistently favourable openings than have been evident for any other equity-seeking group. The Charter's equality language (in section 15) was influenced by what were considered limitations in the rights language of earlier statutes in both Canada and the United States. Section 15 included an extensive list of grounds on which discrimination was prohibited. While it did not explicitly include sexual orientation (and indeed an amendment seeking its addition was rejected), sexual orientation was soon interpreted as a ground 'analogous' to those already there.[19] Courts were quick to signal their readiness to consider analogous grounds, in part based on the widely held view that constitutions were 'living trees' that had to evolve with time.

Attributing the success of lesbian/gay rights claims to widespread judicial 'activism' is tempting, though misleading.[20] It is certainly true that the federally appointed judiciary has delivered a number of rulings with expansive readings of Charter provisions, but the record of adjudication on gender and Aboriginal status displays a mixed record, as it does on labour rights and privacy. There is only a limited and indecisive record on disability and race. On some issues related to sexual diversity – for example, relationship claims – the courts were at first ambivalent. Favourable decisions were eventually made easier by the fact that the courts were judging instances of explicit discrimination, making for more straightforward cases than claims coming from other traditionally marginalized communities.

## Government Systems

When activists in Canada and the United States seek change in public policy, they work through unusually complex governmental systems, though much more so on the American side of the border. In both countries, federalism sometimes divides authority over issue areas crucial for the maintenance of family hierarchies, impeding overall change. But jurisdictional fragmentation also creates opportunities. At the same time, the unusual fragmentation of authority within all levels of American government impedes radical change, but creates entry points though which gains can be secured in particular locations and times.

### Federalism and Multi-Level Governance

The Canadian federation is one of the most decentralized in the world, having moved substantially over the twentieth century towards enhancing provincial power. Provinces have primary or exclusive jurisdiction in health and other social policy realms, as well as education. The greater fundraising flexibility of the federal government has sometimes been used to secure national standards in social policy, but deficit cutting has resulted in much-diminished leverage. Those financial transfers from federal to provincial governments that remain are more likely to be block grants, and less likely than their American counterparts to have strings attached.

The room for local government autonomy in Canada, though greater than in most European systems, is highly constrained by provincial authority. The provinces have the power to alter local government processes, limit spending capacity, and oversee policies in areas ostensibly under local control. They also regularly use that power, even against clear majority opinion at the local level. Schooling is a policy area in which local authority is formally prominent, but the provincial ministries of education exercise firm and wide-ranging powers, increasingly so over recent decades. Most provincial governments have also amalgamated school boards across their jurisdiction, eliminating highly localized governance.

The American system has moved in quite different directions. The twentieth century saw a significant shift from a system once more decentralized than the Canadian to one with a major increase in federal government leverage. Washington now raises about 70 per cent of all government revenues in the country, and it spends a much larger share of the overall pot on social services and education – areas that in Canada are principally funded by provinces. Federal grants to states are more likely than their Canadian counterparts to be specific and conditional, creating what François Rocher calls 'permissive federalism.'[21] Since the 1980s, the rhetoric of states' rights has been reinvigorated by Republican administrations in Washington, and this has led to significant off-loading of responsibilities to the states, but this has not fundamentally altered the weight of federal and state power.

On the other hand, the American distribution of powers gives states leverage over some areas that are federally controlled in Canada, and that are specifically relevant for family policy. Beyond having jurisdiction in criminal law, state governments also have full jurisdiction over not just the administration of marriage (also true of Canadian provinces) but also its definition (in Canada a federal responsibility). As in Canada, many other policy areas that shape the overall regulation of conjugal relationships and parenting are also under state jurisdiction, as is public schooling.

American local governments also have more policy reach than Canadian municipalities. They are constrained by the formal jurisdictional control of state governments, and by funding dependency on federal and state authorities. However, they are routinely given greater political and administrative leeway than could be found anywhere in Canada. And their access to some federal as well as state funding (even with strings) gives them opportunities that are not available in Canada. Their leeway is illustrated by the many local rights ordinances that reach into the private sector, which are much more difficult for Canadian cities, if possible at all. True, there are state constitutions that limit the room for manouevre of localities that wish to legislate in directions that contravene state law, for example in the provision of family benefits to the same-sex partners of local employees. This will sometimes constrain even those cities accorded 'home rule' status that gives them additional latitude. Nevertheless, American cities on balance have more de facto leeway than Canadian cities in any province.

*Fragmentation within Single Jurisdictions*

The American 'congressional' system is unusual (by international standards) in the extent to which power is fragmented within any one jurisdiction. The separation of powers gives legislatures more leverage over policy making than is characteristic of parliamentary systems. Within legislatures, individual politicians have much more freedom than their counterparts in other countries, the U.S. Senate being a particularly striking example. Party discipline may be higher now than thirty or forty years ago (particularly among Republicans), but it pales by comparison to the discipline inherent in parliamentary systems. There is also fragmentation on the executive side. Administrative units are commonly created outside the normal departmental hierarchies, thereby proliferating the policy-making centres and networks operating in Washington, state capitals, and localities.

Further fragmenting the American system is the increased resort to referenda to decide public policy. Religious conservatives have been particularly intent on putting questions before state electorates to prevent or roll back measures that recognize sexual diversity.[22] They do not always succeed, but ballot measures have helped conservatives to effect an end run around local and state politicians insufficiently allegiant to their cause. This creates an extra set of fronts, and expensive ones, on which pro-gay activists must do battle.

Such a system, combined with the important jurisdictional fields of state and local governments, creates huge challenges for activists. To be sure, it opens access points to decision-making systems and creates opportunities even in unfavourable times. Amendments to legislation or small changes in regulations can be effected, and damage that might be inflicted on any particular cause can be minimized with the right alliances. But it also complicates immensely the process of effecting large-scale change. It is a governmental regime, then, that creates room for innovation, but it requires constant vigilance and offers only limited hope of sweeping change.

Political power is much more concentrated in Canadian governmental systems, with the result that opportunities for change are more dependent on the party in power, and the party leadership's willingness to act. The dependence of the executive on a legislative majority, the essential feature of the parliamentary regime, has led to overwhelming dominance of the legislative agenda by the cabinet, and in particular the first minister's office (the prime minister or provincial/territorial premier). This imbalance is exaggerated by the single-member-district electoral system in place across the country, since it tends to create one-party majorities in the legislatures by exaggerating the number of seats held by the largest party. This shores up the power of the major party's leadership, increasing already-high levels of party discipline.

An unsupportive government in power means that shifts towards the recognition of sexual diversity, even minor ones, have been very difficult to secure, whatever the activist resources marshalled. With a party more open to persuasion, though, the application of activist resources that would be considered modest by American standards can be sufficient to effect change. There might still be a pattern of nervousness about taking on such issues, and we will see lots of evidence of that, but once a position is adopted by a government's leadership it is easier to secure legislative approval.

## Party Systems

For almost three decades, American LGBT activists have faced a Republican Party that has portrayed itself (with few exceptions) as explicitly anti-gay. Over that period, most state Republican parties have been dominated by Christian conservatives, intent on rolling back whatever gains have been secured in recognizing sexual diversity. They have lost more battles than they have won, despite appearances created by the struggle over marriage, but they have substantially slowed the pace of change, and in some parts of the country stopped it altogether.

The American party system is very different from the various party systems in Canada's federal and provincial arenas, in ways that are vital to the success or failure of pro-gay activists. At both state and federal levels, the two major parties in the U.S. system are more polarized on 'moral' issues than ever, one measure being that the vast majority of Republican politicians have adopted unequivocally condemnatory views of homosexuality. At the federal level, the Human Rights Campaign (the largest of the LGBT advocacy groups) regularly gives over two-thirds of Republicans in the House and Senate scores of zero (out of 100) in their voting records on issues relevant to it. Only a few Democrats warrant such scores; most get over 50, and between a quarter and a third get a perfect score of 100.[23] The noticeable minorities of Democrats who support anti-gay positions, and the larger number who fear the electoral consequences of appearing too pro-gay, do limit the opportunities for securing legislative majorities in favour of equity. No clearer an illustration can be provided than the disastrous outcome of President Bill Clinton's attempt to lift the ban on gays and lesbians serving in the U.S. military.[24]

At all levels of government, not surprisingly, change is much more likely to come from Democratic legislatures and executive offices. It matters, then, that the strength of the two parties varies from state to state. Democrats are stronger in the northeastern states than elsewhere, and these Democrats there are more likely to lean left than their counterparts in most other regions. In southern states, Republicans are stronger, and where Democrats succeed they are often more conservative (on moral issues at least) than their counterparts elsewhere.

Canada has more than one party system, since the nature of party competition is so variable from one region to another and the links between most federal and provincial parties so frail. In federal politics and some provinces, party alignments have changed radically over the last dozen years, and electoral volatility (always high) is as dramatic as ever. For most of the twentieth century, federal politics were dominated by the Liberal and Progressive Conservative (PC) parties, both of them centrist coalitions 'brokering' regional differences and a variety of social interests. The early 1990s saw the precipitous decline of the Conservatives, inaugurating a period of Liberal dominance and right-wing fragmentation.

From the 1980s on, and especially in the 1990s, the Liberals shifted significantly to the neo-liberal right, preoccupied with deficit reduction and ready to offload some social spending to the provinces. As with American Democrats, this shift did not apply to moral policy, though on gay rights especially the federal Liberals retained a strong and vocal minority of legislators with conservative views. The party slowly shifted towards a willingness to recognize sexual diversity in federal policy during the time it governed in the 1990s and early 2000s, though the threat of open division produced a stubborn streak of political caution.

To its left was the social democratic New Democratic Party (NDP), long the 'third' party in the federal system, and for some time the strongest advocate for gay rights among federal parties. The Bloc Québécois, a sovereigntist party that emerged in the early 1990s and remained influential among Quebec voters, has had a large social democratic core, and has provided relatively strong support on gay rights issues.

On the right, the Reform Party emerged and grew during the 1990s, overtaking the Progressive Conservative Party. Combining neo-liberal anti-statism and neo-conservative morality, it was strongly represented in western Canadian regions. Repeated calls for uniting the right-wing parties first produced the Canadian Alliance and eventually (in 2004) a merger with the PCs under the 'Conservative' label. The new party's leadership was strongly right wing on both economic and moral fronts but tried hard to downplay the latter to protect the party from charges of extremism. Though opposition to the extension of marriage rights to same-sex couples (the one issue that party strategist believed they had majority support for in the population) featured prominently in the party's presentation of itself to voters in its first two years, there have been many within the party (and more so as time passed) who have recognized that seizing that issue too tightly will backfire.[25]

The provincial party systems vary greatly from this pattern and from one another. With the possible exception of the Conservative Party of Alberta, there is no strong provincial party successfully focusing both on neo-liberal and moral conservative issues. Where shifts to the right have been most pronounced – for example, in Ontario during the mid-1990s and in British Columbia from the late 1990s on – the emphasis has been almost entirely on limiting social spending and cutting taxes, not on morality. It is also true that there have been few governments prepared to take major steps to recognize sexual diversity in the absence of court pressure. There are partial exemptions to be found in early and mid-1990s British Columbia, and in Quebec late in that decade, both at times when social democratic parties were in government.

**Religion**

The strength of religious conservatism may well be the most distinguishing feature of the American body politic.[26] It has meant that every single step towards publicly recognizing sexual diversity has been fiercely contested, and that no gain is entirely secure from counter-attack. Although Christian conservatism has provided the core opposition to the public recognition of sexual difference in Canada as well as the United States, its demographic and political weight is much less in Canada. The prominence of conservative religiosity even in the most progressive of American regions means that victories can be won only with enormous effort, and the stark opposition faced by activists forces them to organize on a scale that would be inconceivable in Canada, and to do so as continuously as possible. It also facilitates links to groups and activists confronting the religious right on other fronts – civil liberties, women's rights, labour organiz-

Table 2.1   Measures of Religiosity in Canada and the United States, 2002–4

|  | U.S. (%) | Canada (%) |
|---|---|---|
| Weekly (or more frequent) church attendance, 2002[a] | 42 | 22 |
| Religion is very important in my life, 2002[b] | 59 | 30 |
| Religion is very important in my life, 2004[c] | 55 | 28 |
| The Bible is the actual word of God, to be taken literally[c] | 34 | 17 |

[a]Reported in Michael Adams, *Fire and Ice* (Toronto: Penguin, 2004), 50.
[b]Pew Research Center, 'Global Project Attitudes,' 2002 survey.
[c]Gallup, 2004 survey, available at www.gallup.org.

ing. Canadian activists do not face such a clear and present danger, in addition to working in political contexts that provide only episodic opportunities for change. This makes widespread or sustained political mobilizing difficult, and creates little capacity to build firm organizational bases for the activist movement.

### Strong and Conservative Faith in the United States

American distinctiveness lies most strikingly in the fact that so many Americans are religious, so many of them are conservative in their faith, and so many can be mobilized by the political arms of the religious right.[27] A 2003 Pew Research survey of Americans showed that just under 30 per cent belonged to 'evangelical' churches, this figure omitting conservatives in other Christian currents and in other faiths.[28] When asked if they were 'born again' or evangelical Christians, 35 per cent of Americans polled by Pew answered yes (a 2006 Gallup poll reported 44 per cent responding affirmatively). When asked if they believed the Bible to be the actual word of God, and to be taken literally, fully 36 per cent responded affirmatively.[29]

The survey data in tables 2.1 and 2.2 illustrate the sharp contrasts between the United States and Canada in the level of religious practice, the importance attached to faith, and the extent of literalist belief (particularly important as an indicator of Protestant conservatism). The data do not suggest that the religious right is inconsequential in Canada, but that is represents half, or less, of the proportion of the population that it does in the United States. Environics polling shows about 33 per cent of Americans and 14 per cent of Canadians to be

Table 2.2   World Values Survey Measures of Religiosity in Canada and the United
States, 1990–2000

|  |  | U.S. (%) | Canada (%) |
| --- | --- | --- | --- |
| God is very important in my life | 1990 | 53 | 31 |
|  | 2000 | 57 | 30 |
| Monthly or more frequent church attendance | 1990 | 58 | 40 |
|  | 2000 | 60 | 36 |

Source: Ronald Inglehart, Miguel Basanez, Jaime Diez-Medrano, Loek Halman, and
Ruud Luijkx, ed., *Human Beliefs and Values: A Cross-Cultural Sourcebook Based on
the 1999–2002 Values Survey* (Madrid: Siglo XXI Editores, 2004).
(The WVS now administers a single survey to randomly selected residents of more
than sixty countries, every ten years.)

'fundamentalist' in orientation.[30] Bruce Bibby argues that in overall
terms 30 per cent of Americans and fewer than 10 per cent of Canadians are 'evangelical.'[31]

Data from the World Values Survey (table 2.2) suggest that the
United States is one of the only countries in the industrialized world
where religiosity has been increasing. The prominence of non-traditional Protestant denominations in this picture, as Roger O'Toole and
Seymour Martin Lipset have pointed out, is partly a reflection of the
competitive entrepreneurialism in the American religious landscape,
in turn influenced by the absence of state support for particular
denominations.[32] Explicitly conservative and non-mainstream Protestant denominations are on the rise in Canada too, but the religious oli-
gopoly that has prevailed in much of Canadian history has limited
their numbers compared to their American counterparts.

Canadian and American Christian conservatives differ from each
other. A mid-1990s survey by Sam Reimer of 'core evangelicals' – those
with the strongest beliefs and most frequent church attendance –
showed signs of a subculture that crossed denominations, regions, and
the international border.[33] But there was also less political extremism
among Canadian evangelicals, more tolerance of differences, and a
noticeable contingent of those following in the progressive footsteps
of social gospel leaders such as Tommy Douglas.[34] Dennis Hoover
agrees, citing greater willingness among Canadian religious conservatives to support various forms of government intervention.[35] He and
others have also found that American evangelicals are more 'moralis-

tic' than their Canadian counterparts, and are less concerned about economic inequality.[36]

The numerical strength of Roman Catholicism in Canada (representing about 43 per cent of the population, twice as much as in the United States) and the conservatism of the church's worldwide leadership on questions of gender and sexuality might seem to provide a boost to the Canadian religious right. As in the United States, however, major policy differences in issue areas apart from abortion and homosexuality separate Catholic doctrine from the beliefs of most conservative Protestants, making wholesale alliance impossible.[37] In addition, considerable evidence in both countries suggests that official Catholic opposition to measures recognizing sexual diversity is out of step with the beliefs of most Catholics, who are no more conservative on issues of sexuality than the rest of the population.

In Canada and the United States, many Protestant conservatives are in 'mainstream' denominations, but their claims to represent all Christians are challenged by those with more accepting views of sexual difference. Those progressive voices of faith are influential on both sides of the border but somewhat more widespread in Canada. The United Church of Canada, in formal numbers the largest Protestant denomination in Canada (9 per cent of the population), has moved gradually to a distinctly progressive stance on a range of sexual diversity issues, somewhat more forcibly than its closest American counterpart, the United Church of Christ, which represents a relatively smaller constituency. The influential Anglican Church, though much smaller than the United Church, is slowly moving towards a relatively positive stance on sexual diversity, much like its U.S. counterpart.

Conservatives are more organized within American mainstream Protestantism than they are in Canada. The U.S. Institute for Religion and Democracy, for example, brings together representatives from a number of conservative political organizations to combat progressivism in such denominations as the Presbyterian, Episcopal, and Methodist churches.[38] Their fundraising capacities far outstrip those of pro-gay forces within such churches, and their followers have easy access to conservative media supporting their position.

Conservative Christians in Canada are more likely to appear to be on the margins of social and political life than those in the United States. Their anti-gay campaigning, too, is more likely to be seen as extreme. As in the United States, Canadian opponents of gay rights have learned to temper their language by avoiding scriptural refer-

Table 2.3    Major Anti-Gay U.S. Religious-Right Political Organizations, 2000–5

| Group[a] | Budget ($ millions) | Staff | Members | Radio broadcasts |
|---|---|---|---|---|
| American Center for Law and Justice (1990, Pat Robertson) | $16 (2003) | 50 | – | – 140 stations<br>– weekly |
| American Family Association (1977, Donald Wildmon) | $11 (2000) | 105 | 500,000 | – 200 stations<br>– owned by AFA |
| Concerned Women for America (1979, Beverly LaHaye) | $12 (2002) | 34 | 500,000 | – 75 stations<br>– daily |
| Family Research Council (1983, Tony Perkins) | $10 (2000) | 120 | 455,000 | |
| Focus on the Family (1977, James Dobson) | $146 (2005) | 1,200 | 2.3 million[b] | – 6300 (worldwide)<br>– daily |
| Traditional Values Coalition (1980, Louis Sheldon) | | – | 43,000 churches | |
| Alliance Defense Fund | $16 | | | |

[a]Below the name of each group is the founding date and the name of its most prominent leader.
[b]Subscribers to 10 monthly magazines. Focus on the Family's daily broadcast is carried on about 1300 U.S. radio stations and 82 television stations, reaching an estimated 32 million people.
Source: People for the American Way (www.pfaw.org), with updates from media stories.

ences, employing the language of traditional family values, and citing the rights of Christians to their point of view. But the mobilization of their constituency invariably unleashes a form of vitriol that is far less acceptable in Canada than it is in the United States, where it is still widely accepted as normal.[39]

*Political Mobilizing*

Beyond the contrasts between these two countries in the size and intensity of conservative Christian belief, there are dramatic differences in the extent to which such belief is politically marshalled and the ways in which this marshelling occurs. Christian right organizations in the United States are enormous, are visible across the country,

and devote vast resources to political intervention at all levels of government. From their origins, most such groups included gay rights
alongside abortion as their highest priority political issues, and same-
sex marriage helped them retain a war footing from the mid-1990s
on.[40] James Dobson, head of the gigantic Focus on the Family, has been
particularly obsessed with the marriage issue.[41]

The religious right's organizational network includes groups that
specialize in litigation, such as the Liberty Counsel (founded by Jerry
Falwell), the American Center for Law and Justice (formed by Pat
Robertson), and the Alliance Defense Fund, seconded by a number of
Christian public-interest law firms.[42] In addition, religious denominations themselves have poured untold resources into the fight against
political recognition of sexual diversity. Prominent among these in the
United States is the Southern Baptist Convention, representing sixteen
million members, and a variety of smaller denominations ranging
from Pentecostal to charismatic to fundamentalist. On the marriage
issue particularly, the Roman Catholic hierarchy has been using its
priests and churches to mobilize opposition among parishioners, even
if its capacity to sway its own constituency is lower than that of the
Protestant right.

These resources are powerfully augmented by Christian right media
voices. James Dobson is estimated to have a worldwide audience of
220 million every week, and Pat Robertson's nightly broadcast, *The 700
Club*, has a huge American audience. These and many other media
vehicles, combined with the many networks of conservative churches
and the massive mailing lists compiled by religious right political
groups, facilitate the distribution of massive numbers of messages to
millions of Americans, and of voter guides in each election.[43]

Canadian Christian right organizing is a pale shadow of its American cousin's.[44] The Evangelical Fellowship of Canada is the oldest
such group. Although it began creating a political profile in the mid-
1980s, only in 1996 did it open its National Affairs office in Ottawa,
and near the end of that decade its annual budget was a large but not
formidable $3 million. Focus on the Family (Canada) is a branch plant
of the enormous American group, formed in British Columbia in 1983,
and it has grown in part through its opposition to same-sex marriage.
The Canada Family Action Coalition has risen to the marriage challenge, and older groups like the Campaign Life Coalition and the
anti-feminist group REAL Women of Canada have also focused on the
issue.

The political resources of the Protestant right in Canada remain small by American standards, and its supporters are concentrated in only a few regions. They are able to generate large numbers of letters, emails, and phone calls, but only a fraction of the avalanche that can be mobilized by their American counterparts. Despite the movement's impressive numbers, the urban media regularly portray the Protestant right as extreme. Links to the American right only add to that image.

*Religion and Party Politics*

The organized religious right in the United States has very much focused on gaining leverage over the Republican Party and mobilizing votes for it among religious conservatives. To be sure, there have been periods of disenchantment among conservative Christians about how much policy benefit they have derived from their support for Republicans. Still, they have no obvious alternative at election times, and their votes are strongly skewed towards the Republicans.

Conservative Christians in Canada have never gravitated to one party, although the new Conservative Party was attracting disproportionate numbers of regular church-goers, especially Protestants. There is an important religiously conservative core to that party's electorate in the western provinces and parts of Ontario: one 2006 poll showed that 40 per cent of Protestants attending church at least weekly who voted Conservative pointed to moral issues like abortion and same-sex marriage as the area that mattered most in deciding what candidate to vote for. Strong links exist between party leader Stephen Harper's inner circles and Christian right organizations, and subtle cues in his public language signal to religiously traditional voters that he is one of them.[45] That said, many born-again or evangelical Canadian Christians vote for the Liberals and the New Democrats, and Harper himself is considerably more devoted to his party's neo-liberal agenda than to its moral conservatism.[46] The fact that the Conservatives have not been able to deliver observable change in policy on core concerns of its religious voters is unlikely to provide them the capacity to dominate religious right voting in the way the Republicans have.

**Media Systems**

The Canadian mass media are profoundly influenced by those in the United States. The vast majority of Canadians have readier access to

American film and television than media consumers anywhere else in the world. They watch at least as much American television as Canadian and infinitely more American film. News reports on private television stations in Canada (which have larger audiences than the public networks) rely heavily on American journalists, and their coverage is much influenced by American frameworks. The major Canadian urban newspaper dailies have greater similarities to papers across the border than to newspapers in other parts of the world. In both countries, the 'quality' papers range from centrist to centre right on economic issues and moderately progressive on questions of diversity. In economic terms, the radical right is certainly represented by papers like the *Wall Street Journal* in the United States and the *National Post* in Canada; most other papers are not as far right or as explicitly partisan.

There are, however, important differences across the border. American television and especially radio have many more extremely conservative voices (on both economic and social issues) than would be found almost anywhere in Canada, and the personalities behind those voices are much more influential politically. The Christian right in the United States also has its own media outlets, through religious programming on regular media outlets and through its own stations and networks. Many of these reach into Canada, and changes in Canada's Broadcast Act in the late 1980s allowed more air time for evangelical broadcasters.[47] However, religious broadcasting covers the United States much more densely and reaches huge audiences.

The mainstream American media are routinely portrayed as 'liberal' by religious conservatives, but the truth is that they generally strive for a more conservative 'balance' than their Canadian counterparts. Even at a time when openly gay and lesbian characters proliferate on American television dramas, the major (not public) networks persist in ensuring that religiously conservative voices are given a voice in response to measures recognizing sexual diversity.

What these differences mean is that Canadian activists are more likely to find strong support in most of what we might call the metropolitan media – television networks, large-city newspapers, and radio stations. Support can also be found in a significant number of media outlets in less urban environments, particularly where religious conservatism is not prominent. That is much less true of the metropolitan media environment in the United States, where ferociously anti-gay voices are still routinely heard without apology.

## Political Culture

Seymour Martin Lipset long argued that there were 'foundational' contrasts between the United States and Canada – one revolutionary and visionary, the other counter-revolutionary and pragmatic.[48] He and other writers have portrayed American political culture as profoundly individualistic and suspicious of authority, and Canadian as more collectivist and ready to countenance an interventionist state. They have characterized the United States as having a 'muscular' form of nationalism, inviting newcomers and all who were different to the melting pot. By contrast – at least outside Quebec – Canada has been thought to have a low-key and insecure sense of what being Canadian means and a pattern of pragmatically accommodating differences of various sorts into a mosaic, with few international ambitions except to be liked.

In the United States, as we have seen, liberal individualism has helped strengthen religious currents that defy traditional authority but embrace moral traditionalism and associate it with nationalist mission. Homosexuality and other forms of 'moral decay,' then, strike at the very heart of America's divine calling. In stark contrast to the Canadian case, faith became more integral to American political culture over the course of the 20th century. The media became more bifurcated between secular media largely silent on faith and conservative Christian media framing everything by faith. Political speech across the spectrum became regularly infused with references to faith. In Canada, religious denomination was long central to political debate, and Catholicism was particularly important in francophone and Quebec political culture. But secularization has had more powerful play in Canada, and in Quebec particularly, than anywhere in the United States.

There is much debate about such claims concerning contrasts in political culture between the two countries. The forces of economic and cultural globalization have challenged national distinctiveness everywhere, but the long-intertwined economies of Canada and the United States suggest especially powerful forces for convergence in culture and politics. In music, film, television, and radio, the cultural influence of the United States has never been greater. Elements of Canada's political system have changed in ways that are reminiscent of long-standing American patterns – for example the prominence of rights struggles in the courts.

Table 2.4   Gallup Polling on Canadian and American Moral Views, 2004

| | % calling behaviour 'morally acceptable' | |
| Behaviour | Canada | U.S. |
| --- | --- | --- |
| Divorce | 78 | 66 |
| Sex between unmarried man and woman | 78 | 60 |
| Having baby outside marriage | 73 | 49 |
| Abortion | 53 | 40 |
| Homosexual behaviour | 60 | 42 |

Source: Lydia Saad, 'Can a "Reagan Revolution" Happen in Canada?' www.gallup.com.

Neil Nevitte and his associates have marshalled a great deal of public survey evidence that sets Canada in comparative context from the early 1980s on, some of it challenging widely held views about cross-national differences.[49] George Perlin's analysis comes to roughly similar conclusions, pointing to strong similarities in Canadian and American individualism and egalitarianism. Ray Tatalovich and Alexander Smith compare Canadian and American responses to a variety of policy issues that they place under the rubric of 'moral conflicts,' and find mixed results that fall very short of sustaining the Lipset view.[50]

Michael Adams argues on the other side, pointing to public opinion surveys that demonstrate increasing divergence on a range of core political values, rooted partly of course in religious differences.[51] He cites Pew Research Center data from 2002, for example, showing that Canada is the only country among the forty-four sampled where a majority believes that immigrants have a good influence. The 77 per cent who say yes to that question is well ahead of the 49 per cent of Americans who say the same. Americans are also more allegiant to traditional patriarchal conceptions of family. In 2000, a surprising 24 per cent of Canadians agreed with the statement that men were naturally superior to women, slightly down from eight years earlier. In the United States an alarming 38 per cent agreed, up 8 per cent from 1992. Gallup polling on moral issues would seem to reinforce the Adams analysis (see table 2.4).

The Pew Center's global attitudes surveys of 2002 showed significant differences in 'social anxiety' among Canadians and Americans. Fully 49 per cent of Americans, compared to 29 per cent of Canadians, thought that 'moral decline' was a very big problem in their country. This was paralleled by much larger proportions of the population identifying ethnic conflict, immigration, crime, and political corruption as big problems. Some anxiety, of course, has been produced by real differences in social context, but it is hard to avoid concluding that some of it comes from deep-seated ambivalence over the kind of freedom so celebrated in American life.

So on the one hand, the United States is populated by energetic risk takers who celebrate freedom and competition, but also by increasing numbers of citizens concerned about violence and the decline in traditional sources of authority, and as a result retreating to secure traditions. For many Americans, this dovetails with a deeply felt religious faith, usually paired with conservative values on moral questions. Canadians, in a country born of conservative reaction, are less fearful, less deferential, and readier to accept difference and change. They have, as Adams puts it, 'a penchant for going halfway rather than fighting it out to see who's left standing.' As he says elsewhere, 'America honours the lone warrior fighting for truth and justice, the father who is master of his lonely house on the prairie, and a few good men planting the Stars and Stripes on a distant planet. Canada honours compromise, harmony, and equality. Americans go where no man has gone before; Canadians follow hoping to make that new place livable.'[52]

An entirely different school of analysis portrays the United States as internally polarized – as beset by a culture war between religious conservatives and more liberal or secularized populations. The steady identification of most evangelical Protestant voters with the Republican party has widened the spread of the metaphor (and talk of 'red' and 'blue' states). Kenneth Wald thinks the metaphor inapt, and he cites substantial variation of opinion and partisan preference among adherents of each faith current (including 'evangelical' Protestants) to make the point.[53] Morris Fiorina also questions the culture war theory, arguing that most Americans hold moderate positions on contentious policy issues, and that differences within states outweigh regional divides.[54]

However, the concentration of strongly conservative believers within large and visible religious right organizations, and their close ties to the Republican Party, gives regular voice to extreme and militant language on core issues like abortion and homosexuality. The hold on government power by Republican politicians wedded to such views has also given them a certain legitimacy, even if they do not nec-

Table 2.5  Approval and Disapproval of Homosexuality

| | | Percentage agreeing | |
| --- | --- | --- | --- |
| Date | Proposition | Canada | United States |
| 1981 | Homosexuality 'never' or 'always justified'[a] Negative: 8–10 on 10-pt scale | 7 | 13 |
| 1990 | Homosexuality 'never' or 'always justified'[a] Negative: 8–10 on 10-pt scale | 13 | 24 |
| | Homosexuality 'never justified' | 40 | 57 |
| 1996 | Homosexuality an acceptable lifestyle[b] | 60 | 44 |
| 2000 | Homosexuality 'never justified'[a] | 27 | 32 |
| 2000 | Same-sex sexual relations 'always wrong'[c] | 32 | 59 |
| 2004 | Homosexuality an acceptable lifestyle[b] | 69 | 54 |
| 2004 | Homosexual behaviour 'morally acceptable'[b] | 60 | 42 |
| 2007 | Homosexuality should be accepted by society[d] | 70 | 49 |

[a]World Values Survey, from Neil Nevitte, *The Decline of Deference* (Peterborough, ON: Broadview, 1996), 218; updated with Ronald Inglehart et al., *Human Beliefs and Values: A Cross-Cultural Sourcebook Based on the 1999–2002 Values Surveys* (Madrid: Siglo XXI Editores, 2004).
[b]Gallup polling, most recently reported in Lydia Saad, 'Can a "Reagan Revolution" Happen in Canada?' www.gallup.com.
[c]Reginald Bibby survey on Canada and General Social Survey on United States, reported in Michael Adams, 'Sex and Fire: Religion, Homosexuality, and Authority in Canada and the United States,' *Vue Magazine*, February 2005 (www.michaeladams.ca/articles/pdf/sex_fire.pdf).
[d]Pew Global Attitudes Project, 'World Publics Welcome Global Trade,' October 2007.

essarily get translated into public policy. Voters holding moderate or conflicted views on questions of morality end up by putting into office moral extremists who relish making gains by talking of 'liberals' as if they were tainted meat, and of 'San Francisco Democrats' in tones suggesting perversion.[55]

## Public Opinion and Sexuality

There are two stories here. One is of a significant shift towards greater acceptance of sexual diversity in both Canada and the United States through the 1990s. The other is of a growing though uneven divergence in attitudes across the international border, most pronounced on the question of same-sex marriage. One important measure of that divergence is the sizeable number of Americans who abhore every-thing to do with homosexuality and reject almost all measures giving public legitimacy to it.

Up to and including the 1980s, there was a persistent and strong moral disapproval of homosexuality in both countries. Polls that use the same wording of the question in Canada and the United States are not that common, but those displayed in table 2.5 show a steady decline in disapproval of homosexuality, and a persistent gap between Canadians and Americans.

Numerous surveys of American opinion conducted by the National Opinion Research Center from 1973 to 1991 showed that between 70 and 78 per cent of the population thought that sexual relations between two adults of the same sex was 'always wrong.'[56] By the end of the 1990s, that strong disapproval declined to just under 60 per cent, and in 2002 stood at 55 per cent. Surveys in Canada showed that until the early 1990s majorities of about 60 per cent strongly disapproved of homosexuality (somewhat below American levels), but that at decade's end disapproval had declined to 34 per cent (much lower than American levels).[57]

Other evidence suggests that a widening gap may reflect a stalling of the shift towards more positive attitudes about homosexuality in the United States since the late 1990s. Lydia Saad points out in her analy-sis of a 2005 Gallup survey that in the previous six years support for the statement that the homosexual 'lifestyle' should be considered acceptable rose only slightly from 50 to 51 per cent.[58] Patrick Egan and Kenneth Sherrill's tracking of 'feeling thermometer' scorings of gay men and lesbians in national election studies also shows slight shifts towards negative ratings in recent years after modest shifts towards more favourable ratings since 1984.[59]

The gap between Canadian and American attitudes is not evident across all sexuality issues. As table 2.6 shows, it is obvious on ques-tions about civil unions and especially marriage. But Canadians and Americans do not respond much differently on questions about access to job opportunities and the much tougher question of adoption rights. The similarities owe something to the strong individual rights tradi-tion in the United States, and the willingness of many Americans to extend at least formal rights to segments of the population they do not like. This seems to apply more readily to questions of individual dis-crimination than those involving couples, perhaps because the latter

Table 2.6    Gallup Polling on Rights for Gays and Lesbians, United States and Canada, 1996–2004

|  | United States (% approving) | | Canada (% approving) | |
| --- | --- | --- | --- | --- |
|  | 1996 | 2003–4 | 1996 | 2002–4 |
| Equal rights in job opportunities | 84 | 89 (2004) | 88 | 92 (2002) |
| Adoption | – | 49 (2003) | 34 | 52 (2004) |
| Civil unions | – | 49 (2004) | – | 63 (2004) |
| Same-sex marriage | 27 | 35 (2004)* | 34 | 51 (2004) |

*Three 2004 polls showed support at 39 (June), 35 (Oct), and 31 (Dec) per cent, averaging 35 per cent. Gallup polling in 2006 showed support for equal job opportunities at 89 per cent, and for gay marriage at 39 per cent.

more readily evokes religious associations, and fears about homosexual contact with children. In both countries, there are indicators of similar resistance to parenting by lesbians and gay men.

Public attitudes to homosexuality display extraordinary volatility. This is true on any issue, but particularly so in an area that has been the focus of such intense political debate, but which so many people tried to avoid thinking about for so long. The evidence of sudden shifts in opinion seems particularly striking in the United States, where so many battles over the political recognition of sexual diversity have been fought.

During the early and mid-summer of 2003, the American Supreme Court struck down a Texas sodomy statute that criminalized homosexual activity (*Lawrence v. Texas*), and at about the same time controversy inside the Episcopal Church exploded over the blessing of same-sex unions and the naming of an openly gay man as bishop of New Hampshire. The religious right then intensified its anti-gay mobilizing, and what followed was a significant shift in public response to polling questions on homosexuality. In May 2003, 59 per cent of American respondents responded favourably to a Gallup question asking whether 'homosexual relations between consenting adults should be legal'; in July the same question elicited positive responses from only 49 per cent.[60] Over the same period, support for gay civil unions dropped from 49 to 40 per cent, and polling by other firms in the next several weeks showed even more of a drop.[61] By 2005 response patterns to most gay-related questions had returned to their early 2003

Table 2.7  Support for Equal Rights for Gay and Lesbian Teachers in Canada and the United States, 1988–2004

|  | 1988–89 | | 2000–1 | | 2004 |
| --- | --- | --- | --- | --- | --- |
|  | Canada | U.S. | Canada | U.S. | U.S. |
| Equal rights in job opportunities | – | 71 | 92 | 85 | 89 |
| Equal right to be employed as elementary-school teachers | 45 | 42 | 67 | 56 | 61 |

Source: Gallup, for 1989, 2001, and 2004 U.S., 1988 and 2000 Canada. The 2004 U.S. survey indicated that 67 per cent supported the hiring of gays as high-school teachers.

form, all this replicating the volatility of attitudes towards the military ban on gays and lesbians in the military, at the time of the firestorm that emerged in 1993 when President Clinton tried to lift it.

Canadian surveying in recent years has shown both volatility and sensitivity to the wording of specific questions, but the slippage seems isolated to the question of marriage itself. Environics polling showed a drop in support for same-sex marriage from 2004 to 2005, down a full 10 per cent to 44 per cent. But polling on other issues related to sexual diversity did not show the kind of shifts that were evident in the United States.

*Attitudes on Schooling Issues*

Public anxieties about recognizing sexual diversity in schools are reflected in polling in both Canada and the United States, though relatively few data are available in this area. As we have already seen, public attitudes continue to be conservative about issues related to young people and sexuality. To illustrate, data reported in table 2.7 reveal the slippage in support when the question shifts from the principle of equal rights for gays and lesbians in jobs to a specific question about schoolteachers.

In 2000, the Kaiser Foundation reported that 64 per cent of respondents to an American survey approved the inclusion of discussion about sexual orientation as a normal part of some people's sexuality, but the question was only about sex education classes.[62] Anxiety about 'exposing' young people to homosexuality is reflected in the declared preparedness of fully 32 per cent of respondents to the same survey to not allow children, if they had them, to attend an elementary class if their teacher was openly gay or lesbian.

## The Attitudes of Young People

The attitudes of young people are especially important for any consideration of public anxiety on schools issues, because such attitudes so greatly influence school climate. On the positive side, all surveys in Canada and the United States indicate that adolescents are much more likely than their elders, and more likely than young people a generation ago, to have positive attitudes towards homosexuality, regardless of the question. In fact, shifts in general public sentiment that were characteristic of the 1990s were especially pronounced among young adults and adolescents.

In 1999, a UCLA survey of first-year college/university students across the United States showed that 30 per cent supported laws prohibiting homosexual relationships – in some respects this number is alarmingly high, but it is down substantially from 53 per cent in 1987. One analysis of these data from 1995 to 2004 pointed out an overall shift towards more conservative political values among young people, but not on questions related to homosexuality.[63] In early 2006 a Zogby International poll showed that three-quarters of high school seniors favoured legal recognition of same-sex relationships, and 63 per cent supported adoption rights for lesbian/gay couples.[64] Even more dramatically, a 1999 Kaiser Foundation survey of teens aged 13–19 showed that 54 per cent 'don't have any problem with homosexuality' – in stark contrast to the 17 per cent who answered thus in 1991.

Yet, it is hard to know how to interpret the responses of those many who say they 'don't have a problem.' For over a decade, in both Canada and the United States, there has been widespread talk of the 'coolness' or 'chic' associated with being lesbian or bisexual in school. But this taps into behaviour that plays with and appears to rebel against adult norms. Having 'no problem with homosexuality' is about either an abstraction or 'playing around,' and appears to coexist with persistent personal discomfort when faced with 'real' homosexuality. One mid-1990s national U.S. survey of teenagers (15–19) – admittedly more than a decade ago – found that a startling 89 per cent considered the idea of homosexual activity 'disgusting.'[65] A 2001 American survey of high school seniors found that the majority supported gay marriage, but only 43 per cent said they would be comfortable with a gay lab partner, only 38 per cent with a gay teammate using the same locker room, and only 32 per cent with socializing alongside gay couples at a party.[66] One Chicago high school student was quoted in 2003 as saying that you may not be shoved or beaten, but 'you're just kind of that elephant in the living room that no one wants to talk about.'[67] Even in relatively inclusive schools, sports remain an arena in which deviation from heterosexuality is policed most aggressively, intensified by anxieties about same-sex physical contact, change rooms, and showers.

### Variations by Religious Faith

A major source of cross-border contrast on its own, religion is among the most important influences on attitudes to sexual difference on both sides of the border. In a 2003 Canadian survey, Reginald Bibby showed that only 22 per cent of those who attend religious services at least weekly supported gay adoption, in stark contrast to the 58 per cent of those attending less frequently or not at all.[68] He indicates that among younger Canadians (18–34) the contrast in attitudes towards same-sex marriage is even starker – only 21 per cent of weekly attendees were supportive, compared to 74 per cent of those attending less frequently.

American polling also shows how strongly religious practice shapes attitudes. A 2003 Gallup poll showed that affirmative responses to the statement that homosexual relations ought to be legal varied from 27 per cent among those attending religious services weekly, to 66 per cent among those attending seldom or never. A Pew Research poll, also in 2003, found that among those with high religious commitment, only 12 per cent favoured gay marriage, and among those with low commitment, 50 per cent.[69] In 2006, an ABC News poll indicated that an amazing 72 per cent of white evangelical Protestants favoured a national constitutional amendment banning same-sex marriage, compared to a national average of 42 per cent.[70]

### Regional Differences

Public opinion on sexual diversity has significant regional differences that are equally strong within Canada and the United States. However, we also find that on the controversial issue of marriage, the most conservative of Canadian regions display support that is higher than all

Table 2.8   Attitudes to Sexual Diversity, by American Region, 1998–2003

| | Percentage agreeing | | | |
| --- | --- | --- | --- | --- |
| | Northeast | South | Midwest | West |
| Homosexual relations always wrong | | | | |
| (National Opinion Research Center 1998) | 48 | 68 | 61 | 46 |
| Homosexual relations always wrong | | | | |
| (NORC 2002) | 41 | 71 | 52 | 45 |
| Homosexual relations should be legal | | | | |
| (Gallup May 2003) | 65 | 50 | 58 | 69 |
| Support same-sex marriage | | | | |
| (Gallup Dec. 2003) | 39 | 24 | 32 | 31 |

Source: American Enterprise Institute, 'Attitudes about Homosexuality and Gay Marriage,' 2004.

but a few U.S. states. The strength of unfavourable opinions in parts of the United States is particularly important in light of the prominence of state and local jurisdiction over areas of relevance to sexuality.

In the United States, the Northeast and West have the most favourable attitude mix, and the South the most negative, with no sign whatever of the gap narrowing (see table 2.8). A 2006 survey by Pew Research highlighted in particular the gap between the U.S. South and other regions. Support for adoption rights in the South was 35 per cent, only 4 per cent higher than in 1999. The average across the whole country was 46 per cent in support, up 8 per cent from 1999.[71]

A 2000 National Election Study provided one of the few opportunities to explore attitude differences between American states (rather than roughly drawn regions): it included a question on whether the federal government should do more to stop job discrimination against homosexuals.[72] Of the fifty-one jurisdictions, the most favourable ten states (with positive responses varying from 46 to 64 per cent) were all in the Northeast (including Washington, DC). The eleventh was California (45 per cent affirmative). All other states had fewer than 43 per cent affirmative answers (down to 30 per cent in South Dakota).

On the Canadian side, surveys show attitudes towards sexual diversity most favourable in Quebec, British Columbia, and (surprisingly) the Atlantic region, and least favourable in Alberta and the Prairie region (see table 2.9). The contrast between the most traditional and

Table 2.9   Attitudes to Sexual Diversity, by Canadian Region, 2000–4

|  | Percentage agreeing | | | | | |
| --- | --- | --- | --- | --- | --- | --- |
|  | Atlantic | Quebec | Ontario | Prairies | Alberta | BC |
| Support constitution prohibiting discrimination on sexual orientation (Environics, 1996) | 54 | 65 | 43 | 45 | 52 | 56 |
| G/L couples should have same treatment as heterosexual (Environics 1999) | 56 | 62 | 52 | 43 | 38 | 57 |
| Support same-sex marriage (Environics 2006) | 64 | 67 | 56 | 39* | 51* | 65 |

*These results are comparatively low for the Prairies and high for Alberta compared to other polls, probably a result of the wider variation to be expected from a relatively low sample size. Polling in 2004 by Environics showed support in the two areas at 45 and 37 per cent respectively.

most accepting of Canadian regions is not much different from those we see in United States, though the 'floor' is higher. Scott Matthews sees region as declining as a significant differentiator of Canadian responses, using the marriage issues as an illustration.[73]

## The Broader Question of What Difference Region Makes

No comparative analysis of Canadian and American belief systems, cultural patterns, political activism, and public policies can ignore the question of regional variation. The sheer territorial expanse of both countries gives regionalism a powerful geographic foundation, contributing to diversity in economic structure, migration patterns, and ethnic mix. Federalism provides a vehicle through which regional characteristics can shape political outcomes and create radically different opportunities for social movement activists to secure gains on one side or another of debates over moral issues.

In Canada, regional identities and regionally based political tensions have long been a central feature of political life.[74] A sense of distinctiveness is especially powerful in Quebec, but it is also strong in Newfoundland, British Columbia, and Alberta. The recognition of such identities is regularly accompanied by a belief that provinces or regions have different political cultures and public policy preferences. In the United States, even if the strength of nationalism seems to mute regionalist voices, state and (in some areas) regional identities are strong, most obviously in the South. As in Canada they are usually seen as marking important variations in popular beliefs and policy. World Values Survey data from 1990 show markedly little difference between Americans and Canadians in the proportion of the population identifying primarily with their locality or region.[75]

For decades writers have been arguing that regional boundaries within each of these countries are so significant that they loom larger than the international border. Most of Joel Garreau's famously described nine nations of North America straddle that border, including the central manufacturing 'foundry,' and the west coast 'ecotopia' (in other portrayals called 'cascadia.')[76] After the divisive 2004 American election, a widely distributed cartoon map of North America eliminated the international border and replaced it with an undulating boundary between 'The United States of Canada' (taking in the American West Coast and the Northeast) and 'Jesusland.'[77]

These are of course exaggerations. The international border does matter. Michael Adams's mapping of attitudes on a range of issues certainly displays wide regional variation, especially within the United States, but it also shows a clustering of all Canadian regions in a place quite distinct from the disparate American ones, with only 'New England' even close to the Canadian cluster.[78]

Some regional differences, and indeed international differences, are being eroded by the homogenizing influences of mass communication, increased geographic mobility, and the economic dominance of large corporations with global reach. The uniformity of shopping malls, the ubiquity of mass-marketed brands, the giant waves of popular culture, the orchestrated shifts in style – all these reduce the economic, cultural, and linguistic uniqueness of both cities and the regions around them no matter how distinctive their inhabitants believe themselves to be. The largest cities in Canada and the United States have large numbers of people born and raised elsewhere, including what William Leach describes as 'floating populations of business professionals rooted everywhere and nowhere.'[79]

Differences within regions, in fact, often appear much more important than those between them. The contrasts in social and economic life, and in outlooks, between Atlanta and the rest of Georgia, Montreal and the rest of Quebec, Calgary and farming Alberta surely count more than region. Polling on many issues, including sexuality, shows that community size is an important source of difference in attitudes towards sexual orientation. Electoral maps by district or constituency regularly suggest that the divide between big cities and small communities is more important than that between one region and others.

Nevertheless, regional identity and a *belief* in regional distinctiveness are tenacious. And these can serve to accentuate the political play of variations in popular beliefs. If a particular locality or region comes to portray itself as distinctively accepting of sexual or cultural diversity, for example, that self-image might draw ambivalent inhabitants to a more accepting view, just as a regional self-image upholding 'traditional' family values might do the opposite.

Variations in partisan balance across state and provincial borders can of course strengthen the regional contrasts in how sexuality is debated and policy shaped. The party systems in both countries have powerfully decentralizing features, leaving ample room for regional differences to emerge in the ideological balance within and between parties. The winner-take-all electoral system that operates across both countries then exaggerates the political contrasts between local districts or constituencies, and across regions.[80] Moderate variations in the balance of opinion on issues like sexual diversity, then, can produce major contrasts in the way those issues are taken up politically.

The question of how important geography is in determining how sexual diversity issues play out, and in shaping pro-gay activism, may be usefully explored by a consideration of a few of those regions thought most distinct. Quebec and the American South are two obvious candidates. So is Alberta, widely considered the most conservative province in Canada. The U.S. Northwest and the West Coast in Canada are intriguing in somewhat different ways, in part because their own populations commonly see themselves as very different from their compatriots across the mountains, and in part because many inhabitants see strong similarities across the international border.

*Quebec*

There is no region in Canada with as strong a claim to the status of a distinct society as Quebec. Four-fifths of its population is French speaking, the great majority of them with deep roots in the region. The 1867 federation agreement that created the Canadian political system treated Quebec differently from the other provinces, providing not only special cultural protections but also a legal system built in part on the provincial Civil Code. Since then, a large number of other policy developments have given Quebec a distinct status.

In present-day Quebec, most French speakers would identify strongly as nationalist Québécois, even if only about half are sovereigntist. Francophone social movement activism is almost invariably tinged with such nationalism, and frequently with sovereigntist sentiment.[81] Though all but a tiny minority of French speakers are nominally Roman Catholic, Quebec is now an overwhelmingly secular society, and the church hierarchy exercises almost no political influence.

Over the last few decades, Quebec nationalists have portrayed their society as less bound than English-Canadian (and American) society by traditional morality. Pollsters in the late 1970s eliciting reactions to the statement 'Marriage is an outdated institution' found that 19 per cent of francophones agreed, in contrast to 11 per cent of English Canadians and 7 per cent of Americans.[82] Polling in 2007 showed a similar contrast on marriage, and distinctly less disapproval of extramarital affairs among Quebeckers than among residents of any other province.[83] Writers, media commentators, politicians, and social movement activists across Quebec regularly portray it as categorically more accepting of sexual diversity than the rest of Canada and its political system as being on the leading edge of developing inclusive policy.The reality, however, is more nuanced. In a general sense, the distinctiveness of Quebec society and culture is declining even if the belief in its distinctiveness persists. Its Montreal metropolis has not been immune to the standardizing pressures of mass communication and a globalizing economy. The lived reality of everyday life in Montreal is less a contrast to Toronto and Vancouver than it once was, and countless media accounts of the preoccupations of young Québécois are not much different from stories on young people in the rest of the country.

On sexuality issues, opinion surveys generally show Quebeckers as the most accepting of diversity, but they are usually in the same league as British Columbians (and sometimes Atlantic Canadians), and not radically above Ontarians. On most issues, residents of Montreal, Toronto, and Vancouver are not much different from one another. What we will find in subsequent chapters, too, is that the caution of Quebec's politicians is not much different from that which we find elsewhere, with policy developments only rarely in the Canadian vanguard.

*Alberta*

There has long been a powerful current of conservative individualistic populism in Alberta. This current created the basis for the growth of Social Credit in the mid-twentieth century and of the Reform Party at century's end.[84] Through the 1990s and into the twenty-first century, the province's electorate have been the strongest supporters of federal parties representing a combination of neo-liberal resentment of state regulation and neo-conservative antipathy to changing social codes. The provincial Conservative Party, long in control of the Alberta government, has come the closest of any successful provincial party in effecting the American Republican combination of neo-liberalism and moral conservatism. Alone among provincial leaders, Alberta's former premier Ralph Klein promised a crusade against same-sex marriage as the federal Liberal government prepared legislative steps to enshrine it in 2004. Polling on lesbian/gay rights reveals more opposition in Alberta than elsewhere in Canada, with the neighbouring provinces of Saskatchewan and Manitoba close behind.

However, the economic growth of the province has attracted many Canadians from other regions, particularly to the large cities. The rapid growth in the number of corporate headquarters in Calgary has increased the presence of employees and company executives with no obvious interest in or support for morally conservative crusades. At the time of the marriage debate, in 2005, then-premier Klein spoke about the province's cosmopolitanism, and the outdatedness of its redneck reputation. In 1998, when the Supreme Court of Canada effectively wrote sexual orientation into the province's human rights statute, he mused about invoking a constitutional provision that would allow circumvention of the court's ruling. He soon learned, however, that most Albertans supported that ruling, and he backed off.[85]

*The American South*

Is there a similar story in the American South – a belief in regional distinctiveness exceeding the reality? Certainly allegiance to the region's distinctive identity, particularly in the 'Old South,' has very deep roots.[86] And there can be little doubt that the legacy of the Civil War, of segregation, and of long-standing economic disadvantage reinforced social and political conservatism, particularly among whites. Adherence to conservative strands of Protestant Christianity (Baptist, for example) remains a strong force in the South, among both African Americans and whites, and this strength is amply reflected in the politics of most states in the region. Republicans here are as influenced by the religious right as anywhere in the country, and most state Democratic parties in the South are more to the right than their counterparts elsewhere.[87] Opinion surveys regularly show the South as the most conservative region in the United States, and as more supportive of traditional norms of gender and family. Surveying on some gay rights issues, as we have seen, reveal much the same pattern.

The 'New South,' however, is in some respects a very different region than the Old South. Economic fortunes have improved for parts of the region, starting in the 1930s and accelerating in the last few decades. Change in Atlanta, for example, including large-scale population shifts to it from within and outside the region, makes plausible the claim that it has essentially become a northern city. Assertions of this sort could be made for smaller growth poles centred on the region's best universities (for example, in North Carolina) and for several other major urban centres. And as is true across the country, national media and cultural industries have a profound impact on the tastes and preferences of southerners as well as non-southerners, exercising a homogenizing effect on even this most distinct area.

That said, the possibilities for significant shifts towards recognition of sexual diversity in state-level public policy are limited, or nonexistent. As in Canada, the variations in public attitudes across regions get exaggerated in electoral outcomes, and states have more jurisdictional room than Canadian provinces do on issues related to sexuality. Although cities like Atlanta and New Orleans have had large and vibrant gay communities for decades, conservative religious belief still counts for much, and especially so in state politics. Activists in the American South face challenges more daunting than anywhere else on the continent.

## Cascadia

Descriptions of West Coast political culture in Canada and the American Northwest suggest considerable openness to the acceptance of diversity, including that based on sexuality. Physical and psychological remove from the rest of the continent, shaped by distance and mountains, and a history of economic and political dependence on more powerful regions to the east, it is said, have created a willingness to reject the constraints of more traditional settlement areas. The isolated frontier experience and the early immigration of strongly individualistic fortune seekers can be said to have strengthened the acceptance of difference. Rapid population growth in the last several decades, including waves of immigration from Asia, may also have infused a broader acceptance of diversity into regional identities. This builds on elements of egalitarianism, progressive individualism, and civic-minded collectivism that are thought by many writers and inhabitants to set the region apart from the rest of the continent.

There are, however, forms of populism on both the American and Canadian West Coasts that can veer as strongly to the right as to the left. Religious conservatism has a strong foothold, alongside high levels of secularism. The electorates of these regions, then, provide sustenance for political leaders of a wide ideological range, and unpredictability in political outcome. Gay rights measures regularly provoke intense anti-gay campaigning by religious conservatives in precisely these regions. When Focus on the Family first established a Canadian branch plant, its headquarters was in BC.

There are also major differences across the international border, here as well as further east. Support for government intervention seems to have more hold in BC, and the labour movement is stronger. Most significant of all is the far greater strength of the religious right on the American side. The Northwest may well be the most secular region in the United States, but it does not look very secular by comparison to any Canadian region. As a result, the American Northeast's Republican parties have been much more influenced by moral conservatism, and by the organized religious right, than the major right-wing party in BC (now the Liberal Party) or even the Conservatives in Alberta. The Republicans are strong contenders for legislative and executive office at all levels of government in the region, too, and the strength of religious conservatism is great enough to cow a minority of Democrats.

Pro-gay activists in states like Washington and Oregon also work with political institutions in which (as in the rest of the United States) power is much more fragmented, making radical or sudden change difficult to imagine. Their counterparts north of the forty-ninth parallel may face insurmountable odds in taking even the smallest of steps towards recognition when right-wing parties are in power, but then may suddenly encounter widely opened doors when the New Democrats are in power. The regional distinctiveness that shapes Cascadia, then, does create real opportunities for creating more inclusive political environments for sexual minorities, but the power of the region does nothing to diminish the decisive impact of the international border.

## Conclusion

Pro-gay activists in Canada and the United States face family regimes shaped by similar hierarchies and prejudices, deeply enmeshed in countless statutes and institutional policies. The policy web holding up the privilege of the heterosexual family, though, has come under sustained pressure, starting long before the rise of the modern lesbian, gay, bisexual, and transgender movement. The result was more sustained shift in Canada than in the United States, in ways that would benefit claims by same-sex couples.

Several other contextual factors – institutional, social, and cultural – also lay the groundwork for more comprehensive change in Canada, with sometimes surprising uniformity. The notion that Canadians are significantly more accepting of sexual diversity is not substantiated on the full range of issues being explored here, and attitudes vary across the country. In the United States, however, moral disapproval of homosexuality is legitimized by conservative religious faith, which is an imposing force throughout the United States. Institutional fragmentation compounds the challenge for LGBT activists. Jurisdictional decentralization over the issues that count for sexual minorities, however, provides local and regional opportunities for innovation, at the same time leaving the exclusionary policies and practices of other places almost completely unchanged.

# 3 Broadening Activist Agendas

From the late 1980s on, challenges to heterosexual assumptions about family and the education of children multiplied in both the United States and Canada. This expansion was risky, because the pressure for change confronted complex policy frameworks and deep-set beliefs about what family meant. Advocates for change also met internal resistance from activists who had cut their teeth on systematic critiques of the whole idea of family. On the other hand, activist questioning of what counted as a relationship, who could be publicly recognized as a parent, what freedom children had to develop their sexuality, and what schools taught, could not be stopped.

The lesbian/gay/bisexual/transgendered movement of the late 1980s, the 1990s, and the first decade of the twenty-first century has been more institutionalized and legitimized than in the 1970s, and more open to claims that it was too mainstream, but the challenges to family norms and structures, and to school inattention to sexual diversity, were grassroots movements springing from many different corners of North America. Employees wanting health-care coverage or pension benefits for their partners, parents looking for acknowledgment of their relationship to their children, teachers hoping to be able to respond honestly about who they were, partners of the sick or dying wanting their voices recognized, union members pushing inclusive benefit claims to the forefront of the bargaining agenda, students claiming the right to establish a school group to raise awareness – all these people were pushing against the boundaries of family regimes, and many of them were becoming activists in the process. They may not originally have seen themselves as part of a broader movement, but they usually found themselves seeking information from organizational web sites, or help from advocates linked more explicitly to movement networks. And for most of these claimants, the stakes were concrete, and high. In unprecedented numbers, they were not prepared to back down in the face of organized opposition or structural impediment.

American activists have had access to more resources than those in the Canadian movement, placed marriage on the front burner more quickly than their Canadian counterparts, and engaged with schooling issues with more sustained attention and from an earlier stage. In fact, pioneering challenges to heterosexual family assumptions were registered as early in the United States as in any country. But American activists confronted a formidable opposition spearheaded by the Christian right. Religion counted for much more in politics than it did in Canada, and in no liberal democratic industrialized country was there a conservative religious force as politically mobilized against homosexuality as in the United States. The ensuing struggle produced, as later chapters will show, not so much a transformation as a gradual extension of arenas in which such assumptions were overturned or modified. Canadian activists have mobilized with a much smaller resource foundation and a limited capacity to bridge regional divisions. Even with such handicaps, however, they have had remarkable success in challenging the established family regime.

## Activist Resources

It would be hard to find two queer activist movements that contrast so dramatically in resources as the movements in Canada and in the United States. To be sure, there are strong similarities between the two. They have experienced similar cycles of mobilization.[1] Issues like violence, AIDS, workplace equality, and relationship recognition moved to the front burners at roughly the same time. Each movement was able to build on the growth of visibly gay commercial and residential districts in large cities. Both found opportunities for engagement with mainstream political processes at about the same period (starting in the 1980s). A confrontation with hard questions about movement inclusiveness on lines of gender, race, bisexuality, and transgenderism has been a feature of both.

Among the differences between them, one of the most striking is the scale of organizing. In the United States, at the national, state, and local level, there are innumerable LGBT activist groups operating on a scale

Table 3.1   National LGBT Organizations in Canada and the United States, 2004–5

|  | Annual budget (millions) | Full-time staff |
|---|---|---|
| **Canada** | | |
| Egale Canada | $ 0.5 | 5 |
| **United States** | | |
| Human Rights Campaign | $33.0 | 140 |
| Lambda Legal | 11.7 | 91 |
| National Gay and Lesbian Task Force | 8.5 | 45 |
| Gay, Lesbian, and Straight Education | | |
| Network | 4.5 | 30 |
| Parents, Families and Friends of | | |
| Lesbians and Gays | 2.0 | 16 |
| Freedom to Marry | 1.2 | 7 |

Source: Organizational web sites and interviews.

virtually unknown in Canada. The profile of national groups in table 3.1 provides a dramatic glimpse of such differences. At the provincial level in Canada, LGBT groups are almost all run by volunteers, and on tiny budgets, apart from those groups operating under an AIDS rubric. In the United States, several of the state groups and many local groups are well resourced and staffed.

The number, range, size, and permanence of U.S. groups result partly from the strength of the religious right and the complexity of the political systems through which change must be effected or defended. The American framework creates inescapable pressures on activists to intervene in elections and organize inside political parties. The same compelling attraction also exists in the American court system. For well over half a century, activists seeking equity have tried to effect change through litigation, following in the steps of the civil rights movement.[2] This produces enough positive results to be an attractive option, particularly where few positive results can be anticipated through legislative or administrative action. In any event, activists are inevitably drawn into court by the willingness of conservatives to pursue anti-gay objectives through the courts.

The American LGBT movement, then, has strong incentives to mobilize widely and to institutionalize for the longer term. It also has the capacity to do so. Activist groups have far greater fundraising capacities than their counterparts in any other country, including Canada. This derives in part from a culture of individualistic optimism, which sees progressive change as always possible, and achievable through the efforts of individuals. It also comes from a long-standing pattern of private giving, whether to the arts, to universities, or to political causes. As Seymour Martin Lipset says, the American preference for private giving has been the natural consequence of a reduced commitment to the welfare state and a belief in the free market.[3] This produces stark social inequalities, but it also results in the United States leading the world in philanthropic giving.[4]

The American system creates huge incentives to organize at the national level, and inside Washington, DC. The power of the central government, the number of political openings within it, the near-constant opportunities for making gains and risks of suffering losses – all these factors require continuous and detailed attention. The country's large population allows many groups to establish a presence in Washington on an imposing scale. Groups like Lambda Legal, the National Gay and Lesbian Task Force (NGLTF), Gay, Lesbian, and Straight Education Network (GLSEN), Parents and Friends of Lesbians and Gays (PFLAG), and especially the Human Rights Campaign (HRC) are enormous. They may not have nearly the resources to devote to regional and state campaigns that grassroots campaigners would wish, but in many states and cities their work is paralleled by equivalent groups.

The same forces that create incentives for national group institutionalization also operate at state and local levels. The capacity of governments at these levels to act in quite independent ways on issues of crucial significance to sexual diversity make them inescapable sites of intervention, especially as the range of issues raised by activists extended into the arena of same-sex relationships. The capacity to organize in those parts of the United States in which the prospects of change are slightest – for example, in the South – will be much lower than in those parts where change has been greatest or its prospect most tantalizing. In many such places, though, we see more elaborate organizing than we would see in the most densely mobilized regions of Canada.

Sexual diversity activism at the national level and in every region in Canada has been smaller in scale and more episodic. Apart from AIDS or health-focused groups, only Egale even pretends to have cross-country reach, and it remains a tiny organization by U.S. standards.[5] Canadian activists have striven mightily to extend their informal networks across the country, but they do so in an environment in which such networks are harder to build and sustain. The relative weakness of LGBT organizations is even more apparent at the provincial and local levels. In the larger cities, there are dense networks of community groups and informal networks, but few that are explicitly focused on politics have sustained resources.

Canadian activists are less preoccupied than their U.S. counterparts with creating a continuously visible presence inside the political mainstream, and the concentration of political power in the hands of cabinets and first ministers reduces the incentives to do so. The major exception has been in the courts, where the robust rights platform provided through the Charter of Rights and Freedoms has provided strong inducements to mount court challenges against discriminatory family law. Even there, intervention is more haphazard and is highly shaped by the willingness of claimants to pay legal costs or of individual law firms to take on cases without charge. Some LGBT groups now operate within Canada's bar associations, and more firms than ever are eager to take on cases.[6] Nevertheless, Canada has no activist groups specializing in pro-gay litigation, and nothing like the resources ready to be directed towards mounting significant legal challenges.

One of the few 'resource' advantages that the Canadian movement has over its American counterparts is the strength of the Canadian labour movement and the widespread support for the rights of sexual minorities within that movement.[7] Canadian workers are more than twice as likely as Americans to be union members, and they are more likely to belong to a union that has taken up sexual diversity issues.[8] Activists working inside the American labour movement have made great strides in pushing equal rights agendas to the fore, with notable gains in public sector unions and some other service sector unions. The AFL-CIO provides support for Pride at Work, a national group representing LGBT union members, and even the Teamsters now have a GLBT caucus. The spread of support for the recognition of sexual diversity across American unions, though, is not as great as in Canada, and the labour movement's voice is weaker overall.

American activists are not without important allies. For decades they have benefited from the strong support of the American Civil Liberties Union (ACLU), itself a major group with a large courtroom presence and much more uniformly supportive of LGBT claims than the Canadian Civil Liberties Association.[9] The U.S. movement also benefits from the work of groups who track the religious right, most notably People for the American Way, for which there is no Canadian counterpart. It has also been able to count on support from important national African-American groups that have no real equivalent in Canada.

## The Power of Regionalism within Social Movements

How much does geography matter in the scale of activism, movement priorities, and strategies? Are social movement politics dramatically different in Boston and Seattle, Montreal and Vancouver, Washington, DC, and Ottawa? The slow development and modest size of a national group like Egale speak loudly to the challenge of building a single organization in a far-flung country with a relatively small population. Even at the provincial and territorial levels, geographic size and small population make the sustenance of groups difficult. The on-again, off-again opportunities for change at both the federal and provincial levels, depending on the party in power, also reduce the incentives to support large organizations, in turn reducing the capacity to overcome distances.

Cross-country organizing in Canada is hampered by regionalist identities and resentments. Activist communities across Canada are more likely than their American counterparts to be only moderately aware of developments in advocacy elsewhere in the country, and to believe those developments only marginally relevant to their own work. British Columbia activists, for example, have been known to argue that they have little in common with counterparts in the 'east' (i.e., central Canada).[10] And with some justification they will point to low levels of awareness of West Coast developments elsewhere in the country. Francophone LGBT activists in Quebec take for granted their separateness from developments elsewhere. They see the society they inhabit as significantly more accepting of sexual diversity than the rest of North America and agree with the growing number of sovereigntists outside their movement that such acceptance is part of what defines Quebec as distinct. As a result, they would argue, the movement in that region employs different priorities and strategies. At times, this trend has led to lower levels of activism among francophones than the political circumstances would otherwise predict, although at other times the opposite is true.

Regionalist sentiment in Quebec and western Canada, however, does not mean that activist priorities or strategic choices are all that different. Responses to police raids or workplace discrimination have looked broadly similar, in the arguments marshalled and the tactics employed. Relationship issues, and marriage in particular, came onto the agenda only at slightly different times across Canada. The development of commercial and residential areas where sexual diversity is made highly visible has not been particularly different in Canada's major cities, regardless of regional base. Montreal's Village de l'Est is larger than its counterparts in Toronto and Vancouver, but it does not feel categorically different, and certainly not by comparison to equivalent areas on other continents. Rainbow flags proliferate, and the influence of Americanized gay cultural patterns is pronounced. English names for events and bars are widespread, itself remarkable in a city so long committed to the defence of the French language.

In the United States, regionalism is a less powerful force inside the activist movement than might be imagined, and national networks have been easier to sustain. The reason derives partly from the extent of cross-regional contact among activists. Many of them physically meet in conferences such as 'Creating Change,' organized annually by the National Gay and Lesbian Task Force, or develop close contact through the Internet in more specialized networks. The sheer size of several of the national groups allows them to maintain their own cross-country networks in a way that would be difficult to emulate in Canada.

Of all the American regions, the South might be expected to have a distinctive movement. However, there is no evidence that the political agendas and strategic repertoires of southern activists are that much different from those in other regions. Notions of what issues are worth focusing on are shaped by the distinctively limited political openings outside the most progressive cities. However, the long-term agenda is much the same, and the formidable odds facing most southern activists, and those in other conservative regions, make linkage to national networks that much more important. In all regions, activists have to be wary of the power of their opponents, and conscious of the very real possibility that the religious right will undo their gains.

## Broadening the Activist Agenda from Individuals to Families

Family and schooling issues were taken up as soon as an activist wave emerged in the late 1960s and 1970s. Although liberationist perspectives generally rejected traditional family constructs, popular and legal denial of recognition to gay and lesbian relationships was thought worthy of attack. The threat to parenting rights and the attacks on gay

and lesbian teachers were also seen as embodying insidious stereotypes about homosexuals as sick and predatory. The late 1980s and
early '90s, saw a major increase in attention to relational and parenting
issues, sometimes provoking internal debate over questions of assimilation. But as more same-sex couples had children of their own, and as
right-wing opponents mobilized around defending the heterosexuality of family and the innocence of children, there was no avoiding
these issues.

## The Early Emergence of Parenting Claims

Faced with concrete challenges to their rights to visit or retain custody
of children born in earlier heterosexual relationships, gay and lesbian
parents organized. Toronto's Lesbian Mothers' Defence Fund formed
in 1978, following on similar American groups created a few years
before. This was a small group, but, like other such groups, it represented only a part of the defensive custody movement. Many women
who were too isolated or afraid to join such a group, or be associated
with it, still acted individually to defend their claims. Custody and
access rights were also included in the political agendas of multi-issue
lesbian networks.

Gay fathers' groups also first emerged in the 1970s. What may have
been the first were formed in San Francisco in 1975 and soon after in
New York and Los Angeles.[11] A Toronto group was created largely as
a response to a 1978 article written by activist/academic Michael
Lynch for the *Body Politic*. Most of these were less explicitly political
organizations than most of the lesbian mothers' groups, as prejudice
against gay fathers impelled most of them to seek whatever forms of
access they could through informal means.

In the 1980s and even more in the 1990s, more lesbian and gay
couples were living openly as such, and many of them wanted children or had already expanded their families to include children.[12]
These trends accelerated demands for change in family law, fostering
agencies, adoption procedures, assisted reproduction, and schooling.[13]
Networks were forming among supportive lawyers who were actually
taking relationship and parenting cases to court, and in a sense they
became part of the movement. From an early stage in the United
States, Lambda Legal was prominent in the struggle for parenting
rights, not surprising in light of the centrality of court challenges to the
advancement of parenting claims.

To be sure, there have been sceptics. Writers such as John Malone have worried about the advisability of a political agenda expanded to include such hot-button issues as adoption, fearing they will jeopardize advances in less controversial areas.[14] There are others, like Michael Bronski, who argue the opposite – that parental claims are too accommodating to the status quo and that focusing on them risks draining energy from grass-roots politics, which is, by implication, more radical. In fact, though, parenting issues have arisen almost prototypically from the grass roots – propelled by individuals and groups across the continent making their claims or defending their rights in the face of opponents still prepared to invoke the very worst of stereotypes about homosexuality.

## Expanding the Relationship Agenda in the Late 1980s

Several developments in the 1980s increased interest in relationship rights and to some extent schooling. One was the onset of the AIDS epidemic, which raised urgent concerns about the recognition of partners of those infected – for hospital visits, medical decision making, funeral arrangements, and inheritance.[15] Interest was fuelled by stories of exclusion and denial from across North America. AIDS also made the inclusion of straightforward messages about HIV transmission to teenagers that much more urgent.

Widening opportunities for lesbians and gays to be out also increased the visibility of same-sex relationships within sexual minority communities and the broader public. So did the rapidly growing numbers of gays and, particularly, lesbians who were having children. Many activists strongly shaped by liberationist rejection of traditional notions of family were acknowledging the importance of securing rights for couples and families with children, and they saw in the struggle a potential for radically challenging norms embedded in family regimes. Others were never as radical and simply wanted to be recognized as partners or parents within existing frameworks. In unionized workplaces, the recognition of same-sex relationships in benefit programs was an issue tailor made for activists wanting to press their labour unions to take sexual orientation issues seriously.[16] In jurisdictions where homosexual activity had been decriminalized and individual discrimination on grounds of sexual orientation prohibited, relationship issues seemed a logical next step. For all of them, the denial of recognition to same-sex relationships became an obvious symbol of exclusion.

Greater determination to be visible also reached into religious circles, where the importance of symbolic recognition of relationships was inescapable. The rapid growth of largely gay/lesbian Metropolitan Community Churches gave the broader activist movement an explicitly religious voice. So too did the emergence or growth of openly gay groups within a variety of Christian, Jewish, and eventually Muslim denominations. Among the demands emerging from such circles was the provision of at least some form of ceremonial recognition to lesbian and gay relationships.

The prominence of family and schooling issues rose further as conservative opponents seized on them and sought to mobilize a large public around their particular disdain for sexual diversity. Marriage was an especially appealing issue for the religious right, and as a result this issue above all others came to stand for the threats posed by any public recognition of sexual diversity to an already damaged ideal of family and community. This did not necessarily marginalize other issues, since this was also a time of unprecedented levels of activism on such issues as schooling and transgenderism, though it did provide unprecedented prominence to debates over the family.

The pressure for a more intensive and expansive engagement with relationship issues in particular provoked debate in pro-gay activist circles. There were concerns over assimilation and over what seemed to some a prioritizing of claims by those already most privileged within the movement. The discussions on priorities organized in 1989 by the Coalition for Lesbian and Gay Rights of Ontario (CLGRO), a group strongly influenced by liberationist ideas, illustrate the point.

**CLGRO Struggles Over Relationship Recognition, 1989**

Most of the leadership of Ontario's major lesbian and gay rights group were averse to seeking mere inclusion in existing relationship regimes rather than challenging them more radically. They were uneasy about a political agenda that would end up privileging couples and were distrusting of a strategy that seemed to rely on state approval to achieve legitimacy. But one of the cornerstones of CLGRO's past agenda had been achieved when in late 1986 sexual orientation was added to Ontario's Human Rights Code. With the ink barely dry on that amendment, the group's own activists were talking about relationship recognition as a priority, and planned a consultative conference in 1989 that sparked active debate. The compromise that emerged included a stated preference for social benefit regimes that did not simply privilege cohabiting couples, but also set out demands (in the meantime) for access to the rights and responsibilities applied to heterosexual relationships. Long-time CLGRO activist Tom Warner recalls that he and others 'cringed' at the framing of a later relationship campaign in the language of 'we are family.' At the same time, he recognized that it tapped 'a deep-rooted desire on the part of individual gays, lesbians, and bisexuals – still reviled and viewed as deviant – to achieve mainstream respectability and legitimacy, to have same-sex relationships seen as the same as heterosexual ones.'[17]

Within a decade, the importance of relationship claims was only rarely contested within LGBT groups in Canada and the United States. In Canada, the ability to make significant gains outside the marriage rubric, by claiming equivalence to de facto heterosexual couples, helped to retain unity. Only once such gains were secured was the call for marriage recognition widened. And once the religious right seized upon the issue, there were relatively few activist voices arguing that the battle could be avoided, even if only a small minority would themselves opt for marriage.[18]

American mobilization around relationship issues was hampered for a time by the absence of more elementary rights protections in much of the country. In many states and localities, there seemed little prospect of establishing protections against employment discrimination, the most broadly supported diversity issue, and even less of progress on relationship issues. Criminal penalties against private homosexual activity in several states cast a pall over the sexual activity of even the most respectable of same-sex couples. For some activists, then, there were concerns about shifting priorities away from more basic rights. As Arthur Leonard points out, many of the lawyers in LGBT litigation groups and public interest law firms had little enthusiasm for the marriage fight in its early years, believing that the institution itself was fatally traditional and that the battle had little chance of being won.[19] Until the mid-1990s, advocates for marriage complained about lack of support from the major national groups like HRC and NGLTF.[20]

From the mid-1990s on, relationship issues were on the front burners in both countries, and marriage an intensifying focus in the United States. American activists had only limited opportunities to make gains by securing the de facto status of heterosexuals and were more vulnerable to being treated as legal 'strangers,' for example, in medical decision making and visitation rights. A 1993 Hawai'i victory on marriage (however pyrrhic) widened the range of activists who thought that marriage was winnable; later court victories in Vermont and Massachusetts did the same.[21] Throughout this period, religious conservatives were increasing their mobilization on the issue, and as waves of statutory and constitutional measures barring the recognition of lesbian and gay marriage were enacted, activist mobilization in favour of such marriage became inescapable. Freedom to Marry, a national group focused just on this issue, was joined by all the major national groups and a host of state groups facing anti-gay referenda.

By 2000, American surveying indicated that a strong majority of lesbians and gays treated marriage as very important, with even stronger majorities seeing other family issues as very important.[22] The losses incurred over marriage referenda in the 2004 election provoked some doubts about the strategic wisdom of pursing marriage and nothing less, but not enough to change course. In fact, those favouring a continued focus on marriage included radical activists unwilling to settle for other forms of relationship recognition (e.g., civil unions). In both the United States and Canada, the strength of activism on family issues lay in the multiplication of settings in which claims have been made, and the variety of constituencies with an interest in one or another of the specific issues entailed in recognizing lesbian and gay relationships and their role as parents.

## The Special Case of Schooling

Challenging family regimes inevitably engages schooling issues. Same-sex couples with children, all families with non-heterosexual children, and all other parents interested in developing their children's acceptance of difference are concerned about school inclusiveness. Most of them are still confronted with institutions that have adjusted only very unevenly to the challenge of sexual diversity.

Writing about American schooling in the 1990s, Gerald Unks argued that 'heterosexual students are given no reasons not to hate homosexuals, while homosexual students are given no reason not to hate themselves.' Dances, yearbooks, hallway gossip – all these conspired to enforce heterosexist presumptions. Those who deviated were typically made invisible in what schools teach, conveying the message to sexual minority students that 'no one who has ever felt as you do has done anything worth mentioning.'[23]

School students are still surrounded by strong messages urging conformity to what is supposed to be feminine and masculine behaviour, and most of them bring deep-seated anxieties to their school environments about deviating from these norms even if they challenge authority on other fronts. Students who step outside gender norms in anything other than superficial ways have been ridiculed or harassed by their peers. Teachers have been even more strictly policed, and, as Catherine Lugg has said, those who fail to comply 'have touched the third rail of sexuality politics, the queer stigma.'[24]

Youthful sexuality is the most untouchable of all hot buttons associated with the 'gay agenda,' and social conservatives recoil at the very notion that an institution with responsibility for young people might recognize the sexual diversity among them. They envisage vulnerable children drawn towards unnatural and disease-ridden practices and abused by predatory adults who will ruin their lives.

Inclusive schools would need to acknowledge sexual diversity respectfully, from elementary grades on. Support services would need to address sexual orientation and gender identity supportively. The curriculum would need to acknowledge sexual diversity across the full range of subjects, and school-based resources would need to include materials reflective of that. The 'informal' curriculum, too, would also need to be accepting of diversity – in the casual chat of school staff about their lives and student relationships, in the social and sports events promoted in schools, in the kinds of postering around school buildings. Teachers would need to feel able to come out fully, and to speak about sexual difference in ways that are equivalent to the 'straight' talk that permeates schools.

## The Harm Done by Silence

Mobilization in favour of greater school inclusiveness has been boosted by evidence of the harm done to students by homophobic bullying and harassment.[25] There are dangers in overplaying the extent to which sexual minority students are prone to dropping out and damaging themselves, for this plays into conservative portrayals of homosexuality leading to sickness and destruction, and understates the resilience of many young people who do not conform.[26] Nevertheless, the stark and frightening information available on harm is compelling, and an important stimulant to activism.

Surveys conducted of LGBT adolescents between 2001 and 2005 by Gay, Lesbian and Straight Education Network in the United States, have found persistent levels of harassment of and physical violence towards LGBT students at least three times the average for heterosexual students.[27] In the most recent of these surveys, close to 40 per cent of LGBT students reported being the target of physical harassment, and nearly one-fifth reported violence. A major national study conducted in 2007 by Children's Hospital in Boston showed that gay and lesbian teenagers were three to four times more likely to be bullied than heterosexuals, bisexuals twice as likely.[28] Canadian studies have found the same, and in 2007, a Quebec Human Rights Commission report on homophobia described schools as permeated by homophobia, using language similar to that used by GLSEN for years.[29] Transgendered students would undoubtedly be the most at risk of all.[30]

Many of the targets of such bullying are in fact heterosexual.[31] Insults and harassment are routinely directed at a whole range of behaviours that are seen as deviating from gender norms – in dress, hair, accessories, body shape, friendships. Sometimes the targets are virtually random, but targeted with homophobic language as a vehicle for proclaiming the heterosexuality of the attacker.

Sexual minority youth are much more likely to skip school, at least three or four times the rate among heterosexuals. Even starker evidence of the impact of an anti-gay environment can be found in suicide rates among queer youth.[32] Every significant study of youth suicide in Canada and the United States shows that gay youth are at least three times more likely than heterosexual youth to attempt suicide and succeed in the attempt, and many studies show much more alarming ratios than that.

This experience crosses ethnic, gender, and class lines, though the prospects of isolation and punishment for being different may be greater in ethnic and immigrant groups where the strength of family and church ties are especially strong. The predominance of Caucasian faces within visibly out sexual minority populations, including those displayed in the media, can also make sexual difference seem an essentially white and 'other' phenomenon. Small towns and rural areas will also be more difficult than large cities, and across all community sizes, those with class and educational backgrounds in which there has been little exposure to sexual diversity will be at greater risk of social isolation than those in more privileged milieux.

The other side of this picture is that most sexual minority students pass through their schooling experience with great resilience. Increasing numbers of them are out at school, and at an earlier age than ever. Many of them affirm their right to be out, and form groups alongside straight allies to challenge the patterns of silence and ridicule. They are often critical of the limitations of their schools, but stronger for having found support among friends, family members, teachers, and school-mates.

The enforced heterosexuality of most school climates is harmful not only to students but also to teachers and staff.[33] The vast majority of sexual minority educators remain closeted, and many of those who are out are very cautious about what they say to students. They fear harassment, rumours based on stereotypes about pedophilia, and job loss. Personal anecdotes relayed in class that would be routine for heterosexual teachers are often repressed for fear of provoking complaints and investigations.

In general, educators are less likely to intervene when they see or hear anti-gay behaviour than prejudicial behaviour directed at other groups.[34] Even sympathetic teachers are usually cautious, and reluctant to raise issues they fear as controversial. For others educators, homophobia evokes personal discomfort, and elicits either silence or prejudicial language, colluding in the everyday use of anti-gay language in hallways, schoolyards, and locker rooms. Teachers making casual remarks about their own lives or the lives of others will contribute to the wallpaper-like ubiquity of heterosexual references, usually in the absence of openly lesbian, gay, bisexual, or transgendered teachers feeling equally safe to talk about their own lives.

**Schools Activism**

Schools activism has generally arisen in quite different circles than those making claims about parenting and relationships, but there are overlaps. Parents of sexual minority children, and same-sex couples with children, have been important proponents of change in education. The challenges mounted by all schools-focused advocates, too, confront much of the same prejudice about who does and does not constitute a family as advocates on other fronts, and certainly the same stereotypes about the risk posed by homosexuality to children.

*Sustained American Activism*[35]

Activism on schools issues has a decades-long history, but the pace quickened in the United States during the 1990s, and more modestly in Canada during the early 2000s. In 1972 New Jersey teacher John Gish organized the Gay Teachers Caucus of the National Education Association (NEA), and soon found himself kept out of the classroom.[36] That year, activists in California convinced the California Federation of Teachers to pass a resolution supporting the rights of lesbian and gay teachers. At mid-decade, organizations of gay teachers were formed in New York and San Francisco, the latter including high-profile activist Tom Ammiano as one of its central players. Within a couple of years, such groups also existed in Los Angeles, Boston, Philadelphia, Denver, Oregon, Texas, and Maryland. This was at the height of campaigning by Anita Bryant and other Christian conservatives under the banner 'Save Our Children.'

The AIDS epidemic focused activist attention on schooling, particularly on sex education. AIDS educators insisted quite properly on the importance of reaching the young as they were becoming sexually active, and doing so with frank messages and easy access to condoms. Opponents saw these proposals as an attempt to legitimize youthful sexuality in general, and homosexuality in particular – yet another challenge to traditional morality and the role of the family.

During the middle and late 1980s, the broader LGBT activist movement was devoting more attention to anti-gay violence, and this soon dovetailed with concerns about school safety. By decade's end, teacher organizing was also becoming more concerted and sustained, some of it provoked by concerns about anti-gay bullying. A gay and lesbian caucus formed in the NEA in 1987 and one year later secured passage of a resolution in favour of equal opportunity regardless of sexual orientation. In 1994, the NEA passed a resolution broader than any before it, calling for increased training for educators to address sexual orientation stereotyping in schools. In the American Federation of Teachers, a gay and lesbian caucus was formed in 1988, with a membership that quickly exceeded two hundred. By the late 1990s, support for resolutions calling for greater attention to sexual diversity among youth was coming from other associations of educators, such as the American School Counselor Association, the Association for Supervision and Curriculum Development, the American School Health Association, the National

School Boards Association, the National Association of School Psychologists, and the National Middle School Association.

The formation of an organization devoted entirely to raising the profile of sexual diversity in schooling was a major contributor to the activist wave that built momentum through this period. In 1991, the Gay and Lesbian Independent School Teachers Network held its first conference, spearheaded by Massachusetts-based teacher Kevin Jennings. It attracted 100 participants from both private and public schools, and in two years, the annual conference was attracting 350. Starting in mid-1994, the group formally expanded beyond its private school base and went national, becoming the Gay, Lesbian and Straight Teachers Education Network (GLSEN). Within eighteen months, it had thirty local chapters and 3,000 members. By decade's end, the group had an annual budget of $2.5 million and a staff of eighteen in its New York national office, with 15,000 members nationwide (30 per cent of them heterosexual). Early in the next decade, it was the fourth-largest LGBT political group in the United States, with programs or initiatives operating in forty-seven states.[37] In several areas, state-wide gay/lesbian educator groups were developing alongside GLSEN. Their work was also now being supported by national groups like HRC, NGLTF, the National Center for Lesbian Rights, Lambda Legal, and the ACLU – groups that had previously paid only modest attention to education.[38]

There were now substantial numbers of sexual minority teachers, parents, and students prepared to be assertively out about their sexuality. Students were forming forming Gay-Straight Alliances, pressing for school recognition of them, going to court to challenge homophobic school climates, and lobbying politicians. At the beginning of 1996, the *Washington Blade* began a story that talked of gay issues in schools becoming a 'front-burner' issue nationwide.[39]

## Weaker and Episodic Organizing in Canada

There has been little sustained activism on schooling anywhere in Canada until recently, and much of it has been reactive rather than proactive.[40] In the early years of the modern activist movement, two cases of discrimination against gay teachers (in Saskatchewan and Toronto) had provoked protest. In 1975, Doug Wilson, then completing an education degree at the University of Saskatchewan, was barred from school placement because of his open gayness.[41] He made the discrimination public and took it to the province's Human Rights Commission, which ruled against him. Later that decade, when Toronto teacher and swim coach John Argue came out, he faced restrictions on his activities, a decision born entirely of prejudice about gay men as predatory on young boys. In 1980 he led a group in an unsuccessful bid to establish a school board liaison committee on sexual orientation issues. These causes were supported by lesbian and gay rights advocates, such as those in the *Body Politic* magazine and the Coalition for Lesbian and Gay Rights in Ontario.

As in the United States, the AIDS epidemic spurred calls for the inclusion of AIDS in provincial health curricula and in some cases for the placement of condom machines in high schools. It did not lead to a quantum leap in organizing on schooling, however, not least because of the amount of activist attention devoted to other parts of the HIV/AIDS agenda, though for a time Toronto was an exception. Educators in the public school board had pressed for reform at the beginning of the decade, and they renewed their initiatives in the second half of the decade, forming a lesbian/gay caucus in 1989.[42] Students were becoming more visible too, forming the group Teens Educating About and Challenging Homophobia (TEACH) in 1993 with the support of the Toronto Board of Education's Equity Studies Centre.

In 1990 Vancouver was another important centre of activism, with the formation of Gay and Lesbian Educators of BC (GALE-BC). From its beginnings, it developed resources for counsellors and teachers, and pressed for change within the British Columbia Teachers Federation. The BCTF had a long history of taking up issues of diversity and equity, and from the late 1980s on it was approving pro-gay resolutions.[43] From 1997 on, GALE activists pushed it to ramp up its attention to sexual diversity, and this led to the approval of resolutions supporting the preparation and distribution of resource materials on sexual orientation to schools across the province, and encouraging the establishment of 'gay-straight alliance' student groups.

In the late 1990s and early 2000s, progressive activism on sexual diversity become more widespread among Canada's teacher unions. Apart from the BCTF, the Elementary Teachers Federation of Ontario (ETFO) was a leader, building on earlier work by the Federation of Women Teachers' Associations of Ontario.[44] In 2000, it voted to establish a standing committee for sexual minority members, and in the years to follow the union developed substantial resources for teachers and schools.

In the late 1990s, the Saskatchewan Teachers Federation and the Alberta Teachers' Association began acting in this area. The ATA amended its code of professional conduct to require teaching in a manner that respected sexual diversity, and it created the Safe and Caring Schools Project, to develop proactive programs addressing school violence and intolerance.[45] By 2003, it was providing elaborate guidance to teachers through its website on creating more inclusive schools, and sponsoring workshops. The two Quebec unions to which teachers belong (the Centrale de l'enseignement du Québec [CEQ] and the Confédération des syndicats nationaux [CSN]) also became more visibly supportive at the end of the 1990s, and by 2002 they were pressing for greater public policy attention to anti-gay climates in schools. At about the same time, provincial federations in Manitoba, Newfoundland and Labrador, and New Brunswick were launching initiatives to raise awareness of sexual diversity among educators. Meanwhile, the Canadian Teachers Federation was becoming more visible, producing a resource guide in 2002, and in 2004 endorsing the National Day Against Homophobia.

Most Catholic teacher groups have stayed clear of these issues, but there is at least one exception. In 2002 the Ontario English Catholic Teachers Association approved a resolution supporting the bid by a student in a Catholic school (Mark Hall) to take a same-sex partner to his prom. The union's newsletter also advertised the availability of a resource guide on gay inclusiveness prepared by ETFO in collaboration with the Toronto District School Board.

Activist mobilizing outside teacher groups has emerged – albeit sporadically – in several centres across Canada in recent years. In Montreal, the Groupe de Recherche et d'Intervention Sociale gaies et lesbiennes de Montréal (GRIS) was formed in 1994 to volunteer speakers to school audiences (much like the Toronto based group TEACH, formed one year earlier). The helpline Gai Écoute has highlighted the need for action in schools to address the needs of sexual minority youth. The Rainbow Resource Centre in Winnipeg has developed resources specifically targeting school reform. In various centres, Parents and Friends of Lesbians and Gays (PFLAG) groups have been actively pressuring school boards to change. Student organizing has become more prominent, largely through Gay-Straight Alliances or their equivalent, though not yet on the scale that we find in the United States. There have been only a few court challenges to school authorities by students, or indeed by others, in striking contrast to the United States, and also in contrast to the Canadian pattern on other sexual orientation issues. The national group Egale has helped build what amounts to an English-speaking network of educators across Canada and has recently prioritized schooling issues, but with only a small resource base to support work in the area. No equivalent to GLSEN has been formed, and none appears to be imminent.

## The High Stakes of Schooling Debates

Public debates over what does and does not get taught, and by whom, have been common for at least a century across North America and Europe. Consequently, when sexual diversity issues are raised, they evoke differences that have been aired many times before. A single question about whether a teacher should talk about her same-sex partner ends up entwined with a range of questions over the role of public education.[46] If religious conservative engagement with schools derives in part from distinct views on education, it is also driven by strategic calculations, as anxieties about youthful sexuality and gender conformity, among educators, parents, and students themselves, have the potential to broaden the conservative coalition.[47] Schooling debates escalate more quickly in the United States than in Canada, since so many issues that separate conservatives and progressives remain fundamentally unresolved.

### Religiously Based Morality versus Secular or Pan-Religious Values

The question of what role religion has to play in public schools has obvious ramifications for how schools should respond to sexual diversity. On one side are those who would either keep religious teaching out of the classroom entirely or teach a multiplicity of religiously derived positions. On the other are advocates of public school curricula infused explicitly with a specific faith, and of state support for private denominational schools.

Large numbers of conservative American Christians still advocate prayer in public schools and a curriculum that reflects a literal reading of scripture, including 'creationism' or 'intelligent design.' The feelings of religious conservatives are strong enough in parts of the United States that Supreme Court judgments barring school prayer are simply ignored.[48] Opposing them are advocates of progressive versions of faith or of secular views, many of whom treat the separation of church and state as an absolute imperative. This division brings to the front lines of battle highly experienced and committed protagonists.

Canada has a long history of controversies over the role of religion in education, but it has not been as polarized in recent years as in the United States. When there has been conflict, the combatants were arrayed in ways that were different than in the United States – more likely focused on Catholic schools, for example. The constitutionally formative agreement that federated the British North American colonies in 1867 established a school system in Quebec that was entirely based on religious denomination, and it guaranteed Roman Catholic schooling elsewhere. This was in part a vehicle for assuring francophones education in their own language. There were then, and in the decades since, opponents of such arrangements, and provincial governments who violated these guarantees. But in the past quarter century, Roman Catholic rights to state support for their schools in those parts of the country where they have most wanted them are no longer face sustained opposition. In addition, the two provinces with school systems that were once entirely denominational (Quebec and Newfoundland) are no longer so. Quebec is a particularly striking example of a shift from a regime in which the influence of religion (particularly on the Roman Catholic side) was paramount to one in which such influence is almost entirely absent.

The publicly supported Catholic schooling that remains in Canada might seem to preserve a domain in which strictly conservative views of gender and sexuality would prevail. But many Catholic schools are only modestly influenced by church doctrine. In addition, the very existence of such schools essentially withdraws conservative Catholics from debates over public schooling, which substantially reduces the size of the constituency available for opponents of change in the public sector.

Public schools across Canada gradually became secularized during the second half of the twentieth century, almost entirely without rancorous disputes. Up to the early 1980s religious exercises opened the school day in Ontario, British Columbia, and Manitoba, but such requirements were atrophying in most of the country, and low-visibility court judgments in the 1980s hastened their demise. Some debates over religion and schooling remain in Canada – for example, over whether tax concessions ought to be available for private schools (including non-Catholic denominational ones) – but the larger questions that so polarize Americans are largely settled.

*Conveying Dominant Values versus Reflecting Diversity*

The challenge to increase the recognition of sexual diversity in schools is evocative of another of the great debates over education. On one side are those who insist that schools transmit unchanging values, reflective of the core of what it means to be American or Canadian. On the other side are advocates of schools' reflecting the diversity of the society around them – in the ideas they transmit, the teachers they hire, and the students they recruit.

This debate has a long history and is thoroughly entangled with struggles over equity. The exclusion of African Americans from white-dominated public schools, either by policy or practice, was seen by rights activists as demeaning of the idea of public education. What was taught was also seen as reflecting only part of the American experience. Such views placed public education at the very centre of the civil rights movement's agenda.

This debate about whether schools should be centred around common and 'timeless' values or around ideas of difference has retained its bite in debates over teaching languages other than English (e.g., Spanish in the United States) and has frequently divided minority communities internally. Some minority group members want to see their children treated exactly like everyone else and do not want their cultural or linguistic distinctiveness emphasized. Others advocate separate classes or schools.

These debates have occurred in large Canadian cities, with some flashpoints, but not with the same long and intense history. Recent public discussion of the harm done by residential schools for Aboriginal children can be conflictual, but largely with regard to the means to repair damage, not the inappropriateness of the stark assimilationism of those schools. Debates over the language of education in Quebec centre on the right of the French-speaking majority to secure the place of its language, but virtually no protagonists deny the legitimacy of an English-language school system.[49]

Controversies that have occurred over the recognition of difference in Canadian schools have not been as laden with racial segregation as debates in the United States. In English Canada, too, there is a weaker sense of civic nationalism than in the United States, and therefore a hazier sense of the values to which school students should be assimilated. The notion that schools had a central role in 'making Canadians' was never as powerful as its counterpart in the United States.

*Knowledge Transmission versus Critical Engagement*

The recognition of sexual diversity evokes debate over whether the primary mission of schools is to transmit previously accumulated knowledge or to promote change and critical engagement. The 'preservationist' view emphasizes a core curriculum that includes training in the basics, teaching a traditional 'canon' of literary classics, and conveying respect for established institutions. The alternative view emphasizes the development of critical abilities to discover and adapt to new ideas.

The movement towards 'child-centred' learning associated with the progressivism of the 1960s challenged the content-focused styles of teaching a core curriculum. School systems across North America were influenced by this reformist wave, but opposition to it never disappeared. The move to the right associated with the neo-conservatism and neo-liberalism of the last quarter of the twentieth century strengthened calls for a return to 'basics,' just when sexual diversity was becoming visible and equity claims becoming more forceful.

The swing to the right and away from state spending and regulation was somewhat stronger in the United States than in Canada, and preservationist forces have always been strong on the American side. But reformist voices have also been strong in the United States, where talk of critical engagement has roots going back to John Dewey. On this question, too, therefore, more polarization exists in the United States than in Canada.

*Protecting Children versus Freeing Young People*

A related concern is whether schooling should protect children from influences that might lead them astray or should facilitate their independence and their awareness of the unvarnished realities of the world.[50] Those who see the world as filled with malevolence, and human nature as inherently prone to sinfulness, are likely to see all people, but particularly youngsters, as needing highly directive guidance. In this view, schools need to be shielded environments, imposing strict discipline on children. Proponents usually link such protective views to a belief in the family as the most secure refuge for children, with parental authority trumping all other influences on them. They will see any positive recognition of sexual diversity in schools as an example of exposing vulnerable youngsters to dangerous ideas best left unspoken or subject to parental guidance.

The opposite view holds that children and youth need to develop independence in order to navigate the world as young adults. This view is often built upon a belief in the appropriateness of the self-navigating skills inherent in human nature. Advocates of such a view are more likely to construe the outside world in positive terms, or at least as capable of being shaped in positive ways. Children need their schools to help them observe and understand the world around them, in all its variety. This 'liberatory' view is more acknowledging of the limitations or inadequacies of parental authority, and of the legitimacy of a range of influences on children needed to develop independence.

*Consumer 'Choice' versus State Support for Public Schooling*

The capacity of public school systems to respond to questions of diversity is dependent in part on resources, and the financing of public education is of course tied to shifts in dominant ideas over the proper role of the state. There are two questions here. First, how much public money should go into any state-run institution? Second, should public funds be funnelled primarily to state-operated schools, or should they support a wide array of private arrangements?

Proponents of a minimalist state would see programs to recognize diversity as a wasteful deviation from the core mission of public schooling. Neo-liberal ascendency in the 1980s and 1990s heightened scrutiny of social spending and increased concern that schools were not adequately training students for an increasingly competitive and globalizing world. Across North America and to some extent Europe, this led to more centralized control over a core public school curriculum, and at the same time greater state support for parents opting out of the public system. (Demands for school choice have a long history, often mingled with questions of state support for religious schools in Canada and parts of Europe, and routinely entwined in American racial politics during the 1950s and 1960s.)[51] These patterns have weakened public school capacity to devote resources to diversity, and increased the resources provided for religiously based schools, most of which would avoid any positive recognition of sexual diversity.

*The Fearful Bundle*

The stakes in controversies over schooling, then, are often very large indeed. For many participants in deliberations and struggles over sexual diversity, the issues crystallize aspirations and fears about what schools might become, or what they have already become. When the question of recognizing sexual diversity is raised, of course, a core component of the opposition is driven by abhorrence of homosexuality. That portion of the population that is deeply anti-gay has been slowly declining, but strongly disapproving responses to questions about homosexuality will still come from about 20 per cent of Canadians and 30 per cent of Americans. Beyond that there are 'softer' forms of discomfort with sexual difference, for example based on fears that youthful deviation from heterosexuality will lead to unhappiness.

There are also opponents of change who are relatively 'tolerant' of diversity, but who adhere to a 'preservationist' view of schooling that resists one more in a series of reformist distractions. Many who have no particularly strong religious adherence believe that schools should teach a set of core values that respect tradition. These and many others may also fear exposing children and adolescents to what they would see as excessive doses of the real world – a world they see as full of temptations. In any event, parental teaching pre-empts schools for such issues as sexuality.

Debates over sexuality, then, bring to conservative ranks a variety of sympathizers who do not have a categorical opposition to the recognition of sexual diversity, but who are suspicious of the schools diluting what they believe to be their core mission, and wary of leaving decisions entirely to educational experts. At the same time, advocates of inclusive schooling may also forge alliances with defenders of other reformist perspectives, especially where they are under attack by conservatives. This does not mean that reformers are invariably prepared to address sexual orientation in their school advocacy, for many will themselves be uncomfortable doing so or worried that their inclusion on the agenda will jeopardize other gains. But many will see the links, especially in the United States, where religious-right organizing around schools issues is so prominent and continuous.

The play of these issues becomes further intensified in the United States by party oppositions. Democrats and Republicans generally differ on schooling issues, especially on the role of religion in schooling. At local, state, and federal levels, conservative Republicans will often raise schools issues to frighten electors about the 'gay agenda.' Thus, advocates on both sides have continuing incentives to organize politically. The growth of religious-right interest in school board elections through the 1990s and into the first decade of the twenty-first century, and the increase in numbers of explicitly 'Christian' candidates, has also mobilized reformers and raised the overall stakes in elections that have often been relatively low profile.

## Conservative Backlash

Gains – or the prospect of gains – made in publicly recognizing sexual diversity have almost continuously provoked fierce mobilizing by religious conservatives in the United States. The issues of same-sex marriage, lesbian/gay parenting, and what is taught in school have been the most hotly contested and are often linked to one another. Among the images most persistently held out to intensify public fears has been the vulnerable child, threatened by predatory and disease-ridden homosexuals. Widespread public anxiety about the rearing of children and the risks of threatening gender categories give such stereotypes great power, and Christian-right organizations know it.

### Marshalling the Symbolism of Vulnerable Youth

In the late 1970s, Florida orange juice queen Anita Bryant crusaded against gay rights ordinances with the slogan 'Save Our Children.' Buoyed by the right's success in rescinding local ordinances in several states, California politician John Briggs in 1978 spearheaded a referendum campaign aimed at providing statutory permission for the state's school boards to dismiss gay and lesbian teachers. Though defeated by a margin of 58 to 42, it was followed by many other referendum campaigns across the United States, spearheaded by religious conservatives who regularly invoked the image of vulnerable children.

The American Christian right's control of many state Republican parties during the 1980s allowed it a continuous platform from which to rail against the threats posed to traditional families, and children in particular, by LGBT claims. Mobilization was intensified from the mid-1990s, after lesbian/gay marriage advocates won an important round in Hawai'i, and schooling battles were becoming more visible. The religious right was also attaching a higher priority to state and local politics, partly from frustration at what it felt were inadequate results from the years of Republican domination in Washington.

Canadian conservatives were mimicking their American counterparts by invoking the risks to young people from extending rights protections to lesbians and gays, though still much more sporadically than in the United States. Canadian religious conservatives invited Anita Bryant to Toronto in 1978, highlighting their own campaigning against rights claims by sexual minorities. Despite intense organizing in 1986, they failed to prevent the inclusion of sexual orientation in the Ontario Human Rights Code, and the adoption of similar provisions in other provinces did not meet with protests on nearly the same scale.[52] The addition of sexual orientation to the federal human rights act in the mid-1990s provoked considerable mobilizing across the country, and during that decade, schools controversies in Toronto and BC generated noticeable activism.[53] But none of this protest was sustained.

*Targeting Marriage*

The marriage issue intensified Christian right activism on both sides of the border. In the United States this was apparent from the mid-1990s on, after marriage equality advocates won a court victory in Hawai'i. In 2002 the 'Arlington Group' brought together several large religious-right groups (to a meeting in Arlington, Virginia) to strategize over marriage, and over the following year its membership grew to more than fifty groups. As long-time religious-right organizer Paul Weyrich commented in the aftermath of the 2004 election, 'for the first time, virtually all of the social issues groups are singing off the same sheet of music.'[54]

American conservative focus on homosexuality was strengthened in mid-2003 when the U.S. Supreme Court struck down Texas's sodomy statute and the Massachusetts Supreme Judicial Council ruled in favour of same-sex marriage. As Doug Ireland put it in October 2003, Republican and religious conservatives were anxious to use marriage in particular to stoke up the culture wars in anticipation of the next year's election: 'The Rev. Jerry Falwell recently announced that he will devote all his time and energy to opposing gay marriage and campaigning for the FMA [the federal marriage amendment to the constitution]; the Traditional Values Coalition has been sending out 1.5 million pieces of mail a month on the gay marriage issue; and addicts of Christian and conservative radio have been treated to daily diatribes against gay marriage from the likes of Focus on the Family's James Dobson, who has more radio listeners than CNN has viewers, and the Rev. Donald Wildmon's American Family Association, which has 200 affiliated Christian radio stations.'[55]

The full resources of the religious right were in evidence during the 2004 and 2006 election cycles, when marriage referenda campaigns in several states were run alongside voter mobilization drives to ensure the election of conservative politicians. Prominent leaders of the Protestant right (such as James Dobson of Focus on the Family and Richard Land of the Southern Baptist Convention) were in regular contact with Republican campaign leaders. Although electoral observers debated whether the marriage referenda had much influence on electing George W. Bush, Christian right leaders and Republicans seemed mostly to believe that they had.

The issue of same-sex marriage galvanized Canada's Christian conservatives as never before and produced sustained institutional growth. The issue was given a high profile several years later than in the United States, mostly because so many gains were being secured in the recognition of de facto lesbian/gay relationships. Religious conservatives were resistant to any recognition of such relationships, but most advances were secured incrementally, through court victories. It was a 2003 decision by Ontario's highest court opening the door to full marriage that provided conservatives with a wedge issue, and of course they were able to draw support from American organizations in waging war on gay marriage. American religious broadcasters regularly targeted reformist change in Canada, but never more so than on the question of marriage. Various legal and legislative thresholds on the road to fully securing marriage rights provided continuous incentives for Christian conservatives to organize. By the mid-2000s, a BC-based branch plant of the American Focus on the Family was able to raise over $11 million annually – a huge sum in Canada – while benefiting from its access to broadcasts and written material from its American parent. In 2006 it established a think tank that continuously churned out material on marriage and the family, representing a major enhancement of religious-right presence in federal and provincial politics. The legalization of marriage also energized the more established Evangelical Fellowship of Canada, and spawned new groups like the Defend Marriage Coalition – a joint venture of the anti-feminist REAL Women of Canada, Canada's most established 'pro-life' organization, a 'family action' coalition, and the Catholic Civil Rights League.

In Canada, the new Conservative Party was in a more complex strategic position than the Republican Party in the United States. It depended on core constituencies of religious conservatives, but proportionately this constituency was less than half the size of the American Christian right. The party's leadership seized on same-sex marriage as the one gay issue they thought would not ghettoize them as extremist on social issues, though as time went on, the risks of over-embracing the issue and trying to roll back the clock only increased. Still, religious conservatives were more visible than ever, and more institutionalized.

In both countries, marriage offered the prospect of broadening the political support for the religious right, within the Christian faith and beyond. The issue was as high a priority for the Roman Catholic hierarchy as for conservative Protestant leaders. The Vatican's concerns about homosexuality were heightened as various regimes accorded at least some recognition to same-sex couples, and in a few cases marriage, in countries with large Catholic populations. The recognition of lesbian and gay marriage was characterized as part of 'a new ideology of evil' by Pope John Paul II, and his successor Benedict XVI did nothing to lighten the rhetoric.

The American religious right, and the Republican Party, also saw a potential for campaigning on this issue to increase their appeal among African Americans and Hispanics. Black clergy were usually loath to cooperate with white Christian conservatives in the United States, but many were adamant in their opposition to gay marriage.[56] The Nation of Islam has also harboured deeply homophobic sentiments, and at its 2006 Millions More March, gay African-American activist Keith Boykin was prevented from speaking. Republican campaigning in such circles was not very successful at the ballot box, mostly because minority voters – blacks, hispanics, and others – were unlikely to see marriage as a high-priority issue. Nevertheless, conservative mobilization on the issue helped to keep public support firmly arrayed against lesbian/gay marriage.

*Pro-Gay Religious Activism*

There had long been progressive religious voices among those seeking more inclusive concepts of family and schooling, and LGBT-positive groups had formed within a wide range of faith currents. But progressives working within mainstream American Protestant denominations are vastly outgunned by conservatives, with one study estimating an 8–1 disadvantage in group funding.[57] Nevertheless, reformers were registering advances in the Episcopal church and in more liberal denominations like the United Church of Christ. The same was true of activists in Reform and Reconstructionist Judaism, and even within Conservative Judaism there was pressure to shift towards more inclusive positions. Progressive currents of Protestantism are prominent in Canada, and at less of a numerical disadvantage than their American counterparts.

There have been Catholic priests in Canada and the United States prepared to dissent publicly from the hierarchy's aggressive stand on marriage and its drastic embrace of more exclusionary policy on gay priests. In Quebec, nineteen priests published an open letter in 2006 criticizing their church's stand; a month later the Canadian Religious Conference (an umbrella group with a membership of 230 religious orders) sent a letter to every bishop in the country criticizing the church's intransigence on a range of issues, including homosexuality.[58] In the United States, a number of priests have spoken out, including a group of almost two dozen priests in Chicago who described the Vatican's rhetoric as violent and abusive.[59]

## Activist Limitations

Campaigning for more inclusive family and schooling policies has emerged in a wide variety of settings – in workplaces and unions, among parents and prospective parents, in networks of educators, and among students. In that sense, advocacy on these fronts has arisen from the grass roots. In both Canada and the United States, however, the movements advocating change do not always look like the broader constituencies they want to represent. All social movements most often draw out those who already have some of the resources that make political involvement easier, and this inevitably gives them a leadership that is not demographically representative of the broader population.

The risk of demographic distortion is especially great when it comes to issues that involve young people or that ask for a rethinking of time-honoured institutions. It is here that the urge to portray claimants as 'respectable' and unthreatening is strongest, and it is therefore here that the public face of the activist movement is most likely to be dominated by those who are reassuring to judges, politicians, social agencies, and the general public. This tendency has class and race implications, sidelining those whose sexuality is ambiguous or whose relationships are not reassuringly familiar.

The politics of family and schools routinely sidelines bisexuals and the transgendered. This of course is not new; pressure on the LGBT movement to take those last two letters more seriously has been applied for decades. Transgender activists have been particularly visible and vocal in the last decade, in both Canada and the United States, and have had some success in placing gender identity on the political agendas of national and regional groups. In the United States, the National Center for Transgender Equality has recently increased its profile substantially and helped other national LGBT groups to high-light their issues. (No equivalent group exists in Canada.) On family and schools issues, however, trans struggles are less visible. To be sure, part of the reason is because trans activist priorities lie elsewhere – for example, in securing supportive and affordable medical procedures for transitioning and building up workplace protections. But part of their marginalization comes from the pull towards 'respectability.'

Bisexuals have had an even harder time claiming visibility. Their networks that have emerged over the last decade, on both sides of the border, have been frail, and their work has not yet translated into con-certed campaigns on bisexuality by major national or regional LGBT organizations. They do not have the specific priorities that set them apart from the rest of the movement, in the way that trans activists have in the medical field especially. They also still face hostility or indifference from many lesbians and gay men, even if it is less marked than a decade or two ago.

## Conclusion

The strongest cross-border contrasts in pro-gay organizing are in the scale of American mobilizing, compared to the Canadian, its institu-tionalization, and the prominence of its activity inside maintream political processes. Some of this contrast is a product of long-standing patterns of group formation in American politics, and of the kind of support that organized groups can mobilize in their most relevant con-stituencies. It also comes from the resources available to the religious right, and the complex institutional context in which it operates.

The marriage issue mobilized vast resources in the United States from the mid-1990s on, and even more in the following decade – far more than was ever apparent in the Canadian movement even at the peak of public debate over the issue. Particularly striking have been the resources mobilized to make American public schools more inclu-sive, picking up substantial energy (and alliances) in the early 1990s, at a time when only sporadic activism on schooling occurred in Canada. The sharpening of already clear contrasts between the scale of the two movements was partly a product of the high stakes long associated with public schooling in the United States, and the substantive rights still associated with marriage in that country. It was also a product of the readiness of the American religious right to focus its mighty resources on those two issue areas.

The resources available to the American movement do not, we know, predict success. But they do help us understand the early successes, the capacity of activists to take advantage of occasional openings even in otherwise conservative areas of the United States, and the gradual expansion of public recognition of diversity even during periods of conservative political rule. What Canadians activists have lacked in resources they have more than made up for in political opportunities on family issues, allowing for a kind of 'take-off' in regime change. This has not happened yet in schooling. That, we will find, is a very different and disheartening story.

# 4 Canadian Recognition of Same-Sex Relationships

When marriage was opened up to lesbian and gay couples in Canada, starting in 2003, the public recognition of same-sex relationships had already taken off. By the late 1990s, courts had made it extremely difficult to exclude such relationships from the wide range of rights and obligations already granted to de facto straight couples. At the end of 2006, Conservative prime minister Stephen Harper reacted to the defeat of a parliamentary motion calling for the reopening of the gay marriage issue by saying his government would not revisit the matter. Changes have occurred not only in public policy and law but also in workplaces and the practices of many churches. And while Canada is a decentralized and fractious federation, there is a strikingly common narrative in the increased public recognition of gay and lesbian relationships.

This, as we will see, is very different from the American story. The first steps in publicly recognizing gay and lesbian relationships were taken as early there as anywhere, but in contrast to Canada there was no take-off, and certainly no 'national' storyline. The differences across the border are not a result of a better organized or more skilful activist movement. In fact, the resources that gays, lesbians, bisexuals, and the transgendered have marshalled in the struggle for relationship recognition in Canada have been small in contrast to those mobilized by their American counterparts. The stark difference in outcomes also has little to do with federal government leadership, which has often played a cautious role more prone to avoiding the issue than embracing change.

The distinctive Canadian story, including its surprising commonalities across the country, has a great deal to do with the leverage provided by the Charter of Rights and Freedoms and by the preparedness of the judiciary to apply it to lesbian/gay claims. The exclusive federal jurisdiction over criminal law and the definition of marriage also helped create a single cross-Canada story line. Other factors that helped to produce take-off in the development of a more inclusive family regime were divisions within Canada's right-wing parties, the weakness of the religious right (compared to the United States) across even those regions where conservative faith is strongest, the increased prominence of the celebratory language of diversity in urban Canada, and the prominent equity role assumed by the labour movement.

## Late 1960s to Mid-1980s: First Steps on Basic Rights

In 1969, just as activism on sexuality issues was about to intensify, Prime Minister Pierre Trudeau spearheaded changes to the Criminal Code that included a partial decriminalization of homosexual activity.[1] Though discriminatory elements remained, allowing police to continue targeting gay sexuality, the legislation reduced a legal impediment to the political recognition of same-sex relationships.

The next decade and a half, though, was a period when gay and lesbian activists were mobilizing outside the political process, combatting the worst of their political and social exclusion. Family issues were seen on the agenda, but more attention was paid to the protection of community institutions and basic rights protections against attacks from state institutions, including the police.[2]

### Local Civil Rights Pioneering

Local governments provided the few political openings of the period and were particularly important targets for activism aimed at police abuse. On 10 October 1973, after months of lobbying by the Gay Alliance Toward Equality, Toronto City Council became the first legislative body in Canada to prohibit discrimination based on sexual orientation (following by one year the same move by their municipal counterparts in San Francisco and two university towns in Michigan). There was little debate, and only one councillor voted against the motion. Over the next few years, several other Canadian cities followed suit.

Toronto witnessed an unprecedented surge of gay activism in the late 1970s, following attacks on major gay institutions in the city, and even more in the aftermath of large-scale police raids on bathhouses in 1981. The widespread support such activism received from civil libertarians, labour unions, the media, and reformist city politicians helped pave the way, in 1985, for the city to approve a contract compliance policy that included sexual orientation, requiring employers doing business with the city to show a commitment to equal opportunity. This was the first such measure adopted by any city in Canada, and one of the few in North America to include sexual orientation.

## Isolated Rights Extension at the Provincial and Federal Level

Activism in Montreal had also been provoked by police raids, though the city's political leadership was still in the hands of a majority that was relatively conservative on questions of policing and morality. In 1977, however, Quebec's Charter of Rights was amended to include sexual orientation, at a time when there seemed little chance of effecting such change in any other province or at the federal level. The amendment was supported by the provincial government, in the hands of the pro-sovereigntist and social democratic Parti Québécois. But it was added quietly, in the dying days of a pre-Christmas sitting, away from public glare. No senior government or political party in Canada was yet ready to proclaim from the rooftops its support for gay rights.

In the early 1980s, activists pushing for rights protections, for example, in the Coalition for Gay (later Lesbian and Gay) Rights in Ontario (CLGRO), were able to secure broad support from allies – women's groups, labour unions, religious leaders, and to some extent civil rights groups. They were also given a crucial opening by the enactment in 1982 of the Canadian Charter of Rights and Freedoms. By mid-decade, constitutional experts were increasingly of the view that courts would interpret the Charter to include sexual orientation, effectively forcing provinces to amend their own human rights statutes. Rights advocates in Ontario took advantage of that leverage, and in 1986 the province became the second to add sexual orientation to its human rights code. Over the next few years several other provincial and territorial jurisdictions followed suit.

## 1985–90: Relationship Issues Increase in Profile

Relationship issues increased their profile with the widening protection of individual rights, but also because of the AIDS epidemic. Part-

Table 4.1    Major Canadian Court and Tribunal Rulings on Relationship Claims, 1980s

| Date | Province | Case/level | Issue | Outcome |
|------|----------|-----------|-------|---------|
| 1983 | Manitoba | *Vogel v. Manitoba* (labour arbitration) | Provincial employee benefits | Claim denied |
| 1986 | BC | *Anderson v. Luoma* (court) | Family law | Claim denied |
| 1986 | Quebec | *Re Canada Post Corporation & Canadian Union of Postal Workers* (labour tribunal) | Federal employee benefits | Claim denied |
| 1988 | Ontario | *Andrews v. Ontario (Ministry of Health)* (court) | Provincial health benefits | Claim denied |

ners of men who were infected risked having no access in hospitals, and no say in the event of death. The increased visibility given to sexual difference by the rapid spread of the epidemic also induced more same-sex couples to become open about their relationships. Starting in the early 1980s, lesbian and gay employees began launching grievances or human rights complaints against provincial authorities to get their partners covered by workplace benefit plans or social insurance programs (see table 4.1), and in the second half of the decade such claims were spreading rapidly. Almost all of them, and certainly all the major ones, failed. But at the same time, a few victories were being registered in public policy. In 1986 Hamilton became the first major city in Canada to extend benefits coverage to same-sex partners of its employees. Two years later, the Yukon Territory became the first provincial or territorial jurisdiction to do the same for its employees. By the end of the decade, Toronto's public library system did the same, as did Ryerson Polytechnic Institute.

## 1990–3: Urban Take-Off and Tribunal Victories

The year 1990 was a turning point. The pressure on city governments to extend employee benefits bore fruit across the country, and major victories were won by activists challenging provincial and federal authorities. By the end of this short period, the British Columbia legis-

Table 4.2   Extension of Employee Benefits to Same-Sex Partners in Canadian Cities[a]

| Year | | |
|---|---|---|
| 1986 | **Hamilton, ON** | |
| 1990 | **Toronto** | **Vancouver** |
| | **Montreal** | |
| 1991 | Coquitlam, BC | |
| 1992 | **Windsor, ON** | |
| 1993 | **Ottawa** | Kitchener, ON |
| | Prince George, BC | Richmond, BC |
| 1994 | **Halifax** | |
| 1995 | **Calgary**[b] | |
| 1996 | **Winnipeg** | Guelph, ON |
| | Sault Ste Marie, ON | Saskatoon |
| 1997 | Brampton, ON | **Metropolitan Toronto**[c] |
| | Oshawa, ON | Kingston, ON |
| 1998 | Ajax, ON | Barrie, ON |
| | **Edmonton**[b] | Kamloops, BC |
| | Peterborough, ON[d] | Lethbridge, AB[b] |
| 1999 | Mississauga, ON | Saint John |
| 2000 | Regina | St John's |
| | Thunder Bay, ON | Laval, QC |
| 2001 | Medicine Hat, AB[b] | Cape Breton Regional Municipality |

[a]Pension benefits were usually excluded because of federal income tax rules, until those rules were deemed unconstitutional in 1998. Cities of more than 500,000 are in bold. Three cities – Kelowna, BC, Red Deer, AB, and Sarnia, ON – indicated that they did not offer such benefits. Responses could not be obtained from sixteen cities.
[b]Alberta legislation precluded pension and health benefits until 2002, when a favourable ruling in *Anderson v. Alberta Health and Wellness* forced change.
[c]An 'upper tier' local authority grouping several municipalities that were formally amalgamated in 1998. Benefits extension was forced by a tribunal ruling.
[d]Included only some benefits, additions in 2000.
Source: Survey conducted of the fifty Canadian cities of more than 50,000, under supervision of the author in 2003–3.

lature redefined 'spouse' in three provincial statutes to include same-sex partners – the first such act by a senior level of government in the country.

*Local Take-Off*

In October 1990 an almost unanimous city council made Toronto the first of Canada's biggest cities to extend workplace benefits to the part-ners of its lesbian and gay employees, following a request from Kyle Rae, a long-time gay activist (and future city councillor). Within weeks,

Table 4.3   Major Canadian Court/Tribunal Victories on Relationship Claims, 1990–3

| Date | Jurisdiction | Case/court level | Issue |
|------|-------------|------------------|-------|
| 1990 | Canada | *Correctional Services of Canada v. Veysey* (Federal Appeal Court) | Prison conjugal visit |
| 1991 | BC | *Knodel v. British Columbia (Medical Services Commission)* (BC Supreme Court) | Provincial health benefits |
| 1992 | Manitoba | *Vogel v. Manitoba* (Human Rights Commission) | Provincial employee benefits |
| 1992 | Ontario | *Haig and Birch v. Canada* (appeal court) | Exclusion of sexual orientation from federal HRA |
| 1992 | Ontario | *Leshner v. Ontario (no. 2)* (human rights tribunal) | Provincial pension benefits |

Vancouver acted similarly, despite the relatively rightist slant of its city council. Montreal did the same before year's end. As table 4.2 shows, more than half of cities with more than half a million people followed suit by 1993 (all but a few doing so by 1998), and in only a few places was there active resistence. (Alberta law limited the range of benefits that localities could provide, but this would not long survive constitutional challenge.)[3]

*Court and Tribunals*

Gay and lesbian relationship claims began winning major victories in court during the early 1990s. Tim Veysey's challenge to the prison system's denial of visiting privileges for his gay partner was the first (see table 4.3).[4] Then in 1991, the British Columbia Supreme Court struck down the restrictive definition of 'spouse' in provincial health insurance regulations. One year later, tribunals in Ontario and Manitoba supported challenges by activists Michael Leshner and Chris Vogel. In the 1992 *Haig* case, an Ontario appeal court ruled that the Canadian Human Rights Act (crucial for relationship claims under federal jurisdiction) should be interpreted as if it included sexual orientation.

These rulings intensified the pressures being placed on provincial and territorial governments by public employees and their unions. As

Table 4.4    Extension of Federal, Provincial, and Territorial Benefits for
Same-Sex Partners of Public Employees in Canada

| | |
|---|---|
| 1988 | Yukon |
| 1991 | Ontario, Manitoba |
| 1992 | British Columbia, Northwest Territories |
| 1993 | New Brunswick, Quebec (1993 and 1994) |
| 1995 | Nova Scotia |
| 1997 | Federal government |
| 1998 | Saskatchewan, Newfoundland |
| 1999 | Prince Edward Island, Nunavut |
| 2002 | Alberta |

a result, benefit plans were made inclusive of same-sex partners for at
least major sectors of the public service in Ontario, British Columbia,
Quebec, Manitoba, New Brunswick, and the Northwest Territories in
the short period between 1991 and 1993 (see table 4.4).

*The Remarkable Case of British Columbia*[5]

Across Canada, politicians were loath to recognize same-sex relationships beyond the benefits packages for public employees and were more
than content to let courts take the lead. Legislatures were ap-proving
bills to add sexual orientation to human rights statutes, but this was still
seen primarily through the lens of individual rights. British Columbia
was a remarkable exception. In 1991 the New Democratic Party won a
large majority in that province's legislature, making former Vancouver
mayor and party leader Mike Harcourt the new premier. The long-pow-
erful Social Credit party was decimated, leaving the BC Liberals as the
largest opposition party. By this time, Vancouver had a highly visible
lesbian and gay community, a union movement rapidly taking up
sexual orientation issues, and a network of supportive lawyers prepared
to push the boundaries of political change. Lesbian and gay activists
within the NDP had also worked hard on educating the party's legislative candidates on the party's policy commitments on sexual diversity.

Within the first year of its mandate, the government introduced a
bill to add sexual orientation and 'family status' to the grounds on
which discrimination was prohibited by the province's Human Rights
Code. There was almost no debate over the sexual orientation amend-

ment either in committee or the legislature as a whole. Modest opposition was expressed in letters to newspapers, but little to compare with the large-scale mobilization that had accompanied Ontario's similar move in 1986.[6] Writer Daniel Gawthrup described the bill as passing through the legislature 'with about as much resistance as a highway improvement project in the North.'[7]

In June 1992, the government introduced another bill without much apparent connection to equality rights – the Medical and Health Care Services Act. Bill 71 sought to alter the role of the Medical Services Commission by making it a significant manager of health care services in the province and broadening the range of voices that would have a say in the process. Section 1 of the bill was given over to definitions of various terms used in the sections to follow, and it included somewhat innocuously (and awkwardly) the following: '"Spouse" with respect to another person means a resident who is married to or is living in a marriage like relation with the other person and, for the purposes of this definition, the marriage or marriage like relationship may be between persons of the same gender.' This health focus was not accidental, since the AIDS crisis had highlighted the importance of giving same-sex partners a role in medical decision making. However, the definitional change was not noticed by either opposition parties or the press, and the bill was approved in short order without a single word uttered, resulting in the first explicit legislative recognition of same-sex relationships in Canadian federal or provincial politics.

In June 1993 four bills were presented that aimed to establish a new system of designating adult representatives and 'guardians,' especially for health care purposes, and to reorganize the office of public guardian accordingly (see table 4.5). Bills 48 to 51 all had definitions of 'spouse' similar to that enacted a year before. These were bills that were widely supported among opposition legislators, so the bills proceeded speedily through the requisite stages. Only in connection with the Adult Guardianship Act was the spousal definition raised. A Liberal member of the Legislative Assembly noticed that the definition of spouse had 'expanded.' 'Is this,' he asked, 'an attempt to be consistent with other legislation that has been brought forward by this government?' Colin Gabelmann, the attorney-general, responded yes with a brief explanation. Without another word of debate, the section was then approved.

Table 4.5   British Columbia Legislation Recognizing Same-Sex Relationships, 1991–3

| 1992 | Medical and Health Care Services Act (Bill 71) |
|------|-----------------------------------------------|
| 1993 | Representation Agreement Act (Bill 48) |
| 1993 | Adult Guardianship Act (Bill 49) |
| 1993 | Public Guardian and Trustee Act (Bill 50) |
| 1993 | Health Care (Construction) and Care Facility (Admission) Act (Bill 51) |

## 1993–9: Securing Wide Recognition of De Facto Relationships

Across Canada, by the end of the 1990s there was no longer much legal room (if any) to discriminate formally against same-sex couples. The long incremental process through which de facto heterosexual couples were given most of the rights and obligations traditionally associated with marriage continued through the decade, and in 1999 the Supreme Court of Canada made clear that de facto gay and lesbian couples could not be treated as second class in law or public policy. Private sector employers could see the writing on the wall and were rapidly modifying their benefit plans. At the same time, religious authorities within progressive Christian and Jewish faith traditions were beginning to bless gay and lesbian unions.

### Persistent Political Caution

Throughout this period, federal and provincial government authorities knew that their employee benefit packages would have to recognize same-sex partners, but legislative change (outside BC) was another matter. Political fears were reinforced in 1994 by the failure of Ontario's NDP-led government to secure passage of a bill recognizing gay and lesbian relationships. Bill 167 was as comprehensive as any activist community at the time sought, including the issue thought most controversial – adoption.[8] Opposition to the measure, mobilized primarily by the religious right, was met by effective lesbian and gay organizing, but fierce resistance in both opposition parties and within a minority of the governing NDP defeated the measure in a hailstorm of national publicity. This response seemed to be a warning to any other government seeking such a multi-pronged response to discrimination.

In Quebec, government ministers had been discussing relationship recognition off and on since the late 1980s. In 1994 they were urged to act by Quebec's Human Rights Commission and by activists who had mobilized to highlight discrimination issues in presentations to the commission. But the Parti Québécois government recoiled in fear after the failure of Ontario's Bill 167. In that very year, Quebec's Civil Code was amended to explicitly define marriage as between a man and a woman.[9]

The federal Liberal government remained nervous about sexual orientation issues throughout this period. In 1996, when it was securing passage of legislation adding sexual orientation to the Canadian Human Rights Act (encoding what courts had already effected), the justice minister took pains to assure legislators that the measure was unrelated to relationship recognition.

There were only a few exceptions to this pattern. British Columbia was still in the vanguard, ensuring the passage of major adoption and family law bills in 1995 and 1997 that contained inclusive definitions of spouse. In 1996 Ontario's legislature approved a bill giving people in same-sex relationships decision-making authority in the case of an incapacitated partner. In 1998 the Yukon Territory's legislature approved two statutes that extended provisions on support payments, property division, and inheritance to separating same-sex couples.

*Charter Victories*

It was in this period that the Supreme Court of Canada first ruled on relationship claims, taking at first a cautious lead in signalling the inclusion of such claims within the ambit of the Charter's equality rights provisions. In 1993 the court ruled against a claim by long-time gay activist Brian Mossop against his federal government employer's denial of bereavement leave to him on the occasion of the death of his partner's father. He had argued unsuccessfully that this was discrimination on the basis of marital status. But the chief justice, writing for the majority, suggested that a Charter challenge based on sexual orientation might have succeeded. This was a message not only that the court might be ready to interpret the Charter as including sexual orientation, but that it was prepared to side with favourable lower court rulings in the last few years on relationship claims.

As Cynthia Petersen points out, the impact of the *Mossop* decision was felt almost immediately, and perhaps most obviously on labour tribunals.[10] In provinces with human rights statutes that included sexual orientation and in workplaces with collective agreements that included it, unions and individual employees were now winning on relationship cases almost all the time. Activist pressure on those provinces that had still not added sexual orientation to their human rights statutes was augmented by stronger-than-ever indications that the Charter of Rights and Freedoms would force them to do so.[11]

In 1995, the Supreme Court faced a challenge brought by another long-time gay activist, James Egan, against the opposite-sex definition of spouse in the Old Age Security Act. The court ruled narrowly against Egan, but a majority agreed that the definition of spouse was discriminatory in ways that were covered implicitly by the Charter. They rescued that definition only by relying on section 1 of the Charter, allowing governments to impose 'reasonable limits' on constitutional rights.

Once again, this confused and uncertain judgment sent out more favourable signals than was at first appreciated.[12] In a 1996 ruling, the Canadian Human Rights Tribunal declared that the law was now 'crystal clear,' and that 'denial of the extension of employment benefits to a same-sex partner which would otherwise be extended to opposite-sex common-law partners [was] discriminatory on the prohibited ground of sexual orientation.'[13] In 1998 the Ontario Court of Appeal eliminated the heterosexual restrictiveness of the federal income tax (in *Rosenberg*), thereby removing the impediment to extending pension benefits to same-sex couples. Federal justice officials knew they did not stand a chance of winning on appeal, and let the ruling stand.

In 1999, the Supreme Court faced yet another relationship claim, and this time seemed ready for clarity (see box).

---

**M. v. H. 1992–9**

In 1982, 'M.' began living with her lesbian partner 'H.,' who at that time owned a house and an advertising business. The relationship ended ten years later, and M. sought a portion of the property in their joint possession, as well as support payments stipulated in the Ontario Family Law Act. But the act defined spouse in heterosexual terms, even though it applied to de facto couples cohabiting for at least three years. A trial court judge agreed with M. that this definition was unconstitutional, and this decision was upheld at appeal. The Supreme Court of Canada, in an 8–1 majority, upheld M's claim. For the majority, Justice Cory wrote, 'The exclusion of same sex partners from the benefits of [the statutory section at issue] promotes the view that M. and individuals in same sex relationships generally, are less worthy of recognition and protection' (Par. 7). The majority recognized that its view on this law would affect many other statutes that relied on a similarly restrictive definition of spouse, and it gave the provincial government six months to provide a legislative remedy. This decision would not affect marriage, but would remove distinctions between cohabiting same-sex and opposite-sex couples.

## Private Employers

In 1993 none of Canada's largest corporations included same-sex partners in the family benefit packages of their employees.[14] The first moves by large firms in North America were taken in the United States just a year or two before. However, by 1999 all but a few in Canada had done so, and those who had not knew the writing was on the wall. Pressure had been building from union activists and collective bargaining teams, and from LGBT caucuses and networks among employees. Now they had the enormous leverage of court and tribunal rulings. (Early in the decade, the Canadian labour movement became widely engaged with issues of discrimination based on sexual orientation, and they fixed on same-sex benefits as an obvious sign of discrimination.[15])

Bell Canada and IBM turned down demands from employee groups for an extension of benefits in 1991 and 1992. North American Life may have been the first large firm in Canada to extend benefits, in 1992, and then 1993 saw Dow Chemical do the same. As table 4.6 shows, the first trio of companies among Canada's fifty largest extended benefits in the following year. Only one year later, when the Ontario legislature was seized by debate over Bill 167, business sections of the province's major newspapers were reporting that the extension of benefits to such relationships was being treated as 'ho-hum' in the corporate sector. Imperial Oil had been one of the few corporations prepared to insist on the retention of discriminatory benefits, holding out until 2000. This position reflected the intransigence of its American parent corporation, in addition to the conservatism of its own management. When it finally conceded, it sent a clear message to the other remaining recalcitrants.

Table 4.6    Provision of Benefits to Same-Sex Couples in Canada's 25 Largest Corporations*

| 1994 | General Motors (non-unionized) | Nortel Networks | Bell Canada |
|------|------|------|------|
| 1995 | Bank of Montreal | Manulife Financial | |
| 1996 | Air Canada | General Motors (unionized) | Canadian Imperial Bank of Commerce |
| 1997 | Alcan | | |
| 1998 | Royal Bank Celestica | RBC Dominion Securities | Quebecor |
| 1999 | Ford Motor Co. Bombardier | Canadian Pacific Railway | Kruger |
| 2000 | Imperial Oil | Honda Canada | EnCana Corp |

*The Bank of Nova Scotia and Great-West Lifeco reported that they had extended benefits to same-sex couples, but could provide no date for doing so. Information could not be obtained from some other companies, but none indicated that it did not supply such coverage.
Source: Survey conducted under the author's supervision, based on the *Report on Business* ranking of corporations by revenue (July 2002), excluding holding companies and those wholly owned by others on the list.

## Intensified Pressure on Religious Congregations

The bestowal of religious blessings on same-sex unions was still hotly contested during this period. The United Church moved the furthest of the large Christian denominations. After a difficult debate over the ordination of gay and lesbian ministers, the church had officially approved doing just that in 1988. The church was not yet ready to take so progressive a position on the issue of blessing relationships, but its decentralized structure allowed individual congregations considerable leeway. Thus, by the end of the 1990s same-sex couples in many areas of the country were able to find United Church ministers willing and eager to bless their unions.

Within the Anglican Church of Canada, there was mounting pressure to allow such blessings. Bishop Michael Ingham of New Westminster (covering the Vancouver area) had authority over a number of congregations and priests ready to act, but he knew there was also stiff opposition so he imposed a delay. Within other mainstream faith currents, Jewish as well as Christian, this was an uncertain period, but one in which relationship claims were coming rapidly to the fore.

### 1999–2002: The Aftermath of *M. v. H.*

In the few years following the Supreme Court ruling in *M. v. H.*, provincial, territorial, and federal governments scrambled to adjust their statutory regimes (see table 4.7). A few governments simply redefined 'spouse' in their laws; Ontario's right-wing government grudgingly used the term 'partner' to distinguish same-sex relationships from those designated by the term 'spouse.' Alberta's conservative government went further to avoid the appearance of recognizing lesbian/gay couples, including non-conjugal as well as conjugal 'adult interdependent' relationships in its changes. Some of these legislative measures created full equivalence to heterosexual de facto couples on all issue fronts; some went beyond the existing regime for de facto couples and reduced the gap with married couples. A few governments at first excluded adoption, but the courts were making clear that this exclusion would not pass constitutional scrutiny.

It was in the federal arena that enactment of such legislation was most controversial. The Liberal government knew that some of its own legislators opposed public recognition of same-sex relationships, regardless of court rulings. As recently as 1999, in fact, most of its own members had sided with a non-binding resolution presented by the right-wing Reform Party, defining marriage in exclusively heterosexual terms. When the government eventually introduced legislation recognizing same-sex relationships, it chose the term 'common law partner' rather than spouse to calm protests within their ranks, and then amended its own bill with an interpretive clause making clear that the bill did not affect the definition of marriage. In the end the bill passed with a strong majority, but in the face of angry dissent from a minority of its own MPs, and formidable protest mobilized by the religious right.

### Quebec's Distinctive and Not-So-Distinctive Record

Change in Quebec was effected in two steps, the first in 1999 at the time of the *M. v. H.* ruling. Impatience at government inaction on relationship issues had been building, with some activists pointing out

Table 4.7    Legislative Recognition of Same-Sex Relationships Following *M. v. H.*

| | | |
|---|---|---|
| 1999 | BC | Definition of Spouse Amendment Act. Amending several acts related to surviving partners to recognize same-sex relationships, building on earlier legislative measures. |
| | QC | An Act to Amend Various Legislative Provisions Concerning De Facto Spouses. Amending 27 statutes and 11 regulations, but not family law and parental rights governed by Quebec Civil Code |
| | ON | An Act to Amend Certain Statutes Because of the Supreme Court of Canada Decision in *M. v. H.* Amending scores of statutes equalizing same-sex 'partners' and de facto heterosexual couples, excluding adoption (treated by 1995 court decision). |
| 2000 | Can. | The Modernization of Benefits and Obligations Act (Bill C-23). Changing 68 statutes, recognizing 'common law partners,' excluding immigration. |
| | BC | Definition of Spouse Amendment Act (Bill 100). Changing 31 statutes, including inheritance and property ownership. |
| | NS | Law Reform Act. Changing 10 statutes, recognizing all de facto relationships through a domestic partner registry, excluding adoption (until a 2001 court ruling). An additional statute (2001) amended 5 further statutes. |
| | NB | An Act to Amend the Family Services Act. Changing family law to extend spousal support provisions to same-sex partners. |
| | NF | Family Law Act. Changing some elements of family law to recognize same-sex partners. Additional legislation (2002) enabled same-sex adoption. |
| 2001 | MB | An Act to Comply with the Supreme Court of Canada Decision in *M. v. H.* Changing 10 statutes recognizing same-sex relationships, excluding adoption, inheritence, property division. Additional legislation (2002) amended 50 statutes, and included adoption rights. |
| | SK | Miscellaneous Statutes (Domestic Relations) Amendment Acts. Changing 24 statutes, treating same-sex couples as equal to married couples, including step-parent adoption (joint adoption having already been legalized in 1998). |
| | Can. | An Act Respecting Immigration to Canada and the Granting of Refugee Protection to Persons Who are Displaced, Persecuted, or in Danger. Inclusion of same-sex couples, provisions modified by regulations issued in 2002 and again in 2004 (recognizing marriage). |
| | NF | Same-Sex Amendment Act. Amending several statutes, extending rights to same-sex partners. Additional legislation (2002) included adoption. |
| 2002 | AB | Intestate Succession Amendment Act, and Adult Interdependent Relations Act. Recognizing 'adult interdependent relationships,' extending recognition to any two adults living interdependently |
| | NT | An Act to Amend the Adoption Act and the Family Law Act. Extended definition of spouse to recognize same-sex couples, including adoption. |
| | QC | An Act Instituting Civil Unions and Establishing New Rules of Filiation. Changing Civil Code and 54 statutes creating civil unions open to same-sex and opposite-sex couples. |
| | MB | Charter Compliance Act. Amending over 50 statutes, including those governing adoption and property, extending recognition to all de facto couples. |
| | PEI | An Act to Amend the Family Law Act. Extending provisions on spousal support on separation to same-sex couples. |
| 2005 | ON | Spousal Relationships Statute Law Amendment Act. Amending about 170 laws to redefine spouse, and reaffirm that religious officials could not be compelled to perform same-sex marriages. |

that Quebec was falling behind other jurisdictions in Canada. In the spring of 1999, the Parti Québécois government introduced Bill 32, amending twenty-seven laws and eleven regulations to eliminate the distinction between gay and straight de facto couples in a range of social policy and taxation provisions. The measure passed quickly and easily, supported by the opposition Liberals. As in almost all other Canadian jurisdictions, this did not require the kind of registration that was the norm in those states and localities in the United States that recognized same-sex couples.

This was a major move forward, but certainly not the first by a provincial government, and not nearly as wide ranging as government pronouncements claimed, since it did not include changes to the Civil Code.[16] As a result, same-sex couples were given no recognition in areas of property division, family residence, support payments, inheritance, consent to medical treatment, and parenting, this at a time when courts elsewhere in the country (most recently the Supreme Court) were making clear that such exclusions were unconstitutional.

A year later, the government announced its intention to create a civil union regime that it claimed would establish the same rights as married couples, and include changes to the Civil Code and fifty-three statutes. Family law embedded in the Civil Code did not extend as much recognition to de facto couples as was the norm in the rest of Canada. For both straight and gay couples, then, moving beyond existing rules would make sense by using a 'registration' portal. This was in contrast to other provinces and territories, whose recognition was being extended to same-sex couples living in de facto relationships, as had already been done for heterosexual couples. Nova Scotia was an exception in having already installed a civil union regime, though there could be no serious question that all or almost all of what was available through it would also be extended to unregistered couples.

When details of the civil unions proposal were first unveiled in late 2001, parenting rights were strikingly absent. In response to questioning, the justice minister wondered out loud if Quebeckers were ready for such a change. A few months later, in 2002, as we will see in chapter 6, the government agreed to amend its own legislation, but only after a flood of activist representations. By now, less than a year after government hand wringing over the parenting issues, political support for this very inclusive new regime was widespread, and the amended bill passed the National Assembly without opposition.

## 2003–5: Marriage Takes Centre Stage

There had been isolated challenges to exclusionary marriage earlier than this, but most leading activists counselled against such action in light of the very real prospect of making gains on the substantive rights and obligations associated with heterosexual cohabition. Later in the decade (1998), when major gains just short of marriage seemed within sight, Quebec activist Michael Hendricks and his partner René LeBoeuf launched court action on marriage, but then put it off in part as a response to Quebec government promises on relationship recognition.[17]

*Court Victories*

With substantive recognition largely secured by same-sex couples, the symbolism associated with continued exclusion from marriage acquired much more prominence. This led to a new round of court challenges, supported by the national group EGALE and networks of activist lawyers. In 2000, cases were launched in Ontario and British Columbia against a heterosexual definition of marriage embedded in common law, joining the Quebec case now being reviewed.[18] (The definition of marriage lay within federal jurisdiction; the administration of it lay within provincial and territorial jurisdiction.) Most of the claimants had activist experience, though there was still doubt among many of their movement colleagues about the appropriateness of pursuing marriage or the likelihood of victory.

A BC trial court judge was the first to deliver a verdict, in October 2001. The court rejected the claim, even arguing that the existing common-law definition was sufficiently embedded so as to be beyond the power of the federal government to change. The second and third judgments, first in Ontario and then in Quebec, asserted that the exclusionary definition of marriage was unconstitutional, but suspended implementation to give governments time to formally amend their laws accordingly. All three rulings were appealed. In the spring of 2003, a British Columbia appeal court overturned the negative trial court judgment before it, delaying application of the ruling.

Then, on 10 June 2003, an Ontario Court of Appeal changed everything. As expected, it supported the earlier trial court judgment in characterizing the denial of gay and lesbian marriage rights as unconstitutional. What surprised many is that it applied its ruling

Table 4.8   Canadian Same-Sex Marriage Chronology

| | | |
|---|---|---|
| 1993 | | Ottawa court rules against marriage challenge. |
| 1994 | | Quebec's Civil Code is amended to define marriage in heterosexual terms. |
| 1998 | | Michael Hendricks and René LeBoeuf launch marriage challenge in Quebec. |
| 2000 | Aug. | Hendricks and Leboeuf challenge relaunched. |
| | Aug. | Ontario 'Halpern' challenge (with 8 couples) launched; additional case subsequently launched by Metropolitan Community Church of Toronto. |
| | Oct. | BC challenge launched by Egale and 5 couples; additional case subsequently launched. |
| 2001 | Oct. | BC trial court rules against same-sex marriage. |
| 2002 | July | Ontario trial court rules in favour of same-sex marriage, implementation suspended for two years. |
| | Sept. | Quebec trial court rules in favour of same-sex marriage; two-year suspension. |
| 2003 | May | BC Court of Appeal rules in favour of same-sex marriage, suspended until 2004. |
| | June | Ontario Court of Appeal rules in favour of same-sex marriage, applying immediately. Federal government acquiesces, announces legislation and Supreme Court reference. |
| | July | BC Court of Appeal lifts suspension in application of earlier ruling. |
| 2004 | Mar | Quebec Court of Appeal lifts suspension on earlier ruling. |
| | July | Yukon Territory court rules in favour of same-sex marriage, applying immediately. |
| | Sept. | Manitoba court rules in favour of same-sex marriage, applying immediately. |
| | Sept. | Nova Scotia court rules in favour of same-sex marriage, applying immediately. |
| | Nov. | Saskatchewan court rules in favour of same-sex marriage, applying immediately. |
| | Dec. | Supreme Court of Canada rules on marriage reference. |
| | Dec. | Newfoundland and Labrador Supreme Court rules in favour of same-sex marriage, applying immediately. |
| 2005 | Jan. | Canadian military issues interim policy approving same-sex weddings. |
| | Feb. | Federal government introduces marriage legislation in Parliament. |
| | June | New Brunswick court rules in favour of same-sex marriage, applying immediately. |
| | July | Federal Parliament completes approval of marriage bill. |
| 2006 | Dec. | Parliament defeats Conservative government motion to reconsider marriage. |
| 2007 | Jan. | Same-sex marriages performed outside Canada recognized for immigration. |

immediately. It did so in part because the heterosexual definition of marriage was in fact a construction of the common law, and not statute law. The evolving interpretation of such law was more obviously in the realm of the courts, and could not as easily be characterized as infringing on legislative prerogative as a ruling that explicitly overturned a statute.[19] Within twenty-four hours, long-time activist Michael Leshner and his partner, Michael Stark, became the first same-sex couple married in Canada, and the first in the world to enter into a marital regime that was free of major discriminatory provisions. (The marriages open to gay/lesbian couples in the Netherlands and Belgium had exclusions in the area of adoption.) And because neither federal nor provincial law imposes residency or citizenship restrictions on who can get married, Leshner and Stark were soon joined by same-sex couples from other provinces and other countries. A month later, the BC appeal court lifted the suspension on the application of its ruling. In 2004, the Quebec appeal court did the same, and courts in five additional jurisdictions ruled in favour of same-sex couples seeking marriage rights.

*Liberal Government Divisions and Delays*

In the face of real marriages taking place, the federal government was put on the spot. Martin Cauchon was federal minister of justice at the time, and himself an advocate of broadening the definition of marriage. In the immediate aftermath of the Ontario court ruling, he argued to his cabinet colleagues that the Ontario court's verdict should be accepted, and the ruling not appealed to the Supreme Court of Canada. He was backed by a widening consensus in justice circles that an appeal to the Supreme Court of Canada would result in yet another ruling in support of same-sex marriage. The Liberal government, in power for a decade, had been cautious in dealing with sexual minority rights up to this point, but Prime Minister Jean Chrétien and most of the cabinet were convinced by Cauchon to leave the Ontario ruling alone.

The government then announced that it would introduce legislation formally defining marriage to include same-sex couples, and at the same time seek the opinion of the Supreme Court of Canada on issues raised by the legislation.[20] It did not at first ask the court whether extending marriage to lesbian and gay couples was constitutionally required, since the government had effectively answered that question for itself by failing to appeal the Ontario court ruling (and those that followed from other provinces). Posing other questions in this 'reference' to the court was widely seen as a tactic to delay parliamentary debate until after the next federal election. A favourable response from the court might also soften resistance among dissident Liberals and boost public support.

Liberal dissent was not quieted. Some caucus members wanted the government to abandon its plans to introduce legislation; others wanted a quick vote to avoid marriage being an issue in the next election. Prime Minister Chrétien stuck to the new game plan, however and, backed by his determined justice minister (Martin Cauchon), convinced a majority of his caucus (at an August retreat) to stay on board.[21] In the meantime, as table 4.8 shows, favourable court rulings appeared in additional provinces.

## Conservative Mobilization

The summer of 2003 saw religious conservatives mobilizing to defend 'traditional' marriage. Protestant pastors were urging action among church goers at Sunday services, evangelical radio and television personalities were asking listeners to send messages to Ottawa, Catholic priests were reading letters from bishops asking parishioners to do the same. Groups that had been battling public recognition of sexual diversity for some time mobilized as energetically as ever, most prominently the Christian groups Campaign Life Coalition, the Catholic Civil Rights League, REAL Women of Canada, the Evangelical Fellowship of Canada, the Canada Family Action Coalition, and the well-resourced Focus on the Family Canada.[22] Rallies were organized in several cities across Canada, and members of Parliament were inundated with messages. Public opinion polling was showing a slight decline in public support for same-sex marriage, from the 50 to 55 per cent range to between 47 and 49 per cent.

The religious right had already been mobilizing on another bill aimed at fully including sexual orientation into the federal hate crimes statute. This was a private members bill introduced by openly gay New Democratic MP Svend Robinson, which was given a real chance of passage through the support of the Liberal government. Religious leaders knew this and were mobilizing supporters with the claim that scriptural condemnation of homosexuality, and church sermonizing on the subject, would be prosecuted under the revised hate crimes law.

The Canadian Alliance, inheritor of the Reform Party's moral conservatism, firmly linked itself to religious-right mobilizing in declaring its determination to defeat the government's marriage legislation. When Parliament reconvened in September, the party put forward a motion intended to preserve the heterosexual definition of marriage, directly challenging the government's plans and exploiting Liberal divisions. On 16 September 2003, the motion lost in a close vote, but it drew support from nearly a third of the Liberal caucus.[23]

## The Prime Ministership of Paul Martin and the 2004 Election

In December 2003 Paul Martin replaced Jean Chrétien as Liberal leader and therefore as prime minister. As a cabinet minister in earlier governments, Martin had displayed much of the same caution as Chrétien, and a significant number of his key supporters in caucus were opposed to same-sex marriage. Fearing how the issue might play out in a widely anticipated election, the new Martin government engineered a delay of Supreme Court proceedings on the marriage reference by adding a new question for justices to consider, asking whether the opposite-sex definition was consistent with the Charter.

For a time, Martin benefited from a continuing split in the partisan right. However, final steps were being taken to merge the Canadian Alliance and the Progressive Conservatives early in 2004, and in March Alliance leader Stephen Harper was chosen to head the new Conservative Party. Harper and his team knew that the Reform and Alliance parties had lost potential supporters fearful of social policy extremism, and he had engineered the party's founding convention so as to avoid votes on divisive issues such as abortion. Opposition to same-sex marriage, though, was thought a possible vote-winner, and the convention resoundingly supported a resolution on the subject.

Prime Minister Martin announced a federal election for the end of June 2004, and there seemed little doubt that same-sex marriage would be prominent in the campaign. The Conservatives' national campaign was closely scripted to avoid fuelling fears of a hidden social agenda, but the party was officially committed to oppose lesbian and gay marriage, and a few of the party's candidates used unqualified homophobic language in campaigning against it. Religious-right groups were also mobilizing over marriage, with Focus on the Family Canada announced a $1.5 million campaign – a major sum by Canadian standards.

The Liberals won the 2004 election but with a significant reduction of seats (to less than a clear majority in Parliament, with the losses attributed overwhelmingly to a major spending scandal). The fact that the government survived at all was partly a result of public fears of the Conservatives' 'hidden agenda' – fears well stoked by the Liberal use of the marriage issue.

## The Supreme Court Response

In October 2004 the Supreme Court of Canada heard representations from governments and other intervenors on the marriage reference. On 9 December, it delivered its response, which was short, subtle, and unanimous. Federal jurisdiction over who could define marriage was affirmed, with the court making clear that provinces could not infringe that power indirectly through a manipulation of their powers over solemnization. The court also made clear that any attempt to create a civil union regime instead of marriage would also lie outside of federal jurisdiction, since that was not part of the power to define marriage and divorce. The right of religious authorities to refuse the performance of same-sex marriages was affirmed.

The court declined to say whether the Charter required that marriage be extended to gay and lesbian couples, responding to the additional question added by the Martin government. (Its argument lay partly in the federal government's own decision to not appeal court rulings in several provinces that struck down the restrictive definition of marriage.) This did not prevent the court from subtly indicating where the majority opinion lay. It denied categorically that same-sex marriage created a conflict or collision of rights based on religion and other equity principles. In response to arguments that the meaning of marriage was 'fixed,' necessarily incorporating an opposite-sex requirement, the court declared that 'Canada is a pluralistic society' and that marriage was a civil institution. It asserted what it described as one of the most fundamental principles of Canadian constitutional interpretation 'that our Constitution is a living tree which, by way of progressive interpretation, accommodates and addresses the realities of modern life' (Par. 22).

## Legislating Gay and Lesbian Marriage

The government announced that legislation would be introduced soon after Parliament was reconvened at the end of January 2005. Liberal cabinet members would be obliged to support the bill, but others in the caucus would be free to vote their conscience. Conservative leader Harper immediately thrust his party's opposition to the legislation to centre stage. He argued that Parliament had the full freedom to legislatively define marriage in heterosexual terms without having to invoke a constitutional provision (the 'notwithstanding' clause) that allows legislatures in Canada to override the Charter.[24] This was a legally untenable position, but Harper knew that he had no chance of securing a legislative majority for invoking a constitutional provision that had only rarely been used in Canada, and never by the federal government.[25]

Once again, mobilization of the religious right was intensified. Newspaper ads were taken out, and American-based preachers reinforced the call to arms in broadcasts on Canadian radio and television stations. Again, Roman Catholic bishops and archbishops spoke out publicly, ensuring that lobbying materials were available in parish churches. Some members of Parliament reported getting more than five thousand e-mails or letters on the government's legislation, 90 per cent of them opposed.

Support for the government was mobilized by established LGBT groups like Egale and newly formed ones like the Campaign for Equal Marriage. The latter's staff was small, though it was mobilizing support at levels not previously seen on sexual diversity issues. The work was supported by the United Church of Canada, a considerable number of religious leaders in other 'mainstream' Protestant denominations, and progressives in other faith traditions.[26] The Canadian labour movement was also vocally supportive, with the Canadian Union of Public Employees, the country's largest union, and the Canadian Labour Congress, the largest federation, urging members to send supportive messages.

Even if the campaigning for gay and lesbian marriage had nothing like the resources mobilized in opposition to it, the government's resolve on the issue seemed to be stiffening. Prime Minister Martin, who for so long had dithered on this issue, introduced parliamentary debate over the bill on 16 February with unusually passionate language:

> This bill protects minority rights. This bill affirms the charter guarantee of religious freedom. It is that straightforward and it is that important ...
>
> That is why I stand today before members here today and before the people of our country to say that I believe in and I will fight for the Charter of Rights.

We will be influenced by our faith but we also have an obligation to take the widest perspective – to recognize that one of the great strengths of Canada is its respect for the rights of each and every individual, to understand that we must not shrink from the need to reaffirm the rights and responsibilities of Canadians in an evolving society ...

When we as a nation protect minority rights, we are protecting our multicultural nature. We are reinforcing the Canada we cherish. We are saying proudly and unflinchingly that defending rights, not just those that happen to apply to us, not just those that everyone else approves of, but all fundamental rights, is at the very soul of what it means to be a Canadian.[27]

The government was teetering on defeat by votes on other issues, most importantly a budget, over continuing revelations concerning earlier government misspending.[28] This would have killed the marriage bill and left its fate to whatever new government emerged from an election. The Liberals survived, for a time, and by early June were convinced that the marriage question needed quick resolution. The final House of Commons vote on the bill, held in late June on the last day of sitting before a summer recess, was 158–133 in the government's favour.[29] The bill's approval in the Senate was never in doubt, and final passage was secured in July. Over the course of the next several months, polls showed a slowly increasing majority of Canadians prepared to put the issue behind them.

## A Conservative Government and the Increased Profile of the Religious Right

Near year's end, the minority Liberal government was defeated in the House of Commons, forcing an election for January 2006. Early in the campaign, Stephen Harper promised to allow for a free (non-whipped) vote on a resolution to reopen the marriage question. He did not raise the question again, though, and the heavily controlled party campaign ensured that morally conservative statements were minimized and candidates with particularly strong conservative views on issues like abortion and homosexuality kept away from the media.[30] On the other hand, the Conservatives (like the U.S. Republicans in the 2004 elections) were clearly using the marriage issue to increase their support within ethnic communities traditionally supportive of the Liberals, including East and South Asians.[31] And once again, the religious right was mobilizing intensively on the question, vastly outgunning LGBT groups whose constituencies widely believed the issue resolved.

The final election results gave the Conservatives fewer seats than expected, given the extent of scandal enmeshing previous Liberal governments, but enough to form a government. Paul Martin announced that he would vacate the leadership of the Liberal Party, weakening the party's voice in the new Parliament until a new leader was chosen at a convention scheduled for December. The Bloc Québécois was also weakened by the election of several Conservative MPs in Quebec, reducing that party's eagerness to cause the defeat of the minority government. Whatever its numerical weakness in Parliament, then, this government was destined to survive at least a year.

Whether the marriage issue helped the Conservatives or hampered them was unclear. Reminding social-conservative voters of the issue may have increased their turnout at the polls, but this would have usually helped Conservatives in areas where they were already strong. An Ipsos Reid poll after the election showed that among those voting Conservative, 40 per cent of Protestants attending church at least weekly felt that moral issues like abortion and same-sex marriage mattered most in deciding which party to support. (Twenty-six per cent cited 'cleaning up corruption,' and no more than 7 per cent prioritized any other issue area. ) Marriage was generally not a high-priority issue for moderates who were uneasy about the party's social policy agenda, and it probably hampered the party's success in the country's largest urban centres and in some constituencies beyond these centres.[32] As Egale pointed out, only 10 of 34 non-incumbent Conservative candidates with strongly rightist views on marriage and other social issues were elected.[33]

The new government made a point of downplaying morality in its legislative program, and the promised marriage debate kept getting put off. All this caution was not surprising, since polls were showing that over 60 per cent of Canadians did not want the marriage issue reopened, and support for same-sex marriage itself was now significantly higher than 50 per cent (47 per cent among Conservative supporters).[34]

On the other hand, newly appointed Justice Minister Vic Toews was an outspoken moral conservative. He lost little time before announcing legislation raising the age of consent for sexual activity (from fourteen to sixteen). Prime Minister Harper appointed advisers who included several with morally conservative views, and his office regularly confirmed that they planned a parliamentary debate on reopening the marriage issue. In early October, Harper also announced plans to introduce a Defence of Religions Act to address the right of public officials to refuse performing same-sex marriages, despite its self-evidently unconstitutional intrusion into provincial jurisdiction.[35]

The marriage fight had mobilized the religious right more than ever, and increased its political capacity in Ottawa. In 2003, only the Evangelical Fellowship of Canada had a staffed office in Ottawa; by 2006 so did the Institute of Marriage and Family Canada (formed by the Canadian branch of the U.S.-based Focus on the Family), the Canada Family Action Coalition, and the Institute for Canadian Values.[36] This meant not only more professionalized lobbying, but a steady supply of commentaries on a wide range of policy issues.

On the government side, however, it was increasingly obvious that the parliamentary motion to reopen the marriage issue would lose. A number of conservative legislators known to be opposed to gay marriage now realized that the issue could harm their chances of re-election. The government responded to these conflicting pressures by scheduling a truncated parliamentary debate shortly before a holiday recess, one heavily scripted to avoid inflammatory remarks by Conservative members. The House of Commons, as expected, then voted down the motion on 7 December, with a convincing 175–123 majority. Among the 'nos' were thirteen Conservatives, including six cabinet ministers. When meeting reporters afterwards, Harper announced 'I don't see reopening this question in the future.'[37] There was also no further talk of a Defence of Religions bill.

What remained ominously on the government's agenda was a reorientation of the many judicial appointments within federal jurisdiction. Harper and others within the Conservative leadership had campaigned in the past against 'activist' court rulings, and in early 2007 they made their move. They increased the weight of government appointees on the advisory councils designed to vet candidates for court appointment, and they provided a seat at the table for police forces. Few observers doubted that the Conservatives would also seek out candidates with relatively narrow interpretations of Charter rights.

The government was also prepared to tolerate explicit discrimination in the statute stipulating the age of consent for sexual activity. Raising the age from fourteen to sixteen would have been an opportune moment to reduce the anomalously high age of consent for anal sex from eighteen years to sixteen. Some years earlier, appeals courts had twice ruled the provision unconstitutional, but the rulings did not apply across Canada. There could be little doubt that the failure to address this inequity was deliberate.

## Solemnizing Marriage

Lesbian and gay marriages, with full legal rights, had been performed in Canada since 2003. By the time the federal government introduced its marriage legislation, the vast majority of Canadians lived in regions where gay marriage was legal. By mid-2006, same-sex marriages had been performed between military personnel, on military bases, and two constables of the Royal Canadian Mounted Police had been wed with almost no controversy in a small Nova Scotia town.[38]

Passage of the federal legislation recognizing civil marriage across all jurisdictions in Canada left unresolved the question of whether marriage commissioners (regulated by the provinces and territories) could refuse to marry same-sex couples on religious or conscience grounds. Some provincial and territorial governments made pronouncements (one way or the other), but there was little doubt that it would end up in the courts. In the meantime, few Canadians would find it that difficult to locate a marriage commissioner ready to officiate at a gay or lesbian wedding.

Church weddings were made available to same-sex couples in a few denominations. Individual clerics had been officiating at gay and lesbian weddings since 2003, acting in their capacity as civilly licensed marriage commissioners, and in some cases also able to use their own churches. The Metropolitan Community Church's congregations had actively supported the marriage campaign from its beginnings, and its main Toronto affiliate spearheaded a legal challenge on the basis of its performance of same-sex weddings. Among major Protestant denominations, some United Church ministers and congregations were willing to marry lesbian and gay couples through religious ceremonies. In 2000, the church's General Council had expressed support for the recognition of same-sex relationship rights, and some ministers were including blessing ceremonies in their marriage registries. In 2003, the council supported civil marriage for lesbian and gay couples, giving congregations leeway to allow church weddings.

Anglicans had been struggling over sexual diversity for some years. In May 2003, after years of debate, the diocese of New Westminster in British Columbia (including Vancouver) became the first in the worldwide Anglican communion to approve the blessing of same-sex unions. In June 2004, a national policy meeting put off a motion to approve the blessing the unions, but it did approve a statement affirming the 'integrity and sanctity' of same-sex relationships, expanding room for dioceses and individual churches to bless them and express political support for civil marriage.[39] In 2007, Vancouver Bishop Michael Ingham, long an advocate for change and a target of conservative Anglican attack, published a call for radically rethinking Christian approaches to sexuality.[40] In May 2007, a bare majority of Canadian bishops voted not to approve the blessing of same-sex unions, in contrast to the decision made two months earlier by American Episcopalian bishops. However, they did call for further study of the issue.

## Overview of Change in Law and Policy

In the late 1980s, activists seeking institutional recognition of same-sex relationships in Canada faced a complex web of exclusionary policies and practices, just as their American counterparts did. By the early years of the decade beginning in 2000, the most important issue still to be resolved was marriage, which in Canada was far less distinct from de facto relationship status than anywhere in the United States. As figure 4.1 illustrates, the pace of change in formal government policy and law had accelerated, reaching take-off at the end of the 1990s. By this time, constitutional interpretation left little room for variation across provinces and territories, and by the mid-2000s only the question of marriage provoked much controversy, and that not for very long.

There were some regional variations in the path to change. Among provinces, British Columbia began recognizing same-sex relationships by redefining the word 'spouse,' starting in the early 1990s. These pioneering moves can be explained by the fact that the government was controlled by the New Democrats, led by a former mayor of Vancouver, and influenced by activists who had worked hard to ensure that legislative candidates adhered to the party's formal policy commitments on gay rights. The province's labour movement also included unions that had shown leadership across Canada in pressing for the inclusion of same-sex benefits. The path towards legislative change was eased by the disunity on the partisan right, and especially on that side of the right upholding moral traditionalism.

Figure 4.1    Canadian Public Policy Recognition of Same-Sex Relationships, 1988–2004

| 1988–91 | 1992/3 | 1995/6 | 1997 | 1998 | 1999 | 2000 | 2001 | 2002 | 2003 | 2004 |
|---|---|---|---|---|---|---|---|---|---|---|
| 100% of jurisdictions | | | | | | | | yt | yt | NU |
| | | | | | nf | mb | yt | nu | nu | PEI |
| | | | | | mb | yt | nt | pei | pei | AB |
| | | | | qc | yt | nt | nu | AB | AB | NB |
| | | | | nf | nb | sk | pei | NB | NB | YK* |
| | | | qc | mb | nt | nu | MB | NT | NT | NT |
| | | qc | mb | on | ns | pei | NB | MB | MB | MB* |
| | qc | mb | on | yt | can | NF | NF | NF | NF | NF* |
| | mb | on | yt | nb | sk | NB | SK | SK | SK | SK* |
| | on | yt | nb | nt | nu | QC | QC | QC | QC | QC* |
| qc | yt | nb | nt | ns | pei | CAN | CAN | CAN | CAN | CAN |
| mb | nb | nt | ns | can | QC | NS | NS | NS | NS | NS* |
| on | nt | ns | can | sk | BC | BC | BC | BC | BC* | BC* |
| yt | bc | bc | BC | BC | ON | ON | ON | ON | ON* | ON* |

Note: Lower case = at least one significant legislative or administrative action.
Caps = multiple initiatives but with several important exceptions.
Bold caps = widespread recognition with few exceptions.
*same-sex marriage permitted.

Quebec might have been expected to play a pioneering role on relationship issues, as it had in its adding sexual orientation to the provincial Charter of Rights (1977). Public opinion was more favourable than the Canadian average on most questions related to sexual diversity, in the same league as British Columbians. During most of the 1990s and early 2000s the social democratic Parti Québécois was in power, and it showed no visible internal dissent on such questions. The low levels of religious practice, and relatively high levels of anti-clericalism, reduced the political leverage of the Roman Catholic Church to near-insignificance. However, it was precisely these factors that bred complacency, and led Quebeckers to believe that state policy was ahead of other jurisdictions in Quebec (matching well-deserved credit in some other social policy realms). The faith in Quebec's progressiveness in policy related to sexual diversity was especially strong in the media (gay and mainstream), and among those activists who were well-connected to the PQ.[41] The preparedness to defer to state representatives was reinforced by the relative weakness of legal networks focused on LGBT advocacy, reducing the supports available to challenge existing statutes in court.[42] When change did come in Quebec, the factors that may have produced an early start to legislative change contributed to very quick and uncontroversial passage of major legislation, with unanimous cross-party support and in the face of only modest extra-parliamentary opposition.

Among the provinces, the Alberta government gave most play to morally conservative arguments against the recognition of same-sex relationships and held on to some discriminatory provisions in law as long as it could. When forced to change, it extended some forms of recognition to all interdependent relationships to avoid seeming to acknowledge the legitimacy of gay and lesbian couples. Premier Ralph Klein (alone among provincial and territorial leaders) promised to campaign against same-sex marriage from coast to coast in the face of the federal Liberal government's promise to legislate change. Even Klein, though, recognized the futility of such a campaign and was probably getting the message from business leaders in his fast-growing province that it would harm Alberta's image. He soon shifted his stance to a resigned complaint that the province had run out of legal options.

Characteristic of the whole country is the finding that opposition to the full recognition of lesbian and gay relationships has declined rapidly once major legal or legislative steps have been taken. When individual civil rights were extended to lesbians and gays, there were only isolated calls for rolling back those changes. When marriage surged onto the agenda, most opponents signalled their acceptance of civil unions – something they would have fiercely opposed only a few years before. There has not been any serious talk of boycotting companies for recognizing sexual diversity, at any time or in any region. By the mid-2000s, religious marriage was still provoking stiff opposition within even progressive denominations, but debate over civil marriage was quickly moving out of the public realm.

### Change Beyond Formal Policy?

In any setting, shifts in the formal parameters of a family regime do not in themselves change the day-to-day favouring of some relationships over others. Policies and upper-level court rulings may be unevenly implemented by state officials, lower courts, and social agencies. Family members, co-workers, and spiritual leaders will recognize some relationships as worthy of celebration and others not. Many workplaces that formally allow same-sex partners to be covered by family benefits are still antithetical to members of sexual minorities being out, and even more unfriendly to discussion of same-sex partners.

True, public opinion has shifted towards much greater acceptance of same-sex relationships. Data reported in chapter 2 showed that by 1999 a solid majority of Canadians favoured treating same-sex couples the same as heterosexual couples. By 2004 support for civil unions was close to or over 70 per cent.[43] Marriage was much more contentious, but here too we see dramatic change over a decade, and consistent majority support from the mid-2000s on. A favourable shift in opinion is most evident in the much-increased number of Canadians who support gay marriage strongly, and the much-reduced numbers opposing strongly. In 1993, the Canadian Election Study found that 42 per cent strongly opposed such marriage, and only 12 per cent strongly supported it, but by 2000, the numbers had shifted to 31 per cent very opposed and 21 per cent very supportive. In 2006, Environics polling showed strong opposition down to 24 per cent, and strong support up to 36 per cent (the latter about three times the American figure).

However, Canadians still demonstrate greater ambivalence in their conception of 'family.' When sociologist Reginald Bibby surveyed a cross-country sample in the early 2000s about what constitutes a family, only 46 per cent said 'yes' when probed about 'two people of the same sex with at least one child.'[44] There cannot be much doubt that a significant number of those responding affirmatively retained ambivalent feelings about whether such arrangements were healthy for children.[45]

*Explaining Take-Off in Formal Recognition*

Explanations for change will be revisited in subsequent chapters, but the take-off pattern recorded on relationship issues calls for reflection. Perhaps the most obvious explanation is the preparedness of courts to apply Charter prohibitions on discrimination to lesbian and gay relationships. Many critics frame this as the primary illustration of judicial 'activism,' in defiance of popular and legislative will.[46] However important the role of courts in the cross-country narrative laid out here, it cannot be considered in isolation from other factors. Legislators at the federal and provincial level have usually been more than prepared to allow courts to take the lead, and at times have put up only tepid defences of exclusionary law. Until the late 1990s, the Supreme Court of Canada was extremely cautious in its approach to demands for recognizing lesbian and gay relationships short of marriage, and by that time public opinion was squarely on the side of treating them the same as de facto heterosexual relationships. The widespread judicial belief in Canada's constitutional rights framework as a 'living tree' helped adapt the already flexible language of the Charter.[47] But claims that they were far ahead of public opinion are ill-founded.

The openings to change in courts, legislatures, and other institutions were widened by the already expansive recognition of de facto heterosexual relationships. This was a policy legacy that allowed for an incremental strategy to secure most of the rights and obligations traditionally associated with marriage, without invoking that explosive concept. As much as in any country, the state regulation of marriage had been moving away from moral arbitration and treating marriage as the only legitimate conjugal relationship. The recognition of gay and lesbian partnerships was eventually seen as simply a logical extension of these earlier changes.

This incremental path was eased by partial decriminalization of homosexuality in 1969, at which point legal reformism had begun in the United States but without rapid or uniform change across state jurisdictions. The enactment of the Charter then allowed significant acceptance of individual civil rights for lesbians and gays in the late 1980s and early 1990s, also helping prepare the ground for subsequent relationship claims – a point made by comparative writers such as Robert Wintemute, Kees Waaldijk, and Yuval Merin.[48]

The fact that religious conservatism was a comparatively weak political force was an obvious contributor to the take-off pattern. Divisions within the political right in Canada, and the tensions that regularly arose when politicians tried to marry right-wing neo-liberalism to moral conservatism also weakened the capacity of opponents to resist without seeming extreme. As debate over relationship recognition intensified, there were growing numbers of right-wing public figures who at least acquiesced in the recognition of gay and lesbian relationships using a neo-liberal rationale, on the grounds that individuals should be free to make their own relational choices, and that reinforcement of mutual family-like obligations reduced the drain on the public purse.

The strong support provided by social democratic forces was also an important factor. Most pioneering steps by Canada's provincial governments were taken by New Democratic Party governments, and the backbone of the federal Liberals on marriage was undoubtedly stiffened by support from the NDP and the Bloc Québécois. The New Democrats in some parts of the country were not always solid in their support for gay rights, but they became much more committed through the 1990s. This pattern was also evident in the Canadian labour movement, which acquired widespread conviction on issues such as same-sex benefits from the early 1990s on.

As will be obvious in tracking American developments, Canadian governments, once convinced to act, did not face the same institutional hurdles that U.S. legislators and officials routinely face. The fragmentation of power at the American state and federal levels provides opponents of change many levers, including popular referenda, to stymie progressive administrations. Provincial and federal government leaders have more control over the policy agenda.

None of this would have produced formal policy change, in Canada or anywhere else, were it not for the increased visibility of lesbians and gays, and of same-sex couples. Recognition claims were advanced by activists in workplaces, labour unions, and religious congregations, as well as courtrooms, but without the backing from increasingly visible constituencies their chances would have been much reduced.

This visibility, and the legal and legislative change facilitated by the Charter, contributed to a favourable shift in public attitudes. To some extent, as Scott Matthews argues, court rulings helped establish lesbian/gay rights as a question of basic equality – a framework quite readily understandable and supportable especially in light of the generally positive Canadian views towards the Charter.[49] Perhaps more importantly, favourable rulings and legislative outcomes enhanced the prominence and legitimacy of claims that were new and poorly understood by most citizens.

An additional factor facilitating the take-off is the widespread suspicion of or scepticism about moral conservatism in the United States, intensified during the administrations of George W. Bush. Indeed, the more that the religious right increased its strength and visibility south of the border, and the more intensely it railed against gay rights, the safer Canadians felt in supporting such rights, and the easier it was to treat the opposition to them as extreme.

## Conclusion

This story of political change has a strong cross-country narrative line, for all the complexities of the relationship regimes across the Canadian landscape. Even in Alberta, there was often more bluster and posturing than effective opposition to change. Public opinion reveals important regional variations, showing Quebec and BC with above-average levels of support, and the Prairie and Alberta regions with below-average levels. Even in the most conservative areas of Canada, however, support for recognizing same-sex relationships had become widespread by the late 1990s. In the politics of morality, then, region matters less than Canadians generally believe, and less than in the United States.

Prejudice remains a disturbing and daily reality for lesbians and gays in Canada. Bisexuals and the transgendered are likely to encounter even more severe rejection, and the struggles over relationship recognition have largely ignored them. But the extension of rights and obligations to same-sex relationships, combined with the growing visibility of sexual diversity in all its variety, has produced important change in public beliefs towards such diversity. The many Canadians who remain uncomfortable with such recognition, especially with respect to marriage, are showing more readiness to acquiesce to change and turn their attention to issues they consider more important. The hardest core opposition is not ready to do that, but it is a declining portion of the overall population.

# 5 American Recognition of Same-Sex Relationships

The movement to recognize same-sex relationships became highly visible in the United States at about the same time as it did in Canada, and even earlier in some locales. By any international comparison, the activist resources marshalled for the struggle were substantial, and pioneering victories were won. In the mid-1980s, progressive municipalities like Berkeley, California, were beginning to recognize same-sex relationships of their own employees, and in the early 1990s private employers were starting to do the same. Activism within a range of Protestant denominations was urging the blessing of gay and lesbian unions as early as, or earlier than, such claims were being lodged in other countries. The first major legal victory on same-sex marriage anywhere in the world was won in Hawai'i in 1993.

The early gains, and most advances since, encountered resistance as fierce as that anywhere in Canada, and activist victories were routinely at risk of reversal. Not surprisingly, the gains are uneven across regions. Recognition of sexual diversity was often isolated to one issue area or institutional domain; the overall spread of public recognition in most domains has been slow. Corporate recognition of gay and lesbian partners in benefit programs has spread more rapidly than change in public policy and law. But across the board, there is nothing like the take-off pattern that is so evident in Canada.

On the question of marriage specifically, a backlash has led to a wave of state measures barring recognition of same-sex couples. Public opinion has moved towards equitable treatment of gay and lesbian relationships, but on the crucial issue of marriage a strong majority remains opposed. Only after 2005 was there any sign of slowdown in the entrenchment of such bans in state constitutions: by then over three-quarters of states had encoded such bans in statute. The success of gay marriage bans, as well as the slowness of progress on other fronts, owes much to the organizational strength of Christian conservatives in the United States and to their willingness to cooperate with one another and with Republican leaders to mobilize the 'moral right' behind the Republicans. The fact that marriage became such an effective wedge issue, however, did not noticeably impede the slow march towards recognition of gay and lesbian relationships by other means. The focus on marriage may even have eased public and political acceptance of measures extending benefits and obligations similar to or equivalent to marriage without the symbolic loading of that term.

Taking stock of developments in the American public sector is immensely complex. All three levels of government have substantial influence over relationship regimes, as do courts that have significant room to strike out in different directions on same-sex relationships. The diversity of outcomes builds on earlier variations in the recognition of straight conjugal relationships and the reluctance of federal courts to clearly signal the inclusion of sexual diversity within the constitutional rights framework of the United States as a whole, in stark contrast to the Canadian court record since the 1990s.

One feature of the American pattern that has few parallels in Canada is the creation of 'domestic partner' or 'civil union' regimes to recognize gay and lesbian relationships. An equivalent was created in Quebec and Nova Scotia, and a limited variant in Alberta, but most of the recognition accorded gay and lesbian couples in Canada does not require formal registration. Cohabiting same-sex couples came to be incorporated into the pattern already well established for straight de facto couples, automatically treating them as entitled to most of the rights and obligations associated with marriage. The much more limited legal recognition of de facto couples of all sorts in the United States was precisely what led to the creation of a new category of non-married but registered couples.

## 1960s and 1970s: Pioneering Groundwork at Local and State Levels

U.S. local and state authorities were among the global pioneers in taking first steps to officially recognize sexual diversity, clearing the path to later recognition of gay and lesbian relationships. The

Table 5.1   Decriminalization of Homosexual Activity in U.S. State Law, 1962–80

| 1962 | Illinois | | | |
|------|----------|--|--|--|
| *(1969* | *Canada)* | | | |
| 1971 | Connecticut | | | |
| 1972 | Colorado | Ohio | Oregon | |
| 1973 | Delaware | Hawai'i | North Dakota | |
| 1974 | | | | |
| 1975 | New Hampshire | New Mexico | | |
| 1976 | California | Maine | Washington | West Virginia |
| 1977 | Indiana | South Dakota | Vermont | Wyoming |
| 1978 | Iowa | Nebraska | | |
| 1979 | New Jersey | | | |
| 1980 | Alaska | New York * | Pennsylvania * | |

*Repealed by court action.
Source: http://www.lambdalegal.org.

decriminalization of gay (and sometimes lesbian) sexual activity was the first critical step towards more wide-ranging change, a policy area within state jurisdiction in the United States.

*Decriminalization of Homosexual Activity*

Where sexual activity between consensual adults of the same sex is formally designated a criminal act, arguing for public recognition of lesbian and gay relationships is challenging, even when such 'sodomy' laws are rarely enforced. The first victory over such statutory prohibition was in 1962, in the state of Illinois, five years before decriminalizing reform in Britain and seven before the country-wide change in Canada. As table 5.1 shows, the 1970s saw similar repeals of sodomy laws in twenty states, almost all by legislative action.

By the late 1980s, the possibility of securing change through legislative reform seemed to have run its course. Between 1981 and the decade's end, only the state of Wisconsin repealed its sodomy law, in 1983. Conservative resistance left few options, and the 1986 U.S. Supreme Court ruling in *Bowers v. Hardwick* gave states constitutional shelter in retaining their criminalized response to homosexuality. Only in the 1990s were court challenges to state sodomy laws more widely launched, and with successful outcomes. Finally, in 2003 the remaining sodomy laws were dealt a heavy blow by the Supreme Court in *Lawrence v. Texas*.

*Prohibitions on Discrimination*

The first legislative prohibitions against discrimination based on sexual orientation were at the local level, beginning in 1974.[1] College and university towns (Berkeley, California; Ann Arbor, Michigan; Madison, Wisconsin) and larger centres with well-organized gay/lesbian communities (San Francisco, Los Angeles, Seattle) featured prominently among the pioneers, as they did later in taking further steps in acknowledging sexual diversity. In some places, most famously Dade County, Florida, this action provoked furious response from religious conservatives. Such opposition slowed the pace of reform, though close to fifty localities had enacted basic rights protections by the end of the 1980s.

State-level pioneering began at about the same time as the first provincial steps in Canada, by Quebec in 1977. In 1975, 1979, and 1983, governors in Pennsylvania, California, and Ohio issued executive orders against discrimination covering the public sector.[2] The District of Columbia enacted rights protection in both the public and private sector in 1977, and Wisconsin did the same in 1982. There was, however, no take-off. The next state to enact a comprehensive prohibition on anti-gay discrimination was Massachusetts, in 1989, by which time the pace of change across Canadian jurisdictions was quickening.

## 1980s: First Local and Corporate Recognition of Same-Sex Relationships

The pioneering pattern was evident in the recognition of same-sex relationships (see table 5.2). The first locality to recognize the gay or lesbian partners of civic employees was Berkeley, in 1984, two years before the first Canadian city with a population over 50,000 did so. Los Angeles was the first city of over half a million people to take the step, two years before the first of Canada's largest cities. Some of these steps were accompanied by the creation of domestic partner registries, though many of these were of purely symbolic value beyond their extension of benefit plans in the public sector. Not surprisingly, these measures were generally in places that had already seen basic rights protections extended to sexual orientation.[3]

In 1982, the *Village Voice* became the first private sector employer to agree to inclusive health benefits. The first litigation designed to force an employer to offer benefits to same-sex couples appears to have been led in 1985 by lawyer/activist Roberta Achtenberg of the California-

Table 5.2   U.S. Local Recognition of Same-Sex Relationships, 1984–90*

| 1984 | Berkeley | |
|---|---|---|
| 1985 | West Hollywood | |
| 1986 | Santa Cruz, CA | Madison, WI |
| 1988 | **Los Angeles** | Takoma Park, MD |
| 1989 | Santa Cruz County, CA | |
| 1990 | Ithaca, NY | Laguna Beach, CA |
| | **San Francisco** | **Seattle** |

*Localities are recorded as recognizing same-sex relationships either by extending health benefits to the same-sex partners of their own employees or by creating a domestic partnership registry. For those that have taken both steps, the date recorded is of the first. Cities over 500,000 are in bold.
Source: Human Rights Campaign website.

based Lesbian Rights Project. The case, argued on behalf of a state employee, was unsuccessful.

During this period, some state courts were interpreting state constitutions as requiring them to move above the constitutional floor set by the federal court on civil rights cases, and by the end of the decade this had begun to have an impact on gay relationship cases.[4] In *Braschi v. Stahl Associates* (1989), a New York court affirmed Miguel Braschi's right to remain in the New York apartment that he and his deceased partner had lived in, successfully claiming that they constituted a family for purposes of settling inheritance rights in the absence of a will. This was a year ahead of the major precedent-setting rulings that were to occur in Canadian courts.

### 1990–2: Slow Spread of State and Local Recognition of Same-Sex Relationships

In 1992 Massachusetts and Delaware became the first states to cover the gay and lesbian partners of at least some of their employees in benefit plans. This could be done by administrative order, making reform possible at a time when legislative action would have been next to impossible. Similar moves were slowly spreading at the local level, such as in Seattle and San Francisco.

There was some movement among private employers in making benefit programs more inclusive. In 1990 only about twenty employers (public and private) in the country had done so, but in 1991 they were joined by a publicly traded company (Lotus Development

Table 5.3   Large U.S. Cities* Offering Domestic Partner Health Benefits, 1988–99

| 1988 | Los Angeles | |
|------|-------------|---|
| 1990 | Seattle | |
| 1991 | San Francisco | |
| 1993 | New York | |
| 1994 | Portland, OR | San Diego |
| 1995 | Baltimore | |
| 1996 | Denver | |
| 1997 | Chicago | New Orleans |
| 1999 | Atlanta | Pittsburgh |

*Municipalities with populations in 2000 of more than 500,000. Atlanta and Pittsburgh have sufficiently narrow boundaries to not exceed the half million mark, but are major cities nonetheless.
Source: Human Rights Campaign web site (http://www.hrc.org).

Corporation). Employee groups were forming, and the pressure to change was rapidly intensifying. Again, such pressure was being mobilized, with first wins recorded, just ahead of the work being done in Canada.

Beyond workplace discrimination, the highest-profile relationship claim centred on a guardianship case in Minnesota. Sharon Kowalski was severely injured in a 1983 car accident, and a trial court had ruled that her partner, Karen Thompson, should be denied legal guardianship. After eight years of litigation, an appeals court reversed that decision, concluding that the two of them constituted a 'family of affinity which should be accorded respect.'[5]

### 1993–9: Acceleration without Take-Off

The evisceration of newly elected President Bill Clinton's pledge to lift the ban on lesbians and gays serving in the U.S. military might have cast a pall on efforts to expand the equity agenda. In the first few years to follow, however, the recognition of same-sex relationships spread steadily at the state and local levels within the public sector, and more rapidly in the benefit plans of large corporations.

*Public Sector Employment Benefits*

Before 1993, only three large cities included gay and lesbian partners in the health benefits of their own employees (see table 5.3). By the end

Table 5.4    States Offering Domestic Partner Benefits for Public Employees, 1992–9

|  |  | Health benefits | Other benefits[a] |
|---|---|---|---|
| 1992 | Massachusetts | x (non-union)[b] | |
| | Delaware | | Bereavement leave |
| 1994 | Vermont | x[b] | |
| 1995 | New York | x[b] | |
| 1997 | Hawai'i | | Domestic partner registry |
| 1998 | Oregon | x[b] | |
| 1999 | California | x | |

[a]Other benefits or registries indicated only where health benefits not provided. In subsequent years, benefits were extended in Connecticut (2000), Rhode Island (2001), Washington (2001), Maine (2001), DC (2001), Iowa (2003), New Mexico (2003), Illinois (2004), New Jersey (2004), Montana (2005).
[b]Benefits extended to all de facto couples.

of 1999 there were nine more. This number was still less than half the American cities with populations of more than half a million, and it displayed nothing like the take-off pattern in Canadian cities, but it was a significant improvement.

In 1993–9 five states created inclusive employment benefits (see table 5.4), marking a steady if not accelerating spread. One of the most significant steps was in Oregon, the result of a 1998 court victory in *Tanner v. Oregon Health Sciences University*. The ruling declared 'suspect' any denial of a benefit to homosexual couples that was given to married heterosexual couples, effectively creating a statewide domestic partnership regime. This decision was only shortly before a Canadian Supreme Court ruling was making comprehensive relationship recognition virtually compulsory.

*Private Sector Employment Benefits*

In 1994 only about one hundred employers (public and private) across the United States included gay and lesbian partners of their employees in benefit coverage. Three years later, that number exceeded fifteen hundred, and by decade's end was increasing by 25 per cent a year. Among Fortune 500 companies, the acceleration was even greater.[6] Levi Strauss and Silicon Graphics were the first to offer health benefits, in 1992. The numbers grew steadily for a few years, and then

Table 5.5    Domestic Partner Benefits among the 50 Largest U.S. Corporations, 1993–9

| 1993 | Microsoft | + | | |
|------|-----------|---|------------------|---|
| 1994 | Fannie Mae | | | |
| 1996 | Verizon | | | |
| 1997 | IBM | | Hewlett-Packard | + |
| | JPMorgan Chase | + | Time Warner | |
| 1998 | Bank of America | + | Costco Wholesale | + |
| | AT&T | | Wells Fargo | + |
| 1999 | Target | + | Morgan Stanley | + |

+Benefits provided for heterosexual as well as same-sex de facto couples.
Source: Fifty highest-ranking corporations, taken from the Fortune 500 in 2004, listed in HRC, 'The State of the Workplace.'

accelerated. By decade's end close to half of the fifty largest corporations had extended their benefit plans (see table 5.5).

In 1996 San Francisco's city council pioneered a new kind of measure to force change beyond its own employees. It approved (unanimously) the Equal Benefits Ordinance, requiring firms and non-profit agencies doing business with the city to provide benefit coverage for cohabiting same-sex and opposite-sex couples. Most local governments in the United States (and all in Canada) lack the authority to legislate as expansively as this, but San Francisco survived court challenges of its right to do so.[7] Los Angeles, Seattle, Minneapolis, and a few other city and county governments (mostly on the West Coast) soon followed San Francisco's lead. A 1999 Atlanta ordinance prohibited local businesses from discriminating on the basis of domestic partner status as well as sexual orientation, though the later passage of an anti-gay-marriage amendment to the state constitution placed the enforceability of that measure in doubt.

### Hawai'i and Marriage

A 1993 court ruling in Hawai'i changed the landscape of the American struggle for relationship recognition. Three couples in that state had launched a court challenge on marriage three years earlier, though few Americans expected victory and little activist support was forthcoming from outside the state. The challengers lost the first round, but the Hawai'i Supreme Court supported them in 1993 and sent the case back to trial, insisting that the state set out justifications for discrimination.

Three years later, amidst a continuing firestorm fed by the earlier victory, the trial judge ruled that the state had failed to offer sufficient rationale for limiting marriage to heterosexuals. However, religious conservatives ensured that the issue would be put to a referendum, and in 1998, Hawai'i voters adopted (by a huge majority) a constitutional amendment allowing the legislature to retain its exclusionary definition of marriage, effectively skirting the court ruling.

At a national level, the marriage issue became the centrepiece of the relationship agenda for all sides of the debate. Because court victories seemed possible, the stakes had become much higher. Marriage in the United States also carried more substantive rights and obligations than in Canada. Whatever misgivings LGBT activists might have had about embracing the issue, on principled or strategic grounds, the *Baehr v. Lewin* case and the conservative mobilization around it had made a war over marriage inescapable.

Subsequent developments in Hawai'i demonstrated the contradictory trends that would continue to mark the struggle over relationship recognition until the present. In 1997 the state legislature enacted something of a consolation prize in the form of a 'reciprocal beneficiary' regime open to people not able to marry – same-sex couples, brothers and sisters, elderly mothers and supportive offspring.[8] This was the first statewide domestic partnership legislation in the United States, giving couples access to some health insurance coverage plans and state employee benefits, bereavement leave from employment, hospital visitation rights, and inheritance rights. As in Alberta, where a rightist government enacted a similarly limited and 'de-gayed' regime, this was an attempt to steer clear of recognizing same-sex couples explicitly. Nevertheless, it represented an opening for legal recognition of precisely such relationships.

*Federal Inaction and Counterattack*

The 'full faith and credit' clause of the U.S. Constitution had always given marriage law reformers the hope that changes enacted in one state would be recognized in others. This possibility provided religious conservatives and their Republican supporters in Congress an argument for enacting federal bulwarks against the spread of gay and lesbian marriage. One vehicle was the Defense of Marriage Act (DOMA), affirming the heterosexual definition of marriage, declaring that states did not have to recognize the marriages of same-sex couples performed in other states, and stipulating that all federal laws dealing with spouses be read in opposite-sex terms only. The Republican-dominated Congress passed the bill in 1996, and President Clinton signed it. (That same year saw a setback in immigration law, narrowing a loophole that some same-sex couples had been able to use until then.[9]) State legislatures had already begun passing their own DOMAs. The first was in Utah (1993), the second was in Hawai'i (1994), and then twenty-six more states followed between 1996 and 1998.

*Overview*

By this time, Canadian recognition of gay and lesbian couples had been expanding rapidly but in a piecemeal manner and largely through court and tribunal rulings. Only in British Columbia had a provincial legislature begun taking steps to explicitly recognize them, though more sweeping statutory changes would soon cross the country. As the decade was drawing to a close, then, there was more widespread recognition of same-sex relationships in Canada than the United States, but apart from BC this had little to do with governing parties showing principled commitment or courage.

What remained a characteristic of the American landscape, with little parallel in Canada, was the continuing fragility of even the most elementary gains. The most recent example was a 1997 civil rights measure enacted by Maine's legislature, overturned by popular referendum one year later. Religious conservatives were also routinely threatening referendum drives against local ordinances prohibiting discrimination or extending employee benefit plans.

Conservatives were also challenging local recognition of same-sex relationships in court. As Charles Gossett points out, of the twenty-two states in which at least one city or county had extended benefits to same-sex couples by the end of the 1990s, thirteen had seen lawsuits challenging their right to do so.[10] Most city measures survived such challenges, but even in relatively progressive states some did not (e.g., Minneapolis and Boston).[11]

**1999–2003: First Comprehensive State Regimes**

The end of 1999 marked another major shift in the American landscape. While radical change was occurring across Canada, major regime change was taking place within a few U.S. states. In late 1999

Vermont's Supreme Court provoked lasting change with a positive ruling on a marriage challenge. A few years later, the highest court in Massachusetts did the same. Between those two rulings, wide-ranging recognition of same-sex relationships was being legislated in California, and partial recognition established through litigation in Washington State.

## Vermont

In *Baker v. State* (a case launched two years earlier), Vermont's Supreme Court unanimously ruled that the exclusion of same-sex couples from marriage violated the state's constitution. It created some room for manoeuvre for legislators by suggesting that a parallel domestic partnership regime would suffice, as long as it created full equality to marriage within state jurisdiction. As William Eskridge has suggested, the court's deference to the legislature was informed in part by its awareness that a voter backlash had overturned rulings in other states on this or similar cases.[12]

Vermont's Freedom to Marry Task Force pressed for full marriage, rejecting the negative symbolism inherent in any 'separate but equal' regime.[13] In April 2000, however, the legislature opted for 'civil unions.' This was the first comprehensive regime recognizing gay and lesbian relationships among U.S. states, including parental rights and obligations, though of course it could not extend to federal jurisdiction.

In November 2000 the state's Republicans campaigned aggressively against gay marriage. They made gains on election day, winning control of the state House, but Democrats retained a majority in the Senate and Governor Howard Dean won re-election. By the time of the 2004 elections, civil unions were being described as part of the Vermont 'fabric,' with polls showing that close to 70 per cent of state voters favoured either civil unions or full marriage.[14]

## California Domestic Partnership, 1998–2003

In the meantime, incremental steps were being taken in California to recognize gay and lesbian relationships. The state had long been ahead of the wave in reforming the legal apparatus for heterosexual relationships. In a 1973 case (*Cary*), the state's Supreme Court applied principles of family law to the division of property for a separated heterosexual couple who had never married. California was also among the minority of states that had prohibited discrimination based on sexual orientation, in 1979 by executive order covering the public sector, and in 1992 by legislation covering the public and private sectors.

The first legislative step towards recognizing same-sex relationships was taken in 1999, with the approval of a domestic partnership regime for same-sex couples (and elderly heterosexual couples). It had provisions for some of the rights and obligations associated with marriage and allowed for workplace benefit coverage for the same-sex partners of government employees.

One year later, 61 per cent of California's voters approved Proposition 22, enshrining in the state's constitution a rejection of same-sex marriage. A mere one year after that, however, the state's domestic partnership regime was expanded to include provisions for the adoption of a partner's child, for health-care decisions when a partner was incapacitated, sick leave to care for an ill partner, and some social insurance and taxation benefits.

In 2003, two more bills bringing the state into line with what had been created in Vermont were approved in the state legislature and signed into law by Governor Gray Davis, by then under the shadow of a referendum campaign to recall him, motivated in part by his support for gay rights. The first bill created almost complete equality between domestic partners and married heterosexual couples in policy areas within state jurisdiction – a regime that would take effect in 2005. The second bill (to take effect in 2007) was a contract compliance measure, requiring all companies doing business with the state to recognize same-sex relationships in workplace benefits. This followed the pioneering ordinance that San Francisco had enacted in 1996, and it was the first such measure at the state level. It was signed by Davis in the dying days of his governorship, just days before Arnold Schwarzenegger took his place.

*Other States*

In the state of Washington, a 2001 Supreme Court ruling recognized gay and lesbian couples for inheritance purposes. Frank Vasquez argued that the relationship with his deceased partner should be treated as having been equivalent to marriage, and the court agreed. Another ruling three years later agreed that a separating lesbian couple should be treated as equivalent to a married couple for property division.

New York inheritance law had already been extended to same-sex couples by the 1989 *Braschi* ruling. In 2002 the first of what would turn out to be a cluster of bills extending modest recognition to same-sex couples passed the state legislature. This first step gave partners of victims of the 11 September 2001 attacks on the World Trade Center access to the workers' compensation benefits ordinarily available to spouses.

*Sodomy Law Challenge*

One impediment to the enactment of more inclusive family regimes was removed in June 2003 when the U.S. Supreme Court, in *Lawrence and Garner v. Texas* overturned a Texas sodomy statute that criminalized homosexual activity. The court's majority stated that people with attractions to others of the same sex were entitled to freedom, dignity, and 'respect for their private lives.' The court's decision effectively overturned its 1986 ruling in *Bowers v. Hardwick*, which upheld the right of states to criminalize homosexual activity. It built on a renewal of activist challenges against the sodomy laws that remained on the books, in turn energized by the federal court's favourable 1996 ruling (in *Romer v. Evans*) striking down an anti-gay measure approved by Colorado voters four years before.

Lawrence Tribe, of Harvard Law School, was quoted as saying 'You'd have to be tone deaf not to get the message from *Lawrence* that anything that invites people to give same-sex couples less than full respect is constitutionally suspect.'[15] It was certainly true that the removal of an aura of criminality on sexual minorities, including those in relationships, swept aside an important justification for withholding rights protections, but the reach of the verdict was unclear.

The court majority made clear that its decision on criminality 'does not involve whether the government must give formal recognition to any relationship that homosexual persons seek to enter,' despite the view of Justice Scalia that it would. The majority had in fact relied primarily on the right to privacy in reaching its judgment. They were not yet ready to declare that discrimination based on sexual orientation warranted anything more than minimal 'scrutiny.' This was at a time, of course, when Canadian courts had firmly placed sexual orientation among grounds given full protection by the major equality rights provision of the Charter of Rights and Freedoms.

One analysis of major court decisions in the seven months following *Lawrence* found only one had been successful in making equity claims based on sexual orientation, and that the lone exception (the Massachusetts marriage decision) had relied much more heavily on a reading of the state constitution than of U.S. Supreme Court jurisprudence.[16] The absence of a clear direction from the Supreme Court meant that, as much as ever, the outcomes of activist litigation could vary hugely from state to state and from issue to issue. State legislators were also left relatively free to enact what they wanted, both positive and negative, including amendments to state constitutions prohibiting the recognition of same-sex marriage.

*Employee Benefits*

Public sector employee benefits for same-sex partners continued to spread steadily across other states and localities. In 1999, eight states had extended public employee benefits of one sort or another to recognize same-sex partners. By the end of 2003, four more states had done the same. Minnesota might have been a fifth, after Governor Jesse Ventura and the American Federation of State, County and Municipal Employees came to an agreement, but in 2001 Republicans in the state House led a successful charge against it.

Inclusive benefit plans were also spreading among cities, gradually but steadily. In 1999 ten of the thirty-two cities with populations of half a million or more had approved such plans, and by the end of 2003, four more were added to the list. This represented about 44 per cent of the total of such cities, and all but one (Houston) of the very largest. Court challenges and anti-gay referenda were still being mounted to local measures such as these, but an increasing proportion were withstanding those challenges.

In two sectors the pace of change was more dramatic. By 2001, forty-five of the top fifty American universities (public and private) and thirty-three of the top liberal arts colleges had effected such recognition in benefit programs. The shift towards inclusiveness would have been even greater except that some public universities were constrained by restrictive state legislation, and the willingness of conservative politicians to resist or reverse change in university employment policy.

Private sector employers were also changing at an accelerated rate. By 2003 thirty-four of the country's fifty largest corportions provided domestic partnership benefits, up almost four-fold over a four-year period. American labour lagged behind its Canadian counterparts in pressing for such change in unionized workplaces, but by this time a significant number of public sector and white collar unions were taking up sexual orientation issues at the bargaining table. The Communications Workers were thought to have been a major factor in getting same-sex domestic partnerships recognized by such large firms as AT&T, Bell Atlantic, Pacific Bell, and Lucent Technologies.[17] The United Autoworkers were also crucial in getting such benefits in the big three American auto manufacturers (GM and Ford in 2000).[18]

However, even among very large and visible corporations, resistance to change was sometimes formidable at a stage when such resistance had largely faded from view in Canada (see box).

---

**Exxon Mobil**

On 30 November 1999 a takeover bid of Mobil Corp. created Exxon Mobil, the new company employing 36,000 in the United States and more than 100,000 worldwide. Mobil employees with same-sex partners learned that their newly merged family benefits program would cover only married employees, though Mobil workers who already had such benefits could keep them.[19] The board of the merged company had recommended against inclusion, and shareholders had rejected by a 94 per cent majority a resolution to include sexual orientation in an otherwise wide-ranging anti-discrimination policy. This was the first major rollback of an inclusive benefit plan in the United States, and it provoked considerable activism. Gay and lesbian employees working for the company were joined by the Human Rights Campaign (HRC) and the New York-based Equality Project (a coalition aimed at using investor pressure to fight for workplace rights for lesbians and gays, which included the New York City Employees' Retirement System, the New York State Common Retirement Fund, and HRC). There was also support from Pride at Work (working within the AFL-CIO), and indications from the Paper, Allied-Industrial, Chemical and Energy Workers International Union (PACE) that they would fight to retain the benefits they had already won for their twenty-five hundred former Mobil employees. As a result of activist mobilizing, the company's public relations office received thirty-five thousand letters of protest, one of them signed by twenty-eight members of Congress and three state attorneys. In Vermont, and in a few of the company's subsidiaries outside the United States (The Netherlands, Canada), same-sex relationships of employees had to be recognized. But still the company's American leadership resisted, and year after year a majority of shareholder votes supported them.

Table 5.6  Recognition of Gay/Lesbian Relationships in the United States and Canada, 2003

|  | Percentage recognizing | |
| --- | --- | --- |
|  | U.S. | Canada |
| Employee benefits: | | |
| – states/provinces with coverage for public employees | 22 | 100 |
| – large cities with coverage for public employees | 44 | 100 |
| – large corporations with coverage | 68 | 90+ |
| Recognition in other realms: | | |
| – states/provinces with comprehensive recognition | 0* | 62** |
| – states/provinces with full recognition in their domain | 4 | 62 |
| – states/provinces with recognition on at least one issue | 14 | 100 |

*U.S. figure reflects absence of federal rights and obligations within any jurisdiction.
**Canadian figure reflects extension of rights and obligations under federal jurisdiction.

## Overview

The area in which the public recognition of same-sex relationships had advanced most widely in the United States was workplace benefits, and especially among very large city, educational, and major corporate employers. A few cities had moved more assertively to the forefront by insisting on inclusive policies for companies doing business with them, going beyond where any Canadian city had the power to go. A few states had included domestic partners in their own benefit plans, though the stiff opposition of Republicans, and unease among a minority of Democrats, kept down the pace of change. Beyond employment benefits, policy and law were changing only haphazardly and unevenly, though wide-ranging and inclusive state regimes were beginning to appear (table 5.6).

## 2003 and After: Marriage and Backlash

Gay and lesbian marriage had been in the foreground of American debates over relationship recognition since 1993. Ten years after that, though, the very real prospect of gays and lesbians getting married in Massachusetts, San Francisco, a few other U.S. localities, and Canada pushed the issue even more prominently to the front pages. Religious-right mobilizing intensified, and setbacks multiplied.

## Massachusetts Marriage

In 1996, when Julie Goodridge was going through the extremely difficult birth of her daughter Annie, her partner, Hillary, was facing one barrier after another in getting to her side.[20] Medical officials at the hospital did not recognize her as family, and only tears and lies overcame the resistance. Neither Julie nor Hillary forgot that episode, and in a few years (2001) they became the lead plaintiffs in a challenge to Massachusett's discriminatory marriage regime.

Mary Bonauto, the legal director of the New England activist group Gay & Lesbian Advocates & Defenders, and a major figure in the Vermont case of *Baker v. State*, was the lead attorney in the Goodridge case. Because Massachusetts was strategically attractive, the case was supported by political groups and legal networks extending beyond the state. There had been a statewide prohibition on anti-gay discrimination since 1989, and the Supreme Judicial Court (SJC) had ruled positively on adoption rights in 1993. Since then, the struggle for relationship recognition had been actively supported by some of the state's largest trade unions, with some, like the Service Employees International Union (SEIU), aggressively bargaining for same-sex benefits and supporting the call for marriage.

In November 2003, the SJC ruled 4–3 in Goodridge's favour, saying that the denial of marriage rights contravened the state's constitution. The court's written decision cited the Ontario Court of Appeal ruling that, only five months earlier, had overturned the existing common-law meaning of marriage in Canada. In contrast to that court, which had allowed marriages to take place right away, the SJC gave the state legislature six months to respond.

Republican Governor Mitt Romney was quick to denounce the ruling, and fierce opposition was soon being mounted from religious conservatives. The state's Roman Catholic bishops (still reeling from child sex abuse charges) were prominent among these voices, calling on parishioners to mobilize. The state's Protestant right benefited from the resources of large national groups eager to use the Massachusetts court ruling as a mobilizing instrument, and an alliance builder to conservative African American clergy.

In December, the state Senate requested a clarification from the SJC as to whether a civil union regime would pass constitutional muster. In February 2004 the court responded with an unequivocal no, declaring, 'The history of our nation has demonstrated that separate is seldom, if ever, equal.'

The next step for political opponents was to press for a constitutional amendment banning gay marriage. On 11 February, state legislators met in special convention to consider just such an amendment. Just one day later, same-sex couples in San Francisco were being 'married' following Major Gavin Newsom's decision to provide civic approval for them in defiance of state law. In several municipalities across the country, local officials were trying to figure out ways to do the same. These marriages were not destined to survive legal challenge, but they appeared on the front pages of newspapers from coast to coast.

In late March, the constitutional convention narrowly approved an amendment that would allow civil unions but bar same-sex marriages. But this was only the first step in the formal amendment process. Another convention vote would be needed, and then a referendum. In the meantime, gay and lesbian marriage was soon going to be legal, as the SJC's self-imposed delay period was coming to an end. Romney had tried various delaying tactics, but in the end he was able only to invoke a 1913 statute to bar out-of-state couples from marrying if they lived in states that would not recognize their marriage (this limitation was confirmed in a 2006 court ruling).

At midnight on Monday, 17 May, ten thousand supporters gathered in front of Cambridge City Hall, across the Charles River from Boston, as the first marriage licences were issued for 250 couples. Here and elsewhere, the United Church of Christ was organizing volunteers to offer refreshments to couples going to municipal offices to marry, and many of its four hundred congregations in the state were preparing themselves for full-fledged marriage ceremonies. Clerics in other faith communities were also declaring their willingness to marry same-sex couples or were pressing for change within their denominations.

As in Vermont, the scope of the rights and benefits that marriage brought was limited to state and local jurisdiction. The many important benefits regulated by the federal government would not be affected, and the extension of employee benefits to same-sex partners was still liable to taxation that would not be levied against heterosexual married couples. Massachusetts marriage, too, was not transportable, because so many other states had passed 'defense of marriage' bills.

The marriage issue remained controversial within and beyond the state through to the general election of 2004, but statewide legislative results revealed no damage to politicians who backed same-sex marriage in the constitutional debates, and an overall increase in the numbers of politicians likely to oppose a constitutional change banning such marriage. The constitutional amendment drive remained active, but looked unlikely to place the issue on the 2008 ballot.

## Firing Up the Anti-Marriage Backlash

In the summer of 2003, the Bush administration and Republicans in Congress and state capitals were renewing their offensive on gay rights in the wake of the Supreme Court's June decision on the Texas sodomy law and the publicity generated by the Ontario appeal court marriage ruling. They were encouraged by a dramatic decline in positive public attitudes to homosexuality in the few weeks following those decisions.[21] President Bush, pressed hard by religious conservatives who saw this as an ideal mobilizing issue, was soon talking about finding ways to stop gay marriage.[22] The focal idea to emerge from this period was a constitutional amendment to affirm the exclusively heterosexual character of marriage – an idea that was advanced even more assertively in the wake of November's court ruling in Massachusetts. The installation of the Episcopal Church's first openly gay bishop in New Hampshire only added fuel to this fire. In January, Bush reiterated his support for a constitutional amendment in the State of the Union address, and again when marriages started occurring in San Francisco.

In mid-2004, the amendment was killed for the time being by a procedural defeat in Congress.[23] But the idea of state-level constitutional amendments was gaining appeal, doubly so because constitutional change could be secured in many states by referendum, a tool that the religious right was well equipped to wield. In the spring of 2004, for example, when signatures were being sought to place a ban on the Oregon ballot, five thousand were gathered at a mere dozen churches in Portland and the state's Defense of Marriage Coalition had already heard from four thousand potential volunteers.[24] Across the United States, opinion polls were showing 60–70 per cent opposed to same-sex marriage, even if opinion was more evenly divided on whether constitutions should be changed to prevent it.

The Bush Administration seemed fully prepared to benefit from the issue and to take advantage of religious networks that were already on high alert. Months before the 2004 election, the re-election campaign was sending detailed strategy guides to religious volunteers across the country.[25] They believed that placing gay marriage issues on state ballots would help bring out conservative voters, and religious right groups believed that successful mobilizing around the issue would secure their standing within the Republican Party. Religious leaders were reminding President Bush that many conservative Christians stayed home in the 2000 election because of his apparently tepid response to their concerns.

## The 2004 and 2006 Elections

Still, the Republican leadership was playing a delicate game. They wanted the votes of religious conservatives, and they knew they needed to use the issue of gay marriage to embarrass a divided Democratic Party. But they generally attached higher priority to lower taxes and reduced government regulation than to the moral agenda. Clyde Wilcox has argued that during his first term in office and during the election, Bush's public pronouncements were not preoccupied by moral issues.[26] The policy legacy from his first term was, he points out, much more dominated by a pro-corporate neo-liberal agenda than by the morally driven policies favoured by Christian conservatives. The Republican leadership was also wary of being linked to voices that would be seen (even by American standards) as extreme. The late-summer Republican National Convention was heavily scripted to keep its most conservative voices from the podium, even though hard-line delegates insisted on toughening the language of a resolution supporting a constitutional amendment, making clear that the prohibition they favoured would extend far beyond marriage itself.

Democratic standard-bearer John Kerry claimed that he opposed gay marriage, and his campaign highlighted his religious belief. Other Democratic candidates tried simply to avoid the issue. But Republicans used attack ads and shadowy groups to paint the Democrats as pro-gay. And of course the placement of marriage referenda questions on state ballots made the issue inescapable. Republicans and conservative religious groups believed that the issue afforded them opportunities to make inroads among African Americans and Hispanics, who were shown in repeated polling to have strong majorities opposed to lesbian and gay marriage.

In November, voters re-elected Bush and secured Republican gains in the House of Representatives (of five) and the Senate (of four), producing solid majorities in each. In races for state governor, though,

Democratic and Republican gains were about equal, and in state legislative races, only modest changes were recorded, Democrats winning control of five houses they previously did not control, Republicans four.

Most post-election analysis suggested that the marriage issue had not been as significant as first thought. Allan Abramowitz highlighted the continuities with partisan patterns in earlier elections, and attributed Bush's victory to the advantages of incumbency and to shifts deriving from the 9/11 aftermath.[27] Morris Fiorina and Ken Sherrill agreed, rejecting the 'moral values' line of explanation for Republican gains at the federal level.[28] They pointed to the fact that states with anti-gay referenda showed turnout rates only fractionally higher than other states, and that the rise in turnout among evangelicals was not greater than for other groups.

The plain fact is, however, that the American voting public was more polarized by party on morals issues than ever, and the federal governing party had mobilized its core constituencies with a self-conscious and elaborately applied anti-gay strategy, working in close quarters with groups and pastors on the religious right. In the past, Republicans (and Democrats) had usually run to the ideological hearts of party activists during the lead-up to nomination, and then to the centre during the election. This time, the Republicans made electoral gains while attacking the rights claims of a minority group. The result was that those voters who regularly attended religious services and held traditional religious views voted Republican more than ever, and those who did not more Democratic. In some key states, there was even evidence of significant increases in African-American support for the Republicans.[29]

Although the war in Iraq would soon lead to drastic decline in the public approval of Bush, there was no sign of moderation in the administration's rhetoric, and its policy agenda in areas that mattered for sexual minorities. Most notably, congressional majorities and Republican discipline around a strongly right-wing leadership provided enough support to sustain the appointment of conservative judges to federal courts. Two vacancies on the U.S. Supreme Court gave the president an unusual opportunity to shift its direction towards conservative jurisprudence. At the state and local level, religious conservatives were threatening judges with organized opposition at their next election.[30]

Two years later, the 2006 election was fought alongside increased public preoccupation with the Iraq war and growing doubts about the

Table 5.7   U.S. State Constitutional Amendments Prohibiting Same-Sex Marriage[a]

|  |  |  | Percentage favouring amendment | |
| --- | --- | --- | --- | --- |
| 1998 |  | Hawai'i[b] | 69 | |
|  |  | Alaska | 68 | |
| 2000 |  | Nebraska | 70 | + |
|  |  | Nevada[c] | 70 | |
| 2004 | August | Missouri | 71 | + |
|  | September | Louisiana | 78 | + |
|  | November | Arkansas | 75 | + |
|  |  | Georgia | 77 | + |
|  |  | Kentucky | 75 | + |
|  |  | Michigan | 59 | + |
|  |  | Mississippi | 86 | |
|  |  | Montana | 66 | |
|  |  | North Dakota | 73 | + |
|  |  | Ohio | 62 | + |
|  |  | Oklahoma | 76 | + |
|  |  | Oregon | 57 | |
|  |  | Utah | 66 | + |
| 2005 | April | Kansas | 70 | + |
|  | November | Texas | 76 | + |
| 2006 | June | Alabama | 81 | + |
|  | November | Arizona | 49 (defeated) | |
|  |  | Colorado | 56 | + |
|  |  | Idaho | 63 | + |
|  |  | South Carolina | 78 | + |
|  |  | South Dakota | 52 | + |
|  |  | Tennessee | 81 | |
|  |  | Virginia | 57 | + |
|  |  | Wisconsin | 59 | + |

[a]Most of these measures are under court challenge.
[b]Amendment did not explicitly bar same-sex marriage, but empowered the legislature to do so, which it subsequently did.
[c]Nevada requires a reaffirmation of constititutional amendments, and in 2002 a ballot measure was supported by 67 per cent.
+Denotes measures with broad language prohibiting 'marriage-like' recognition.

Bush administration. However, there were eight state ballot measures aimed at gay marriage (see table 5.7), and across the country religious conservatives and Republican strategists worked hand in hand to rally morally conservative voters to the Republican side. On election day itself, Republicans and religious voters heavily supported these measures, and exit polls showed that even with the high profile of the Iraq war, 36 per cent of voters considered 'value' issues such as same-sex marriage and abortion 'extremely important,' and an additional 21 per cent 'very important.'[31] Still, overall support for these measures was slipping, and there was even less evidence than in the 2004 election that these measures pulled undecideds or those inclined to stay home to the Republican side.[32]

The election produced Democratic majorities in the House and (by the slimmest of margins) the Senate, and saw the defeat of a few notoriously anti-gay federal politicians. On the other hand, relatively few of the new Democratic members were distinctively progressive on the question of same-sex relationship recognition. Only nine of the fifty surveyed by the *Washington Blade* supported marriage equality, with an additional sixteen prepared to go as far as civil unions.[33]

## State Constitutional Amendments on Marriage

By the time of the 2004 election, thirty-eight states had Defense of Marriage statutes on the books, denying recognition to same-sex marriages performed elsewhere. It was in that election, too, that referenda to enshrine such prohibitions in state constitutions spread rapidly. Previously, in Hawai'i, Alaska, Nebraska, and Nevada, these amendments had been approved by large majorities, whetting the appetites of conservatives in the 2004 election cycle.

All of the fourteen constitutional prohibitions on gay marriage voted on that year won strong majorities. Three-quarters of them went beyond marriage, with wording that could effectively prohibit the recognition of civil unions or the extension of benefits to same-sex couples. The wording of Ohio's measure was the most explicitly all-encompassing: 'This state and its political subdivisions shall not create or recognize a legal status for relationships of unmarried individuals that intends to approximate the design, qualities, significance or effect of marriage.' In Michigan and Georgia, the breadth of their constitutional amendments led officials to question local government benefits plans that covered same-sex partners.[34] In Virginia, lawmakers were speculating that their new anti-marriage provision could threaten even corporate plans extending such benefits.

All this activity provoked a flurry of legal challenges from equity advocates, alongside continued litigation on marriage claims for same-sex couples. In 2006 Washington State's Supreme Court upheld the statutory ban on gay marriage (*Anderson v. Kings County*), as did appeal courts in Georgia and Nebraska. In the same year, New York's Court of Appeals rejected a marriage claim by same-sex couples (*Hernandez v. Robles*). In all these cases, the courts were prepared to retain the very limited 'scrutiny' accorded by most U.S. courts to discrimination based on sexual orientation.[35] Early in 2007, a Michigan appeals court ruled that the provision of health benefits to same-sex partners of state and local public sector employees violated the state's recently amended constitution, this being the first major ruling on an expansively worded constitutional amendment.

The 'success' of the marriage referenda in 2004 spurred religious-right groups and Republican politicians to introduce similar measures for the next available electoral round. Kansas legislators were first off the mark, and an overwhelming majority of voters approved a constitutional amendment in an April 2005 ballot. In November, three-quarters of Texas voters supported a similar amendment on November's ballot.

Where legislative approval was given for a ballot measure, state house votes in 2005 and early 2006 were usually very lopsided: 96–3 in South Carolina, 78–18 in Virginia, 88–7 in Tennessee, 55–14 in South Dakota. Hardly a Republican could be found among the brave few resisting these measures, and most Democrats supported the constitutional amendments. By election time in 2006, eight states had constitutional bans on gay marriage on the ballot.

But in this round there was a noticeable shift. In Arizona, voters narrowly defeated one, and in four other states, the majorities supporting them were only in the 52–59 per cent range.[36] It could be that religious and political conservatives were running out of states where passage of such measures could be guaranteed, and where they could be strategically deployed to assist Republicans. Public opinion was shifting only slightly towards more positive views of same-sex marriage, not yet at 40 per cent levels, but support for entrenching prohibitions constitutionally could no longer be assumed.

*Gains outside Marriage*

The marriage backlash did not stop the slow spread of comprehensive regimes at the state level recognizing same-sex couples. In some respects, the focus on marriage created a certain political opening even for wide-ranging programs, as long as they avoided the loaded term 'marriage.' Public opinion polling was suggesting that support for civil unions or domestic partnership regimes was approaching or crossing the 50 per cent mark (depending very much on the question asked).

In 2004 New Jersey became the fourth state to enact a measure granting significant recognition to same-sex couples.[37] Although the legislation was not directly forced by court challenge, some of the substantive rights and obligations associated with marriage, most notably in parenting, had been won through litigation. The New Jersey bill created a domestic partnership registry, which like California's was open to same-sex couples and heterosexual ones eligible for social security. This was not as wide ranging as changes in California, Massachusetts, and Vermont, but it was extended in 2006 by two other bills. Later that year, the state's Supreme Court ruled unanimously that same-sex couples were entitled to the same rights and obligations as married heterosexual couples, though a slim majority of the panel turned down the claim that this necessarily required marriage itself (*Lewis v. Harris*).[38]

In 2005 Connecticut's creation of a civil union regime made it the fifth state to extend wide-ranging recognition to same-sex couples. At the beginning of 2006 the District of Columbia joined this group when its legislative council approved a broad domestic partner regime, which then survived a waiting period during which Congress had the right to intervene. In the same year, California enacted additional laws extending coverage of its regime. And then in 2007 New Hampshire, long the most reluctant of New England states, created a civil union regime with rights and benefits in state and local law mirroring those for married heterosexuals.

More limited measures were approved in other states. In 2004 Maine's legislature created a domestic partnership registry, granting rights to same-sex couples in relation to decision making and inheritence. This was significant in a state where a simple non-discrimination law had been so persistently controversial. (Voters had once before repealed a civil rights measure, though in November 2005 they rejected a measure aimed at undoing legislation prohibiting discrimination based on sexual orientation.) Alaska's Supreme Court ruled in 2005 that state and local governments had to provide domestic partners of their employees with benefit coverage (*ACLU v. Anchorage*). The following year, New York State took a couple of modest steps beyond those already taken by courts or the legislature, extending recognition to same-sex partners in unemployment insurance, state pensions, and decision-making rights. Also in 2006, Maryland's legislature extended medical decision rights to non-married partners, gay or straight, and resisted calls for a constitutional ban on same-sex marriage. A year later it passed a bill requiring health insurance firms to provide coverage for same-sex partners if employing institutions requested such coverage. Washington State's legislature approved a domestic partnership bill in 2007 covered hospital visitation, healthcare decision making, property inheritance, organ donation, and funeral arrangements.[39] In neighbouring Oregon, the legislature and governor approved a domestic partnership regime that granted many benefits and recognized obligations offered to married couples. At the same time, the state enacted a civil rights measure including both sexual orientation and gender identity.

## Corporate Recognition

The now-rapid spread of workplace benefits recognizing same-sex couples continued through the period of marriage backlash. By 2006 just over half of Fortune 500 corporations – including three-quarters of the largest fifty – had extended health benefits coverage. This was partly a result of increased organizing by LGBT employees and greater assertiveness on this issue by American labour. It was also the product of growing management recognition that more inclusive policies helped attract the highly educated employees they sought. This extension of benefits was a concrete example of the claims made by Gary Gates and Richard Florida, who argued that acceptance of diversity (including sexual diversity) was a hallmark of communities and regions that were experiencing economic growth.[40] Companies were pitching their products and services to what they saw as an important LGBT market, or promoting their inclusiveness through the provision of visible support to sexual diversity, partly to attract more business, but also to establish their reputation for welcoming diversity among their own and prospective employees.

When Procter & Gamble agreed to extend its benefits, in 2002, its home base of Cincinnati had an ordinance on the books preventing the enactment of any further local measure prohibiting anti-gay discrimination. Some elements in the business community, P&G a leader among them, argued that the city had to become more gay friendly if it was to reverse the steady decline in population that had been plaguing it. In 2003 P&G supported an activist campaign for repeal of the ordinance – a campaign that carried the day in the 2004 election.[41]

Changes in corporate response to sexual diversity did not go unnoticed by the religious right, which has had a long history of mounting protests against corporations displaying a gay-friendly face. Boycotts against firms like the Walt Disney Company and American Airlines had been generally seen as failures, though the prospects of publicity around such an issue might still deter some firms from taking their first steps. Even Microsoft, one of the earliest of the large corporations to extend benefit programs to same-sex couples, seemed vulnerable to threats from the Christian right: in early 2005 it suspended its support for a non-discrimination measure being hotly debated before the Washington State legislature (its home base being in Seattle). A local pastor had threatened to organize a national boycott, and to all appearances the company buckled. Microsoft employees, however, had a long history of organizing inside their company, and the networks built up over the years were quickly mobilized, alongside many supporters outside the firm. They soon forced a restoration of the corporation's earlier supportive policy, though the legislation at issue had since died in a close vote.

Threats against Procter & Gamble seemed not to diminish its contribution to the repeal of Cincinnati's anti-gay ordnance, but the fact that its ads were no longer being placed in gay magazines and on television programs featuring gay characters was thought by some observers to be a response to Christian-right opposition.[42] Phil Burress, a leader of Ohio's Christian right and vocal opponent of the corporation's role in the Cincinnati campaign, was quoted as saying 'P&G has quietly backed away from promoting homosexuality, but they'll never admit it.'[43]

In late 2005 the Ford Motor Company appeared to have recoiled in the face of a boycott threatened by the American Family Association, agreeing to stop advertising some of its brands in gay publications. It soon reversed itself after criticism from LGBT groups, maintaining its preparedness to sponsor gay community events, retain inclusive benefits, and advertise in the publications it had placed ads in before. A few months later, 95 per cent of shareholders voted down a proposal that benefits be withdrawn for same-sex partners. Although Christian-right groups have attributed declining car sales to the boycott they have maintained against the company, Ford continued its record of donations to LGBT groups through 2007.

Despite such attacks, we see widespread acceptance of formal policy changes recognizing same-sex relationships, among large corporations especially, and indications that many are prepared to go beyond formal policy.

## Religious Recognition

Though the most vocal religious voices in the United States were strenuously opposing gay marriage, steps were being taken within some faith traditions to recognize same-sex relationships. Individual Protestant churches, especially within such denominations as the Unitarian Church and the United Church of Christ (UCC), had been blessing same-sex couples for years. The Metropolitan Community Church as a whole had also been doing so for twenty years – not surprising given its explicitly association with LGBT communities. In 2001, a convention of the Presbyterian Church in the United States had approved the blessing of same-sex unions, and in 2004 the church sent a letter to President Bush supporting the recognition of civil unions (while still barring openly lesbian and gay ministers). The Lutheran Church has retained its policy of not blessing same-sex unions, but has decided not to discipline ministers and congregations deciding to do so. The national Methodist conference has not adopted a denomination-wide policy approving blessings, and still had policies officially barring openly lesbian or gay clergy and blessings for same-sex unions, but it has publicly called for an extension of civil rights to lesbian and gay couples.

In 2003, the year that openly gay Gene Robinson became bishop in New Hampshire, the Episcopal Church's national convention voted to allow the blessing of same-sex unions, a practice that had been occurring in some individual churches already (as it had been in England).[44] In the early 1990s great controversy had accompanied such actions, but quietly there were now bishops simply ignoring the practice, neither supporting nor condemning it. In 2004 and 2005 the bishops of New Jersey and Utah affirmed their preparedness to allow such blessings in their dioceses, and the Bishop of Los Angeles personally blessed the union of a gay couple, all of this in the face of growing international condemnation within the Anglican communion, and urgings to avoid stirring up further controversy. In 2006 the dioceses of the District of Columbia, Arkansas, and Connecticut came to similar views. A year later the American Episcopal Church's executive council rejected demands that same-sex blessings be stopped.

The United Church of Christ had often been in the forefront of main-stream Protestant debates on issues related to homosexuality. In 2005, 80 per cent of the delegates at a UCC General Synod approved a reso-lution allowing gay and lesbian marriage services and calling for support of inclusive legislation, though leaving individual congrega-tions the choice as to applying the resolution. In the year to follow, much internal controversy persisted, though the great majority of con-gregations remained in the fold.

As in Canada, there was dissent over these issues even within the Roman Catholic Church. When Vatican policy radically shifted from a policy of clerical celibacy to one that targeted those with 'deep-seated' homosexual tendencies, dissent broadened.[45] The intensity of the hier-archy's campaigning on marriage also troubled many clergy, and its prohibition on Catholic agency placement of even the neediest chil-dren with same-sex couples (in 2005 and beyond) provoked many Catholic priests as well as lay supporters.

Reconstructionist rabbis in the United States voted overwhelmingly in 2004 to support the extension of civil marriage to include same-sex couples. Ordaining of gay and lesbian rabbis had been supported since 1984, and blessing same-sex unions was approved in 1993. Many Reform rabbis have also performed marriages in their synagogues. The Rabbinical Assembly, representing the Conservative branch of Judaism, had decided in 1992 that rabbis should not perform same-sex marriages and commitment ceremonies, but it did not encode this as a binding standard.[46] In 2006 conservative Judaism's highest legal com-mittee approved a variety of measures that essentially left it up to individual synagogues and seminaries to decide whether to perform commitment ceremonies and whether to accept openly gay rabbis.[47]

These changes and debates have been broadly similar to those within the religious mainstream in Canada, though Catholics are less numerically prominent in the American religious landscape, and mainline Protestant denominations more obviously overwhelmed by explicitly conservative ones. Even more than in Canada, U.S. religious progressive voices are drowned out by those condemning any public recognition of homosexuality.

## Overview of Change

In the first decade of the twenty-first century, conservative religious leaders remained focused on anti-gay compaigning while becoming

Figure 5.1   American State Policy and Legal Recognition of Same-Sex Relationships, 1989–2005

| | 1989 | 1991 | 1992 | 1994/5 | 1997 | 1998 | 1999 | 2000 | 2001 | 2002 | 2003 | 2004 | 2005 | 2006 | 2007 |
|---|---|---|---|---|---|---|---|---|---|---|---|---|---|---|---|
| 41% of jurisdictions --------------------------------------------------------------- | | | | | | | | | | | | | | mt | mt |
| | | | | | | | | | | | | | | il | il |
| | | | | | | | | | | | | | mt | ri | ri |
| | | | | | | | | | | | | | il | ak | ak |
| | | | | | | | | | | | | il | la | md | la |
| | | | | | | | | | | | | la | dc | la | de |
| | | | | | | | | | | | dc | dc | de | de | ia |
| | | | | | | | | | | | de | de | ri | nm | mn |
| | | | | | | | | | | | ma | ct | nm | ia | ny |
| | | | | | | | | | dc | dc | ct | ri | ia | mn | MD |
| | | | | | | | | | de | de | ri | nm | mn | ny | ME |
| | | | | | | | | dc | ma | ma | nj | ia | ny | or | WA |
| | | | | | | | dc | de | ct | ct | nm | mn | or | ME | HI |
| | | | | | | dc | de | ma | ri | ri | ia | ny | ME | WA | NH |
| | | | | | dc | de | ma | vt | mn | mn | mn | or | WA | HI | OR |
| 12% of jurisdictions ----- | | | | | de | ma | vt | cn | ny | ny | ny | WA* | HI | DC | DC |
| | | | | dc | ma | vt | mn | mn | or | or | or | HI | NJ | NJ | NJ |
| | | | | de | vt | mn | ny | ny | wa* | wa | wa | NJ | CT | CT | CT |
| | | | dc | ma | mn | ny | or | or | HI | HI | HI | CA | CA | CA | CA |
| | | de | ny | ny | or* | HI | HI | CA | CA | CA | VT | VT | VT | VT | VT |
| | mn* | ny* | ma | vt | HI** | HI | CA | CA | VT** | VT | VT | MA* | MA | MA | MA |

**Canadian provinces/territories**

| | 1992 | 1994/5 | 1997 | 1998 | 1999 | 2000 | 2001 | 2002 | 2003 | 2004 | 2005 | 2006 | 2007 |
|---|---|---|---|---|---|---|---|---|---|---|---|---|---|
| % minimal recognition: | | 61 | 61 | 77 | 92 | 92 | 92 | 100 | 100 | 100 | 100 | 100 | 100 |
| % comprehensive recognition: | | 0 | 0 | 0 | 8 | 23 | 46 | 62 | 62 | 69 | 100 | 100 | 100 |

Note: Lower case = at least one significant area, by legislative action or court ruling (including extension of public employee benefits).
Caps = more than one significant area of policy but with several important exceptions.
Bold caps = widespread recognition with few exceptions.
*By court judgment.
**Court judgment followed by legislative action.

increasingly emboldened politically. But despite setbacks on marriage, lesbian/gay relationships were becoming more widely recognized. Nine states had established civil union, domestic partner, or marital regimes, six of them extending wide recognition to same-sex couples. Three of them did so in 2004–5 when anti-marriage organizing by

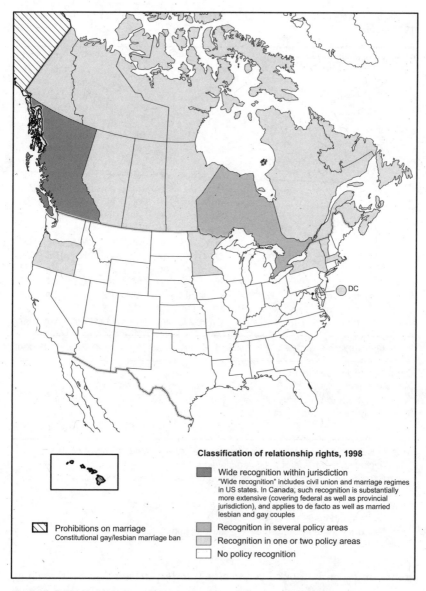

Figure 5.2  Relationship Recognition in the United States and Canada, 1998

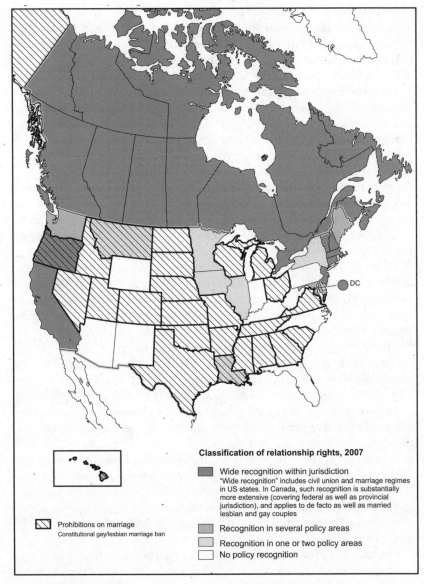

Figure 5.3  Relationship Recognition in the United States and Canada, 2007

conservatives was at its most effective. As figure 5.1 shows, 41 per cent of American state jurisdictions had extended recognition to same-sex couples in at least one domain, 18 per cent in several, and 12 per cent had done so across a wide range of policy areas.

In the United States there are strong regional variations in response to pressure for recognition, much more so than in Canada. Comprehensive change at the state level is entirely restricted to the Northeast and far West (including Hawai'i). At the local level, most of the cities that have pushed furthest to recognize gay and lesbian relationships are located in these same regions, though some large cities in otherwise conservative regions have adopted inclusive policies.

Outside the public sector, the recognition of same-sex relationships has also been spreading. The inclusion of same-sex partners in employee benefit packages was more likely in large than small workplaces, but the pace of change across the country was impressive, extending to three-quarters of the country's largest private corporations by 2007. This spreads the recognition of same-sex relationships, in effect, into urban areas of otherwise conservative regions, especially as competition for investment in the educational sector and in high-tech innovation pushes up the standards for inclusive benefit programs. (One example is in Kentucky, where the two largest universities have extended benefits plans to domestic partners.[48])

Most religious authorities have resisted gay marriage, but the number of Protestant and Jewish congregations prepared to bless gay and lesbian unions in one way or another is growing steadily. Many newspapers across the country began listing commitment ceremonies alongside marriage announcements before gay/lesbian marriage was possible. The *New York Times* was not the first when it made the decision to do so in 2002, but it was a crucial marker. Now more than half of the major dailies do so. For all its limitations, the immensely popular television program *Queer Eye for the Straight Guy* publicly displayed gay men delivering what the audience was to read as sage advice on the sustenance of intimate relationships. In the midst of battle, the terrain was indeed shifting.

In Canada, public sector recognition of same-sex relationships was almost entirely completed by 2005, and the controversy over marriage was dying down. Public policy and law in the United States never experienced the kind of take-off that had occurred north of the border, but steady gains in recognition continued, even in the face of the most intense mobilizing by the religious right that equal rights advocates had ever seen. The adoption of inclusive benefit policies in the private sector may have been somewhat slowed by religious-right opposition, but it was far from stopped. The relationship recognition secured in the United States is more vulnerable than those gains effected in Canada, especially in the face of broadly worded constitutional amendments on marriage, but the steady pace of change has not yet slowed.

*How Much Change?*

The absence of any significant change in federal policy prevents full recognition of same-sex relationships even in the six states (plus Washington, DC) with the most inclusive civil union regimes. In other words, no same-sex couple in the United States has the full rights and responsibilities accorded straight married couples. And of course, as is also true in Canada, formal recognition in any particular issue area does not in itself guarantee full or consistent acceptance in public regard or institutional practice.

Public recognition of gay and lesbian relationships has indeed expanded considerably over the last two decades. As chapter 2 showed, the general public responds relatively favourably when asked about the extension to gays and lesbians of the specific benefits and responsibilities traditionally associated with marriage. It also favours rights associated with inheritance, social insurance, and employment. Support for civil unions has spread widely and grown significantly. A form of comprehensive recognition that was not even on the popular radar screen until 2000 has increasingly become a surprisingly comfortable middle ground.[49]

Yet opposition to marriage remains powerful, as does moral opposition to or disapproval of homosexuality, even if it has declined significantly since the early 1990s. Such discomfort or antipathy increases the volatility of support for substantive recognition of gay and lesbian relationships – a tendency evident in 2003, when positive responses to a range of gay-related questions dropped so markedly.

The strong regional and urban/rural variations in support for greater policy inclusiveness are not much different from those in Canada, but there are some indications that they may be increasing. PSRA/Pew polling has, for example, shown that opposition to gay marriage in the South remained stable over the decade following the mid-1990s, at around three-quarters of the population. In the Northeast, on the other hand, there was growing support for marriage over this period, and in New Jersey, New York, Vermont, and Massachusetts, at least as much support as opposition. In the United States such regional contrasts have greater 'play' in public policy than they would in Canada. Across the South, for example, the average response to relationship issues, or any other question about gay rights, is persistently conservative enough that centrist and progressive politicians give voice to inclusive stances at their peril. This is not just because of popular responses to issues of sexual diversity, but also because polling has shown that Southerners are more likely than others to weigh party positions on gay marriage in making voting choices.[50] The more favourable views in states like Massachusetts and California do not eliminate the electoral caution of moderate politicians, but they reduce it significantly.

If one of the important gains to be made in recognizing same-sex relationships is the visibility and legitimacy it potentially extends to those whose sexuality varies from the norm, one of the costs is that it 'normalizes' only a small band of such variation – a point made in chapter 1. Indeed, claimants to marriage rights almost invariably present themselves in respectable forms that are familiar to those in more traditional family relationships. Gender ambiguity and gender crossing are rarely in the picture. Even when bisexual or transgendered people make relational claims, they will often censor themselves or get cut out of the public picture. In 2004, for example, high-profile bisexual activists were among the first to be married in Massachusetts and San Francisco, but mainstream media reports ignored that event entirely.[51] This form of constrained presentation may help in generating more popular acceptance of gay and lesbian relationship recognition, but it does come at a cost.

*Explaining National Patterns of Change*

The slowness and unevenness of the policy shift towards recognizing gay and lesbian relationships stand in contrast to the Canadian pattern of take-off. They result most obviously from the large numbers of religious conservatives in the American population, the resources of the political groups representing them, and their influence on the Republican Party. The religious right has long seen gay rights as effective mobilizing issues, and at least until recently same-sex marriage has been the most effective of all. Its power lies in the religious trappings of marriage and the heavy weight of tradition loaded onto it. The issue has also shown more capacity to bridge religious and political divides among conservatives than other sexual diversity issues.

The unity of the political right on these issues is also an important factor in slowing change. The peculiar American coalescence of neo-liberal, anti-government sentiment with morally conservative support for state regulation is embodied in the political platforms of major religious-right groups and the Republican Party. There has been a high level of disciplined opposition to all attempts at recognizing sexual diversity by Republicans in almost all parts of the United States from the 1980s on, and an eagerness to use these issues at election time.

The power of the religious right to resist or slow change in policy, law, and institutional practice is bolstered by conservative media that regularly attack any claims based on sexual diversity in the framework of 'special rights.' There are such media voices in Canada, but they are modest in comparison to the ubiquity of Christian broadcasting, right-wing talk radio, and conservative commentary on American television portraying gay rights claims as hallmarks of moral decline.[52] All of this reinforces the kinds of contrasts in political culture that have been pointed out by writers such as Seymour Martin Lipset and Michael Adams.

The relative weakness of American labour is another factor in slowing the rate of change. Proportionately, the membership of the Canadian labour movement is over twice that of the American, and Canadian unions have been a world leader in taking up sexuality issues. Some U.S. unions have made important moves on these and other equity issues, but the reach and visibility of the activism is modest.[53]

As several writers have pointed out, the policy legacy in areas related to relationship recognition is clearly a factor affecting all of the United States.[54] There has been no U.S. Supreme Court ruling that comprehensively extends rights protections to sexual minorities. Discrimination in federal employment was proscribed by an Executive Order issued by President Clinton, but that is open to narrow interpretation or reversal and represents only partial coverage, with no obvious ramifications for relationship recognition. Only a minority of states have extended rights frameworks to cover sexual orientation and gender identity (even if over half of Americans live in state or local jurisdictions which prohibit discrimination based on a sexual orientation). Such basic rights create platforms on which relational claims can be made, and their very partial spread weakens the case.

Across the United States, too, family law has moved substantially slower than in Canada towards a recognition of de facto straight relationships. This has deprived activists of opportunities to aim for an equivalent treatment of de facto same-sex relationships, before taking up the highly charged marriage question. In the United States, much change has occurred in the legal regulation of marriage itself, and non-marital cohabitation has increased substantially over the last few decades, but much more than in Canada this has fueled anxiety about social order.

The American health-care system also increases the stakes of relationship claims. The expenses associated with broadening workplace benefits to same-sex partners may be modest, but they are a good deal higher than in Canada. More seriously, the recognition of gay and lesbian relationships has risked destabilizing the exclusion of de facto heterosexual relationships from such plans. Some employers have opened up their benefits to gay and lesbian partners but kept them closed to cohabiting straight couples, aiming to contain additional costs. Other corporations have included both categories, but many others would resist moving on any of these fronts for fear of the expense.

The slow pace of change is also a result of the fragmentation of power in the American political system, one of the institutional factors emphasized by Miriam Smith.[55] Within state and local governments, there are far more checks on executive power than there are in Canada, so that even a determined government administration has difficulty overcoming strong opposition. With Republicans almost invariably opposed to any recognition of sexual diversity, and prepared to campaign on the issue, securing policy gains is bound to be challenging. In most regions of the country, too, there will be a minority of Democrats who oppose such gains on moral grounds, or on the basis of electoral fear. Such fear can be enhanced by threats to use referenda to encode anti-gay barriers, especially because referendum campaigning is well-suited to the organizational strength and depth of the religious right.[56]

Slow and uneven progress effected through the courts speaks to a national constitutional rights framework that has not yet been interpreted to clearly prohibit anti-gay discrimination.[57] This is in part the product of conservative appointments to the federal bench, and a shift away from the readiness of the court majority to read constitutional rights provisions broadly. On race and then gender issues, most dramatically in *Roe v. Wade*, the U.S. Supreme Court had dramatically shifted the regulatory regime governing reproduction, at a time when finding a legislative majority to do the same in Congress would have been impossible. The shift back to greater caution was made possible by a rights apparatus laid down much earlier than its Canadian counterpart, and more open to a wide range of interpretations. The drafters of Canada's Charter of Rights and Freedoms, and the activist intervenors in the debate over its provisions, were able to benefit from what they saw as the weaknesses of the American framework and earlier Canadian rights instruments. Since then, courts have generally come down on the side of interpreting the rights framework as a 'living tree' that should be interpreted in a way that reflects broad social and political changes. This has been an extremely important factor in changing the legal and public policy construction of 'family' in Canada, and an important boost to favourable changes in public opinion.

No ruling of the U.S. Supreme Court has clearly enunciated a prohibition on discrimination based on sexual orientation, even if decisions on Colorado's Amendment 2 and Texas's sodomy law have imposed some limits on making lesbians and gays strangers to the law. The appointment of conservative judges to the high court by President George W. Bush makes any significant shift towards equity very unlikely in the next several years.

## Explaining Regional and Local Variations

If slowness of change is one hallmark of the American experience, another is the pioneering advances made in some regions, particularly at the local level. On most of the issue fronts related to the recognition of gay and lesbian relationships, we can find victories being secured, somewhere in the United States, as early as anywhere in the world.

One factor explaining the early gains in some parts of the United States is the density of networks and the scale of resources that activists were able to mine from an early stage. The sheer size of the country's population provided the wherewithal to build substantial national groups, which has helped (even if imperfectly) to provide resources for local activism.[58] The complexities of the American political system also create pressures to develop stable institutional structures at all jurisdictional levels. This increases the support available to those groups and individuals wanting to challenge existing regimes.

One study in the late 1990s, which ranked states by per capita membership in the National Gay and Lesbian Task Force, found those with the greatest activist density tended to also be in areas with the most progress in policy recognition of sexual diversity.[59] Haider-Markel, Wald, Button, and Rienzo have pointed to variations in activist resources as important contributors to variations in policy outcomes at state and local levels.[60]

The weight of religious conservatism is a potent force of resistance to change in virtually every community and state in the country, but it does vary across locale. In those regions where the religious right is weaker, pro-gay activism is enhanced by the real possibility of securing gains.[61] The fact, too, that the religious right is a consequential political presence everywhere stimulates LGBT mobilization and increases fundraising capacity, volunteer recruitment, and alliance building, especially so where the right's weight does not appear socially or politically overwhelming.[62]

Not surprisingly, areas of Democratic Party strength are generally going to be more open to activist pressure on relationship issues. Quantitative work by Haider-Markel, Wald, and their associates identify this factor and low levels of conservative religiosity as significant contributors to progressive policies on sexual diversity.[63] Naturally, those areas where attitudes are more favourably disposed to homosexuality and gay rights are more likely to see policy changes on relationship issues.[64] This favours activists in the Northeast particularly and disadvantages their colleagues in the South.

Elaine Sharp explores the role of political culture in sorting out uneven change across the American landscape, while acknowledging the elusiveness of the concept. She suggests that variations in social capital and other factors pointed out in Daniel Elazar's classic study of regional differences have a role in explaining differences in the outcome of 'culture wars' such as those we are surveying here.[65]

The fragmentation of power in American political life, while slowing large-scale change, also creates openings for activist success where other factors are favourable. The relative permeability of American parties has also meant that LGBT activists could make substantial inroads into the Democratic Party, and in some regions secure policy commitments on the recognition of sexual diversity. Party permeability allowed for a few quite early electoral ventures by openly gay/lesbian candidates, who would often become policy champions on issue fronts related to sexual diversity.

At the local level, as is true in Canada, large cities are more likely to have taken steps to recognize same-sex relationships than smaller centres and rural areas.[66] States with a more urbanized population, too, are more likely to have moved in the same direction. Regions with ethnically diverse populations are also more likely to have inclusive policies on sexual orientation, even though African Americans and Hispanics have more traditional views on issues like gay marriage than Euro-Americans (controlling for other factors).[67] Such areas are of course more likely to vote for Democrats.

The absence of a clear direction from the U.S. Supreme Court on issues of sexual diversity has created substantial room for the play of variations in state law prior to activist claims on relationship issues. The rights statutes of American states vary significantly, and the fact that some of them have explicit protections against discrimination based on sexual orientation (and in a few cases gender identity) has provided an opening for court challenges on relationship issues. This is especially relevant in the Northeast, and a few of the progressive states on the West Coast and in the Midwest.

Earlier enactment of measures decriminalizing homosexual activity and providing basic civil rights protections is a factor pointed to by various writers with an interest either in cross-national or cross-regional variation. Among the latter, Button, Rienzo, and Wald, for example, argue that changes in rights protections encourage members of sexual minorities to come out, and this obviously helps to provide a platform on which relationship rights can be claimed.[68]

Unevenness of change in heterosexual family regimes has also created openings for lesbian and gay activists in some states, and not at all in others. Where de facto straight relationships have acquired partial recognition in law, for example in Washington State and California, incrementalist strategies are more available for those seeking the accommodation of gay/lesbian relationships.

## Conclusion

In their day-to-day lived experience, same-sex couples in large American cities are more accepted than they ever have been. In a substantial number of cities and university towns, the social service supports, employment benefits, and religious acceptance available to them rival those in any Canadian or European region. We can find in the United States the first steps towards recognizing such relationships in public policy, religious ceremonies, and employment practices anywhere in the world. But years after those pioneering steps, official recognition accorded them is weaker than in Canada and most of northern Europe.

What gay and lesbian couples encounter in policy terms is an unstable but slowly shifting regime. The idea of family, and the lived reality of heterosexual relationships, has been in great flux for most of the last century. The recognition of same-sex relationships has intensified anxiety already on the rise, even if in the meantime lesbian and gay activists have found political openings for change. There are fewer signs of social anxiety in Canada, and of course less of a religious revival embodying such anxiety. Public discomfort with some aspects of same-sex relationship recognition remains north of the border, but less of it is intensely felt, less of it is tied to apocalyptic vision, and less of it is translated into a yearning for greater moral regulation. The resistance to same-sex marriage was strong enough, but only a few months after federal legislation encoded country-wide change the issue's power as a mobilizing instrument was largely deflated.

More than any country, the United States has seen more constant challenge to the traditional family regime by changes in everyday life, and yet there are few countries in which the resistance to those changes is more intensely felt and mobilized. Some steps towards recognition of lesbian and gay relationships may be secure, and we might on that basis chart steady progress that seems unlikely to be rolled back. But other changes, we know from past experience, are unstable and at constant risk of repeal.

# 6 Parenting in Canada

In 1995 British Columbia became the first regional or national jurisdiction in North America, and probably the world, where adoption rights were extended to lesbian and gay couples. Only one year earlier, a legislative measure designed to recognize same-sex couples in Ontario, introduced by a social democratic government, had been defeated – many said because it included adoption rights. Acknowledging rights and responsibilities for same-sex couples was one thing – still controversial to be sure – but bringing children into the picture engendered much more fear.

Over the next decade, northern European governments continued to exclude parental rights from civil union regimes. The Quebec government, portraying itself as far in advance of other Canadian provinces in the equitable treatment of sexual minorities, excluded adoption from wide-ranging legislation enacted in 1999 and at first tried to do the same in additional legislation unveiled in late 2001. Pundits and politicians widely agreed that their fellow citizens were not yet ready for such radical change.

However, the treatment of sexual diversity in Canadian family law was undergoing dramatic change, and parental policy could not easily be left behind. Despite official resistance in some provinces and territories, activist pressure and the growing willingness of parents to challenge exclusionary law in court ensured that the victories won on relationship recognition would be extended to parenting. Theoretically, the lack of a significant federal role in areas such as parenting left much room for variation in policy from region to region, but as in other areas related to sexual diversity, a cross-country narrative thread emerges. We find a scattering of claims in the 1970s and early 1980s, and then a substantial broadening of activist interest in the early 1990s, which started to bear fruit in the middle of the decade. By the turn into the next decade, most formal discrimination against lesbians and gays as parents was doomed to collapse in the face of constitutional challenge.

## The 1970s, 1980s, and Early 1990s: Resisting Custody Losses and Planning for Children

Lesbian and gay parents groups emerged in Canada in the 1970s, providing access to political advice and social networks for women and men who mostly had children from previous heterosexual relationships or marriages.[1] Lesbian mothers' groups were more politicized, helping to bolster defences against hostile custody claims. Gay fathers' groups were more focused on mutual support and friendship, since any court action on custody claims seemed unlikely to succeed.

In the 1980s, increasing numbers of same-sex couples were planning to become parents. Some became foster parents, taking advantage of the shortage of homes for children, and especially for those with special needs. Many others were arranging for one or the other partner to become a biological parent, either through informal arrangements for conception or one or another form of assisted reproduction. This trend raised the question of securing recognition of the non-biological parent's role, in health-care and schooling systems, in access to family benefits at work, and in the web of laws that recognized some families and not others.

Changes in the treatment of heterosexual families might have smoothed the path towards recognizing parental rights for same-sex couples. The broadening recognition of de facto conjugal relationships in Canada entailed a shift away from a purely biological construction of parenthood, including a recognition of step-parent obligations in heterosexual relationships. Over thirty years ago, for example, the Canadian Divorce Act imposed child-support obligations on spouses who have stood 'in the place of a parent.'[2] (This would not generally have applied to Quebec, with its separate Civil Code regulating divorce and marriage, and with greater reluctance to formally recognize rights and obligations of de facto partners.) From the 1980s on, federal pension and income tax statutes included de facto parental roles in their determinations of eligibility for benefits.

Table 6.1    Selected Court Rulings on Custody for Lesbian or Gay Parents, 1974–9

| | | |
|---|---|---|
| 1974 | SK | *Case v. Case*<br>First reported case: custody awarded to father and not to lesbian mother, for fear of contact with people of 'abnormal tastes and proclivities.' |
| 1975 | AB | *K. v. K.*<br>Custody awarded to lesbian mother, based on discretion. |
| 1978 | ON | *D. v. D.*<br>Bisexual father awarded custody partly on grounds that he was not militant or active in gay organizations, and kept his sexual orientation hidden from all but close friends. |
| 1979 | MB | *Bernhardt v. Bernhardt*<br>Custody denied to mother, her lesbianism cited as one factor. |

## Custody and Access

Most early claims for recognition focused on custody and access. The first recorded court case was in 1974, when a Saskatchewan judge ruled against awarding custody to a lesbian mother for fear of contact with people of 'abnormal tastes and proclivities' (*Case v. Case*). Prior to that, few lesbian mothers and even fewer gay men would have risked contesting custody at all, and would more likely bargain it away in exchange for liberal access.

Until 1980 it is hard to find a single reported court case anywhere in Canada in which the ruling sustained the child custody rights of a lesbian, bisexual, or gay man without heavily discriminatory conditions requiring that children be guarded against displays of homosexuality (see table 6.1). A positive ruling by an Alberta provincial court in 1975 (*K. v. K.*) was remarkable for its rejection of arguments that societal homophobia would harm a lesbian mother's children, suggesting that conceding to such sentiment would be equivalent to awarding custody in a mixed-race relationship on the basis of persistent racism. Still, the favourable ruling was made conditional on the discretion of the mother.

There seemed a shift in the early 1980s, with courts in the three largest provinces arriving at relatively favourable conclusions on custody (see table 6.2). Their rulings reflected a growing view that the best interests of the child ought to be the central criterion in adjudicating custody and access: homosexuality was to be considered

Table 6.2   Selected Canadian Court Rulings on Custody/Access for Lesbian or Gay Biological Parents, 1980–9

| | | |
|---|---|---|
| 1980 | ON | *Bezaire v. Bezaire*<br>Appeal Court ruled that sexual orientation in itself was not a ground for denying custody. |
| 1982 | QC | *J. v. R.*<br>Appeal Court struck down clause requiring that access only be in the absence of same-sex partner, ruled as discriminatory according to Quebec rights charter. |
| | BC | *Nicholson v. Story & Nicholson*<br>Lesbian maternal grandmother awarded custody of granddaughter (already in her care for years), judge noting that homosexuality was a factor, but not a bar. |
| 1983 | QC | *Droit de la famille – 31*<br>Superior Court ruling includes overtly hostile remarks on lesbian/gay parenting. |
| 1984 | ON | *Elliot v. Elliot*<br>Court awards custody to lesbian on condition of discretion. |
| 1985 | SK | *Worby v. Worby*<br>Court denied access as long as present lifestyle (cohabiting with partner) continued. If allowed access in future, could not expose son to lifestyle that was confusing, disruptive, and contrary to moral upbringing. |
| 1986 | BC | *Templeman v. Templeman*<br>Court ruled that homosexuality was not a bar to custody or access, though child's exposure to promiscuous lifestyle allowed shift in access rules. |
| 1987 | BC | *Elliot v. Elliot*<br>Court denied lesbian custody of daughter despite support from experts, on grounds of her resuming cohabitation with partner. |
| 1989 | NL | *E.(A.) v. E.(G.)*<br>Supreme Court restored access to gay father, partly on grounds he remained discreet and apolitical. |
| 1989 | BC | *Saunders v. Saunders*<br>County Court denied custody to gay father, alarmed at child's exposure to same-sex relationship. |

only if there could be a link established between that and harm to the child.

Still, courts were imposing severe restrictions on the custody of lesbian or gay parents, or denying it on the basis of what was thought

Table 6.3    Custody Cases Involving Non-Biological Lesbian or Gay Co-Parents, 1980s

| | | |
|---|---|---|
| 1986 | BC | *Anderson v. Luomo*<br>Supreme Court ruled that even though two lesbians and two children had formed a family-like unit, the statutory definition of spouse meant that the more financially advantaged had no financial responsibility for children or spousal support after separation. |
| 1989 | ON | *In Re L. & S.*<br>Family court granted sole custody of two children to birth mother, one of them conceived by artificial insemination during lesbian relationship. |

to be indiscretion. The best interests of children, in other words, was contingent on a definition of 'normal' upbringing that was routinely considered incompatible with 'exposure' to sexual diversity.[3] In British Columbia, a province thought to have a relatively progressive bench, the judge in a 1989 case involving a gay man wrote, 'surely it cannot be argued that exposure of a child to unnatural relations is in the best interest of that child of tender years' (*Saunders v. Saunders*).

The 1980s saw the first attempts to secure legal recognition of parental rights for non-biological parents in a same-sex relationship, one in BC and one in Ontario. Not surprisingly, both claims failed, at a time when non-parental claims by lesbian and gay couples were not yet being recognized (see table 6.3).

*Fostering, Adoption, and Assisted Reproduction*

In the 1970s informal networks were developed to assist lesbians with at-home insemination using donated sperm – typically from gay men – usually accompanied by private agreements on parenting rights and obligations. Until the mid-1980s medical clinics rarely treated single heterosexual women, let alone lesbians, for fertility problems.[4] As recently as the early 1990s, a survey conducted for the Royal Commission on New Reproductive Technologies found that 76 per cent of medical practitioners would refuse donor insemination to women even in a stable lesbian relationship.[5]

If lesbians had children with donors known to them, which was common throughout this period, there was continuing uncertainty about whether the donor could legally claim parental rights (against the wishes of the same-sex couple), especially in a context where the parental rights of the non-biological lesbian partner were not legally recognized. In cases of heterosexual marriage and cohabitation, artificial insemination would almost never compromise the presumption of parenthood residing with both spouses.[6] Lesbian couples were some distance away from such presumption, and gay male couples even further.

The foster system provided an outlet for lesbians and gay men wanting children, although agency willingness to agree to such placements is not much documented and difficult to track. As in other countries, officials have long faced challenges in placing all the children and adolescents who need homes, and this difficulty has increased over time. It was probably only from the mid-1980s on that officials would knowingly place children with couples presenting themselves as lesbian or gay, and such placements were handled quietly. One activist's account in British Columbia talks about the early steps being taken at a time in the late 1980s when the provincial premier was extremely conservative (see box).

### Lesbian/Gay Fostering and Adoption in British Columbia

'Even in [right-wing Premier] Vander Zalm's day, there was a network of public service social workers who were doing foster home recruitment in the gay and lesbian community, and doing adoptions. Everybody knew it and nobody owned it – it would have been stupid and reckless. These straight-laced older women – social workers some of them – needed homes and as the women's labour force participation began to increase, the pool of available foster homes decreased. But there was an untapped pool of potential foster care givers in the gay and lesbian community. [With the cooperation of gay and lesbian activists in social work networks] when they did recruit gay and lesbian homes, they did use a higher standard, because they wanted them to work. The children involved were often either very special needs or terminally ill – kids who were not going to be adopted by anyone else. There were people in the gay and lesbian community who were deeply offended, but they did it anyway, mostly because they wanted to establish a track record. And what that did was to build a record and an institutional memory within the public service that said, "this has been done, and we know that these placement have been successful." So when they raised the question about equal rights under the Adoption Act [of 1995], the answer was ... "we've already been doing this."'[7]

Adoption was another matter. Individuals could legally adopt across Canada, and undoubtedly there were many lesbians and gay men who acquired parental rights and obligations as individuals. From 1983 on, Canadian courts had been mandated to assess adoption applications not according to some mythical or ideal alternative but on the basis of the qualities of the actual applicants. Realistically speaking, though, there was not yet any legal room to obtain public recognition for a co-parent of the same sex, and even less for the joint adoption of a child who was not biologically related to either partner.

## The 1990–3 Transitional Period

The early 1990s was a transitional period on relationship issues, with important tribunal rulings extending recognition to lesbian and gay partners for selected benefits. Although such shifts were not much in evidence on parenting, there were some exceptions. Amendments to Ontario's family law in 1990 provided that a person other than a parent could apply for a custody or access order.[8] Parents were defined in gender-neutral terms and included those who had demonstrated a settled intention to treat a child as part of his or her family. This amendment would help partners in existing or now-ended same-sex relationships in making claims for recognition down the road.

In 1992 a BC court (in *N. v. N.*) upheld a custody claim of a mother who was in a lesbian relationship. The ruling depended in part on there being 'no evidence whatever that the lesbian relationship was in any way notorious in the community or in the school.'[9] Despite the condition, the ruling accepted the relationship. Beyond this decision, increasing numbers of positive but unreported cases passed without notice.

## 1993–9: Pioneering Steps in British Columbia and Ontario

The mid- and late-1990s were a period of legal and institutional take-off in the recognition of gay and lesbian relationships, even if anxiety about extending this pattern of rights and responsibilities into parenting continued.

### Pioneering British Columbia

In June 1995 British Columbia's social democratic government headed by Premier Mike Harcourt introduced a major bill on adoption, designed to modernize a statute that had not been substantially revised for decades. It proposed bringing private adoption agencies and international adoptions under public regulation, increasing the range of options for adoptees to obtain information about and contact with birth parents, and establishing special provisions for Aboriginal children. It also proposed a change to the existing statutory stipulation that only single people or legally married couples could adopt. Section 5 of Bill 51 included simply this: 'a child may be placed for adoption with one adult or two adults jointly.' There was not a single mention of gay, lesbian, or two people of the same sex, but this provision would clearly allow for same-sex couples, as well as common-law couples, to adopt. That is what the media focused on, and that is what then dominated the debate time in the legislature.

Legislators from the right-wing Reform Party quickly voiced their opposition.[10] Just two weeks before, the party's convention had passed a resolution proclaiming the traditional family as the basic unit of society, and defining it as a legal union of two people of the opposite sex. By this time, members of the Legislative Assembly were receiving a number of large petitions, the overwhelming majority opposing same-sex adoptions. The majority of Liberal MLAs, however, were in favour of the change, and it was the largest of the opposition parties. So in the final legislative vote, only nine members (of sixty-eight) voted against the bill. Final passage was secured on 4 July. The right-wing opposition mobilized during debate on the legislation was widely viewed as extremist, and it had little long-term impact.

The new regime retained some disparities between the adoption rights of same-sex couples and those of married couples.[11] Nevertheless, it represented the first substantial legislative breakthrough on same-sex adoption in the world. In 1997 the province extended the language of a variety of family law statutes to same-sex couples, including laws dealing with child maintenance in the event of a breakdown of the relationship. These changes gave gay and lesbian couples the same rights and obligations as cohabiting opposite-sex couples and retained only a few important distinctions between cohabiting and married couples. This time, even some quite right-wing politicians in the provincial Liberal and Reform Parties supported the changes, in part on the basis of neo-liberal rationales. One cited a hypothetical instance of a professional woman leaving a less-advantaged partner and her children with no provision for support: 'And that person decides to leave the relationship, and away she goes on her merry way, footloose and fancy free, and has left this mother and her children out there presumably without means. There are things like division of assets that couldn't happen properly, or the division of pensions. For these reasons, I thought it would be best if they could be called "spouse."[12]

During the same years, lesbian access to health services specializing in assisted reproduction was slowly increasing in Vancouver, as it was in Toronto. One of the only Canadian legal challenges to exclusionary practices was mounted in the mid-1990s by a British Columbia lesbian couple who had been refused access to insemination treatment by the only doctor in the province who maintained a frozen sperm bank.[13] In response, a human rights tribunal held (1995) that they had been discriminated against, and in 1996 this ruling was confirmed by the BC Supreme Court (*Korn v. Potter*).

## Parenting Rights in Ontario

In no Canadian province or territory was anxiety about lesbian and gay parenting more public than Ontario. The New Democratic government led by Premier Bob Rae introduced legislation intended to comprehensively recognize same-sex relationships in 1994. The whole bill was controversial, but no part of it more so than the provisions related to adoption.[14] The bill was defeated amid nationwide publicity, and it seemed as if even otherwise-supportive politicians would avoid the parenting issue for some time. However, in that same year, the Children's Aid Society of Toronto declared that they welcomed lesbian, gay, and bisexual foster parents. No doubt fostering placements with same-sex couples had already been made quietly, but this was a strikingly public policy statement.

And one year later, in the same year as BC's new adoption law was passed, an Ontario court ruling (*Re K. and B.*) recognized the parental status of the non-biological partners in four lesbian relationships and cited the restrictive language of the relevant provincial legislation as unconstitutional. The status of joint adoptions remained unclear, and the new premier, Mike Harris, a Conservative, made clear his discomfort with adoption by same-sex couples. The government was therefore disinclined to move beyond the narrow confines of the judgment. But at that time, some legal experts believed that the court ruling meant that joint adoption, and not just second-parent adoption, would be available to same-sex partners. By 1999 that view was widely accepted, and one year later a gay male couple became the first to take advantage of this interpretation.[15]

## Alberta Surprises

In early 1997 Stockwell Day, the Alberta government's most prominent social conservative, a one-time Pentecostal pastor, and then social services minister, issued an order denying the right of a lesbian ('Ms T.') with a eighteen-year-long history of fostering over seventy children to have custody over any more. A provincial election in March of that year returned the Conservative government of Premier Ralph Klein to power, and in the ensuing cabinet shuffle Lyle Oberg replaced Day. He lost little time before expressing support for his predecessor's policy of barring gays and lesbians from adopting children or becoming foster parents.[16] In July, supporters of 'Ms T.' threatened court action to reverse the Social Services Department decision, and in the face of Oberg's intransigence, the legal challenge was launched.

The challenge was given a boost in the early spring of 1998, when the Supreme Court of Canada delivered its *Vriend* judgment, reading sexual orientation into Alberta's human rights law. This decision provoked a tidal wave of opposition in the province, and when the provincial government finally acquiesced, many of its legislators were determined to narrow the policy spin-offs from the ruling. In March 1999, however, a cabinet committee designated to fence in the *Vriend* judgment seemed to create an opening in the opposite direction. It declared that there was no province-wide policy on the placement of children in same-sex parented homes, an intriguing observation in light of the incumbent social services minister's continuing policy of excluding such homes, and one probably recognizing that the government was doomed to lose the Ms T. court case.

Oberg now claimed that foster care placements were being made on the basis of the best interest of the child. And though he also insisted on personally reviewing every file of same-sex foster parent placement in the province, Ms T. was soon granted permission to foster parent.[17] A few weeks later, Oberg announced that there might be legislation in the spring allowing step-parent adoptions for lesbian and gay couples.[18]

Meanwhile, another court challenge had been launched in the wake of the 1998 *Vriend* ruling, by a lesbian couple seeking second-parent adoption. They won their case in 1999, and in the meantime two other lesbian couples in Calgary began litigation on the same point. The government was fighting these challenges, but in the spring of 1999 it presented a multi-purpose Miscellaneous Statutes Amendment bill effectively conceding the case. A deeply buried provision simply substituted 'stepparent adoption' for 'spousal adoption,' without defining step-parent. The head of the province's largest adoption agency was soon quoted as ready to approve adoptions by homosexuals.[19] Later that year, a Calgary court confirmed their right to such adoption, though leaving unresolved the question of joint adoption (Re 'A' and 'K').

By this time, even some very right-wing members of the governing party recognized that the absence of step-parent adoption rights could leave children stranded in the event of their biological parents' death or the separation of the couple parenting them. As one opposition legislator put it, 'This is about a same-sex relationship, and if the biological parent dies, the child would end up in foster care because the other partner had no legal relationship with that child. This is about protecting that child – they'd be hauled out of their home, stuck in a foster home – how is that good for the child? When you develop those arguments, people start going, "oh well yeah, that's not such a good idea."'[20]

*Developments Elsewhere*

Across Canada, some court judgments were still heavily skewed by fears about exposing children to homosexuality, but on custody battles, for example, courts produced fewer blatantly discriminatory rulings.[21] There was undoubtedly a spread of unreported cases of second-parent adoption, following the lead of the influential Ontario court.

Quebec remained something of an anomaly. A 1991 amendment of article 546 of the province's Civil Code allowed that any adult person could, alone or jointly with another person, adopt a child. However, the intent of that change was not to recognize same-sex relationships rights, and it was not clear that it would do so. In 1997 the legislature had amended forty provincial statutes that recognized de facto heterosexual couples without extending these amendments to same-sex couples. When the Parti Québécois government introduced legislation recognizing same-sex relationships in 1999, it failed to address any parenting issues.

In that same year, Mona Greenbaum and Nicole Paquette launched a court action to ensure that both of them were formally recognized as parents – the first such action in Quebec. After a false start, they sought a second-parent adoption, but since a precedent might be established, the judge wanted the provincial attorney general involved. The government wanted to stay entirely out of the case, hoping that a favourable court ruling would eliminate the need for legislation – an avoidance pattern not much different from that which prevailed in most other provinces. The long delays meant that the court challenge was eventually overtaken by the new civil union regime put into place early in the new decade.[22]

During this period, access to assisted reproduction services was also more restrictive in Montreal than in either Toronto or Vancouver. Lesbians were effectively denied access to both private and public fertility clinics, usually on the grounds that they were not infertile women. According to Sarah Rose Werner, those who wanted access to assisted reproductive services would travel to Ontario, British Columbia, or the United States.[23]

## 1999 and After: Parenting Take-Off

The 1999 Supreme Court of Canada ruling in *M. v. H.* didn't specifically address parenting, but there was little doubt about its broad significance for the recognition of lesbian and gay family rights. Such a belief was strengthened by the court's decision in a parenting case that same year, confirming that de facto parents (in this case heterosexual) could not easily shed their obligations to children (*Chartier v. Chartier*).[24] This finding would eventually reduce some of the differences between provinces in the extent to which de facto parental bonds were recognized, though it would have less of that effect in Quebec.

In the wake of *M v. H.*, one province or territory after another secured legislative approval of multi-pronged bills recognizing same-sex relationships (see table 6.4). Some of these measures immediately included adoption; those that didn't were amended within a few years to include such rights. Ontario excluded adoption from its 1999 relationship legislation, but by then it was clear that a 1995 court ruling was being read as covering both joint and co-parental adoption. Nova Scotia excluded adoption from its 2000 legislation, but one year later the province's high court ruled definitively that the exclusion of a lesbian couple and all cohabiting couples from statutes reg-

Table 6.4   Canadian Provincial Recognition of Adoption Rights of Same-Sex Couples, 1995–2004

| 1995 | ON | step-parent (and joint)[a] | court |
|------|-----|----------------------------|-------|
| 1995 | BC | step-parent and joint[b] | legislation |
| 1998 | SK | joint adoption[c] | legislation |
| 1999 | AB | step-parent | court & legislation |
| 2001 | NS | step-parent and joint | court & legislation |
| 2002 | SK | step-parent | legislation |
| 2002 | NL | step-parent and joint | legislation |
| 2002 | MB | step-parent and joint | legislation |
| 2002 | QC | full rights[d] | legislation |
| 2002 | NT | step-parent and joint | legislation |
| 2004 | NB | step-parent | human rights tribunal |

[a] Later (1999) read as including joint adoption.
[b] The BC adoption law was passed in 1995 but came into effect in 1996.
[c] Partial change in 1998, redefinition of spouse in 2001.
[d] The civil union legislation of 2002 allowed women who had engaged in a 'parental plan' (projet parental) to both be registered on the child's birth certificate.
Note: the wording of Yukon adoption law was open to interpretation in ways that might well include same-sex couples.
Source: Various, including Egale, *Outlaws and Inlaws* (Ottawa: Equality for Gays and Lesbians Everywhere, 2004).

ulating joint adoption was unconstitutional (*Re S.C.M. et al.*). These steps provoked little controversy.

*Quebec's Distinctiveness*

Quebec was an intriguing example of continuing political anxiety about the issue of same-sex parenting, but also of rapid change. In late 2001 the Parti Québécois government announced the creation of a civil union regime, claiming that it would recognize registered gay and lesbian partnerships as fully equal to married heterosexual couples. This regime included changes to Quebec's Civil Code, which had been excluded from the province's 1999 legislation granting extensive rights to same-sex couples. The bill unveiled at the time, however, completely excluded parenting rights, though government representatives (and some activists) argued that the measure would create a level of equality for gay couples unprecedented in Canada. At the time, the rationale was that inclusion of parental issues in the legislation would probably not be supported by the public. Yet this excuse was offered at a time when court rulings were making clear that parental discrimination would be unconstitutional in Canada. Also at this time, the federal Department of Justice was providing background documentation for new marriage legislation suggesting that same-sex parents were no less suitable than heterosexual parents.

Quebec activists, particularly Mona Greenbaum, Nicole Paquette, and other women associated with the Association des mères lesbiennes (AML; Lesbian Mothers Association), mobilized quickly and effectively in response to the bill. The group had been formed only a few years earlier (1998), at a time when parenting issues were not firmly on the activist agenda. The winter of 2002 was very different. The mothers' group was now large, energetic, well organized, and was able to marshal powerful briefs to the legislative committee examining the government bill.[25] They were joined in this struggle by Coalition Québécoise pour la reconnaissance des conjoints et conjointes de même sexe (Quebec Coalition for the Recognition of Same-Sex Couples), which mobilized strong presentations from Quebec unions and the largest of the province's women's groups. By late winter 2002, they convinced provincial justice minister Paul Bégin that adoption rights had to be included in the bill. In the end, the amendments provoked little controversy, though Catholic bishops and conservative Protestant groups did speak out against them. The bill was then passed in the National Assembly without a dissenting vote. This was a remarkable activist achievement, and a telling commentary on both the levels of political fear about parenting and the rapidity of change.

The new civil union regime extended full parental rights to same-sex couples who had undertaken to have a child together either through adoption or assisted reproduction, and rights were extended retroactively to parents who had already done so. Both parents would be registered on the child's birth certificate, without any distinction between the two and without the need for the kind of adoption procedures still required across most of Canada. Such provisions took a step beyond what existed in other Canadian jurisdictions.[26]

The Quebec regime was facilitated by already existing law that precluded parental claims from anonymous sperm donors. The new legislation reinforced the point by stipulating that the 'contribution of genetic material for the purposes of a third-party parental project' does not in itself create parental rights and obligations. Another provision made clear that if a child were born of a parental project involving assisted procreation between married or civil union spouses, the spouse of the woman who gave birth to the child is presumed to be the child's other parent.[27]

What was not covered in Quebec's new regime were the parental rights of the non-biological parent in the case of children with a known father from an earlier heterosexual relationship. In some ways, the complete absence of parenting rights in such cases reflected Quebec's continued differentiation of marriage and de facto heterosexual relationships in determining formal parenthood.[28] In most other parts of Canada, courts would be open in principle to arguments that the de facto relationship of the non-biological parent in the current relationship warranted formal recognition, though there would be no guarantee of their accepting such a claim in the face of a biological father claiming parental rights.

On the ground, clinics offering reproductive assistance had been slow to accept lesbian clients. As recently as 2001, an AML brief responding to federal legislation on assisted reproduction indicated that lesbians had no access to fertility clinics in the province, either public or private, since such clinics in Quebec were effectively restricted to married (and therefore heterosexual) couples.[29] This forced most lesbians seeking assistance to use sperm banks in Ontario, BC, or the United States. At the time that the new civil union law was passed, Procrea, the largest clinic in Quebec, opened up access to lesbian couples. The newly established Montreal Fertility Clinic acted similarly at about the same time.[30]

Change was less obvious in the province's adoption and fostering agencies, especially on the francophone side. In 2004 Mona Greenbaum, still AML coordinator, argued that systematic homophobia still pervaded the Direction de la protection de la jeunesse (the province's child protection agency).[31] On the English-language side of the system, gays and lesbians were welcomed by child protection agencies; Batshaw Youth and Family Services of Montreal had been promoting its services to gays and lesbians since 1998. But the francophone side still widely refused to place children with gays or lesbians. The manager of adoption requests at the Centre jeunesse de Montréal rejected the accusation of homophobia, claiming that two children had been placed with same-sex couples. She then stated, without embarrassment, that the centre looked for the best possible milieux, and that society still considered the traditional family of father and mother the best for children. Further, she argued that children in the care of the centre, who had often experienced marginalization, generally should not be placed in situations that are also marginal.[32]

Across the province, access to social agencies, as elsewhere in Canada, could be made dramatically more inclusive by local staff. Nevertheless, it is striking that a secular adoption agency in the province's largest city would assume that explicit discrimination was acceptable, in the same year that Toronto's largest such agency (the Children's Aid Society) was distributing thousands of flyers at June's Pride march, having openly welcomed gays and lesbians as foster parents for ten years. There were signs of change in 2005 and 2006, with provincially sponsored training made available to adoption agency staff. The Centre jeunesse was also meeting with the AML, a clear signal of readiness to change.

International adoptions were, as elsewhere, becoming increasingly difficult in the face of resistance from those countries from which most infants were adopted. An extra barrier in Quebec was an almost inexplicable decision by the provincial para-state agency through which such adoptions were secured. Among the agencies in various countries with which the Secretariat à l'adoption internationale (International Adoption Secretariat) had links, there was only one in the United States – a Tennessee agency that would not accept applications from any other than heterosexual couples married for at least ten years!

*Assisted Reproduction and Birth Registration in Other Provinces*

In 2002 Quebec moved most assertively in the direction of acknowledging two parents as full and equal co-parents of children conceived of in a joint parental project. The clearest symbol of such change was the inclusion of both parents' names on the child's birth certificate. Elsewhere in Canada, change on this front in particular has been incremental. In the late 1990s two lesbian couples in BC had challenged the refusal of the Vital Statistics Branch to register the names of two mothers on their children's birth certificates. A 2001 Human Rights Tribunal ruled in favour of the lesbian couples, agreeing that they had been discriminated against on the basis of sex, sexual orientation, and family status. A 2003 BC Supreme Court concluded that the specific remedy applied by the tribunal was beyond its jurisdiction, but agreed that the couple had encountered unacceptable discrimination (*Minister of Health Planning et al. v. B.C. Human Rights Tribunal et al.*).

In 2003 Manitoba changed its birth registry system to accommodate same-sex couples. In 2006 an Ontario judge ruled in favour of lesbian couples seeking to register both names on the birth certificate of an infant conceived through artificial insemination (*M.D.R. v. Ontario [Deputy Registrar General]*). Until that ruling, same-sex parents had generally had to secure a 'declaration of parentage' or a second-parent adoption through a court. By the time the MDR ruling took effect in January 2007, both women in a lesbian couple could be registered on their child's birth certificate in cases of anonymous sperm donation.[33] A 2005 Alberta ruling (*Fraess v. Alberta*) did not focus on birth registration, but it did extend to a lesbian couple a provision of the Family Law Act securing the parental status of the male spouse of a woman using assisted reproduction. In 2007, the Nova Scotia government changed rules to allow two lesbians to register themselves as parents of their newborn after they filed a human rights complaint.

There is no question that Canadian law still presumes parenthood much more easily in heterosexual relationships than in lesbian and gay ones. As Angela Campbell points out, lesbian parents have to go to extra steps that straight couples do not, and the law has been particularly reluctant to recognize two men as 'natural' parents.[34] A male couple wanting children is likely to consider a surrogacy arrangement, but such arrangements are not recognized in Quebec and Alberta and so would have no bearing in the case of a change of heart by the woman involved. In other provinces, it cannot be presumed that courts would always side with the gay couple if parenthood were challenged by the surrogate mother. Whether marriage would tilt the balance in favour of the gay couple remains to be tested in court. In any event, the prohibition on payment for surrogacy within Canada places an additional impediment in front of men across the country.

*Access and Cost*

In the meantime, federal policy change was destined to make assisted reproduction less available. In response to growing concern about the commercialization of reproduction, and in particular about the potential for exploitation in surrogate motherhood, the federal government introduced legislation (passed in 2004) that, among other things, prohibited payment for surrogacy and for sperm and egg donation. Such measures could well drastically reduce the availability of anonymous sperm and have an even greater impact on the number of potential surrogate mothers.[35] The bill did prohibit discrimination based on sexual orientation or matrimonial status in the provision of reproductive assistance, but the effective availability of assistance was severely compromised. In a 'transition' period, fertility clinics were allowed to import sperm from the United States. Canadians could also travel to unregulated clinics in the United States, but at considerable financial cost and inconvenience.

The issue of cost was present even for assisted reproduction secured entirely within Canada. Few provincial or territorial jurisdictions fully covered the health care costs involved, and some covered none. At one clinic in Toronto, the minimum cost of anonymous donor insemination was about $700/month, so four attempts would cost close to $3000.[36] (This would not be reduced by the modest donor fees once paid but now illegal.) The class issues entailed here are particularly pronounced for men because of the high costs associated with surrogacy.

## Multiple Parents?

The openness to considering de facto parental status alongside biological parenthood in most of Canada raises the question of whether more than two people could be given public recognition of their relationship to a child (as was done first in the United States). In early 2007 an Ontario appeal court ruled that two women who had decided to have a child in 1999, and the male friend who contributed sperm to the effort, would all have parental rights, this judgment reflecting the will of all three (*AA and BB and CC*). This overturned a 2003 lower court ruling from a judge who believed that existing legislation prevented him from recognizing the parental role of the non-biological mother, in light of the fact that both the biological mother and the biological father were being treated as parents. The court did not rule on the constitutionality of the existing law, instead using the court's powers to act as a guardian for children and to grant requests outside the existing statutory framework.[37] This outcome may have widespread application, since in Canada most lesbian couples use known donors, usually gay male friends or acquaintances (in contrast to American couples, most of whom use anonymous donors), and in most cases the donor retains some relationship with the child.[38]

Such cases have elicited mixed reactions from those favouring the recognition of same-sex parental rights. On one side are those who want the law to fit the complex realities of the family relationships formed by lesbians and gays. On the other are those, like Nancy Polikoff, who worry that moving beyond the two-parent model opens the door to the retention of biological pre-eminence, or to assumptions about children's need to have a mother and father figure in a full parental role.[39] In the Ontario case, formal opposition was registered only by groups informed by religious conservatism, for example, the Evangelical Fellowship of Canada, the Catholic Civil Rights League, Focus on the Family, and REAL Women of Canada. The province's attorney general had declined to intervene at the appeal court level in defence of the existing statute. There is no doubt, though, that some element of ambivalence pervades the networks of those seeking recognition for same-sex parents.

## Assessing and Explaining Change

Between 1995 and 2005, but particularly from the turn of the century on, formal policy recognition of lesbian and gay parenting took off. The acceleration of change began somewhat later than it did for relationship recognition, and some issues are still unresolved. The parental side of family regimes in Canada still privileges biological linkage and in some respects makes assumptions about parentage for opposite-sex couples that are not made for same-sex couples. There is also more room for discretion in parental issues than there is in most issues related to adult conjugal relationships, discretion that can easily allow for prejudicial decisions based on what family form is thought best for children.

### Limits to Change

The administrative and court-based systems that form part of the Canadian parenting regime – part private, part public – are invariably only partially affected by change in law. The everyday practices of adoption agencies, foster placement officials, family courts, and fertility clinics can still be shot through with heterosexual assumptions, and sometimes worse. When lesbians and gay men do have children, they are still likely to encounter prejudice and misunderstanding in schools, in health-care institutions, and in myriad social settings. Institutional inattention to diverse family forms is still ubiquitous, and of course public prejudice can survive legal and regulatory change.

As we have seen, even in those Canadian jurisdictions in which the most dramatic gains have been made, formal inequalities remain. The changes to adoption and family law approved by the BC government in 1995–7 were path-breaking, but legal disparities in presumptions of parenthood remain. Legal discourse moves only with great reluctance in the direction of treating two women as 'natural' parents, and even more so with two men.

Across the country, lesbian and gay partners who are without any biological children and are seeking joint adoption face extra barriers outside Canada. Most 'stranger' adoptions are arranged overseas, and most countries that have been major sources of placement have formal prohibitions on gay and lesbian couples. Chinese authorities now require that applicants formally declare that they are not lesbian or gay. This demand at the very least requires camouflage.

Within Canada, those seeking to secure custody of children, to adopt them, or to foster parent will still encounter officials and judges who privilege some applicants over others on the basis of traditional relationship hierarchies. Stranger adoption typically requires a preliminary assessment of parental suitability, a home study, and the approval of the biological mother, before a trial period and legal finalization. There is much room for discretion here, and prejudice. One study from the 1990s showed that 84 per cent of adoption workers would reject an application from a woman in a stable lesbian relationship, and it is unlikely that such prejudice has been wiped out in one decade.[40] Officials placing children for fostering or adoption are still likely to place a disproportionate number of children and adolescents with special needs or difficulties in homes that do not reflect the most widely acknowledged family ideals.

Prejudice is especially widespread in confronting claims by those whose sexuality does not fit easily into clearly delineated categories. It is one thing to extend rights to a stable, monogamous gay or lesbian couple. It is quite another to do the same to those whose sexual relationships are more open or fluid, to recognize rights for bisexuals, and especially the rights of the transgendered. There have been very few publicized cases involving transgendered claimants. In one 1995 Alberta case (*Ghidoni v. Ghidoni*), joint custody was granted but not without the judge expressing concern about the gender 'disorder' of one claimant.

The opportunities for parenting also vary by class and race. The costs associated with having children are usually higher for same-sex couples than heterosexuals, since they more frequently entail reproductive assistance, and often require formal co-adoption procedures. Equitable access to adoption and fostering systems is also influenced by class-based assumptions about what homes are more worthy than others. Sexual diversity activism in Canada, too, has a predominantly white face, and that is at least as true for parenting activism as on other issue fronts. Lower-class and racial-minority aspirants to parenthood are more likely than comfortably well-off whites to live in communities that associate homosexuality with whiteness and middle-class status, making it harder for parenting lesbian and gay couples to claim and achieve visibility.

There are gender issues in parenting. Lesbians seeking assisted reproduction have more options available to them than gay men, and at less cost. To some extent, female couples also gain some leverage through the persistence of assumptions about the nurturing instincts of women, even if they are partially undercut by stereotypes that portray lesbians as masculinized and therefore not real women.[41]

Gay male parents or would-be parents on average have higher incomes than lesbian couples, so are more able to manage the everyday costs associated with parenting. But they are also more likely to encounter public views that this is unnatural on two counts, the homosexuality of the parents and the absence of a mother. Gay men are also more tainted than lesbians by the prejudicial construction of homosexuals as posing a predatory threat to children.

However important the shifts in the policies and practices of individuals and institutions with discretion over parenting decisions, there is still widespread insensitivity to the existence and the needs of children and adolescents whose sexuality is other than heterosexual. Activist claims and policy response emphasize that children of lesbian and gay parents are just as likely to be heterosexual as other children, and cite evidence about the 'normalcy' of childhood development. This leaves little room for public discussion of lesbian, gay, bisexual, or transgendered children and youth, and little opportunity to express a positive response to that eventuality.[42]

## The Persistence of Public Doubt

Public acceptance of the idea that lesbians and gays might be parents has increased dramatically in recent years (see chapter 2). A 1988 Gallup poll found that only 25 per cent agreed that homosexuals should be allowed to adopt children; subsequent years showed a steady rise in that number, to 31 per cent in 1992 and 38 per cent in 2000. Angus Reid polling showed 48 per cent support in 2002; a Strategic Counsel poll showed the same in 2005. This marks considerable progress, but it also means that support for parenting is lower than for marriage.[43]

Other survey evidence is more worrying. A late 1990s survey undertaken by Charlene Miall and Karen March asked how acceptable various kinds of potential adoptive parents were to Canadian respondents.[44] Ninety-two per cent responded 'very acceptable' to married heterosexual couples; 40 per cent to common-law heterosexual couples; 25 per cent to single women; 20 per cent to lesbian couples; and 19 per cent to gay male couples. 'Somewhat acceptable' responses increased the overall willingness to acquiesce in same-sex couple adoption, but only to 48 per cent for lesbians and 46 per cent for gay men. As the authors point out, this was virtually indistinguishable from polling results in the United States.

Reginald Bibby conducted a survey in 2003 (for the Vanier Institute of the Family) on Canadian attitudes towards family issues, and included questions related to sexual diversity.[45] On the encouraging side, 61 per cent of his respondents agreed that same-sex couples can do a good job of raising children, but only 48 per cent agreed that they should be able to legally adopt them. When asked about what constituted a 'family,' only 46 per cent answered 'yes' when asked specifically about 'two people of the same sex with at least one child.' When asked about how they would feel if they were informed that their children were gay or lesbian, only 35 per cent said they would both approve and accept it (42 per cent saying they would disapprove but accept, 23 per cent saying they would disapprove and not accept).

In other words, the near-comprehensive change in formal state policy on parenting issues that has taken effect over the last decade has not been followed by the kind of substantial shift in public beliefs that seems evident on marriage. This comes in part from stark homophobia, but more often from unease about what might be thought to be insufficient gender modelling. This translates into a fear that children will grow up confused about gender, and possibly lesbian or gay. In any event, having same-sex parents would expose children to ridicule among their peers. The fears about gender confusion are bound to be intensified by claims for parenting rights made by those whose relationships challenge gender binaries more radically, for example bisexuals and transgendered people.

Another reason for the persistence of public doubts is that advocacy on parental issues has been relatively low key. Outside of Quebec, activist groups have generally not given parenting issues the same priority as other family-related issues, like workplace benefits, decision-making power, and marriage. Egale has been committed to full equality on parenting to be sure, but with other issues more urgently pressing at the federal level. The Coalition for Lesbian and Gay Rights in Ontario had defended parental rights for years, but was an even smaller group. The Toronto-based LGBTQ Parenting Network helps fill gaps in providing information and a network useful for activism. Provincial groups focused on parenting have been scarce and poorly resourced, again with Quebec an important exception. The critical mass of activists and resources needed to ensure that favourable court rulings in one part of the country translated into action either there or elsewhere has been difficult to marshall in Canada. The regional isolation of Canadian activist networks, too, means that it has been difficult for those in one centre to learn from work done elsewhere.

*Explaining Change*

The factors that explain the take-off in Canadian public recognition of gay and lesbian relationships have also been at play in parenting. Indeed, it would be difficult to hive off parenting issues from overall shifts in family regime. The Charter has obviously been a factor, and so has earlier policy recognition of relationship rights for cohabiting heterosexual partners and for the official recognition of non-biological partners acting as de facto parents. In most of Canada, such shifts in parental regulation were already under way when lesbian and gay parenting claims were being launched.

The increase in numbers of gay and especially of lesbian parents, and of children being raised by same-sex couples, drastically intensified the pressure for change. Courts, social agencies, and policy makers were confronting real families asking for public recognition of what existed in practice. In cases of relationship breakdown, demands were being presented by partners who had established solid relationships with children, and in some cases were prepared to accept the obligations that went along with rights. This is true in American cases, of course, but in Canada this 'presence' helped parenting issues remain on the coat tails of the shifts towards recognizing same-sex relationships.

There were also, of course, child-centred reasons for supporting parental claims. Judicial focus on the best interests of children had formally occurred long before, though it would take some time before policy makers and judges would see the logical extension into the realm of lesbian/gay parental arrangements. In courts and legislatures, such a shift could be strengthened by neo-liberal arguments that the death of a partner or separation of partners ought not to lead to the legal or financial abandonment of the child, and a consequent drain on the public purse. Such arguments are made in the United States too, but they are much more counteracted by the religious right, inside a political setting in which many judges are not as insulated from public pressures as in Canada.

There was, to be sure, a religious right prepared to oppose the public recognition of lesbian and gay parenting, and to some extent able to play on public anxieties of half of the population or more. But many in the public, and many of those in positions of decision-making responsibility in parenting cases, knew all too well that the parenting ideal so often did not reflect the reality. The capacity of the religious right to mobilize, too, was weakened by the incrementalism of most political and legal shifts (apart from Quebec), and the absence of public decision points around which objections could be mobilized.

By the time that parenting rights were most at play, substantive adult relationship rights were basically settled, and the central mobilizing issue was marriage. The religious right did indeed evoke the spectre of gays and lesbians raising children when it mobilized against same-sex marriage, but by then it was almost too late.

## Conclusion

There is no doubt that family policy regimes have shifted comprehensively in Canada in favour of recognizing lesbians and gays as parents. This has happened partly as a result of overall change in adult relationship regimes, and even more from the long-standing pressure of actual parents insisting on recognition.

How much change has been effected beyond formal policy is hard to assess. Parenting regimes are constituted by a complex web of laws, institutional policies, and individual decision makers that has long upheld traditional distinctions between worthy and unworthy families. The tenacity of such frameworks is both evident in and reinforced by public unease about the link between homosexuality, childhood, and adolescence.

The gains that have been secured by activists have been framed in cautious terms. As in other countries, most challenges have been advanced by lesbians and gay men with children, and the high stakes militate against raising fundamental questions about existing regimes. Although the religious right is not nearly as formidable in Canada as it is in the United States, and not nearly as likely to make a cause célèbre of individual parenting claims as in American cases, the popular unease with any association between homosexuality and childhood is widespread. Also, as in the United States, many of the claimants in Canada for rights are content with the features of the existing parental regime other than its heterosexist exclusions, or feel they can live within the parameters of the existing regime.

Still, such claims make for profound change simply by the visibility of the families involved, challenging stereotypes and fears about lesbians and gay men. Like other parents, they seek everyday recognition from medical professionals, teachers, social workers, tax officials, and adoption agencies. In doing so, they assert the validity of their relationships clearly and unapologetically. This broadens the boundaries and shifts the foundations of family regimes.

# 7 Parenting in the United States

One might think that the recognition of lesbians and gays as parents would lag behind other forms of relationship recognition, and that the gap between Canada and the United States would be significant. Public fears about what would happen to children in such cases persist, and religious conservatives have never flagged in their readiness to mobilize around the image of vulnerable youth. Anxiety about the strength of family life and shifting morality is high in the United States, and as both Sean Cahill and Valerie Lehr argue forcibly, opponents of gay and lesbian parenthood continue to make persistently politicized claims that every child needs a mother and a father.[1] For even more people in the United States than in Canada, same-sex families seem to be, as Renate Reimann puts it, 'unintelligible.'[2] Lesbian and gay couples will simply not be 'framed' in the public imagination as parents.

And yet we find a growing number of American couples, especially lesbians, deciding to have children, at first using informal networks to facilitate pregnancy, and later on taking advantage of clinics prepared to help in sufficient numbers that there was talk of a lesbian baby boom from the mid-1980s on. At the same time, a surprising number of jurisdictions recognized the rights of lesbians and gays to parent, and facilitated their doing so – this at a time when little on this front was happening in other countries. Change is not nearly as radical as it has been in Canada since the late 1990s, but as Yuval Merin points out, shifts in law and policy can be found more widely among American states than they can in Europe.[3] There is also no country in the world where we are able to find more research demonstrating that children raised by same-sex couples are as healthy as those raised by hetero-sexual couples, or as wide an array of professional associations ready to support this view.[4] The irony is particularly rich here, for all but a few U.S. states have statutory or constitutional language barring lesbian and gay marriage, justified by its ill effects on children.

A lot of American same-sex couples have children. Over a quarter of the 600,000 same-sex couples reported in the 2000 census were raising children at home (33 per cent of lesbian couples, 22 per cent of gay male). There were undoubtedly many more couples who did not declare themselves as such, so the total number with children was higher. And of course these numbers do not reflect the non-partnered lesbians, gays, bisexuals, and transgendered people who were parent-ing on their own. This is a lot of families.

A full survey of change in parenting regimes entails an analysis of a complex web of public policies, legal precedents, and institutional practices. These determine who is recognized automatically to be a parent, who can claim parental rights and obligations, who can adopt and foster and under what circumstances. As in Canada, courts are vital to the policy-making process, as much in this as in any policy area. When couples separate, courts are the forum through which res-olution of conflicts over parenting responsibilities is sought and enforced. In some jurisdictions, courts have to formally approve adop-tions and usually have enough manoeuvring room to approve adop-tion by same-sex couples even when it is not explicitly included in statute. Because so many politicians are content to let courts confront these difficult issues, state policy is usually set by a series of individ-ual court rulings. Sometimes they move in a coherent and consistent direction; often they do not.

Jurisdiction over parental issues is as decentralized in the United States as it is in Canada.[5] Although the U.S. Supreme Court has taken cases in which parenting issues have been at stake, it has never done so in a case involving same-sex couples, leaving great leeway for divergence among state courts. What we will see here is that a sur-prising number of victories have been won, some in places we would not expect. Even in the face of religious-right campaigning that con-stantly invokes the spectre of vulnerable children being abused or ill served by homosexual adults, the chances of lesbian and gay parents making gains have improved significantly over the course of the last decade.

Table 7.1    Selected U.S. Court Cases on Gay/Lesbian Custody, 1967–84

| 1967 | CA | *Ellen Doreene Nadler v. Walter Robert Nadler*<br>Appeal Court overruled earlier decision that the homosexuality of lesbian mother itself makes that parent unfit to have custody, saying trial court should have weighed best interest of child. |
|------|------|------|
| 1973 | OR | *A. v. A.*<br>Appeal court upheld decision retaining custody with father said by divorced mother to be homosexual, though retaining lower court conditions precluding any other man living in. |
| 1979 | OR | *In the Matter of the Marriage of Ashling and Ashling*<br>Appeal Court affirmed shift of previously joint custody to father, but removed condition on visitation with lesbian mother that prohibited presence of other lesbian(s), so long as mother is discreet. |
| 1983 | WA | *In the Matter of the Marriage of Cabalquinto and Cabalquinto*<br>Supreme Court returned a case to trial, requiring that a father's right to visit his child be determined by the child's best interests and not the father's homosexuality. By 1986, the father won his case, without restrictions on visitation. |
| 1984 | U.S. | *Palmore v. Sidoti*<br>U.S. Supreme Court ruled that state judges should not award custody on basis of society's prejudice (in this case race). |

## Mid-1960s to Mid-1980s: Early Custody Claims, Baby Planning, and Backlash

As in Canada, custody was the first parenting issue to arise from sexual diversity, and the first to be the subject of activist organizing. From a very early stage, American lesbians were prepared to go to court to retain custody of children born into earlier heterosexual relationships, contesting discriminatory claims about their unfitness as mothers.

Early claims were unsuccessful, with notable exceptions (see table 7.1). In 1967, a few years before the first Canadian case, a California appeal court overruled a trial court decision that the homosexuality of a lesbian mother itself made her unfit for custody, insisting that the best interests of the child ought to have been the primary consideration. A 1972 lower court ruling in Washington State allowed a lesbian couple to retain custody of the children that each of them had given birth to in previous heterosexual marriages, as long as the partners did not live together. That condition – a variant of commonplace restrictions to 'protect' children from exposure to homosexuality – was removed two years later. In 1979, an Oregon appeal court removed a similar condition imposed on a joint custody ruling. There is no reported case in Canada up to this time representing a clear-cut custody win for a lesbian claimant, without discriminatory conditions.

By the 1980s, courts across the United States had in theory adopted the standard of 'the best interests of the child' in adjudicating disputes over access and custody. In a 1984 case that centred on race (*Palmore v. Sidoti*), the U.S. Supreme Court added that state judges should not award custody on the basis of society's prejudice. A Washington State case that had begun early in the decade seemed to reflect a shifting tide (see box).

> *In the Matter of the Marriage of Cabalquinto and Cabalquinto*, 1980–6
> The King County Superior Court in Washington denied Ernest Cabalquinto's request for an adjustment of visiting rights with his child, siding with the mother's argument that the father's homosexuality precluded a favourable ruling. The judge claimed that the ruling derived from an assessment of the best interests of the child, but he laced it with prejudicial comments. He acknowledged that the father had made an altogether favourable impression, but argued that a child 'should be led in the way of heterosexual preference, not be tolerant of this thing [homosexuality].' The verdict was appealed, and in 1983 the state's Supreme Court concluded that the lower court did make its determination on the basis of the claimant's homosexuality itself, without any evidence of harm to the child's best interests. It therefore sent the case back for further consideration, making clear that harm had to be shown. One year later, the Superior Court authorized a change in visitation rules, but attached the condition that the father's partner not be present in the house except as a casual friend. In 1986, the Court of Appeal concluded that there was no evidence that the child would be harmed by knowing of the father's relationship, and eliminated the restriction.

## Other Parenting Developments

For those same-sex couples planning children of their own, and with the money to pay, the largely privatized health-care system allowed for comparative early access to clinical assistance in cities with visible lesbian/gay populations. Commercial sperm banks began emerging in the 1970s, largely unregulated, and in 1982, the Sperm Bank of California (opened by feminists in Oakland) became the first to welcome lesbians (and single straight women).[6] The spread of AIDS, and the public fears that became so widespread later in the decade, increased interest in and availability of frozen sperm, expanding the geographic reach of large clinics.

Fostering regimes were slowly opening up to lesbians, gays, and bisexuals in this early period, away from public scrutiny. As in Canada, fostering was presenting public officials and lawmakers with circumstances that in some ways are diametrically opposed to those in adoption. Declining birth rates meant that there were fewer American-born children up for adoption. There was a growing proportion of them who were children or infants of colour, but until the mid-1990s a number of states banned cross-race adoption.[7] The increased number of women in the paid labour force, on the other hand, reduced the number of foster homes to meet a steady need for parents. The difficulty of placing particularly challenging children, and the availability of same-sex couples and of LGBT individuals prepared to accept them, created low-visibility flexibility in the system, eased by the fact that placements do not need the approval of a court.

The first known placements of children or adolescents in gay or lesbian foster homes were of teenagers evicted from their 'natural' families because of being lesbian or gay themselves. In the mid-1970s, the newly founded National Gay Task Force worked in conjunction with child welfare agencies in New York City to place such adolescents with gay couples. Apart from these sorts of cases, most early placements were of troubled or handicapped children and adolescents.

Public fears about parenting by same-sex couples was at least as acute in the United States as in Canada, and fuelled more aggressively by religious conservatives. Anita Bryant's 1970s crusade against equity policies used the slogan 'Save Our Children,' and while it had made an expedition to Canada, it had a much higher profile in the United States. In 1977, Florida expressly prohibited homosexuals (as individuals or in couples) from adopting children, the first state to do so. In 1985, Massachusetts (under Democratic governor Michael Dukakis) banned gay fostering, after a political firestorm erupted over a gay couple serving as foster parents.

## 1985–93: Slow Gains, and Broadening Claims

The second half of the 1980s and the early 1990s saw a number of important victories in custody cases, and the first successful adoption claims. Not surprisingly, results were still mixed, even with courts being told to make judgments based on the interests of children, and not on the basis of societal prejudice.

It was during this period that there was talk of a lesbian baby boom, and one result was a building wave of claims made by non-biological parents within the framework of a same-sex relationship – either a prospering one in which dual parenting roles were being secured, or a collapsing one in which parenting roles were being defended. These claims were obviously even more challenging to courts than those made by biological parents, but there were a few successes.

### Custody

The mid- and late-1980s saw a few important rulings on the West Coast that overturned denials of custody or the imposition of discriminatory restrictions. Courts in Alaska (1985) and California (1988) agreed that any argument seeking the denial of custody based on sexual orientation, or the imposition of conditions, had to be fortified by evidence of harm, and that social stigma was inadmissible.[8] But prejudice did not fall away, and in some respects the U.S. Supreme Court reinforced it. By upholding Georgia's sodomy statute in *Bowers v. Hardwick*, the court effectively allowed a significant number of states to continue treating homosexual activity – and gays/lesbians themselves – as criminal.[9] As table 7.2 shows, appeal court rulings in 1991 (in California and New York) treated non-biological parents seeking access to children as legal 'strangers.'

### Adoption

During this period adoption was becoming the highest-profile parenting issue in the United States, and a few gains were being secured in court at a time when little was happening officially in Canada. Individuals had long sought and secured the adoption of children through private arrangements or private agencies, or of children already in their foster care. They were often able to secure a formal parenting rela-

Table 7.2  Major U.S. Lesbian/Gay Custody Cases, 1985–91

| | | |
|---|---|---|
| 1985 | AK | *SNE v. RLB*<br>Supreme Court reverses lower court change of custody from mother, saying her lesbianness was relevant only if shown to negatively affect child, and barring evidence of social stigma as inadmissible. |
| 1988 | CA | *In re Marriage of Birdsall*<br>Appeal Court removes restriction on visitation with gay father prohibiting presence of any third person known to be homosexual, saying that no evidence of harm was shown. |
| 1991 | CA | *Nancy S. v. Michele G.*<br>Appeal Court affirmed denial of shared custody claim by ex-partner of birth mother of two children born through artificial insemination during relationship, despite both partners being listed on birth certificates, and both earlier agreeing to shared custody. |
| 1991 | NY | *Alison D. v. Virginia M.*<br>Court of Appeals rules that lesbian co-parent could seek neither custody nor visitation rights with ex-partner's biological child. |

tionship to their children by concealing their sexual orientation, or by admitting it to sympathetic officials. Only two states expressly banned gay adoption, Florida having done so since 1977 and New Hampshire since 1986 (the latter covering fostering too). By the 1980s there were private adoption agencies – the predominant vehicle for adoption – willing to work with individuals who were openly lesbian or gay.

Adoption applications were now coming from same-sex couples seeking a formalization of the parental relationship between the child and the non-biological partner – 'second parent' adoptions.[10] In the United States, this requires filing a petition for adoption with a court, which will hear evidence, and in contested cases receive the views of opposing parties. An Alaska court granted what was probably the first second-parent adoption in 1985, quickly followed by courts in Oregon, Washington State, and California. These were all trial courts, unreported and without precedent value. The first 'reported' victories were in 1991 and 1992, the latter in New York (*In re Adoption of Evan*).

### 1993–9: Continuing Incrementalism

During the mid- to late 1990s marriage claims were thrust to the centre of American political debate. In response, conservative rhetoric warning about the risks to children intensified. Yet this was also a

Table 7.3   Major U.S. Second-Parent Adoption Cases, up to 1999

| Year of decision | State | Judgment for (+) or against (−) same-sex adoption | Case |
|---|---|---|---|
| 1992 | NY | + | In re Adoption of Evan |
| 1993 | VT | + | In re Adoption of BLVB |
| 1993 | MA | + | In re Adoption of Tammy |
| 1994 | WI | − | In re Angel Lace M. |
| 1995 | NJ | + | In the Matter of the Adoption of Two Children by HNR |
| 1995 | IL | + | In re Petition of KM and DM |
| 1995 | DC | + | In re M.M.D. v. B.H.M. |
| 1996 | NY | + | In re Christine G. |
| 1996 | CO | − | In re TKJ and K.A.K. |
| 1998 | OH | − | In re Adoption of Jane Doe |
| 1999 | IL | + | Petition of CMW and LAW; Petition of MM and JS |
| 1999 | CT | − | In re Adoption of Baby Z. |

period in which parenting claims were successful in a steadily widening circle of states. Such gains were court led, and often little noticed.

Legal victories were most dramatic in the area of second-parent adoption. By the end of the 1990s, significant shifts had occurred in the law in five or six states, with especially wide-ranging ones in Vermont and New Jersey, and parenting options were spreading more widely than that. Single-parent adoption and assisted reproduction were more available to lesbian and gay couples in the United States than in most of Canada, even though the costs created unequal access across class and ethnic lines (especially for men).

### Second-Parent and Joint Adoption

From 1992 through 1999 at least eight appeal court rulings (across five states and Washington, DC) agreed to the co-adoption requests of non-biological parents in same-sex relationships.[11] In several other states, trial court rulings did the same (see table 7.3).

In 1995 Vermont became the first state where second-parent adoption was legislatively approved; these changes came two years after a favourable appeal court ruling. This was the same year that the British Columbia legislature approved wide-ranging adoption changes. The

New Jersey legislature granted full adoption rights in 1997, also following a favourable court ruling. There were defeats in this period, as well – two in states (Wisconsin and Connecticut) with otherwise progressive records, a reflection of specific statutory language impeding the extension of adoption rights. (The Connecticut ruling was later 'repaired' by legislation.)

The mid-1990s saw the first court approvals of joint adoptions by lesbian and gay couples, of children not biologically connected to either partner, in Vermont, California, New York, and New Jersey. The New Jersey ruling contributed to the legislative enactment of sweeping changes in adoption policy.[12]

The vigilance of the religious right meant that a few adoption cases that would pass unnoticed in other countries became the subject of public controversy. Even in a relatively progressive state like Washington, adoption applicants risked attack from religious conservatives (see box).

**The Megan Lucas Case**

Amid intensive debate during the early 1990s over extending basic civil rights protections to lesbians and gays in Washington State, an adoption case exploded into view. As early as 1978, the state's Supreme Court had upheld the right of lesbians and gay men to retain custody of their children, and other court cases since then had allowed same-sex adoption rights in cases where neither of the partners in a couple was a birth parent. The state's Social and Health Services policy itself forbade discrimination based on sexual orientation in determining the suitability of fostering and adoptive parents, one of six states in the United States at that time to grant adoption rights, and in the late 1980s sexual orientation was included in diversity training for departmental staff.[13]

In late 1993, a highly publicized court case spotlighted the issue. Megan Lucas, a resident of Orcas Island, wanted to reclaim her three-year-old son from a gay couple who were foster parenting him and wanted to adopt him. She had relinquished parental rights in 1992 after being investigated for child neglect but she had changed her mind when she heard that the prospective parents were gay. With the support of the religious right she was appearing on national television shows to put her case before the public.

Some state legislators – mostly Republicans – quickly went on record as favouring legislation that would ban adoption and fostering by gays and lesbians.[14] Megan Lucas became what Chris Bull and John Gallagher describe as a 'poster girl of the religious right's anti-gay parenting campaign.'[15] The Citizens Alliance of Washington used the case to stimulate signature gathering for an anti-gay initiative that included an adoption ban. But the case soon turned into an embarrassment for Lucas's allies. In January 1994 her husband obtained a legal separation and accused her of threatening to kill him and their two-year-old daughter.[16] He won custody of that girl and soon after of another daughter (following an attempted suicide by Lucas). In September the state's Supreme Court ended the court battle by refusing to hear an appeal of a lower court ruling that favoured the gay couple.

## Custody

What seemed like slow but steady gains on adoption, and particularly second-parent adoption, were not as obviously matched on the custody front (see table 7.4). Right through the 1990s and into the 2000s we find examples of starkly prejudicial rulings either fully denying custody to biological parents or prohibiting visible displays of homosexuality during visits. In 1996 a Florida appeals court ruled that a man convicted of murdering his first wife was a more appropriate parent than his lesbian ex-wife. In 1999, Virginia's Supreme Court denied custody rights to Sharon Bottoms, placing her daughter with Sharon's mother and denying visitation either in the home that she shared with her partner or in any other place with her partner present. Outrageous rulings continued to be delivered in other states, including *Weigand v. Houghton* in Mississippi (see box).

*Weigand v. Houghton*, **Mississippi, Supreme Court, 1999**
A gay man seeking to gain custody of his son from his former wife was turned down in a lower court, despite the child's mother having married a man who had twice beaten her. On one occasion, the beating was severe enough to prompt the son to call 911, and the accumulated history of violence prompted their landlord to evict them. The new husband also threatened to kill the child. The trial judge responded to

the father's claim by saying, 'The conscience of this Court is shocked by
the audacity and brashness of an individual to come into court, openly
and freely admit to engaging in felonious conduct on a regular basis and
expect the Court to find such conduct acceptable, particularly with
regard to the custody of a minor child.' The Supreme Court upheld the
refusal of custody.[17]

Parental custody and access claims by non-biological parents in separated couples fared worse. Even in states like California, courts were
treating such parents as 'strangers,' even when they had taken on the
bulk of parenting responsibilities until the separation.

*Other Parenting Changes*

Two encouraging developments on fostering occurred during this
period. The Massachusetts ban on gays and lesbians serving as
foster parents had been rescinded in 1990. In 1994 a Florida court
ruled against an informal policy prohibiting gay fostering in that
state (*Matthews and Kohler v. Weinberg and Williams*). And in 1999
a New Hampshire law preventing both fostering and adoption
was rescinded. True, ominous signs warned of a growing backlash,
with bills being introduced by conservative state lawmakers
proposing new prohibitions on parenting by same-sex couples. But
there was no significant slowing of the expansion of parenting
rights.

**1999 and After: Backlash Alongside Incremental Progress**

By 1999 a backlash marshalled primarily around same-sex marriage
was underway, with particular attention on the 'threat' of gays and
lesbians in parenting roles. In 1999 two states had official barriers to
one or another form of lesbian/gay parenting. By 2006 there were
seven states in which courts had explicitly disallowed parental rights
for same-sex couples, or new legislation to the same effect had been
passed. And by then state electorates were facing a mounting wave of
constitutional amendments banning same-sex marriage, most of them
with expansive language that could well end up curtailing parental
rights. As recently as 2007, appeals courts in the states of New York
and Washington upheld anti–gay marriage laws in part on the basis of

Table 7.4   Major U.S. Court Cases on Custody for Gay or Lesbian Parents, 1993–9

| Year of decision | State | Judgment for (+) or against (−) same-sex adoption | Case | Claimant a biological parent? |
|---|---|---|---|---|
| 1995 | MI | − | McGuffin v. Overton | No |
| 1995 | FL | − | Music v. Rachford | No |
| 1995 | TN | +/− | In re Michael Lee Parsons* | Yes |
| 1996 | WA | + | In re the Marriage of Wicklund and Wicklund | Yes |
| 1997 | CA | − | West v. Superior Court | No |
| 1998 | MI | − | DeLong v. DeLong | Yes |
| 1998 | AB | − | JBV v. JMF | Yes |
| 1998 | NC | − | Pulliam v. Smith | Yes |
| 1998 | MD | + | Boswell v. Boswell | Yes |
| 1999 | VA | − | Bottoms v. Bottoms | Yes |
| 1999 | MS | − | Weigand v. Houghton | Yes |
| 1999 | MA | + | ENO v. LMM | No |
| 1999 | FL | − | Kazmierazak v. Query | No |
| 1999 | IL | − | In re the Matter of Visitation with CBL | Yes |
| 1999 | CA | − | ZCW v. Lisa W. | No |

*Award of custody but on condition of no 'inappropriate' conduct between mother and partner.

the 'reasonableness' of arguments that children were better served by having a mother and father.

At the same time, the number of states in which significant gains had been secured in at least one parenting area increased from about seven to at least fifteen, with an additional dozen having witnessed court rulings covering at least a portion of the state. By 2004, the two states that had enacted widespread recognition of parenting rights earlier (Vermont and New Jersey) were joined by California, Connecticut, and (through state marriage law) Massachusetts. More were added to this list within the next couple of years, with no signs of slowdown.

*Assisted Reproduction*

More real change has occurred in the area of assisted reproduction than in any of the policy areas related to same-sex parenting. And even if the costs associated with such assistance were high, restricting access for many, there may well be no other country in which access for those who can afford it is as easy.

Most reproductive services in the United States are private, and no state expressly prohibits the provision of services to lesbians and gay men. Some religious conservatives and Republican lawmakers have called for legislation barring anyone but heterosexual couples from access to reproductive clinics, but so far without success. There are certainly many sperm banks, fertility clinics, and doctors who balk at providing service to them, but clinics ready to do so have proliferated in large U.S. cities, especially those with sizeable and visible gay/lesbian populations. One 2005 *New York Times* story reported that about half of the American legal firms and agencies that help secure surrogacy arrangements were open to gay couples.[18] *Gay Parent Magazine* listed gay-friendly firms in 2006 (and 2007), among which was California Cryobank, thought to be the largest sperm bank in the country.[19]

Fertility assistance is both expensive and often not covered by insurance. Even in states requiring that medical insurance cover reproductive services (there were fourteen in early 2002), coverage is generally restricted to cases of infertility.[20] In 2005 Sandra Barney estimated that the monthly cost of donor insemination (without qualifications) was close to $600/month (U.S.), though the cost was higher for sperm from donors with more 'attractive' profiles.[21]

Gay male couples are in a more difficult position, and one marked by even more severe inequalities in de facto access, though not as much as in Canada. Because they can secure biological parentage only through the cooperation of a surrogate mother, the costs are extraordinary, easily US$100,000 or more.[22] And because of legitimate concerns about the rights of the mother and the potential for the exploitation of women, policy makers in just under a quarter of American states have imposed restrictions or outright prohibitions on such arrangements.[23]

### Birth Certificates

There are other elements of state regulation that maintain a parenting hierarchy even in as privatized a system as this. The question of registration of parents on birth certificates has been as problematic as in Canada. A Massachusetts court ruled in 2001 that two women could be listed as mother on a birth certificate, but this was an unusual case in which one of the women supplied the egg and the other carried it to term. (Late in 2004, months after marriage became legal in that state, birth certificates issued by hospitals would still not permit the entry of two mothers or fathers.)

A 2003 court ruling in New Jersey allowed two lesbians registered as domestic partners in New York, and married in Canada, to be entered onto their newborn's birth certificate.[24] One year later, California started allowing the registration of two people of the same sex on birth certificates. Remarkably, Virginia's broadly worded prohibition on same-sex marriage, now embedded in its constitution, did not prevent a court from ordering the Division of Vital Records (in 2005) to issue gender-neutral birth certificates to three same-sex couples who had secured co-parent adoption elsewhere.[25] In some states, gay couples with surrogacy arrangements have obtained court declarations of parentage prior to birth, allowing the name of both men to be registered on the birth certificate.[26]

Because same-sex couples invariably require the intervention of a third sexual partner, whether known or unknown, there are extra challenges entailed in legally establishing parenthood. As in other countries, American policy and law only rarely deviate from the two-parent model, a point emphasized by Valerie Lehr in her warning against seeking inclusion within established family frameworks.[27] While some states stipulate that a sperm donor is not a legal parent, the issue is less clear elsewhere, and in flux. Same-sex couples who want to be treated as the only legal parents of a child will sometimes encounter a legal regime that is prepared to accord parental status even to sperm donors and surrogate mothers who have signed contracts giving over their parental rights.

*Fostering*

There have been a few attempts to formally prohibit gays and lesbians from fostering. Arkansas and Utah instituted sweeping bans on parenting in 1999, though Arkansas's was overturned in 2004. Two years later, a Missouri Department of Social Services decision to turn away a foster parent application on the grounds that she was a lesbian was overruled in court.[28] The continuing shortage of foster parents nationwide made it unlikely that political campaigns targeting lesbian and gay foster parents would be widespread.[29]

There is little doubt that fostering agencies are still prone to preferential judgments informed by traditional family hierarchies. As a result, foster parent applicants who deviate from the married middle-class heterosexual norm will be seen as offering less than optimal home environments. There is also no doubt that there are supportive social workers and officials across the United States who are fully prepared to place children in such families without prejudice. The political volatility of this and any other policy issue involving children, and the importance for the religious right of denying the very existence of sexual minority youth, forces discretion and even silence on such policy networks, and often on parents themselves. But shifts in de facto policy are nonetheless undeniable.

On the other side of this parenting relationship, it is also clear that sexual minority youngsters – by estimate 10 to 20 per cent of the total in care – are inadequately served by the fostering system.[30] Many receive hostile or unresponsive treatment, and most try to escape their foster placements. In 2001, a Lambda Legal Defense and Education Fund report on foster care found that 'a few' states had taken positive first steps, and not a single one had system-wide policies and practices designed to prevent discrimination and abuse.[31] Only a few had optional training for parents on sexual diversity, and only Los Angeles and New York City had facilities specifically geared to lesbian/gay/bisexual/transgendered youth. One surveyor was told by a child welfare official that her state did not need such programs because there were no sexual minority youth in their foster care system. Since then there have been encouraging signs in states like Connecticut, Washington, and California, but they remain isolated examples.

*Adoption – Still the Hottest Button*

A few states have explicit prohibitions on same-sex couples adopting children. Florida's 1977 ban has continued to withstand legal challenges. In 2004 a federal appeal court (*Lofton v. Secretary of the Florida Department of Children and Families*) stated that 'it is rational for Florida to conclude that it is in the best interests of adoptive children, many of whom come from troubled and unstable backgrounds, to be placed in a home anchored by both a father and mother.'[32] The Arkansas Child Welfare Agency Review Board approved a ban in 1999. In 2000, lawmakers in Utah and Mississippi enacted laws that explicitly or effectively prohibited gay/lesbian adoptions, the former framed more broadly to apply to anyone cohabiting with another person outside of marriage, the later citing same-sex couples explicitly. In 2003 North Dakota legislators passed a law allowing adoption agencies having contracts with the state to refuse child placements on religious grounds – a measure targeting adoption by homosexuals – and a de facto ban was undoubtedly widespread in the state. In 2004, the Oklahoma legislature enacted a measure preventing the recognition of adoptions by same-sex couples in other states, though two years later the law was struck down by a federal judge.

In other states, including those as different as Oregon and Virginia, Republican lawmakers are still introducing bills to create impediments for same-sex couples and in some cases gay or lesbian individuals wanting to adopt. Conservatives in some states were considering ballot measures, and religious groups were as prepared as ever to mount legal challenges on adoption cases, bolstered by a U.S. president prepared to go on the record as arguing that same-sex parenthood was less than ideal. Their success in entrenching constitutional bans on same-sex marriage were emboldening them to move on the parental front, and in states where expansively worded bans had already been approved (such as Michigan and Ohio), they were sure to challenge adoption rights.

As they had always done, religious conservative groups and conservative think tanks were publicizing disreputable 'scientific' findings on the harm done to children by lesbian/gay parenting. The Traditional Values Coalition was quoting work by the widely discredited psychologist Paul Cameron characterizing lesbians and gays as child molesters, mentally ill, and highly prone to substance abuse. The Family Research Institute was also using such 'research,' as was a small but expert-sounding group calling itself the American College of Pediatrics, aiming to counteract the favourable research relied upon by mainstream professional organizations.[33]

In Massachusetts, a 2005 controversy revealed that Catholic Charities of Boston, which had managed 720 fostercare adoptions over the previous two decades (more than any other private agency in the state), had approved placements for same-sex couples. The Vatican had already described such adoptions as 'doing violence' to children. Then in 2006 the Prefect of the Vatican's Congregation for the Doctrine of the Faith instructed bishops that they should not allow Catholic agencies to permit adoptions by same-sex couples, calling such adoptions 'gravely immoral.' Charity officials defended their past placements by pointing out their responsibility to place very challenging children, and seven board members resigned in opposition to discrimination against citizens 'who want to play a part in building strong families.'[34] The state's bishops responded by ending all its adoption services. The issue was soon spreading to other parts of the United States, though Catholic Charities of San Francisco developed a creative way of facilitating the placement of children in fostering and adoptive homes regardless of sexual orientation, and with the help of local government authorities.[35]

Foreign adoptions have become more difficult in the United States, as they have for Canadians. On the positive side, the Immigration and Naturalization Service was instructed by the U.S. Justice Department in 1993 that applicants' 'personal relationships with other adults' cannot be used to deny an orphan visa petition. That said, none of the countries allowing non-nationals to adopt permit gays and lesbians to do so openly.[36] China, the source of more foreign adoptions than any other country, now obliges agencies to formally attest to the fact that adoptive parents are not homosexual, requires prospective parents to sign a statement saying that they are not lesbian or gay, and limits the number of adoptions approved for single parents.[37]

There are of course several states in which there has been no progress towards recognizing lesbian and gay adoption rights. In some of them, appeal courts have ruled that state adoption laws preclude second-parent adoptions within same-sex couples (e.g., Colorado, Nebraska, Ohio). Connecticut had similar rulings until turn-of-the-century legislation effected wide-ranging change in parenting. Only small gains have been won in a few other states where we might have expected more sweeping change, such as Oregon. California saw pioneering court rulings on some aspects of adoption, but up to the installation of the broad relationship regime enacted in 2003 there were still appeals courts refusing to acknowledge rights for non-biological parents. These oddities often result from the peculiarities of wording in statutes enacted years before, without lesbian and gay adoption being on the agenda. And because the chances of passing more explicitly flexible adoption statutes are remote in all but a few states, even gay-positive legislators are reluctant to raise the issue.

For all these difficulties, judicial acceptance of second-parent adoption has continued to spread steadily. By 2007 statewide acceptance was secured by high court or legislative decision in nine states plus the District of Columbia.[38] Court rulings had allowed second-parent adoptions in some regions within an additional fifteen states, including Alabama, Louisiana, and Texas – surprising by any other measure. Half of the American states, therefore, had seen at least some favourable shift in the treatment of second-parent adoption claims by same-sex couples, and the Human Rights Campaign points to anecdotal evidence of favourable but unrecorded court rulings in other states. Joint or 'stranger' adoption was still more challenging, but in 2007 it was recognized at least in some parts of ten states plus Washington, DC.[39]

Adoption of children through private or public agencies depends not only on favourable hearings in court, but also on the availability of gay-positive institutions. Here too surprising gains had been made. One 2003 survey of private and public adoption agencies showed that 60 per cent accepted homosexual applicants, and 19 per cent actively sought out gays and lesbians as adoptive parents.[40] Even in Florida, which explicitly bans homosexual adoption, some agencies have developed a 'don't ask, don't tell' policy that effectively allows such adoption.[41] In 2005–6, a gay male couple successfully sued Adoption.com, the largest adoption internet business in the country, after the company said they did not provide services to same-sex couples.[42]

*Custody*

Favourable rulings on custody claims made by lesbian and gay parents continue their gradual spread. State supreme courts had ruled affirmatively on custody and visitation rights in Wisconsin (1995), Massachusetts (1999), Maryland, New Jersey, Rhode Island (2000), Pennsylvania (2001), Maine (2004), California (2005), Washington (2005), Delaware (2006), and Minnesota (2007).[43] The Massachusetts case broke new ground, recognizing the rights and obligations of non-biological parents who could establish a de facto parental relationship. The California case made clear that parental rights extended beyond the end of same-sex relationships even in the absence of a formal adoption or registration as domestic partners, and the Washington Supreme Court followed the same logic.[44] This was also based, in other words, on evidence of de facto parental relationships. Less senior appellate courts had done the same not only in several West Coast and Northeast states, but also in states like Arkansas, Tennessee, and North Dakota.

The last few years have seen a new twist on custody battles, as parents in now-ended same-sex relationships have tested the transportability of parental status across state boundaries. One notorious case involved a Vermont couple who had registered under the state's civil union regime, and succeeded in having a child using assisted reproduction. After the breakup of the relationship, the biological mother defied a court order by moving to Virginia, where a court refused to recognize the legal standing of the non-biological mother.[45] Finally, in late 2006, an appeal court in Virginia conceded that the Vermont courts had jurisdiction in the case. Another case involving similar principles was ruled on in 2002 by the Nebraska Supreme Court (*Russell v. Bridgens*), recognizing a Pennsylvania second-parent adoption in a case of a custody claim by the non-biological mother. In 2005, a Florida court supported Hannah Wood's claim to parental rights, deferring to a Colorado court after her partner moved to Florida to escape that court's ruling.[46] On the other side of the ledger, a 2007 Utah Supreme Court overturned a lower court ruling that had granted Keri Lynne Jones visitation rights with a child conceived of in Vermont under that state's civil union regime.[47] Her former partner and the child's biological mother, Cheryl Pike Barlow, was a born-again Christian who had turned away from homosexuality and did not want her daughter in contact with it.

Kate Kendell argues that there are at least six states where courts deny custody and access claims on the basis of homosexuality as such (including Alabama, Mississippi, North Carolina, and Virginia).[48] Writing for the majority of Alabama's Supreme Court in *D.H. v. H.H.* (2002), the Chief Justice described homosexual behaviour as 'a crime in Alabama, a crime against nature, an inherent evil, and an act so heinous that it defies one's ability to describe it.' Courts in many other places effectively do the same but under the cover of other rationalizations, or they impose restrictions that make it impossible for children and parents to have a full and honest relationship.[49] As with adoption, the passage of state constitutional amendments barring same-sex marriage may slow or reverse progress on custody cases. Ohio's amendment is notoriously broad, and in 2005 there was already a case in which the biological mother was citing it to prevent her former lesbian partner from seeing their child (*Fairchild v. Leach*).

Despite important gains for non-biological parents, courts in most states do not grant them legal standing. This is despite a nationwide trend in heterosexual cases that leans towards retaining continuity in parent-child relations after separation or divorce by ensuring shared custody or at least generous access for non-custodial parents. Such logic has only been sparingly transferred to same-sex relationships. As David Chambers puts it, 'no matter how long the gay "stepparent" lives with the child, no matter how deeply they become involved in the care of the child, they and the child will rarely be recognized as having a legally significant relationship with one another.'[50]

Very much in contrast to such reluctance, a Pennsylvania Superior Court ruled in 2007 that for custody purposes, three parents would be recognized. Two women who had conceived of children with a known sperm donor, and in the context of their relationship, were now separated. On appeal, the court decided that all three had visitation rights and an obligation to share in support (*Jacob v. Shultz-Jacob*). This ruling followed by three months a similar Ontario court judgment, and had no parallels in any other Western country.

Overall, important favourable shifts in custody and access are amply evident. Full statewide acceptance of custody claims by lesbians and gay men extends beyond those states that have enacted sweeping changes in relationship regimes, even if not quite as widely as with adoption. In contrast to adoption cases, custody and visitation claims arise out of conflict, creating more unpredictability and more room for prejudice and the privileging of biological parenthood.

### Change in Other Institutional Settings

Parenting regimes, as we have seen, are built up and maintained through the policies and practices of institutions beyond the state. As was chronicled in chapter 5, workplace benefit plans contribute to defining some family arrangements as worthy and others as not. In the United States, too, and especially in large corporations, such plans have been expanding to include same-sex partners at a faster rate than we find in any public policy realm. This development is important for parenting, since such benefit plans usually extend supports related to parenting. Over half of Fortune 500 companies now recognize same-sex partners, and 90 per cent of those plans cover the dependent children of such partners. Sixty per cent also extend adoption assistance to those partners.[51]

## Assessing and Explaining Change

As in the broader area of relationship recognition, significant legal and policy change in American parenting began only in the 1990s. A few

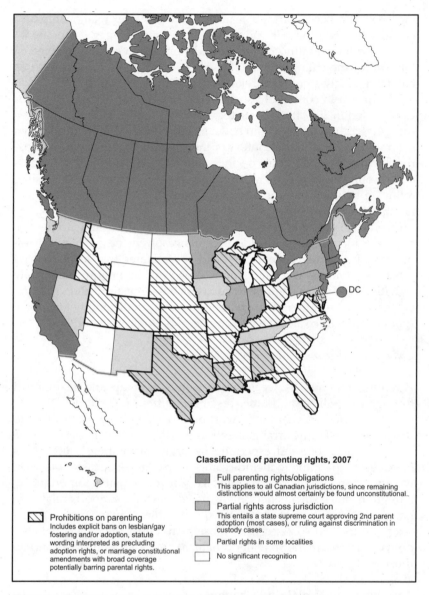

Figure 7.1  Parenting Rights in the United States and Canada, 2007

senior court rulings in the early years of the decade moved the yard-sticks on custody or adoption, at least as early as favourable court rulings on parenting appeared in Canada. The first major legislative step was taken by Vermont in 1995, the same year that British Columbia's legislature passed inclusive adoption legislation. Since then, we have seen a steady spread of favourable court rulings and a few legislative moves recognizing the rights and obligations of sexual minority parents, even if we have also seen a growth in efforts to stop such developments.

There is no take-off to parallel that in Canada. In 2000, when the Canadian courts had clearly signalled that formal discrimination on parental issues was unconstitutional, only three U.S. states had moved towards inclusiveness on at least two parenting issues. Still, that number increased to seven over the next five years. An additional nineteen states had legislation or appeals court rulings covering all or part of a state opening the door to same-sex parenting rights on at least one major front. Positive developments, then, were being recorded in just over half of all jurisdictions – a significantly better record than on other relationship fronts.

We also find progress in unusual places, such as Texas, Alabama, Louisiana, and Tennessee. In fact, no policy area so illustrates the incoherence that has become such a hallmark of American state family policy, where judges and social agencies are struggling with real families that do not correspond to the family models that prevailed when statutes were first being drafted. This produces breakthroughs in some policy areas (like second-parent adoption) in the absence of change on other parenting or familial fronts.

*Limits to Change*

Opposition to parenting by lesbians and gay men remains fierce. The advances being made on parenting have intensified political mobilizing by religious conservatives, already strengthened by the battle against same-sex marriage and emboldened by the federal Republican administration of George W. Bush. Republicans at the state level show increasing willingness to press for legislation that limits parenting options, and religious conservative groups specializing in litigation are throwing more resources than ever into court room battles over parenting rights.

Across the United States, court challenges to lesbian and gay custody or adoption have often come from relatives and intervenors whose views are informed by the religious right, sometimes leading to highly public mobilization designed to whip up the worst of anti-gay prejudice. John Malone recounts a late 1990s story of religious-right groups in Texas rousing controversy over a fostering placement with a lesbian couple.[52] In the aftermath of that controversy, Hilary Rosen and Elizabeth Birch, two of the most prominent politically active lesbians in Washington, DC, sought the adoption of the twin infants of a Texas woman. The Family Research Council took up the issue and used the case to lobby Texas politicians on a proposal to ban such adoptions. As an *Advocate* reporter put it, 'if Birch and Rosen – well-connected Washington power brokers – could be threatened with losing a child, it could happen to anyone.'[53]

The wide discretion given judges, officials, and medical practitioners in making decisions about fostering, adoption, custody, and assisted reproduction provides room for progressive change, but also for the injection of homophobic or heterosexist prejudice. The strength of religious conservatism in the United States ensures that the range of outcomes resulting from such discretion will remain much wider than in Canada.

Heterosexual married couples are still widely assumed to be the closest to ideal parents; indeed, they are thought to be unfulfilled if they have no children. Where adoption by individuals is permitted, openly lesbian and gay applicants are likely to be treated as less worthy than heterosexuals, more likely to get children with special needs, and more likely to encounter insensitive home investigations. When they seek custody of or access to their own children, they may still reduce their chances if they are thought to be 'indiscreet' about their homosexuality. When they seek access to children they co-parented in previous same-sex relationships, they are frequently treated as strangers to the children. The radical disparities between states may mean that parental recognition secured by parents in progressive states will not be transportable to other states, particularly where anti-gay marriage language has been inserted into state constitutions. Even in states where sweeping change has been enacted, federal social benefits and tax entitlements available to families with children will not be available to same-sex couples, sharpening a poverty gap already large for straight families with children.

As in Canada, the barriers facing lesbians and gay men wanting recognition as parents are more formidable for those who do not fit 'respectable' moulds, and especially for those who in one form or another cross gender boundaries. The difficulties facing bisexuals and the transgendered who want to parent are sufficiently great that few have risked testing them in court. The threat of religious-right opposition adds extra pressure on all real or prospective parents to frame their recognition claims in ways that minimize rocking the boat. Whatever the legitimacy of radical challenges to the familial ideologies underpinning public policy and social agency practice in areas like adoption and fostering and custody, those directly involved in the politics of parenting are rarely in a condition to present them.

Whether in a courtroom or in the media, then, individual parents and activists are virtually obliged to insist that their children will grow up 'normal'– that their children will develop appropriate masculine and feminine traits. In 1995, friend-of-the-court brief from LGBT advocates in support of a Colorado applicant for co-parental adoption illustrated this point in a summary of the available research on the subject: 'Research regarding lesbian motherhood has consistently failed to provide any evidence for necessarily inferior parenting styles. Children of lesbian mothers have not demonstrated aberrant gender identity development, increased preference for homosexual object choice, nor enhanced social/emotional maladjustment, when compared with children raised by single heterosexual mothers.' The brief also pointed out that 'numerous studies have disproved the hypothesis that children might acquire a lesbian or gay identity by imitating a lesbian or gay parent.'[54] A footnote flags the contradiction, saying that the fear that children will grow up queer embodies the prejudicial notion that it is preferable that they grow up heterosexual. Still, as the note points out, the prevalence of the fear forces rebuttal. In this and innumerable other cases, the recognition being asserted here is almost always framed as constituting no threat to the existing order.

Arguments pointing to the advantages of children being raised by a same-sex couple almost never get made. In fact, such families can offer new models of intimacy to children, expanding their horizons and reducing the likelihood of their being swayed by prejudice.[55] Their public display of adult lives lived as openly lesbian, gay, bisexual, or transgendered parents makes it more likely that children whose affectional pulls are similar will be comfortable in that skin. Until now, such arguments have seemed too risky, and give way to claims that lesbian/gay parents are the same as heterosexual parents. In light of the discretion available to those making decisions about adoption and fostering, to do otherwise would be folly, and to counsel otherwise irresponsible.

Risk derives from the continuing power of the idea that all children are 'naturally' heterosexual, or will naturally become so – an idea so often paired with the belief that becoming homosexual would lead to harassment, confusion, and unhappiness. The religious right repeats such views constantly, and couples them with the argument that homosexual behaviour is shaped by unnatural forces. Elements of such ideas have far broader resonance than the religious right and its normally receptive constituencies.

The pressures for claimants to portray themselves and their parenting in respectable garb comes also from parents and activists who are not particularly critical of the existing regime apart from its exclusion of them. They may have no particular objection to the privileging of marriage so long as same-sex couples are included within it. Others may support the privileging of biological parentage, fearing that to do otherwise would leave their own co-parenting rights jeopardized by claims from others. As in Canada, there are many parents and activists who are not so sure about moving towards forms of flexibility that would leave them vulnerable to claims of paternity or of parent-like access that they wish to shield themselves from.[56]

The advances made by lesbian and gay parents almost inevitably mean that they encounter greater financial costs than heterosexuals, more so in the United States than anywhere. Co-parents often have to formally adopt when partners in heterosexual couples would not. Prospective parents may well have to search further afield to gain access to inclusive reproductive assistance or adoption agencies. Parenting initiatives of all sorts more likely require legal advice when coming from same-sex couples than from heterosexual couples. The greater leeway given to free-market forces in the fields of adoption, and especially assisted reproduction, created relatively early openings for same-sex couples. But the costs, particularly of assisted reproduction, also ensured inequality of access across class and race lines, especially for gay men, across all regions, and particularly where in-state services are not available.

Inequalities, privileging gays and lesbians over bisexuals and the transgendered, and creating additional advantages along class and race lines distort the public face of parenting, and of the activism pressing for change. In some cases this comes from the unequal access to expensive procedures. It also comes from the pressures towards 'respectability' foregrounding those claimants who provoke the least public anxieties – white, middle class, monogamous, and unambiguous in gender.

*The State of Public Opinion*

There is no doubt that the barriers to acceptance of sexual diversity in the general public are greater for issues involving children than others. Indeed, an important part of the opposition to same-sex marriage comes from a view that the parenting of children by lesbians and gays is inappropriate. Some opponents fear that children would fail to develop appropriate gender roles or would be ridiculed by their peers. Others go much farther, characterizing lesbians and especially gay men as predatory. As in Canada, only a small minority of people would fully accept the possibility of children of these or indeed any relationships being themselves lesbian or gay.

Roper polls conducted in the 1990s show just how reluctant Americans are to think of gay and lesbian couples with children as 'family,' and how slow to change those sentiments are (see table 7.5). Even in a political setting in which formal recognition of de facto straight couples is limited, three-quarters of the general public is ready to see them as family. However, only a little more than a quarter do so for same-sex couples with children. A comparison with data gathered in Canada by Reginald Bibby four years later shows (surprisingly) less inclination to use a family label for non-traditional heterosexual relationships than is evident in the United States, though Canadians are more ready to accept same-sex couples. Other American polling shows that opposition on adoption rights is persistent, and that for 40 per cent or more of the population it is strongly felt (41 per cent in a 2004 Pew survey).[57]

That said, public readiness to accept or at least acquiesce in same-sex parenting has increased dramatically in the United States through to the early 2000s. In 1994, polls were showing that just under 30 per cent supported adoption rights; by 2004 this had increased to over 40 per cent, and in 2006 it was between 46 and 49 per cent (not substantially different from Canadian polling).[58]

*Explaining Positive Change*

What explains the shift towards recognizing sexual minority parenting claims? As in Canada, the sheer numbers of same-sex couples with children, and their growing visibility, has pressed against existing regimes. For a variety of reasons, the strength of moral conservatism has not substantially limited the growth of opportunities for same-sex couples to arrange for children, in numbers as large as in any country. This presents courts, social agencies, health-care institutions, and

Table 7.5    Public Definitions of 'Family' – Americans, 1992–9, and Canadians, 2003

| Living arrangements 'definitely a family' | United States (% affirmative response) | | Canada (% affirmative response) |
|---|---|---|---|
| | 1992 | 1999 | 2003 |
| De facto couple, raising children | 77 | 75 | |
| Unmarried man and woman with at least one child | | | 68 |
| Woman never married, living with her children | 81 | 82 | |
| Man never married, living with his children | 73 | 78 | |
| Unmarried person with at least one child | | | 61 |
| Lesbian couple, raising children together | 27 | 29 | |
| Gay male couple, raising children together | 26 | 26 | |
| Two people of the same sex with at least one child | | | 46 |

Source: For U.S.: RoperASW polls. For Canada: Reginald Bibby, *A Survey of Canadians' Hopes and Dreams* (Ottawa: Vanier Institute for the Family, 2004), 1. The Bibby question asked which of the above arrangements respondents saw as constituting a family.

schools with already-existing families, often at stages when the family relationships are functioning well. Same-sex couples usually confront judges with the question of whether the children in that family unit would be better served with two parents than one. As Nancy Polikoff is right to point out, judges who hear requests for second-parent adoptions also hear many other cases shot through with family dysfunction. She quotes the judge granting New York State's first second-parent adoption to help make the point: 'Today a child who receives proper nutrition, adequate schooling and supportive sustaining shelter is among the fortunate, whatever the source. A child who also receives the love and nurture of even a single parent can be counted among the blessed. Here this court finds a child who has all of the above benefits and two adults dedicated to his welfare, secure in their loving partnership, and determined to raise him to the very best of their considerable abilities. There is no reason in law, logic or social philosophy to obstruct such a favorable situation.'[59]

The statutory frameworks in some U.S. states also facilitate change. Parenting law across the country has for some time accepted the rights of individuals to adopt and foster children, which is in itself a major challenge to traditional parenting regimes. In many states, too, laws governing parental rights are not phrased in ways that preclude, for example, second-parent adoption. And in that minority of states in which formal equality rights have been extended to lesbians and gays, courts are empowered to push against the limits of parental traditions. The substantial decentralization of political and judicial authority in the area of parenting allows room for the same kind of variation across states that we saw in other areas of family law.

Parenting claims by same-sex couples can be framed in neo-liberal, conservative, as well as progressive ways. The parental qualifications of an adopting couple; the commitment to fostering of another – these present circumstances where the best interests of children may simply overwhelm the ideological orientation of decision makers. Some with deeply conservative values will see in the affirmation of family bonds a blow for social stability; neo-liberals may see in it a potential saving for the public treasury. Those with progressive orientations will support a shift in law towards a more inclusive conception of family in which they may themselves have a stake.

Parental claims, too, get framed in terms of formal equality rights, and this draws support from many Americans who are still uncomfortable with homosexuality. We have already seen that basic protection against discrimination in employment, for example, is supported by very strong majorities in the United States, and this has to include many people who 'disapprove' of homosexuality. Here we find a moderate version of the same bifurcation; stronger support for the rights of same-sex parents and their children than for the idea that they might together constitute a legitimate family. The strength of the rights tradition in the United States brings popular support up to the level we see in Canada, even though other conditions, including moral conservatism, would suggest otherwise.

## Conclusion

Demands by lesbians and gays that their parenting rights and obligations be recognized have not yet spread widely enough across the United States to constitute a sea change in the family regime. But there are impressive changes nonetheless and across a surprising range of jurisdictions. Furthermore, on most of the specific issues that arise with parenting, and especially assisted reproduction, American developments have occurred as early as those in Canada, and earlier than anywhere else.

Parenting claims by lesbian and gay couples have embodied a major challenge to the fundamentals of traditional family regimes. The social, economic, and political changes that gave rise to second-wave feminism, and the radical challenges to traditional family forms raised by that feminism, have significantly altered the way that families work and the way that we talk about the idea of family. When same-sex couples succeed in making parenting claims, the cracks in traditional family forms widen, no matter how much the claims are framed in accommodating and respectable ways.

The very fact that the two parents are of the same sex cannot help but undermine the gendered constructs that are at the heart of traditional family ideology. Many lesbian and gay couples with parenting claims will live their family lives in unconventional ways, and continue to do so despite being pressured to present their court case in conventional terms. Will the growing recognition of same-sex couples' parenting rights confine such couples or pull future couples towards more conventional models? Probably not.

The gains chronicled here also have an impact far beyond the often-privileged claimants who are able to go to court. The changes in law and policy that those parents and their children have wrought provide all same-sex parents with more room for manoeuvre, and empower those with no previous activism to work with their children in counteracting the prejudice of their peers, to insist that schoolteachers, health-care providers, and social workers provide support. The symbolic power of policy and law reform, too, cannot help but erode the most insidious and tenacious stereotypes of lesbians and especially gay men – those linked to children.

The gains secured by activist groups and individual claimants can be measured in part by the sheer number of lesbians and gay men who are visibly parenting in the United States. The scale of the parenting boom was evident in the 2000 census, which showed that close to 40 per cent of same-sex couples with partners between twenty-five and fifty-five years of age were raising children, and the figures were high across all major ethnic and racial categories. Most of those who take up the parenting challenge do so far removed from the limelight, wishing to lead ordinary and undisturbed lives. They manage to raise children often without needing legal or political recognition. They find reproductive services, clinics, and schools that are more or less supportive of what they are doing, or they manage with less than that. But the very act of raising children forces couples and individuals to be more open than they might otherwise be, and the impact of such openness on the part of so many parents is incalculable.

# 8 Canadian School Lethargy

The 'take-off' pattern displayed in changes to relationship and parenting policies during the 1990s and early 2000s might anticipate widespread change in Canada's public schools. But it does not. Until recently, the activist challenge on schools issues in most of the country has been strikingly modest, and so has the response of educators and officials.[1] The stark truth is that, with only one important exception, Canadian school boards and provincial education ministries took almost no significant steps in developing policies and practices accepting of differences in sexual orientation and gender identity until the end of the 1990s. At the provincial level, no provincial government had taken serious steps to acknowledge sexual diversity before the mid-2000s. Even on the issue of harassment and bullying, around which so much evidence of harm was available, there is next to no evidence of concerted action beyond generic prohibitions on discrimination and harassment.

There is no obvious way in which mobilizing by religious conservatives could be blamed for this policy failure. Neither could a significant portion of the popular media be blamed for fomenting opposition to inclusive change, as it could be in the United States and Britain. Part of the reason must lie in the relatively low levels of activist pressure for change until the late 1990s; part, too, in the political caution that permeates the ranks of Canadian educators and policy makers when it comes to issues related to sexuality.

**Before the Mid-1980s: Almost Unbroken Silence**

The oppressiveness of schools for sexual minorities received only sporadic attention within the lesbian and gay movement through the 1970s and early 1980s. Explicitly discriminatory treatment of educators Doug Wilson (in mid-1970s Saskatoon) and John Argue (in Toronto later in the same decade) briefly raised the profile of schooling. The refusal of Montreal's Catholic school board to rent facilities to a gay group also led to a successful court ruling in 1980. Some time would pass, however, before sustained activism focusing on schools was to emerge.

Toronto saw the beginnings of an activist network among educators in the early 1980s, supported by reform trustees on the city's public school board, though with little impact on policy. A proposal for a lesbian/gay liaison committee was defeated in 1980.[2] A year later sexual orientation was removed from the board's anti-discrimination policy governing students, and a new policy set limits on discussion of homosexuality in schools and banned 'proselytization.'

### 1985–90: Cautious Gains on AIDS and Formal Equality Rights

The rapid spread of AIDS, and the media dramatization of the epidemic in the mid-1980s, provided an opening in schools, as it did in other policy areas. The urgent need to reach adolescents with public education on the spread of HIV put pressure on schooling authorities to include AIDS education in the curriculum and, in the process, to acknowledge gay sex. AIDS policies were in fact widely developed across Canada, although only a minority required preventive action and, as Morgan Vanek points out, even fewer discuss even the basics of human sexuality.[3] The gains secured by activists in this period, in other words, were isolated and half-hearted. In 1987 Ontario's provincial government required AIDS education in all schools from the seventh grade on – the first large province to do so – but the fears associated with homosexuality remained strikingly in place. In 1988 provincial policy was changed to allow the inclusion of sexual orientation issues in the physical health education curriculum, but there is no evidence that this opportunity was widely taken up. Sexuality in general was still largely avoided in Canadian schools, and what passes for sex education remained sequestered in small curricular moments that were as antiseptic as teachers and administrators could make them.

After Toronto school librarian Kenn Zeller was beaten to death in 1985 by high school students who were described in court as ordinary and normal, activists called for the school board to address anti-gay abuse and the acquiescence in homophobic sentiments by most educators.[4] Rights issues were also being raised, with the Charter of Rights and Freedoms enacted only three years earlier, and its major equality rights section (15) coming into force in 1985. One year later, the addition of sexual orientation to the province of Ontario's Human Rights Code provoked intense and prolonged debate in the legislature and the media. That debate seemed to re-energize activism within educator networks and among students and parents. The school board's take-up of race-focused equity policy in the years leading up to this period also provided room to broaden the diversity agenda.[5]

In 1987 the Toronto public school board began allowing gay and lesbian speakers in school programs, though only after prolonged debate, and with its 'non-proselytizing' policy still in place. A year later, it established a program in human sexuality – a staff training and student counselling initiative – in the face of opposition from religious conservatives. These cautious steps were the first significant openings to change in any of Canada's major school boards.

Across the country, the inclusion of sexual orientation in provincial and territorial rights codes in the second half of the 1980s and the early 1990s extended formal protections to teachers, and potentially to students. By this time, some general anti-discrimination and harassment measures adopted by school boards included sexual orientation, but were accompanied by little or no discernable action. With rare exceptions, school officials ignored the subject, and teacher unions were generally not proactive in taking advantage of what openings there were, even if several unions in other sectors were. Informal networks of lesbian and gay teachers were forming, but with little visibility.

**1990–9: Spreading Activism, Backlash, Isolated School Response**

The 1990s saw continued incremental change in Toronto's public school system, and at decade's end encouraging signs of change in a few other boards across the country. In the late 1990s teachers in British Columbia developed a highly visible campaign to confront homophobia and heterosexism in schools. Yet there was still no cross-country take-off in activism among educators, nor was there an equivalent to the growing wave of student groups that was emerging in the United States. Provincial and territorial education ministries showed no signs of seizing the issues being raised by activists.

*Toronto's Public School Board*

In 1990 Toronto's public school board debated an equity policy that included a provision for an instructional unit on sexual diversity in senior high school health education.[6] This proposal grew out of pressure applied in earlier years to recognize sexual diversity in the student population and to the consequent 1987 creation of the human sexuality counselling program. Once again, religious conservatives mobilized against what they saw as the promotion of homosexuality, but pressure from progressive schooling networks and community supporters helped secure approval in principle.

One year later, local elections increased the number of progressives on the board, including an openly gay trustee, John Campey. Soon after, the board approved the creation of a new equity office responsible for curricular development related to the full range of diversity issues, including sexual orientation. In 1992 Campey pressed forward with motions to the board securing the staffing for the Human Sexuality Program, removing the prohibition on proselytizing homosexuality, adding sexual orientation to the board's harassment and anti-discrimination policies, and approving the fleshed-out curricular plan on sexual orientation. Religious-right opposition was mobilized once again, but the whole package of motions carried.

Just as importantly, a student-led group, TEACH (Teens Educating Against and Confronting Homophobia), was formed in 1993, supported by the board's Equity Studies Centre (later in the decade by Planned Parenthood and Toronto's East End Community Health Centre). TEACH's young volunteers made themselves available to schools as guest speakers or workshop leaders, and by the end of the 1990s they were leading about 150 such interventions a year.

In the fall of 1995, the board launched the Triangle Program, a form of alternative school modelled on the Harvey Milk School in New York, but different in that it was a fully academic program operated by the board. It provided up to twenty students at a time with a gay-positive curriculum and a counselling support system beyond what would be available in other schools.

These developments were just at the time that a new Conservative government of Ontario was threatening to cut school spending and return to basics. It was also forcing an urban amalgamation that would by decade's end combine the relatively progressive Toronto School Board with more traditional boards in neighbouring municipalities. In 1997, the year that measure was passed, the Toronto board approved its most expansive equity statement yet, aiming to set a new benchmark for the amalgamated board.

The first signals from the expanded board were not encouraging. In late 1998 and early 1999, a new equity policy draft covered only race issues. Only after pressure from both inside and outside the board was it broadened to include the full range of equity issues, sexual orientation among them. It covered each area comprehensively, addressing harassment, teacher training, support for student programs challenging homophobia, even curricular inclusiveness. This was the most expansive board policy yet developed in Canada, and it aimed at change in both elementary and secondary schools.

This policy provoked an intense debate within the school system and the local press, and encountered particularly virulent opposition from the very conservative Toronto District Muslim Educational Assembly and other right-wing religious groups. Late that year, however, the new policy was approved (with 'implementation' documentation approved the next year). By this time, there were signs of favourable change elsewhere in Canada, and particularly on the West Coast.

*Gay and Lesbian Educators in British Columbia and the
BC Teachers Federation*

In British Columbia, Gay and Lesbian Educators (GALE-BC) had been working to address homophobic school climates from the beginning of the decade, but in small numbers and with little impact until the late 1990s.[7] In the fall of 1996, a GALE delegation met the New Democratic government's education minister, Paul Ramsey, to press his department to take action. One of the teachers was James Chamberlain, an elementary school teacher in Surrey, a suburb south of Vancouver, where the school board was dominated by Christian conservatives. Soon after the meeting, the director of the ministry's curriculum branch sent a letter to the Surrey Teachers Association indicating that a variety of families, including those with same-sex parents, should be included in discussions of family units in elementary classes.[8]

Early in 1997 Chamberlain asked his board if he could use three children's books for his kindergarten class: *Asha's Mums, Belinda's Bouquet,* and *One Dad, Two Dads, Brown Dads, Blue Dads.* He heard nothing for three months. In February, fellow GALE activist and teacher Murray Warren (with the backing of his local teachers association) proposed to no avail that the Coquitlam School Board establish a committee to study the challenges facing lesbian and gay students.

Both teachers, and the other members of GALE, also worked inside the province's teacher union. This bore fruit in March 1997, when the

BC Teachers Federation (BCTF) annual convention approved (with 96 per cent support) a resolution to create a program to eliminate homophobia and heterosexism in the BC public school system. The convention was picketed by conservatives brandishing signs that read 'No Homo Promo' and 'Stop Homosexual Recruitment in Schools.'[9] BCTF's offices were besieged by up to two thousand phone calls a day.

Right-wing opponents, dominated by the Christian right and spearheaded by a group calling itself the Citizen's'Research Institute (CRI), were soon organizing across the province. Ten thousand copies of a 'Declaration of Family Rights' were distributed to encourage parents to pressure schools and school boards to reject any teaching or teaching materials that 'discusses or portrays the lifestyle of gays, lesbians, bisexuals and/or transgendered individuals as one which is normal, acceptable, or must be tolerated.' Public forums, featuring CRI leader Kari Simpson, were announced in a number of communities, among them Surrey, where debate had already been heating up over 'exposing' youngsters to homosexuality.[10]

Six of the Surrey board's seven trustees were linked to the Christian right, and the board chair was a director of CRI, as well as an activist in the anti-abortion group Operation Rescue.[11] On 10 April, in a meeting attended by two hundred people, the board approved a resolution informing school staff that gay-positive resources prepared by GALE and distributed widely to the province's teachers had not been approved for distribution or use.[12] A few days after that, on 24 April, at a school board meeting packed with delegations and spectators, the board voted to ban the three books that James Chamberlain had asked about earlier in the year.[13]

BC premier Glen Clark condemned the action, and Education Minister Ramsey looked into whether the Surrey trustees had violated provincial curricular regulations. On 3 May, Ramsey, who was in his home constituency of Prince George, a small city deep in the province's interior, joined a rally in protest against homophobia in schools outside a public forum featuring the CRI's Kari Simpson.[14]

It was in this context, with the religious right as fully mobilized as it had ever been in BC, that the government introduced two new legislative bills aimed at recognizing same-sex relationships in family law. For anti-gay activists, this was another threat to the family, and in the late summer 'recall' campaigns were organized against NDP MLAs, Paul Ramsey being the prime target.[15] Rallies organized by the CRI that fall attracted hundreds of supporters.

The campaigns ultimately failed to obtain enough signatures, but they were effective enough to have scared the NDP government and education ministry officials. For example, a resource centre created as part of a 1997 Safe Schools initiative by the provincial government contained no materials on homophobia and heterosexism, at a time when the risks facing sexual minority students were widely known. In addition, rather than add gay-positive resources to a provincially approved reading list, which is what GALE had been demanding, the ministry eliminated the list altogether to leave such choices entirely in the hands of local boards.

The 1998 annual convention of the BCTF entrusted to GALE the development of a program to eliminate homophobia and heterosexism in schools. Workshops for teachers were developed by the summer, and before long several were mounted across the province. One held in Surrey was particularly well attended by teachers.[16] These were encouraging grassroots developments, but there was still nothing in the provincially mandated curriculum that obliged or even induced schools, or boards, to take advantage of the resources now made available to them.

A large 1999 adolescent health survey across the province showed what had been found elsewhere, namely, that there was pervasive anti-gay harassment in schools, and widespread alienation among sexual minority youth.[17] In response, no one even pretended that any board in the province had made much progress in confronting the problem.

### Developments Elsewhere

There were signs of activism in a few other Canadian centres, often first provoked by concerns over harassment and bullying. In 1993, Winnipeg school officials found widespread anti-gay sentiment in a student survey, and proposed action to confront it. When the possibility of board action became publicized, though, enough opposition was mobilized that trustees took no action.

Calgary's public school board added sexual orientation to its harassment policy in 1994, after the publication of evidence on the risk to sexual minority youth in the city. (The Roman Catholic board also began discussing policies to ensure respect for gay and lesbian students.) Proposals for further action by the public board, however, were met by a wave of opposition, and resources required for effective implementation of new policy were dissipated.

In Ontario, the provincial Ministry of Education and Training approved a 'violence-free schools policy' that included sexual orientation in 1994 (when the NDP was still in power). It was a tough policy on the face of it, obliging boards to take responsibility for ensuring that abuse and discrimination were treated as unacceptable, and urging a curriculum that reflected social diversity. But little came of it, especially with a new Conservative government in power in 1995.

In Quebec, provincial curricular materials on homosexuality – reasonably well thought out ones – had been prepared in the early 1990s. The regional health and social services coordinating agency in Montreal also provided training for teachers and school officials who wished to address issues related to homosexuality. But all this was optional, and through the 1990s only rarely taken up in any school system, especially in Catholic boards.

When Quebec's Human Rights Commission held hearings on sexual orientation in 1993, provoked by violence directed at homosexuals in Montreal, the issue of schooling was largely absent. Officials told gay/lesbian activists that they were open to discussion of a wide range of sexual orientation issues, but not education.[18] They were afraid that such talk would mobilize conservatives and disrupt the commission's clear intent to provide at least some response to issues of discrimination in the community at large. In the end the commission report did suggest that schools had some responsibility to treat the issue of sexual orientation, but no response or action came from the Ministry of Education. (Some provincial social and health agencies did develop and support programming for sexual minority youth in the years to follow.)

Activist attention to schooling was growing at mid-decade. In Montreal, the Groupe de Recherche et d'Intervention Sociale gaies et lesbiennes de Montréal (GRIS) was formed in 1994 by educators, community members, parents, and students. The group was focused on opening up opportunities to speak about sexual diversity in schools, and providing trained speakers to do just that. The youth help-line Gai Écoute was also aiming to publicize its service to schools, and in 1996 it sent letters to every French high school in Quebec, asking them to list the group's telephone number in school diaries issued routinely to students. But school response was tepid. Only 5 per cent of Catholic schools in the province responded positively to Gai Écoute's request.

Across Canada, only a few teacher unions had placed sexual diversity issues on the front burner. The Elementary Teachers Federation of Ontario was active, building on the women's public teacher union that was one of its predecessors. The Saskatchewan Teachers Federation was starting to take action at decade's end, as did the Alberta Teachers Association, which approved (by overwhelming majority) a code of professional conduct that required teachers to instruct in a manner that respected sexual diversity. And of course the BCTF continued to be a leading advocate for change.

## 1999 and After: Slowly Widening Local Engagement

Activism in a few large-city school boards across Canada started bearing fruit at the end of the 1990s and the first years of the new decade, in Winnipeg, Vancouver, Victoria, and Montreal. A few other boards, for example in southern Ontario, were also taking up issues of sexual diversity. The inclusion of sexual orientation in school board non-discrimination and harassment policies was now routine across Canada. The spread of these initiatives, though, had none of the character of the policy take-off that we saw on relational and parenting issues.

### Provincial Lethargy until the Mid-2000s

School violence was in the headlines during 1999, the year of carnage at Columbine High School in Littleton, Colorado. Soon afterwards, a shooting occurred at a high school in Tabor, Alberta, increasing pressure on educational authorities to treat bullying and violence seriously. In the United States, as will be evident in chapter 9, such calamities provided an opening for educators, students, and parents who had long pointed out how much school violence and harassment had homophobic elements. Such events had some impact in Canada, too, but only modest.[19]

The Ontario legislature approved a Safe Schools Act in 2001, dramatically increasing penalties for bullying and violence. It was not tailored specifically to any one form of harassment, and its strategic focus on punishment came under attack for being used to target visible minority students. All this ensured that there was no focused debate on the specifics of homophobic violence, and little in the way of effective and widespread change in practice.

The pattern of provincial inaction prevailed in Quebec until the middle of the 2000s. Homophobic bullying became a front-burner issue early that decade in Montreal's French-language school board, and among unions representing the province's teachers, but the provincial education ministry remained unmoved by the mounting evidence that the province's schools were just as rife with prejudicial climates as schools in the rest of the country.[20]

British Columbia seemed it might be an exception. GALE activists had been pressuring provincial authorities for years on a variety of gay-related school issues. And then in 2000 a dramatic story unfolded. In March, Hamed Nastoh filled his knapsack with rocks and jumped off the Patullo Bridge over the Fraser River in Surrey. He left a suicide note that talked of being relentlessly picked on. He was called a variety of names, some just for being too good a student, but there was one part of the bullying that was especially difficult, as he recounted in his suicide note: 'I couldn't take it anymore. School is the main reason. It was horrible! Every day I was teased and teased. Everyone calling me Gay! Fag! Queer!, and I would always act like it didn't bug me and ignored them, but I was crying inside. It hurt me so bad! Please tell the people at school why I did this. I don't want somebody else to have to do what I did.'[21]

Pressure to act also came from the provincial auditor general, who in 2000 recommended that the risks facing students because of anti-gay climates be addressed promptly and effectively.[22] In the meantime, the first legal case challenging school inattention to homophobic bullying in Canada was heading to a BC Human Rights tribunal (see box).

---

**Azmi Jubran and the North Vancouver School Board, 1996–2005**
Students at North Vancouver's Handsworth Secondary School hurled the words 'fag' and 'queer' at Azmi Jubran from Grade 8 on. Jubran was straight, but that did not prevent homophobic students from harassing him, threatening him, spitting on him, throwing bottle rockets and base-balls at him, setting his shirt on fire. Finally, Jubran took his case to the BC Human Rights Commission in 1996 (when he was in Grade 11), charging the North Vancouver school district with discrimination in their failure to respond sufficiently to anti-gay bullying. This was the first such formal case in Canada charging school officials with responsibility over bullying of any sort. A tribunal of the commission heard the case in 2000, and ruled in favour of Jubran in April 2002. This came only a week after a BC court convicted a high school student of criminal harassment for

threatening another student, who later committed suicide. The Jubran ruling rejected school official arguments that they could not be held responsible for the conduct of students, stating that schools had an obligation to provide an environment free from discrimination and harassment, and that failure to do so was discriminatory. The monetary award was only $4,000, but the message to school officials was clear. The school board appealed the ruling to the courts, winning in 2003 on the astonishing ground that because Jubran was not himself a homosexual the Human Rights Code's prohibition on anti-gay discrimination did not apply. In 2005 the BC Court of Appeal upheld Jubran's claim, ruling that the school board had to adopt a proactive and broad educative approach to such issues as harassment, homophobia, and discrimination.

A right-wing Liberal provincial government, elected in 2001, seemed ill-inclined to take up sexual diversity initiatives, but they did establish a Safe School Task Force in 2002, which then heard substantial testimony about homophobic bullying. The task force delivered a report one year later, though with no recommendations specific to anti-gay school climates. Later, in 2004, the provincial education ministry's guidelines on safety failed to specifically address harassment and violence based on sexual diversity. A year later, openly gay Liberal Lorne Meyencourt, who had chaired the task force, introduced a safe schools bill in the provincial legislature. Like most private members' bills, it died before getting approval, in part because some members of his own government were worried about constituency backlash.[23]

In 2006, the provincial education ministry agreed to the creation of an optional Grade 12 social justice course that would include attention to sexual diversity, in response to a human rights complaint against the limitations of the provincial curriculum, launched several years earlier by a Coquitlam teacher and his partner. If it is launched, it will probably be the first such course in Canada, and one that is provincially mandated, but it is hardly a breakthrough. By announcing that it would be optional, the ministry was once again planning to pass the buck to local school boards.[24]

*Teacher Caution*

In legal terms, public school teachers have been protected against discrimination based on sexual orientation for years, and by the end of the 1990s no denial of benefits to same-sex partners could withstand constitutional scrutiny. Also, by the early years of the new decade, several provincial unions were taking up sexual diversity issues, most prominently in BC, Quebec, Alberta, and Ontario. The national LGBT rights group Egale was prioritizing schools and developing a network of educators, even it its tiny staff and broad mandate allowed for the allocation of no significant resources to the network.

Still, few teachers were out enough to take advantage of the formal supports available to them. In 2000–1, a survey of the Elementary Teachers Federation of Ontario membership gave respondents an opportunity to self-identify as members of a variety of disadvantaged groups, and only 0.9 per cent flagged sexual minority status.[25] Teachers remain a cautious lot, and the great majority seem reluctant to rock the boat. Coming out, or talking freely about sexual orientation, is still considered controversial, as illustrated by a story not long ago from just north of Toronto (see box).

**Elmcrest Public School and the Peel School Board, 2000[26]**

Some of the ten-year-olds at Elmcrest Public School began gossiping after one of them saw their Grade 4 teacher accompanied by another woman at a social function. On a Friday in June shortly afterwards, they asked her about her sexual orientation. She answered truthfully that she was a lesbian. Several parents were angered that this had happened without their knowledge, and they let the school principal and the board know it. The principal sent a letter to parents, making clear that the topic had arisen because of questions from students, but also saying that 'the manner in which the discussion unfolded was not consistent with board protocol,' which stipulated that classroom discussion of 'sensitive issues' must be preceded by notice to the school principal and parents, and that parents had a right to ask that their children not be present. A spokesperson for the school board later described the teacher's action as an error in judgment, and one of the trustees argued that there was 'no educational value' in what she did.

This story could easily be repeated in school boards across Canada, many of which impose strict guidelines on discussion of 'sensitive issues,' with human sexuality regularly cited as an example.[27]

Across Canada, there has been little teacher education on sexual diversity issues. Pioneering work was undertaken in the late 1990s at the University of Saskatchewan, and the University of Alberta's Faculty of Education has developed some prominence in teaching and research related to sexuality. The Ontario Institute for Studies in Education has several faculty interested in questions of sexual diversity, and early in the 2000s it created an in-service course on homophobia for teachers. As course instructor Tara Goldstein has pointed out, though, teachers are still worried about including the work on such a course in their teaching portfolios.[28]

*Students Claiming Visibility*

Pressure for change from students themselves has increased noticeably in the last few years. There are also, of course, more students than ever who are out at school, especially in urban areas. This obviously makes it hard to keep the issues that relate to them completely invisible. An important part of the story of American student activism has been the formation of Gay-Straight Alliances, and while the spread of such groups in several major urban centres in Canada has lagged behind the major U.S. surge in the late 1990s and early 2000s, the numbers are now becoming significant. In 2000 the BC Teachers Federation approved a resolution supporting the formation of GSA's in the province's high schools and middle schools. GALE also produced guidelines and modest bursaries to stimulate their spread, so it is not surprising that BC saw the first significant cluster of such groups. By late 2004 about half of Vancouver's public high schools had them, and in total there were about thirty across the province.

In Alberta, the first GSA to form (in 2000) was in Red Deer, the centre of religious conservatism in an already relatively conservative province. Local schools had already confronted questions about racial prejudice, since the community was home to James Keegstra, one of Canada's most notorious purveyors of prejudice against religious and racial minorities. That seemed to arm schools with a willingness to take on other diversity issues. In 2004, interest in the formation of such groups spread rapidly in Edmonton, and by year's end there were five in that city (one in a Catholic school). There was evidence of similar expansion in Toronto's public schools and in some of the surrounding suburban areas.

In 2006 the Canadian Teachers' Federation issued a handbook on the development of GSAs, which may have helped spread the idea beyond the areas in which they are now prominent. By mid-decade, the 'Day of Silence,' an idea first developed by the U.S. Gay, Lesbian and Straight Education Network in 1996 to dramatize the silencing of sexual minorities in schools, and much facilitated by GSAs, was starting to spread in Canada.

In a growing number of schools across Canada, students were also claiming the right for same-sex partners to attend school social functions, and proms in particular. Many have secured that right without publicity, and with little opposition, so it is difficult to know how widespread this challenge to such bastions of heterosexism have been. One Ontario student's prom plans, though, did gain notoriety (see box).

**Marc Hall and Monsignor John Pereyma Catholic Secondary School** [29]
In early 2002, Oshawa's Marc Hall had never been to a Pride march, and he didn't see himself as a gay activist. He just wanted to take his boyfriend to the senior prom. But the principal told him that allowing a same-sex couple to attend would contradict school policy and Roman Catholic teaching. This was unsurprising in some ways. The leadership of the Roman Catholic archdiocese supported the Vatican's conservative line on homosexuality, and the Oshawa community was relatively traditional, with only modest gay visibility. On the other hand, a few other Catholic school boards in southern Ontario had allowed lesbians and gays to bring their dates.

Hall soon found backing from a variety of local groups, including PFLAG. He was also supported by the Canadian Auto Workers – one of the country's largest unions and a major force in this car-manufacturing city. In March, the CAW's nationally prominent president, Buzz Hargrove, wrote to the school principal, urging the acceptance of sexual diversity in the community and the student body: 'Today we spend a great deal of time in our educational programs working to dispel myths and stereotypes about gays and lesbians, and challenging our members to understand these issues as fundamental rights and freedoms. We call upon you as an educator to do the same.'

Hall's cause was supported by the leader of the generally cautious provincial Liberal Party. Dalton McGuinty was himself a practising Catholic, and he headed a party that in the past was not reliably supportive of gay rights. But this time, his public appeal to the Durham Catholic School Board was unequivocal: 'By refusing to allow him to attend the prom with his companion, Marc Hall is being denied some of the most basic rights as a human being and as a Canadian. I cannot understand how the decision to invite his boyfriend to his high school prom poses a threat to Catholic education.'

But the board was unmoved, voting unanimously against changing their prom policy. Hall took the case to court in May, supported by a coalition of groups that included Egale. On 10 May, just hours before the prom, Justice Robert MacKinnon ruled in Hall's favour, clearing the way for Hall and his partner to attend.

*Policy Change at the School Board Level*

Bullying was often the wedge issue that students and other proponents of change could most effectively use to apply pressure on school boards. The power of stories of harassment, and sometimes violence, coupled with growing social science evidence on the prevalence of anti-gay behaviour, was not lost on advocates for change at the local level.

In Winnipeg, for example, the issue of anti-gay school climate had been first raised in 1993, though it would take another six years before concerted action was taken in the city's largest board (District Number One). A committee was created in April 1999 to look at gay bashing in high schools, a move recommended by lesbian trustee Kristine Barr, and supported by an openly gay city mayor, Glen Murray. At meetings on the subject in the same month, many students and parents spoke in support of the committee's mandate.

At the same time, anti-gay positions were staked out by many of the sixty delegations who appeared to speak before the board. The group Parents Against Heterophobia warned of the dangers of children becoming confused if they were to hear talk of homosexuality as an accepted lifestyle. One spokesman dismissed claims about homophobia in schools: 'It's a bunch of malarkey. Sure kids in the hallway call each other fag or zitface or spaz. There's always kids that have to tease one another. [But homosexuals] are so afraid of heterosexualism, and they are so desperate to have their lifestyle accepted by society, that they fabricated this whole thing.'[30] Two conservative radio show hosts then picked up the issue, and accused Barr of attempting to recruit children.

The board reacted by moving ahead cautiously, restricting the committee's mandate to high schools, but the policy deliberation process gained momentum. Once the storm of opposition had passed the board put into place the most concerted awareness program of any school system in the country. Workshops were planned for the 2000–1 school year and made compulsory for all high school staff across the system.

In Ontario, a few school boards in the areas surrounding the metropolitan region of Toronto were beginning to address the issue. Beyond that, an initiative was being spawned in the relatively conservative southwestern Ontario city of London (see box).

**Thames Valley District School Board**

In 1992 a working group on heterosexism and homophobia in schools has been spun out from the long-standing Homophile Association of London Ontario (HALO), and for some time thereafter it pressed the local school board to address gay issues, to no avail. Pressure was remobilized in 2002, in part as a result of a student being beaten outside a dance at South Secondary School – an attack widely seen as homophobic. The now-expanded Thames Valley District School Board faced calls from students (many from the Seen & Heard Anti-Violence Education Project at the University of Western Ontario's Faculty of Education) to address the harassment and discrimination faced by sexual minority youth. A committee headed by trustee Peggy Sattler was soon convened to address sexual diversity issues, and it reported back with a broad range of inclusive recommendations. The board remained cautious, accepting only four of seventeen recommendations in the spring of 2003. A year later, though, it approved most of the remaining ones even in the face of concerted opposition from groups of parents and religious conservatives. In 2005, a London community group launched a fund raising campaign to allow it to get books promoting acceptance of sexual difference in every area school.[31]

Elsewhere in Ontario, two cases of homophobic bullying were challenging school inattention to the issue. In 2002 high school student David Knight and his sister launched a legal suit after years of bullying directed at him and his sister in elementary and secondary school. His sister Katie had been harassed to the point of leaving school. In northwestern Ontario, the Ontario Human Rights Commission mediated a settlement in 2005 between the Lakehead District School Board and Gabriel Picard, with the board committing itself to the development and application of policies addressing sexual diversity. (Neither of these challenges produced the kind of large settlements that shocked many school authorities in the United States.)

*Local Developments in BC*

Even in the face of an unresponsive provincial government, schools issues retained a high profile in BC, and activist networks remained active. James Chamberlain launched a court challenge, with the support of GALE, the BC Teachers Federation, and the BC Liberties Association, to the Surrey School Board 1997 ban on gay-themed books. In 2002, a 7–2 majority of the Supreme Court of Canada rejected the board's argument that these books were unsuitable for five- and six-year-olds, reasoning that children could not learn tolerance 'unless they are exposed to views that differ from those they are taught at home,' and that such teaching was always age-appropriate.[32] The court also cited the BC School Act in asserting that boards could not apply the religious views of one part of a community 'to exclude from consideration the values of other members of the community.' Writing for the majority, Chief Justice Beverley McLachlin of the Supreme Court of Canada then said, 'The requirement of secularism in s. 76 of the School Act, the emphasis on tolerance in the Preamble, and the insistence of the curriculum on increasing awareness of a broad array of family types, all show, in my view, that parental concerns must be accommodated in a way that respects diversity. Parental views, however important, cannot override the imperative placed upon the British Columbia public schools to mirror the diversity of the community and teach tolerance and understanding of difference.[33]

The Supreme Court's *Surrey* ruling could be cited across Canada in response to right-wing resistance to curricular change, even if it would not oblige any board to be more inclusive in its curriculum. Another gay-related ruling by the Supreme Court just a year earlier, also arising from BC, was also likely to provide leverage for advocates of greater recognition of diversity. The *Trinity Western* case might have seemed a defeat for equity advocates, but its argumentation affirmed the importance of schools creating an inclusive environment (see box).

**Trinity Western University and the British Columbia College of Teachers**

Trinity Western is a privately funded university – that itself is unusual in Canada. It describes itself as Christian and adheres to conservative Protestant biblical tenets. Students are obliged to sign a 'community-standards waiver' that forbids a number of condemned behaviours, including premarital sex and homosexual activity. TWU launched a teaching degree program in 1985, but its graduates had to complete a fifth year practicum at Simon Fraser University, in the Vancouver area. In 1995 Trinity Western sought approval for its own full five-year program, but the BC College of Teachers refused to lift the Simon Fraser component, arguing that its absence would allow the imposition of discriminatory teacher views on public school students. TWU challenged the decision in court, supported by the Evangelical Fellowship of Canada, the Canadian Conference of Catholic Bishops, and the Canadian Civil Liberties Association.

TWU won its day in court in 1997, and again at appeal. In May 2001 the Supreme Court of Canada confirmed the earlier rulings, arguing that the College of Teachers had never presented evidence that training at that institution fostered discriminatory behaviour in public schools. But in doing so, the court asserted that schools were obliged to create environments free of bias and prejudice. In fact, one of TWU's chief administrators had already asserted in the university's defence that there was no evidence of any of their graduates having mistreated gay students in their care. He was effectively siding with the court in agreeing that school authorities could insist on non-discriminatory behaviour in the classrooms, regardless of the religious beliefs of the teacher.

In Vancouver, the 2002 local elections had produced reformist majorities in the city council and the public school board, for the first time in years. Not surprisingly, given the string of controversies over recent years, progressive school board candidates had raised the issue of school safety, and specified the importance of inclusiveness for sexual minority students and staff. Early in the following year, school trustees approved the creation of a Lesbian, Gay, Transgendered and Bisexual Issues Advisory Committee (later renamed the Pride Education Advisory Committee) with a very broad mandate to suggest changes to address sexual diversity. The committee had close working relationships with such groups as GALE, PFLAG, and Gay Youth Services, and so had lots of support in thinking expansively about what needed changing. In early 2004, the board approved a wide-ranging policy extending far beyond homophobic harassment, including curricular reform.

In 2003, the Greater Victoria School Board adopted recommendations aimed at fostering respect and safety for sexual minority students, including the transgendered, after being pressured hard by students in area schools. The code of conduct developed for schools included a prohibition of discrimination based on sexual orientation, gender identity, and gender expression, and educators were to take proactive steps to counter homophobic harassment. Support services were to be established; students groups taking up these issues were to be supported; and curricular resources were to reflect diversity. Elsewhere in BC, in Prince George, a site of so much controversy a few years earlier, the public school board approved recommendations on raising awareness of sexual diversity in 2004. The Gulf Islands and the North Vancouver school districts enacted anti-homophobic policies in 2006.

## Quebec's Distinct Pattern

In Quebec significant uptake of sexual diversity issues in schools began only in 2002, but then spread quickly. During the 1990s, the Catholic school system had resisted any public acknowledgment of these issues. Secularization was more powerful in Quebec than anywhere else in Canada; however, the province's largest school board, the Conseil des écoles catholiques de Montréal, had been dominated by relatively conservative voices. (All publicly funded schools in the province were still formally Catholic or Protestant.) The rapid decline in the proportion of Montrealers with school-aged children, coupled with a pattern of lopsided municipal elections, contributed to electoral turnouts of as low as 20 per cent, creating opportunities for more highly motivated conservative Catholics to retain control over schooling. The city's Protestant school board had long had relatively secular leadership, though it too had never developed proactive policies on sexual diversity.

In 1998 the province's schools were reorganized on linguistic rather than denominational lines, resulting in a new French-language and secular Commission scolaire de Montréal. The new board had a progressive majority that included openly gay councillor Paul Trottier, though it would still take time to overcome fears associated with discussing sexuality in schools. Increased community activism and heightened attention to high rates of suicide among Quebec's gay and lesbian youth helped push the board towards more inclusive policy.[34] By 2002 sexual orientation and transsexualism were added to its harassment policy, and a resolution on initiatives to support sexual minority students was approved with virtually no vocal dissent.

There was no doubt that schools in the board's jurisdiction needed change. A 2002 study of teachers and administrators, commissioned by the board, showed widespread awareness of school-based homophobia, with three-quarters of respondents agreeing that they knew little about homosexuality and were in need of more information.[35] Another study showed, not surprisingly, that few teachers were out.[36] Faculties of education were giving virtually no attention to sexual diversity in the professional training they offered. Research published in 2003 and 2005 portrayed the province's schools as dramatically unfriendly to sexual minorities, using language indistinguishable from that used in studies of schools across most of North America over the previous decade.[37] A report issued by Quebec's Human Rights Commission in 2007 found little evidence of systematic school uptake of what resources were available to combat homophobia in schools in Montreal, let alone in other regions of the province.[38]

Quebec's unions representing teachers were now taking up the issue of homophobia. In late 2002 the Centrale des Syndicats du Québec (one of two unions to which Quebec's teachers belonged) launched a video entitled *Silence SVP* (Silence Please) on homophobia in school environments that was destined for students and educators across the province. In the meantime, student groups had been forming in several of the province's regions, joining together to form the Regroupement de jeunes allosexuelles de Québec (Queer Youth Coalition of Quebec). The Lesbian Mothers' Association, an influential force, was also engaging issues related to elementary schooling.

In Montreal, the Groupe de Recherche et d'Intervention Sociale gaies et lesbiennes de Montréal (Gay and Lesbian Research and Information Group, GRIS) was better resourced, and finding expanded opportunities to speak about sexual diversity in schools. It had two hundred volunteers by the mid-2000s, and a staff of three (largely through funding from the provincial ministries of health and justice). It was now visiting a few hundred schools a year, up from about thirty in the late 1990s, widely distributing resource guides for teachers, and recruiting well-known media personalities to publicize its work.[39]

Still, as recently as 2004, 40 per cent of Montreal's French-language schools, and 60 per cent province-wide, were still unwilling to list Gai Écoute's contact number in student diaries, and the group felt obliged to offer assurances in its materials that it was not trying to recruit students. At this late date, too, the provincial ministry of education appeared largely inactive. A day-long information workshop organized in 2002 by the Human Rights Commission on youth and homosexuality in schools, and attended by school officials, teachers, and agency representatives from across the province, was not attended by officials from the ministry. As one youth agency worker commented in 2004, 'At the Commission scolaire de Montréal, things are really changing; and on the ground in some schools, things are really changing. But when we go to the ministry of education, it's like a desert – nobody talks, nobody moves.'[40]

Since then, there are signs of significant movement, at last.[41] The provincial ministry has begun showing real interest in school homophobia. A 2007 Human Rights Commission report on homophobia in all sectors of society called for all schools (including religious ones) to engage in campaigns to combat homophobia, training for all school personnel on issues related to sexual diversity, and more inclusive curricula in faculties of education. What may result is a pattern reminiscent of policy change in the recognition of same-sex relationships – not particularly ahead of the curve by Canadian standards, but wide-ranging once it comes.

*Policy Development and Implementation Gaps in the Toronto District School Board*

Toronto District School Board's policy legacy provides an opportunity to explore questions of implementation. Recall that the year 2000 saw the passage of an equity implementation plan by the school board that had been first in the country to develop a comprehensive approach to sexual diversity, including gender identity. This plan – obligatory from kindergarten to grade twelve – stated that 'ideals related to anti-homophobia and sexual orientation equity be reflected in all aspects of organizational structures, policies, guidelines, procedures, classroom practices, day-to-day operations, and communication practices.' It specified that the curriculum should reflect these and other forms of diversity, and that all learning materials should be checked for bias.

Implementation was another matter. Radical cuts to provincial spending on schools during the second half of the 1990s and the early 2000s, and a prioritization of basic skills, effectively moved equity issues farther away from the core mission of schools. There were drastic cuts to the Toronto Board's Equity Department in 2003, and a reduction in counselling support provided to the Triangle Program. The absence of administrative support for diversity programming was destined to leave teachers relatively unpressured and unprepared to change. No doubt many of them were already using gay-positive resources in their classrooms, but most were not, either because they were personally uncomfortable with the issues, fearful of taking any steps beyond the provincial curriculum, or uneasy about parental reaction. Most teachers seem only dimly aware of their board's equity policies, and many of those who are more aware seem disinclined to act assertively on them.[42]

Attempts to teach inclusively were also still encountering vocal opposition from religious conservatives. The Campaign Life Coalition warned of the prospect of graphic sex education becoming ubiquitous in Canadian elementary schools, its president predicting that children would be provided with depictions of anal sex and other homosexual practices as appropriate alternatives.[43] In some parts of Toronto, conservative Muslims were among the most vocal of critics (see box).

---

**Market Lane Public School, 2004**

In 2004 a large group of parents, most of them Muslim, protested a workshop on sexual diversity held for staff and some students at their children's school.[44] A few parents talked about the school corrupting their children and insufficiently accommodating their faith. They were supported by the Toronto District Muslim Educational Assembly, which had intervened forcibly a few years earlier in opposition to the inclusion of sexual orientation and gender identity in the school board's equity policy. Its print materials accused the school board of indoctrination and the promotion of a homosexual lifestyle, and provided parents with forms requesting that their children be withdrawn from all discussions of moral corruption that were offensive to their faith.

The principal of Market Lane Public School convened a special information session for parents in November, though from the outset he made clear that board policy mandated the kind of workshop he had approved. At the meeting, school officials set out the board's equity policies, making clear that the recognition of religious differences could not extend to the infringement of other people's rights. After the formal presentations, various audience members raised objections to the workshop, more than one suggesting that it trampled on their religious rights. But a couple of the intervenors who identified as Muslim made clear that they were struggling with the issue and were open to the board's policy. One cited rulings of the Supreme Court of Canada that recognized lesbian and gay rights as human rights. Another talked of the need to live together, and to work on what he acknowledged was a sensitive issue for all religions. The meeting ended calmly, as it had begun.

Soon after, provincial premier Dalton McGuinty addressed Muslim parents concerned about their children being exposed to school discussions of homosexuality, arguing that teaching students to respect differences was important. Education Minister Gerard Kennedy spoke in similar terms when he said he did not think there was harm in exposing children 'to ideas that are different than the ones they teach at home,' perhaps coincidentally echoing the language of the Supreme Court of Canada in the Surrey School Board case.[45]

In some ways the Market Lane school story affirms the possibility of change even in a community of largely first-generation immigrants, from parts of the world where no recognition is accorded to sexual diversity. On the other hand, it demonstrates that taking up these issues requires clear-headed determination from school leaders on the ground. There is no doubt that few principals would have welcomed workshops on sexual diversity, or other forms of teaching about it, even in a board that technically obliged them to act inclusively.

Tim McCaskell, long a member of the equity staff at the Toronto School Board, has come to discouraging conclusions about the absence of effective means to implement the policies that are in place.[46] He tracks the gradual whittling away of resources devoted to equity initiatives of all sorts, hastened by provincial cuts to educational spending, just as formal board policies were developed for the full range of equity issues. Financial crises sharpened the focus on what was said to be the curricular core, and longer-term political shifts were highlighting the practical utility of public education. Faced with a new and more demanding provincial curriculum, few teachers and principals were rushing to fully incorporate equity principles into everything they taught.

The Toronto experience is a vivid illustration of an implementation gap that is inevitable in the translation of schools policy into practice. Try as they might, education departments and school boards cannot monitor everything that goes on in classrooms, and they would not even aspire to do so. Teachers and principals are professionals, and even if they are generally a cautious lot they are expected to exercise discretion every hour of the day. They are also expected to do far more than they are realistically able to, in the face of students with highly disparate learning skills. Schools are expected to respond to students with an extraordinary range of social and cultural circumstances. When a set of issues associated with sexuality gets added to the mandate of schools and teachers, even well-meaning educators will fail to respond proactively enough, or respond at all.

Implementation gaps work both ways, though, and we know that many teachers and principals have taken up the challenges of sexual diversity without the pressure or guidance of board policy. This would undoubtedly have been true before Toronto's school board developed inclusive policy. It is also true of many teachers in the Roman Catholic school system in Toronto, and undoubtedly of some school principals. These are not publicized, for school officials have a delicate path to follow between church doctrine and what they often know to be the needs of their students. But anecdotal evidence in Toronto and elsewhere indicates substantially more positive recognition of sexual diversity in Catholic schools than would be predicted by the stance taken on questions of sexual difference by the Vatican and the Canadian hierarchy.[47]

## Explaining Lethargy

In Canadian schools, talking about sexual diversity in positive terms is still widely avoided. Until 2000 there was only sporadic talk of challenging homophobic school climates, and outside Toronto there was almost no policy development on the subject at either the local or the provincial level. Curricular change was almost entirely absent, even in that school system where most change in formal policy had occurred.

The slow start to the development of inclusive school policy, and the equally slow spread of practices that recognize sexual diversity in Canadian schools, are out of synch with developments on same-sex relationships and parenting. Why this should be so, especially in the face of overwhelming evidence that action is urgently needed, and in a political system with clear constitutional prohibitions on discrimination, is not altogether clear.

One institutional reason is that the substantial provincial leverage over schooling reduces the room for local innovation.[48] Canadian provincial and territorial governments tend to develop more detailed curricular guidelines than state authorities do in the United States, and across most of the country this regulatory detail is increasing.

School boards are also larger than they were, and more uniformly large than in the United States. This can act as a constraint on educational ideas coming from particularly progressive urban areas. This does, to be sure, reduce inequities between schools and districts, allows for economies of scale that are unavailable to very small boards, and in theory allows for a wider spread of inclusive policies once adopted. But it makes change more difficult to effect, and discourages many who might otherwise try.

Where questions of diversity have assumed high priorities in urban Canada, the very rapid growth in numbers of visible minority students has also given pride of place to race in recent years. This will sometimes push sexuality issues to the side, and may sustain nervousness about the controversy that might arise if such issues are raised. Such fear will often rest on unproven stereotypes of social conservatism among immigrant populations, though it is also reinforced by the opposition to public recognition of sexual difference by vocal representatives of visible minorities in such centres as Toronto and Vancouver.

Teachers, as we have seen, are generally cautious about pushing against boundaries. They are heavily circumscribed by curricular expectations, and by the rules and norms associated with a profession that is in the public limelight. The fact that their work brings them into close contact with young people, in a position of authority, increases the concern about being seen to step out of line. Until provincial curricular guidelines clearly direct educators to address questions of sexual diversity, and education faculties spend more time developing skills in addressing sexual diversity, most teachers will not fill in gaps.

Most activist teachers who seek change have only recently had support within their unions. And just at the time when those unions are taking up sexual diversity issues, they have also been confronted by provincial government retrenchment in a range of social policy sectors. Public schools have been under siege in several provinces, and this has often driven teachers and their unions towards a defence of what are seen to be core concerns.

Student activism has also not been as widespread in Canada as in the United States, at least not until very recently. At some level this is understandable, given the power of sexual and gender anxieties among young people. However, the same is true in the United States, and we shall find surprising levels of activism in schools there, and a preparedness to confront authorities even in very conservative areas.

One reason for modest levels of activism among educators and students is the weakness of organizational support for challenges to school complacency. The major national LGBT group, Egale Canada, has begun attending to schools issues only in the last few years. And even if it had begun earlier, it has nothing close to the scale of resources available to its American counterparts. The kind of litigation that has been an important part of the American schools story is especially hard to sustain in the absence of substantial outside support. Unions have intervened on gay-related cases, but so far only rarely on schooling.[49]

Canadian complacency might be reinforced by the relative weakness of the religious right in Canada. Conservatives do raise alarms about schools, but their arguments have less and less credibility across most of Canada. And because they are less likely than their American counterparts to resurrect the whole litany of reformist schools policies that they have fought against in the past, they arouse less activism among non-gay reform advocates. In any event, because Roman Catholics have their own school systems in much of Canada, the voices of Catholic conservatives are inactive on debates over public schooling, reducing the strength of claims by religious conservatives of other faiths.

Complacency, too, is reinforced by the extraordinary gains made in other policy realms. Most Canadians believe that the acceptance of same-sex relationships, up to and including marriage, speaks to overall policy inclusiveness, and they probably believe that schools have moved further than they have. LGBT activists without children, or whose own school experiences are far behind them, may also not be aware of how resilient past patterns are, especially in the absence of high-profile struggles over education.

## Conclusion

The Canadian story on school inclusiveness is a late starter, and it has been moving at a slow and cautious pace in most of the country. In the late 2000s, across the country, great anxiety persists among educators when the subject of sex or sexuality gets raised. Proposals to address sexual diversity routinely confront patterns of hesitation and avoidance, and policy implementation meets the same barriers. Where policies have moved in adventurous and encouraging directions, we do not yet have evidence of effective curricular change and of the kind of personal and principled commitment required among teachers, principals, and staff on the ground. Significant policy improvement has been effected in a few school districts and in a minority of schools. In many schools and classrooms students, teachers, and school principals have made real changes to the classroom and extracurricular climate with the leverage of progressive board policy and sometimes independently of policy silence. But most of the story is riddled with complacency, with educators and politicians avoiding the subject.

# 9 School Reform and the American Culture Wars

Conservative commentators regularly portray American public schools as targeted and influenced by homosexual activists. Sex education in schools, they claim, has been infused with messages that being gay is okay, and student clubs glorifying the lifestyle are proliferating. The triumph of 'secular humanism' has effectively given homosexuals access to school children. More reasoned analysis leads to a quite different conclusion: schools are still shot through with homophobic messages, and words like 'gay' are flung about as insults by students of all ages.

If the state of Canadian school inclusion is disheartening, the American picture must surely be worse. The resistance of both religious and secular conservatives to school reform has been of long standing, and the Christian right in particular has been prepared to challenge every single small move towards inclusiveness. The U.S. public school landscape has been littered with bitterly fought trustee elections and courtroom confrontations. What systematic change could possible emerge from such a pit?

One version of a short answer is 'not a lot'; the great majority of schools still sustain climates that marginalize queerness. Another version of the answer is that more change has occurred, and across a greater range of schools, than would have been predicted by the slow change on other fronts associated with sexual diversity. Some American school districts and individual schools, in fact, have been pioneers in a global sense by putting sexual diversity on the educational map and taking action to shift cultural norms and practices. The very fact that American schooling has so long been a focus of 'cultural warfare' has intensified activism among students, educators, and parents intent on challenging heterosexism and has expanded their capacity to build progressive coalitions. Sexual minority students themselves are out in greater numbers than ever, and they are coming out at younger ages – very often in their high school years. Change in American schooling, then, is slow and dramatically uneven, but there is more of it than we find in Canada.

Where schools have taken up sexual diversity issues in a positive way, homophobic bullying has often been seen as the most urgent issue, even more so than in Canada. In some cases that becomes a wedge issue for a broader array of policies promoting inclusiveness; other schools respond only to safety concerns. As in Canada, curricular change is the most challenging, and the most hotly contested.

As in relationship recognition and parenting, there is no period of political or legal take-off in responding to LGBT activism, but there is a steady increase in the inclusive visibility of issues related to sexual difference. Starting from the middle and late 1980s, not long after Anita Bryant was touring the United States mobilizing conservatives to save their children from homosexuals, we find students, educators, and parents making important gains.

## Before the Mid-1980s: Emerging Activist Challenges

As we saw in chapter 3, gay and lesbian teacher activism was first evident in the early 1970s and had spread to several major cities by decade's end.[1] During this time, activist teachers convinced the National Education Association, the California Federation of Teachers, and the San Francisco Board of Education to include sexual orientation in their non-discrimination policies. This was a time of intense mobilization by religious conservatives against what they portrayed as the homosexual threat to children, and California became a vital battleground. The 1978 statewide Briggs initiative directly threatened the jobs of gay and lesbian teachers in the state, and though ultimately unsuccessful, it was an organizing wake-up call heard across the country.

The willingness to challenge school discrimination and complacency extended to students. In 1980 Aaron Fricke was denied permission to bring another young man as his date to the Cumberland High School prom in Rhode Island, but he went to court and won the right to do so. This was one of the first significant court cases demanding school inclusiveness – one of many to follow.

## Mid- to Late 1980s: Early Innovations on Anti-Gay Harassment

The stark toll of the AIDS epidemic dramatically increased the visibility of sexual difference in the second half of the 1980s and produced a wave of activism insisting on public recognition of that difference. Heightened concern about the spread of HIV among young people, and about the potential for AIDS to intensify anti-gay sentiment, meant that schools were called upon to expand their sex education curriculum and acknowledge the risks that school environments posed to sexual minorities. In 1986, an evangelical Christian surgeon general, C. Everett Koop, added his voice to such calls. Prior to this time, as Catherine Lugg points out, the 'vast majority' of public school districts in the United States did not even have basic sex education classes.[2]

At the same time, conservatives were starting to erect barriers to change, compounding the widespread resistance to discuss sexuality in American schools. Over half of the U.S. states, plus the U.S. military, had sodomy laws on the books that treated homosexual activity itself as a criminal offence, with the U.S. Supreme Court affirming the constitutionality of such radical exclusionism in its 1986 *Bowers v. Hardwick* ruling. Whether enforced or not, such laws were a powerful tool used by conservatives to keep homosexual teachers out of the classroom, and any talk of homosexuality – other than condemnatory – out of the school.[3]

Using the powerful seat he held in the U.S. Senate, Jesse Helms began in 1987 to attach amendments to education spending bills prohibiting the 'promotion' of homosexuality. These were almost always passed with large majorities, since opposition to them could so easily be framed during election time as supporting such promotion. The force of these amendments was sometimes limited by tacking on additional language indicating that schools should not be promoting any sexual activity, or affirming that curricular control was the jurisdiction of states and school boards. Still, the preparedness of Republicans to use federal spending powers to limit school freedom could not help but send cautionary signals to school officials, and it encouraged Republicans in several states to pass similar measures.

Republicans in Washington were also prepared to support Christian right claims that they be allowed use of school facilities for religiously based and other non-curricular student groups, in the face of opponents who argued that this violated the constitutional doctrine of church-state separation. The Equal Access Act was passed in 1984, and six years later withstood constitutional challenge (*Board of Education v. Mergens*, 1990). This was one of the vehicles used by the administration of George W. Bush to increase the presence of faith-based initiatives in schools during the 2000s, though the act also had the unintended consequence of bolstering claims on behalf of student groups combatting anti-gay school climates.

During the mid- and late 1980s, anti-gay school bullying and its costs began to acquire prominence, some time before it did in Canada. In 1984, Virginia Uribe inaugurated Project 10% in Los Angeles, a program centred on confronting high dropout rates among sexual minority youth.[4] Soon afterwards, another approach to the same issue was developed in New York (see box).

**New York's Harvey Milk School[5]**
The Harvey Milk School was created in 1985 by the Hetrick-Martin Institute, an established social service agency with a six-year-long record of working on sexual minority youth issues. It began operation in a dilapidated space donated by a Greenwich Village church, with six female and thirteen male students – mostly Latina/o and Black. After sustained pressure from the agency's staff, the Board of Education provided accreditation and a teacher, as it had done for other social service agencies with at least twenty-two clients not otherwise attending school.[6]

In early 1989, a report on youth suicide commissioned by the U.S. Department of Health and Human Services included a surprisingly comprehensive look at the particular dangers facing lesbian and gay youth.[7] Radical for its time, and this under a Republican administration, it called on schools to

- establish and enforce policy that prohibited harassment based on sexual orientation;
- institute support groups for gay/lesbian/bisexual students;
- establish access to supportive adults through specialized counselling, and by identifying openly lesbian/gay teachers and counsellors;
- include sexual orientation in the curriculum, preferable across a number of subjects and at all grade levels;

- institute changes in school environment to promote acceptance of lesbian and gay youth.

Though suppressed until 1993, some copies of this report were available, strengthening the voice of educators, parents, and students who already knew that anti-gay bullying was ubiquitous in schools, and broadening alertness to sexual diversity among those who were concerned with other dimensions of student harassment.[8]

## 1990–5: Steady Spread of Activism and Policy

Schools activism, particularly by teachers, had been slowly expanding in the late 1980s. Formalized gay and lesbian caucuses were established in the NEA and the AFT in 1987 and 1988, the latter with a membership that soon exceeded two hundred. Nineteen ninety-one saw the birth of the educator activist group that came to be known as the Gay, Lesbian and Straight Teachers Education Network (GLSEN) – the most prominent such network in the world. Student groups aiming for greater acceptance of sexual diversity – Gay-Straight Alliances – were also slowly spreading across the high school landscape, even if still in modest numbers. The first had appeared in the late 1980s, and encouraging their formation became an important part of GLSEN's mandate.

### Policy Change

The risk to students posed by unrelentingly anti-gay school climates remained the primary wedge issue inducing policy change at the school board level. In 1991 the hostility of school climates was formally recognized by the National Education Association. The 1993 release of the federal Health and Social Services report on youth suicide gave the issue prominence, and so did an early 1990s report from the federal Justice Department claiming that lesbians and gays were the most frequent targets of hate crimes, and that schools were the primary settings for such hate-motivated violence.[9]

San Francisco's board was a leader in taking up the challenge, though it encountered heavy seas at first. After a reformist shift in 1990 elections, the school board approved an affirmative counselling program aimed at sexual minority students. By 1993 it was distributing resource materials across the district, and supportive educators were designated for every school. During this time, the Bay Area Network of Gay and Lesbian Educators (BANGLE) spearheaded the establishment of a program aimed at making books and other curricular materials on sexual diversity available to all schools in the region.

The twin cities of St Paul and Minneapolis also saw pioneering work, in conjunction with favourable developments in Minnesota's education department, with all of this bolstered by the enactment of a statewide prohibition on discrimination based on sexual orientation and gender identity.[10] The St Paul school district created an 'Out for Equity' program in 1994, and the same year the state published a guide encouraging schools to assess and change anti-gay climates.[11] Both survived withering attacks by religious conservatives.

At the state level, we can see the beginnings of change in the early 1990s. (The District of Columbia and Wisconsin had non-discrimination laws that included students before this, but there was little focus on anti-gay harassment and bullying, nor any other matter related to the specifics of discrimination based on sexual diversity.) In 1991, Wisconsin's education department required all school districts to develop a policy prohibiting bias and harassment of lesbian, gay, and bisexual students, and the Connecticut Board of Education published suggestions for educators designed to create more inclusive school environments for sexual minority students. However, it was Massachusetts that provided the most impressive lead on these issues in this period.

*Massachusetts Initiative*

In 1992, Massachusetts's Republican Governor William Weld convened the first state-level Commission on Gay and Lesbian Youth.[12] Weld was unusual among American Republicans in his preparedness to take up sexual diversity issues, and in the previous election, running against a socially conservative Democrat, he had promised action on youth suicide. The commission's report was delivered in early 1993 (about the time that the federal report of 1989 was made public), and it recommended that all of the state's high schools establish policies protecting lesbian/gay students from harassment and discrimination, school staff be trained in sexual orientation issues, student support groups be created, library collections include relevant materials, and sexual orientation issues be incorporated into the curriculum.

That year, state education officials developed the Safe Schools Program for Gay and Lesbian Students, the name reflecting the focus

Table 9.1    U.S. Discrimination and Harassment Laws Covering LGBT Students, 1973–2002

| State | Date | Type of law | | | Application |
|-------|------|----------------|------------|-----------------|-------------|
|       |      | Discrimination | Harassment | Gender identity |             |
| DC    | 1973 | x              |            | x*              | includes private schools |
| WI    | 1986 | x              |            |                 |             |
| NJ    | 1992 | x              | x          | x               | includes private schools re discrimination |
| MA    | 1993 | x              |            |                 | includes charter schools |
| MN    | 1993 | x              |            | x               |             |
| VT    | 1994 | x              | x          |                 |             |
| CT    | 1997 | x              |            |                 |             |
| CA    | 1999 | x              |            | x               | includes private schools with state funding |
| WA    | 2002 |                | x          |                 |             |

*Personal appearance.
Note: States that have issued regulations or codes forbidding discrimination based on sexual orientation include Alaska, Florida, Hawai'i, Maryland, Oregon, Pennsylvania, and Rhode Island.
Source: Jason Gianciotto and Sean Cahill, *Education Policy: Issues Affecting Lesbian, Gay, Bisexual, and Transgender Youth* (Washington, DC: National Gay and Lesbian Task Force Policy Institute, 2003), 46–7.

on the prevention of harassment and violence. In fact, it stopped short in not following through on recommendations for libraries and curriculum, to avoid the kind of controversy that had recently enveloped New York City's 'Rainbow Curriculum' (see below).

At the end of 1993, the state legislature easily passed a bill adding sexual orientation to existing non-discrimination policies for public schools. A large-scale lobbying campaign had been mounted, with student activists and their stories given particular prominence.[13] One year later, the state board of education went further, stipulating that teachers' certification depended on their mastering strategies to combat discrimination, including that based on sexual orientation. The Education Department then contracted for three-hour workshops in teacher education faculties across the state.

In the few years to come, hundreds of workshops and presentations were coordinated, and more than one hundred Gay-Straight Alliances were established, soon covering almost half of the state's high schools. Arthur Lipkin, measuring the change over these years, quotes a high school principal who admitted that something was wrong in the fact that his school was the only one in the area without a GSA[14]

The harassment issue gained prominence in other states. Some had already formally included sexual orientation in school discrimination and harassment legislation, at the time that sexual orientation was first added to statewide anti-discrimination codes (see table 9.1). But there was now a more concerted focus on homophobic bullying, reflected in the small wave of measures approved in the middle and late 1990s. Though none of these measures was as ambitious as the safe schools program in Massachusetts, they gave greater profile to the specific risks created by homophobic climates than any provincial or territorial measure enacted in Canada. They were also backed by activist networks, or groups like Washington State's Safe Schools Coalition, with a particular interest in the homophobic dimension of the bullying issue.

*Resistance*

This was not, however, a period of easy sailing. It would be years before Washington State activists could secure passage of a statewide safe schools measure, despite the early formation (in the late 1980s) of an activist coalition pressing hard on the issue. In the relatively liberal state of Connecticut, Latin teacher John Anderson was thought to be the first school teacher to come out when in 1991 he authored a lesbian/gay column in the *New Haven Register*. The formation of GSAs, too, was routinely contested (see box).

**Chapel Hill, 1991**
David Bruton, an English teacher in Chapel Hill High School, suggested the formation of a support group for sexual minority students in 1991. Most students supported the creation of a such a group, and in the fall of 1993 it changed its name to the Gay-Straight Alliance. The next spring, it successfully urged the school's prom committee to adopt an inclusive policy towards same-sex couples. But right-wing resistance was angry and powerful from the outset. Windows in Bruton's classroom were shot out or shattered with stones. 'Bruton's a faggot' was painted on the pavement, on school buses, and on the school building. Some of the school's small buildings were set on fire. Right-wing opponents were mobilizing throughout this period, and they got the school board to delay the inclusion of sexual orientation in its multicultural education action plan.[15]

Curricular change was even more controversial, and a high-profile conflict in New York City over just that issue reverberated across the country.

## New York's Children of the Rainbow Curriculum

In 1985 New York's public school board approved a resolution on multicultural reform aimed at eliminating disrimination against students and staff.[16] This arose in part because of a growing sense that the many students from culturally marginalized populations were not being well served by their schools, and that insufficient numbers of teachers and guidance counsellors came from those populations. The resolution dealt with a range of equity issues, including sexual orientation. This was controversial, but reflected the long history of organizing around LGBT issues in New York, and the activist work of the Lesbian and Gay Teachers Association.

The resolution's approval led to the creation of new teacher guides and curricular materials. One product of this was a 443-page draft of the *Children of the Rainbow* guide for Grade 1 teachers. It included a few pages on sexual orientation, referring to families with two mothers or two fathers as part of a larger diversity in family form, and offered advice on how to counteract anti-gay bias.

When the new guide was ready for local school board review in 1992, five of the thirty-two local school boards within the jurisdiction of the central board refused to adopt it because of its gay content, and others urged amendments. But the central board and school chancellor Joseph Fernandez, a veteran of controversy over AIDS programming, insisted that the curriculum be adopted fully and uniformly. Roman Catholic opponents soon forged links with Latino/a Pentacostals, conservative Muslims, and other religious-right groups, characterizing the gay content of the new curriculum as the product of inside lobbying by a rich gay elite seeking the right to impose their ideas on more disadvantaged groups, and in the process to teach young children about sex.

At the end of 1992, the intensity of conflict over the curriculum induced Fernandez to propose revisions to some of the language used in it, but opponents were unmoved. Early in 1993, in what seemed an escalating and intractable conflict, the central board voted narrowly to remove Fernandez as chancellor. This, alongside talk of a right-wing assault on the school system, fired up progressive mobilization that secured major gains in the 1994 elections. But the range of forces energized in the process was not uniformly supportive on sexual orientation issues, and the chronic financial woes of the New York school system imposed constraints on the implementation of the curriculum that had been so controversial over the previous year. In February 1995 the central board approved a resolution limiting the scope of multicultural education in the city's schools – revising *Children of the Rainbow* and making it a resource for teachers only rather than a required curriculum. At just the time of the first wave of American concern over risks faced by sexual minority youth in schools, then, the New York story was persuading many reformers (including those in Massachusetts) to limit the curricular implications of their work.

## 1995–9: Growing Concern over School Safety, Growing Backlash

This was a period of dramatic contradictions, marked by intensified opposition to the 'promotion' of homosexuality in schools, mixed with successful challenges to school complacency. (In Canada, during this time, dramatic progress was being secured on relationship issues, but little mobilizing on either side in the area of on schooling, at least outside British Columbia and Toronto. Canadian religious conservatives in many parts of the country were not aiming much fire at school policies quite simply because so little was changing, and so little progressive pressure was being sustained.)

*Securing the Promotion of Heterosexuality*

Renewal of Republican congressional strength in the mid-1990s ensured that federal conservatives would continue their attempts to curb school inclusiveness. In 1995, House Speaker Newt Gingrich derided as propaganda and recruitment any curricular change that referred to homosexuality in other than negative terms. That fall, House Republicans even devoted scarce legislative time to a hearing on whether homosexuality was being promoted in public schools – this initiative supported by the notoriously anti-gay Reverend Lou Sheldon of the Traditional Values Coalition.

Similar developments were occurring at the state level. A 1994 North Carolina statute required schools to teach students that homosexuality was illegal under the state's sodomy law, and that marriage was an exclusively heterosexual union. In 1995, the Arizona legislature amended an earlier statute on AIDS instruction by prohibiting school districts from any classroom instruction that promoted a homosexual lifestyle, portrayed homosexuality as a positive alternative lifestyle, or suggested that some forms of homosexual activity were safe. At decade's end, Utah legislators approved a bill outlawing positive or neutral discussion of homosexuality in state schools.

'No promo homo' policies proliferated at the local level, spearheaded by religiously conservative school trustees and parents. One of the battle grounds in this domain was school libraries and resource centres. From the earliest days of schools controversy, the acquisition of books like *Heather Has Two Mommies* and *Daddy's Roommate* were becoming famous because of the hysteria provoked by their crossing into school property. Over the course of the 1990s, the American Library Association recorded almost five hundred cases where attempts were made to remove books from libraries on the grounds that they promoted homosexuality.

*Progressive Activist Surge and the Rapid Spread of GSAs*

By 1996 GLSEN had 3,000 members, and by decade's end, 15,000 (and a staff of eighteen in its national office). In the process it became an invaluable source of advice and information for teachers, officials, and students across the United States. Their work was also being reinforced by such national groups as the Human Rights Campaign, the National Center for Lesbian Rights, the National Gay and Lesbian Task Force, Lambda Legal Defense and Education Fund, the Gay and Lesbian Alliance Against Defamation, and the American Civil Liberties Union. In many parts of the country, teacher unions were also prepared to intervene assertively in defence of sexual minority educators, at a time when almost all Canadian teacher unions showed only tepid interest.[17] The support embodied in the commitment of such activist resources, and particularly those in GLSEN, encouraged the spread of GSAs, and helped students and their educator allies confront their opponents (see box).

## Salt Lake City and the GSA Earthquake

In 1995 Utah became the first state to enact legislation banning the recognition of same-sex marriages. But in the middle of that same year, Salt Lake City saw its first major Gay Pride parade – a remarkable event in such a religiously conservative place. Then in early 1996, fifteen students in East High School proposed the formation of a Gay-Straight Alliance. Seventeen-year-old Kelli Peterson, openly lesbian, was one of the leaders of the group, motivated in part by wanting new students to not have to go through what she did when she first got into high school.

Utah's attorney general, citing the 1984 federal Equal Access Act, confirmed that schools receiving federal funds could not ban one club while accepting others. However, this did not prevent right-wing groups from mobilizing against the club's formation, raising the spectre of homosexual activists recruiting youngsters. In February 1996 a Salt Lake City school board meeting that drew more than one hundred speakers voted 4–3 to ban all non-academic clubs from meeting on school grounds – apparently the only way they could prevent the recognition of GSAs.

Three days later, hundreds of students walked out of East High School and protested at the state capitol. Early in March, another protest against the school board's policy attracted one thousand gays, lesbians, and allies to the state capitol. Utah legislators were then approving a bill that would bar teachers from condoning or supporting illegal conduct – this in a state that still had a sodomy law criminalizing homosexual activity. Among the bill's objectives was the discouragement of teachers becoming faculty advisors to GSAs – a prerequisite for their recognition by school authorities – and the imposition of severe limits on teachers who wished to discuss homosexuality in any forum. The legislators also required school boards to deny recognition to any student group whose activities would encourage criminal or delinquent conduct or involve 'human sexuality,' and allowed them to demand parental permission for students to join clubs.

In 1998, East High's Gay-Straight Alliance launched a legal challenge to the school board policy, supported by Lambda Legal Defense, the National Center for Lesbian Rights, and the ACLU. In that same year, the GSA's president committed suicide, no doubt in part because of the harshness of the battle over the group's right to exist.

In October 1999 a federal court ruled that the school board's policy violated the Equal Access Act, since the elimination of all clubs was so clearly designed to prevent the formation of the GSA. The school board appealed the verdict. In the meantime, East High students attempted to form another club – this one explicitly academic and designed to circumvent the board's policy on non-academic clubs. PRISM was its name – People Respecting Important Social Movements – and its declared intent was to discuss gay-related issues that arose from courses in history, government, and sociology. School officials refused to allow it to meet on school property, but the groups backing the earlier suit won a preliminary injunction (in April 2000) to allow the new group to meet until the court case was completed. The school board appealed that ruling too.

In September the board approved a policy that denied approval to any club if its purposes or activities would 'advocate or approve sexual activity outside of marriage, or involve presentations in violation of laws or regulations governing sex education or privacy rights of individuals or families.' But because board officials had so adamantly insisted that they were not trying to introduce their earlier ban through the back door, it was widely read as lifting the ban. Closely watched by the media and by the groups that had supported the legal challenges against them, school officials gave their approval to both the GSA and the PRISM club that same month.

Republicans in the state legislature and their Christian-right supporters refused to give up, and years later they were still trying to place roadblocks in front of GSAs. In 2007, they passed legislation requiring parental consent to participate in any school club, and allowing principals to forbid clubs that they believe exceed the boundaries of socially appropriate behaviour.[18]

By late 1999 attempts to prohibit the formation of GSAs had been overturned in Colorado, South Carolina, and New Hampshire, largely on the basis of the 1984 Equal Access Act. A similar story began unfolding at that time in Orange County, California. The school board rejected a proposed GSA at El Modena High School, calling the name itself inflammatory. Like their East High colleagues in Utah, the students at El Modena High, assisted by Lambda Legal Defense and People for the American Way, forced the board to back down in September 2000.

Some religious conservatives now realized that they had little chance of winning these battles, especially because they were beneficiaries of the Equal Access Act now being used so successfully to secure recognition of GSAs. A representative of the Pat Robertson–backed American Center for Law and Justice said that as much as he and his colleagues might regret it, 'this is simply a battle we cannot win, and thus, should not fight.'[19] Another conservative activist from Focus on the Family described attempts at excluding GSAs as self-destructive.

*Student Challenges to Bullying*

Student readiness to challenge school inaction was also evident in the number of protests against anti-gay bullying taken to court. As the activist resources available to support such cases increased, so did the capacity of students to pursue them assertively (see table 9.3). One such case made headlines in 1996 (see box).

**Jamie Nabozny's Trials**

In his small Wisconsin home town, Jamie Nabozny was targeted for being gay from the seventh grade through to the eleventh, when he finally dropped out. In one incident, two boys mock raped him as twenty others looked on and laughed. When Jamie went to the school principal, she offered only the observation that 'boys will be boys' and took no action against the offending students. On other occasions, school officials suggested to him or his parents that a student who was openly gay should expect to be harassed by other students. They did not ignore all harassment, for they had a record of responding to girls complaining about the behaviour of boys, but they declined to act on this case.

On one occasion, several boys knocked Jamie to the ground and kicked him in the stomach hard enough to send him to the hospital. Twice Jamie attempted suicide, and eventually he quit school altogether. But then he and his parents, supported by Lambda Legal Defense, launched a court challenge to school officials that became the first in the United States to go to trial over a school's failure to stop anti-gay abuse. In late July 1996 a three-judge panel of the Seventh Circuit (federal) Court reversed a negative lower court judgment and ruled that school officials had violated Nabozny's constitutional rights when they failed to protect him against harassment and assault. The court then returned the case to the district court to give Nabozny an opportunity to make claims relevant to school liability – in other words, to make an argument about damages.

This was a huge victory, and school officials knew it. They quickly settled with Nabozny, awarding him costs and damages totalling $900,000. This settlement sent waves across the country. Lambda Legal Defense, which until then had received only a trickle of calls for help on schools issues, was now getting many more.[20]

In early 1997 the U.S. Department of Education cited this judgment when it issued guidelines indicating that some instances of anti-gay harassment could be considered a form of sexual harassment, and thereby prohibited by Title IX of the 1972 Education Amendments Act (for those schools receiving federal funding, that is, most public schools).[21] In 1999, the U.S. Supreme Court ruled on a schools case that did not arise from sexual diversity, but reinforced the directions adopted by lower courts in cases of anti-gay harassment (see box).

*Davis v. Monroe County Board of Education*, **U.S. Supreme Court**
By a narrow 5–4 margin, the Supreme Court ruled against the school board in Monroe County, Georgia, for 'deliberate indifference' in the face of the persistent harassment of LaShonda Davis, a fifth-grade girl. LaShonda had repeatedly asked teachers and officials to do something to stop the harassment, to no effect. As a result, she became severely depressed, and her loss of concentration led to a major drop in school performance. The court's majority decided that Title IX of the 1972 Education Amendments Act, in prohibiting discrimination based on sex, required any school receiving federal funds to ensure that students were not subjected to sexual harassment. The harassment had to be severe, and the school had to show deliberate indifference. This was not a case about harassment of gays, but the Supreme Court had ruled a year before that workplace sexual harassment included same-sex harassment.

One illustration of the attention that anti-gay bullying was receiving was in Washington State. The Safe Schools Coalition, formed in the late 1980s shortly after an official state report pointed to the risk to sexual minority students of inaction on harassment, seemed now to be having an impact. It issued reports in 1995 and 1999 describing a pattern of gang rapes, physical assaults, and harassment based on sexual diversity. State legislators were not yet ready to pass a comprehensive safe schools bill, but in 1997 the state governor sent a message to every school superintendant in the state urging the adoption of policies to counteract discrimination and harassment based on sexual orientation, whether perceived or real.

The public resonance of anti-gay bullying violence was strengthened in the fall of 1998, when Matthew Shepard was brutally murdered in Wyoming. This tragedy re-energized calls for the inclusion of sexual orientation in hate crimes statutes, and to some extent it challenged the religious right's trivialization of the risks facing lesbian/gay youth. The 1999 shootings at Columbine High School added fuel to concerns about violence, and strengthened the safe schools movement. Guidelines from the U.S. Department of Education and the National Association of Attorneys General issued that year advocated comprehensive and proactive policies, and included references to harassment based on sexual orientation throughout.[22]

### Teacher Visibility

Most American teachers did not have the protection of human rights law barring anti-gay discrimination that Canadian teachers did. Even if many had tenure protections against arbitrary dismissal, the spectre of teachers corrupting and confusing young people was a crucial mobilizing frame of the religious right, who were more than prepared to publicly attack educators who were out or open to talking about sexual diversity.[23] Nevertheless, more and more teachers were asserting their right to be out, and to speak out, and some were successfully taking their cases to court with the help of their unions and other advocacy groups.

Two related issues are at stake here. One is the right to speak about homosexuality as an issue; the other is to disclose one's lesbianness, gayness, bisexuality, or transgenderness in a manner similar to the routine disclosures made by straight teachers. Teachers had been asserting their right to speak on 'controversial' issues for many years, and the late 1990s saw important victories. As early as 1968, in *Pickering v. Board of Education*, the U.S. Supreme Court upheld the right of teachers to speak out on matters of public interest, so long as it did not affect their performance in class or interfere with the regular operation of the school. But for years, decisions such as this did not provide the strong lead it should have, since many courts and legislatures still gave schools considerable leeway in dictating what could and could not be taught.

Karl Debro, an English teacher in the San Francisco area, was taken to court by Vicki and James Godkin, claiming that pro-gay comments in their son's classroom violated their religious rights and privacy rights.[24] In the fall of 1999, the first court to hear the case ruled that Debro had violated neither, and the case ended with confirmation of that verdict. In the same period, two California teachers were plaintiffs in court, arguing that the transfer of students out of their classrooms by parents, only on the grounds of their homosexuality, was discriminatory. In one of the cases, Grade 8 teacher Jim Merrick saw fifteen of his students transfer from his classes as a reaction to his speaking out publicly against a county official who described gay people as sick. Both claimants ended up with rulings that such transfers violated state law prohibiting discrimination based on sexual orientation.

In 1998, Ohio elementary school teacher Bruce Glover was reinstated and compensated after convincing the court that he had been discriminated against when his contract was not renewed. In the same year, Wendy Weaver won a suit against the Nebo School District, which had fired her as volleyball coach after she responded affirmatively to student questions about whether she was lesbian. School officials had also imposed a gag order prohibiting her speaking about her sexual orientation to students, staff, or parents, and it too was struck down.

## 1999 and After: Steadily Increasing Visibility in the Midst of Culture War

The new decade saw more resources than ever being put into the struggle over schooling, by both sides. Christian-right mobilization was intensifying, and centred as always on the image of the vulnerable child and predatory homosexual. But sexual minority students and teachers were becoming more visible with each passing year, and widening the discussion of school inclusiveness. And when, in 2003, the U.S. Supreme Court struck down the Texas sodomy law that criminalized homosexual activity, one important weapon used frequently by American conservatives was blunted.[25]

### Curricular Promotion of Heterosexuality

Curricular change was always destined to be the most difficult. Several state governments had already enacted policies requiring

Table 9.2    U.S. States with Laws Explicitly Requiring Schools to Promote
Heterosexuality

|  | Prohibiting positive portrayals of homosexuality | Requiring promotion of heterosexual marriage |
|---|---|---|
| Alabama | x |  |
| Arizona | x | x |
| California |  | x |
| Florida |  | x |
| Illinois |  | x |
| Indiana |  | x |
| Louisiana |  | x |
| Mississippi | x | x |
| North Carolina |  | x |
| Oklahoma | x |  |
| South Carolina | x |  |
| Texas | x |  |
| Utah | x |  |

Note: This table does not include provisions mandating abstinence-only sex education.
Source: GLSEN, *State of the States 2004: A Policy Analysis of Lesbian, Gay, Bisexual and Transgender Safer Schools Issues* (http://www.glsen.org).

schools effectively to condemn homosexuality, and the new decade swelled these ranks to over a dozen (see table 9.2). Even in relatively progressive states, authorities were not immune to attacks from the religious right. In 2005, the school board in Maryland's Montgomery County felt the sting of an attack from the conservative group Citizens for a Responsible Curriculum, supported by the national group Parents and Friends of ExGays and Gays (PFOX). They launched a court challenge against a more inclusive curricular proposal on the grounds that newly approved course materials criticized the views of certain religions, and they won their case. The board was forced to put a PFOX member on the committee drafting new lesson plans, and modified the language in its sex education curriculum. Although there were still inclusive elements in the program, the fear of backlash was evident in the board's warning to teachers that when covering the section on sexual orientation and gender identity, 'no additional information, interpretation or examples are to be provided.'[26] Even that wasn't enough for Christian conservatives, who filed a lawsuit against a pilot program testing the new curriculum, claiming that it paid insufficient heed to 'ex-gay' programs. Some progress was eventually secured in 2006, but with tightly scripted and studiously uncontroversial lesson plans. Conservatives showed no sign of relaxing their guard and continued to challenge even this very cautious curriculum.[27]

In other states, conservative Christian groups were launching or supporting court challenges asserting their right to present their views on homosexuality to school audiences. PFOX was prominent among the groups spearheading such claims, alongside Liberty Counsel (a Christian law firm).[28] In 2006, PFOX was launching a national campaign encouraging conservative students to form 'Gay to Straight Clubs' and threatening litigation if schools did not allow the ex-gay message into the classroom.[29] Even in a progressive city like Boulder, Colorado, school officials were thinking of including an ex-gay pamphlet in a resource package for teachers, to help them respond to questions about sexuality. The Ex-Gay Caucus of the National Education Association was also adopting the language of choice in claiming the right to present alternative views to students with same-sex attraction.[30]

Sex education remained a crucial target. Going back to 1996, federal funds had been made available to schools for sex education that emphasized mutually faithful monogamous relationships within marriage. The Bush administration then ramped up funding dramatically, to almost $200 million per year in 2006 – this despite evidence that the general public would prefer a broad approach, that abstinence approaches distort evidence, for example, on condom use, and that they do not increase rates of sexual abstinence.[31] Federal funding provisos, combined with similar measures adopted by many states, led most schools in the United States to teach abstinence-until-marriage sex education.[32] One study published in 2002 asserted that only 9 per cent of students in grade six or higher were in school districts that had comprehensive sex education policies.[33]

But the 2006 elections produced Democratic majorities in Congress, posing a threat to at least some of the funding for abstinence programs. By mid-2007, eleven state health departments rejected abstinence-only programs. California turned down federal funds from the beginning. The opting-out rate increased significantly in 2006 and '07, when New Jersey, Wisconsin, Connecticut, Rhode Island, Montana, and Massachusetts declined funds.[34] School boards in other states (e.g., in Oregon, Maryland, Washington State) were also pushing the envelop, and including discussion of condom use and topics beyond abstinence. In 2005, Washington State adopted voluntary sex education guidelines that also moved significantly beyond abstinence, and an early 2007 report from the Healthy Youth Alliance found that only 20 per cent of state schools taught abstinence-only sex education (with just under a quarter prohibiting discussion of homosexuality). The Kansas Board of Education tweaked its sex education policy in 2007, removing the obligation to stress abstinence and calling for 'comprehensive' sex education.[35]

In response to these developments, conservative groups had access to resources to mount a new offensive. As Catherine Lugg points out, the Bush administration had established faith-based centres within various federal departments, including Education, Health and Human Services, with mandates to press for an increased role of religion in schools and to fund initiatives by outside groups – in some cases over the constitutional lines established by courts.[36] Heritage of Rhode Island, for example, was using federal funds to offer abstinence-only programs to 'supplement' existing sex-ed classes, and managed to do so in six hundred public schools across the state.[37]

*Books and Other Media*

Making school texts more inclusive has also been very difficult. Pressure to do so had been mounted by students and educators from the 1990s on, but such work has had only scattered impact. Publishers have been wary of moving into controversial terrain, and their vulnerability to lost sales in states like Texas reinforced caution (Texas being one of the two large states that centralize decisions over books, the other being California) (see box).

**Texas Texts**

The Texas Board of Education controlled the second-largest school textbook purchase orders in the United States. In 2004, five of its fifteen trustees were conservative Christians, and they were on the offensive to ensure that only particular kinds of messages got transmitted to students. Five more trustees were Republican 'moderates' who frequently sided with their more conservative colleagues. That year, a majority of the board secured changes to high school health textbooks to ensure the clarity of the message that marriage was a lifelong union between a husband and wife. They also got agreement from the publisher to remove the word 'partner' – thinking it a stealth reference to same-sex relationships – and insisted on textbook support for abstinence-only sex education. Trustees also succeeded in getting a reference to one ice age occurring 'millions of years ago' altered to ensure that literal creationist views would not be undercut.[38]

In California, the other large state with centralized decision making on books, Governor Arnold Schwarzenegger vetoed a 2006 bill that would have extended prohibitions on discrimination, including that based on sexual orientation and gender identity, to school-sponsored activities, instructional materials, and textbooks.[39]

Conservative opposition to the positive portrayal of homosexuality to youngsters extended beyond schools. In early 2005, the federal education secretary (a conservative Christian) objected to an episode of a children's cartoon show that included a Vermont eight-year-old who had two mothers. This episode was to be shown by the Public Broadcasting System (PBS) as part of its series *Postcards from Buster*. The Republican cabinet secretary's letter to PBS suggested that 'many parents would not want their young children exposed to the life-styles portrayed in this episode,' and that public funding was not intended to introduce this kind of subject matter to children. She also suggested that the money be returned. PBS then decided not to distribute the episode to its 349 stations across the country, saying that it recognized that the issues raised in it were 'sensitive.'[40] Only about forty stations persisted in airing the episode.

*Curricular Gains*

Where books and other materials with positive mentions of sexual difference have been made available in schools, conservatives have been not so successful in getting them banned from schools. In its 1982 ruling in *Board of Education, Island Trees Union Free School v. Steven Pico*, the U.S. Supreme Court had condemned the removal of books (in this case not gay themed) from a California school library. Schools could remove material if it was pervasively vulgar or educationally unsuitable, but not if the removal was intended to deny exposure to ideas with which school authorities disagreed. Most challenges to book banning since then have won in court. This of course does not oblige schools to acquire books portraying homosexuality in positive or neutral terms, and does little to impede political protests at their acquisition. However, it does give some room for manoeuvre to school officials and librarians determined to expand their resources.

There has been some evidence of expanding curricular attention to sexual diversity, even in the face of statutory impediments and a vigilant religious right. San Francisco's school board remained in the vanguard here. The 1993 approval of a program designed to supply resources to teachers in every middle and high school led to only uneven uptake by teachers.[41] In 1998, authorities pushed further by voting to require that curricular reading lists include works of openly lesbian/gay/bisexual/transgendered writers, identified as such. In other places, programs designed to address anti-gay school climates were sometimes expansive enough to encourage curricular change, and there were unquestionably many teachers across the country who taught inclusively without the need for board policy urging them to do so. A 2005 GLSEN survey of sexual minority youth, however, suggested only modest progress on this front.[42] Fewer than a fifth of respondents reported any coverage of LGBT topics in their classes (about the same as reporting any coverage in textbooks), and of that only about 40 per cent was clearly positive.[43]

*The School Safety Opening*

Programming to confront the harassment and bullying of students based on real or perceived sexual difference was still a wedge issue. Students were more prepared than ever to challenge school authorities in court, and most outcomes were forcing policy change and costing boards a great deal of money.

One of the most significant statewide advances was in Washington, following years of activist pressure. A long-fought-for Safe Schools Bill, spearheaded by openly gay state legislator Ed Murray, was finally passed in 2002. It required all school districts to develop policies prohibiting all forms of harassment, intimidation, and bullying, but it was the inclusion of sexual orientation that had stalled it. Only with secure Democratic control of both legislative houses and the governor's office could the bill be brought forward and approved, and this some time before the state had a basic human rights protection against discrimination based on sexual orientation or gender identity. By 2007, eight states other than Washington and of course Massachusetts had safe

Table 9.3    Major U.S. Court Victories in Anti-Gay Bullying Cases

| Date | State | Case | Monetary settlement |
|------|-------|------|---------------------|
| 1996 | WI | *Nabozny v. Podlesny* | $962,000 |
| 1998 | GA | *Wagner v. Fayetteville Public Schools* | – |
| 2001 | KY | *Putnam v. Somerset Schools* | $135,000 |
| 2001 | NV | *Henkle v. Washoe County School District* | $451,000 |
| 2002 | PA | *Dahle v. Titusville Area School District* | $312,000 |
| 2002 | CA | *Loomis v. Visalia Schools* | – |
| 2003 | CA | *Flores v. Morgan Hill Unified School District et al.* | $1,100,000 |
| 2003 | CA | *Shaposhinikov v. Pacifica School District* | $100,000 |
| 2005 | KS | *Theno v. Unified School District 464, Tonganoxie* | $250,000 |
| 2005 | CA | *Ramelli and Donovan v. San Diego School District* | $300,000 |

Source: http://www.glsen.org.

schools laws that explicitly included sexual orientation (a total of five also including gender identity).[44]

There were a number of local measures of the same sort, in cities like Boston, Chicago, and Oakland. One was in Cincinnati, a city with a powerful strain of religious conservatism (see box).

**Cincinnati Schools, 1991–2001**

Cincinnati's school board approved the inclusion of sexual orientation in its anti-discrimination policy for employees in 1991. It did so with relative ease – impressive in a city that had seen its share of anti-gay mobilizing by the religious right. A network of gay and lesbian teachers had formed, eventually becoming a chapter of GLSEN. They gained support from their teachers union, which then secured recognition of same-sex relationships in the board's bereavement policy. But then in 1993 Cincinnati voters rejected the city's gay rights ordinance and unseated the school board member who had proposed the 1991 non-discrimination policy. Teachers were now more fearful of losing their jobs if they were seen to be gay or advocating for gay causes.

Times change, though, even in this conservative city. At the beginning of the school term in the fall of 2001, the school board overwhelmingly approved the inclusion of sexual orientation in the district's policy on student discipline. It was a policy that addressed only serious harassment or intimidation, and would not deal with much of the name calling that so damages sexual minority students. But it was a shift in outlook, and was backed by in-service training for school administrators on sexual orientation (and disability, the other addition to the discipline policy).[45]

Even at the federal level, an opening was provided for proactive anti-bullying initiatives, in a measure that was largely driven by conservative agendas. The 2001 No Child Left Behind Act contained much that was regressive in school policy, but it reaffirmed earlier legislation that provided funding to promote school safety, 'such that students and school personnel are free from violent and disruptive acts, including sexual harassment and abuse, and victimization associated with prejudice and intolerance.' It did not name specific grounds for prejudice, such as gender and race, and may well be weaker because of that. But neither did it preclude programs covering sexual orientation and gender identity.

Conservatives still resisted any but negative references to homosexuality, and data about the risk to sexual minority students could easily fuel their arguments about the sickness and unhappiness associated with deviance. More often, they simply denied that there was a problem at all. In 2002 Virginian state officials took steps to prohibit local measures to address the needs of LGBT students. At about this time, the New York State Education Department refused even to ask about sexual orientation, and about bias-related harassment of all kinds, in its public school Youth Risk Behavior Survey. Attempts to legislatively prohibit discrimination and harassment based on sexual orientation in New York schools was regularly failing before implacable Republican opposition.

*GSAs and Other Forms of Student Advocacy*

In 2007, three thousand six hundred GSAs were registered with GLSEN; undoubtedly there were others with no link to the group. Melinda Miceli estimates that in 2005 about one in seven high schools had GSAs, and GLSEN itself estimated that about one in five students were in high schools that had GSAs.[46] Evidence was mounting that their spread has made a difference in school climates, and in the development of policies recognizing sexual diversity. In an assessment of the Massachusetts Safe Schools Program, Catherine Lugg describes

GSAs as often 'the most potent forces for institutional change,' and for that reason usually the principal target of conservatives.[47] Her data (from 2000) suggest that they have a favourable impact on school climate, though the full complement of policies developed in Massachusetts produced still more favourable results.

Incredibly, opponents persisted in trying to prevent GSA formation, reflecting their devotion to keeping homosexuality invisible in schools and their preparedness to dismiss earlier court rulings as the product of 'activist' judges.[48] In 2002, conservative parents in the California school district of Clovis pressured officials to prevent the formation of a Gay-Straight Alliance in the local high school, though the board was soon informed that they would lose in court if they buckled to the pressure.[49] In Hawai'i, students aiming for the state's first GSA met resistance from the beginning, though they eventually won official status after mobilizing support from parents, teachers, the National Center for Lesbian Rights, the American Civil Liberties Union, and the Hawai'i Safe School Coalition. In 2006, the principal of Okeechobee High School in southern Florida denied permission to students wishing to establish a GSA, though an ACLU court challenge seemed destined to overcome that resistance.[50]

The determination of student advocates of inclusiveness was dramatically illustrated (in 2002) by students at Boyd County High School in rural Kentucky. They wanted their GSA to meet at school, but faced a wall of opposition from the teacher-parent council, religious conservatives in the surrounding community, and many of their fellow students. In this community of fifty thousand, more than two thousand people rallied against the club, and a third of the school's students boycotted class in opposition to it. A lawsuit finally forced the school board to acquiesce, and to sponsor anti-harassment workshops for students and staff.

Students have taken other steps to make sexual diversity visible, and have fought for the right to do so. The 'Day of Silence' has been one such vehicle, calling on students to refuse speaking for a full school day to protest the forced silence of sexual minorities and their allies. The idea was first launched in 1996 at the University of Virginia, and by 2003 GLSEN estimated that there were 150,000 students in about two thousand high schools participating, those numbers more than doubling over the next few years.[51]

Creating more inclusive social events in school was another front on which American high school students continued making claims. More than twenty years after their right to do so was affirmed in *Fricke v. Lynch*, there were still school boards trying to prevent same-sex dates attending student formals, but groups like the ACLU and Lambda were prepared to provide a quick course in the legal risks involved. Sexual minority students inaugurated their own dances in cities like Boston, New York, Seattle, New Orleans, Cleveland, Minneapolis, and St Petersburg, Florida.

### Teacher Rights and Advocacy

The readiness of Christian conservatives to attack teachers whose own sexuality or whose teaching deviated from traditional norms has continued to the present. In 2000, the notoriously anti-gay Oregon Citizens' Alliance rallied 47 per cent of the state's voters behind an initiative directed at such teachers, in an echo of the Briggs initiative in California more than twenty years earlier. In other states, attempts by teachers to secure family benefits for same-sex partners have encountered predictable opposition from the same quarters. Even in an otherwise progressive state like Connecticut, only 22 of 166 school districts had inclusive teacher benefits at mid-decade. In other states, anti-gay marriage amendments to state constitutions were threatening such benefits. Michigan, Ohio, and Wisconsin were examples where such amendments had broad enough wording to jeopardize benefits plans in schools and universities. Even where rights and employee benefits are securely in place, few teachers are open enough to avail themselves of them. In late 2003, a safe schools coordinator for Boston's public schools estimated that of the five thousand teachers in that system, only about twenty were openly lesbian or gay.[52]

With all these constraints, the number of American teachers ready to challenge school authorities and conservative parents is remarkable. In the 2002–5 period, several teachers took on their boards to protest against harassment, discrimination, intimidation, and attempts at silencing, winning significant victories or six-digit settlements.[53] Of the students who responded to GLSEN's 2005 school climate survey, 45 per cent said they knew of at least one openly lesbian/gay/bisexual/transgender teacher in their school, most of them knowing of more than one. Fully 90 per cent knew of at least one teacher or staff person who was LGBT-positive.[54] Another GLSEN report, this one a random sample of secondary school students and teachers, showed that 73 per cent of the teachers strongly agreed that they had an obli-

Table 9.4   Ratings of State Education Policies on Sexual Orientation, by Ronald Russo

| Score (out of 8) | |
| --- | --- |
| 8 | Massachusetts |
| 5 | Connecticut, Rhode Island |
| 4 | California, Minnesota, New Jersey |
| 3 | Washington, DC, Washington State, Wisconsin |
| 2 | Pennsylvania, Vermont |
| 0 | 40 states |

Source: Ronald Russo, 'The Extent of Public Education Nondiscrimination Policy Protections for Lesbian, Gay, Bisexual, and Transgender Students: A National Study,' *Urban Education* 41 (March 2006): 144.

gation to ensure a safe and supportive environment for LGBT students.[55] This does not tell us how many would take action, and student responses indicate that only a minority of teachers who are present when homophobic remarks are made do in fact intervene. Nevertheless, there is widespread awareness that a problem exists, and recognition by teachers that they bear responsibility for action.

## An Overview and Explanation of Change

Ronald Russo assessed state education policies in the early 2000s and scored them according to the extent of their inclusiveness in areas such as non-discrimination measures, safe schools policies, curricular guidelines, and support for student groups.[56] On his eight-point scale, only three states received more than four points, and three-quarters of them got zero (table 9.4). The regional patterns offer no surprises. Six of the eleven states with any equitable attention to sexual diversity are in the Northeast; two are on the West Coast; and the rest are Minnesota, Wisconsin, and Washington, DC.

GLSEN itself prepares an annual score card for state school policies. The scoring (up to a maximum of one hundred) is based partly on overall levels of support for public education, but more so on policies providing rights protections and supports based on sexual orientation and gender identity. Unlike the Russo scoring, points are subtracted for explicitly prohibitive laws. GLSEN is clear that favourable policies acknowledged in this scoring constitute only a starting point, with much dependant on application, so it implicitly recognizes that the

Table 9.5  GLSEN Scoring of States on Schools Issues, 2004

| | |
|---|---|
| 90 + | New Jersey, Minnesota |
| 75–89 | California, Connecticut, Washington DC, Vermont |
| 60–74 | Massachusetts, Rhode Island, Wisconsin |
| 50–59 | Maryland, Nevada, Washington |
| 40–50 | Alaska, Hawai'i, New Hampshire, New Mexico, New York |

Source: http://www.glsen.org.

scores are generous. Even at that, only eleven states and the District of Columbia received more than fifty points (table 9.5). Only nine (plus DC) have comprehensive anti-bullying statutes that explicitly include sexual orientation, and only three of these include gender identity. Two-thirds of the states got scores of thirty-five or lower.

Comparing such scores with achievements in Canadian provinces and territories is difficult. Equality law in Canada has provided formal protections against discrimination based on sexual orientation across the country, fully covering school systems. Court rulings have made clear that sexual harassment is a form of discrimination. These factors have eliminated the need for school policies to explicitly address sexuality in their discrimination language, and perhaps also in respect to harassment. As we saw in chapter 8, however, this has also facilitated complete silence on sexual orientation and gender identity in provincial and territorial policy beyond their formal inclusion in generic policies, and has reduced the perceived need for proactive policies that address the homophobic climates that still pervade Canadian schools. It is also true that prohibitions or constraints on conveying positive or even neutral messages about homosexuality are not in place, and there is no serious talk of installing them. The result is that most or all Canadian provinces and territories would score more than fifty on GLSEN's scale, and get at least two points from Russo. But none would get scores as high as the top five or six performers among U.S. states.

In the United States, as in Canada, inclusive developments are much more commonly found in large cities, and in the United States particularly they are often found in the more prosperous white suburbs within and around them.[57] American college and university towns also figure among pioneering school districts. Still, the successful mobilization of pressure for change in the United States has often occurred outside the usual regions and locales. Students in the southern and mountain states have formed clubs that push against

Table 9.6   U.S. and Canadian Schooling Benchmarks

|  | United States | Canada |
| --- | --- | --- |
| First sustained local/regional activism | 1987–8 | 1993–6 |
| First national pro-gay group or national group program | 1991 | 2005 |
| First major national union action | 1987–8 | 2002–5 |
| First major harassment/bullying legal challenge | 1996 | 2001 |
| First state/provincial/territorial safe schools program | 1992 | none |
| First major local program supporting LGBT youth | 1984–5 | 1988–90 |
| First GSA | 1989 | 1998–9 |
| Student group coverage (% of high schools) | 15% | unknown |
| Wide-ranging state/provincial policies (% jurisd's) | 12% | 0% |

the silence in their communities and have fought to secure the right to do so.

Serious activist attention to schooling does not have a long history in the United States, but a longer and more widespread one than in Canada. By the late 1990s students and educators had a range of large organizations to draw from in gathering information, and if necessary in going to court. This included not only the major national LGBT groups, but also civil liberties groups and organizations devoted to monitoring the religious right, and safe schools coalitions. Canadian groups like Egale and GALE-BC were tiny by comparison, and though labour unions were coming on board during the 2000s, they had nothing like the schools expertise of American groups.

There are unquestionably implementation gaps in the United States, just as there are in Canada. Wide-ranging policies in states like Massachusetts are only partially applied at the level of schools and classrooms, especially where formal commitments are not matched by funding and staff time. At the same time, there seem to be so many stories of individual teachers, school leaders, and students taking initiative in the absence of official policy pressure or guidance. Even factoring in population size differences, that kind of initiative appears more widespread in the United States than in Canada, not least because local activists have access to the resources of state and national organizations. And because policy gains at the state level have usually come only after long struggle focused on sexuality, American activists are likely to be attentive to administrative application.

*Limits to Change*

American schools remain largely unfriendly places for those who appear to deviate from gender and sexual norms. LGBT students responding to a GLSEN 'climate' survey in 2005 were three times as likely as other students to not feel safe at school (22 per cent vs. 7 per cent), and 90 per cent reported being harassed over the previous year (compared to 62 per cent of other students saying they had been harassed).[58] For transgendered students the figures would be much higher than for lesbians and gays. The vast majority of sexual minority teachers are not fully out; most are probably not even partially out. In some regions and most small towns and rural areas, school climates are especially grim.

The strength of the religious right in all regions of the United States, and its fixation on preserving the heterosexuality of publicly funded schooling against the incursions of predatory homosexuality, makes any progress a struggle against formidable odds. Even the smallest steps towards recognizing sexual diversity in school settings is at risk of producing the kind of controversy that ends up on the evening news or the front pages of the newspapers. Social conservatives will rail against the threats to their children and the insult to their religious values; politicians running for election will warn of 'rampant lesbianism' or of the sickness and death inherent in homosexuality.[59]

Change, when it has occurred, has been easier to effect in policies aimed at increasing the protections for sexual minority students against bullying. School harassment and violence have become front-burner issues in the United States, and several widely reported studies have pointed to the vulnerability of lesbian, gay, bisexual, and transgendered students. Even in the face of stark evidence, change has been slow, but shifts have occurred in several states and many localities.

Such change, however, often does not spill over into other policy areas, and especially those related to what students are formally and informally taught. The emphasis on dangers to sexual minority youth, which has been even greater in the United States than in Canada, also has risks. Such students can be too easily cast only as victims of homophobic bullying.[60] In some respects, the emphasis on dropout rates, depression, substance abuse, and suicide pathologizes sexual minority students in ways that feed the propaganda of the religious right on the dangers of the homosexual 'lifestyle.' It denies the real strength and agency that so many sexual minority adolescents acquire during their schooling years, ignores the dramatic increase in teens feeling able to come out in high school, and sidesteps the remarkable stories of them leading activist challenges to existing school norms.[61] Strategies for change that target only LGBT students also miss the extent to which homophobic bullying regulates and delimits gender in all students. Many targets of harassment and violence are simply perceived to be gay or lesbian, or seen as deviating in other ways from traditional gender norms.

There is no easy answer to this pattern, for the evidence of the harm done by school failure to recognize sexual diversity is real, and is an important lever for policy development. Many school districts would not have moved at all on the road to greater inclusiveness were it not for the starkness of the evidence of the risks entailed in avoidance. It is therefore hard to expect advocates for change to avoid invoking the issue of harm to LGBT students.

Another limitation on change is its very unevenness across school districts and within them. As Melinda Miceli points out, Gay-Straight Alliances are much more likely to be found in states that have already created rights protections for sexual minorities, in urban centres and suburbs, and in relatively privileged areas.[62] Schools with high proportions of Hispanic or African-American students are also less likely to have signs of student activism.

Inclusive policy change, and particularly in disadvantaged areas, has been more difficult to effect as neo-liberal approaches to education have taken firmer hold. This has led to constraints on public spending and augmented calls for practical education focusing on the basics. Such shifts in public opinion and policy outcomes reduce the capacity of educators to develop policies in areas regarded as peripheral to core missions, and limit educators' capacity to allocate resources to implement equity policies. The impoverishment of public education in areas other than relatively wealthy suburbs is especially constraining.

### What Has Produced Change?

What, then, explains the change that has occurred in American schools? No policy take-off has occurred, to be sure, and the overall record is far from good. Still, change began earlier than just about anywhere else, and the spread of inclusive policy has been steady. The very fact that activist networks formed at a relatively early stage, and have grown, is vital to any explanation. This is partly reflective of the high levels of activism we find on a wide range of fronts related to sexuality. The American movement is virtually unique in having substantial organizations (GLSEN at the national level) focusing entirely on schooling issues, and the well-staffed support of large LGBT and civil rights groups.

The sustained activism of educators is an important piece of this picture, and it is reflected in the willingness of teachers to launch challenges to their school authorities and support student groups. Such activism is a striking break from the caution that is so pervasive among teachers. In recent years, there have been signs of teacher activism in Canada, primarily through their unions, but not on the American scale. This may well come from the continuous availability of major organizational channels for such activism in the United States.

The scale of school-focused activism also reflects a sense of urgency created by the political power of religious conservatism. As the right focused more of its resources and rhetoric on schools, activist mobilization and vigilance on the other side became obligatory. The power of the religious right, and the expansiveness of its agenda, also raised the stakes for all school reformers in debates over sexual diversity, and created the opportunity for broadening the base of support for gay-positive initiatives. Many advocates of religious conservatism, after all, are still fighting against the teaching of evolutionary theory, and advocating newly dressed versions of creationism. This mobilizes a wide range of progressive activism, much of it recognizing that the attack on homosexuality is only part of a broad and frightening agenda.

Another major factor contributing to change is the urgency associated with school 'safety' at precisely a time when research findings were pointing to the prevalence and cost of anti-gay bullying. Among western industrialized countries, violence in general and in schools particularly is more widespread in American schools than anywhere. It has also surfaced in particularly tragic forms, most dramatically at Columbine. What has happened in at least some parts of the United States is that the escalating concern over school safety has provided an opening for those who seek greater attention to sexual diversity.

There are structural explanations for American gains. The long history of equity-seeking advocates resorting to litigation to get around political resistance has served LGBT activists well on some of their issues. This strategy has become possible, of course, because of the availability of legal and financial resources from groups experienced in pro-gay litigation. Schooling governance in the United States also allows for innovation. In many states and urban centres, school districts are much smaller than in Canada, less forced into larger boards by waves of amalgamation. This creates very poor schools in many rural and central city areas, stifling innovation, but in other areas it allows for new equity programming. In most states, too, local school boards are less closely monitored by state educational authorities than their Canadian counterparts.

Change in the United States may also be a product of student, teacher, and parent optimism that change is possible and that they bear responsibility for effecting change with or without formal policy permission to act. This argument may reflect a stereotype about American political culture, but the stories recounted here and elsewhere of teachers and students fighting for rights against great odds have far too few Canadian equivalents.

## Conclusion

There is strong pressure to retain what one American writer has called 'the heterosexual parade, marching daily through America's classrooms.'[63] Religious conservatives, and most Republican politicians, evoke the threat of homosexual activists recruiting children to their depravity, some of them ringing the alarm that the proselytizing is well under way in schools across the country. Centrist politicians remain nervous of the issue, and even progressive voices are tempered by the public's anxieties over youthful sexuality.

Such campaigning helps preserve one of the essential foundations for a traditional family regime. It aims to ensure that gender roles are clearly delineated, and that families are portrayed in exclusively heterosexual terms. Most importantly, it denies that young people might naturally become anything other than heterosexual. If they should happen to be drawn to homosexual practices, the lessons they learn in schools must make clear the abnormality and danger of such practices, and the availability of programs to return them to normalcy.

We have seen, however, how forcefully activism has pushed against the resistance. Most remarkable of all has been the work of students. GSAs are not cure-alls, but student determination to form them has raised the profile of sexual diversity, sometimes in places where there cannot be many positive portrayals of homosexuality. GSAs, now widely scattered across the American school landscape, act as stimulants to critical discussion of a once-taboo subject and help mobilize further activism. They raise the visibility of sexual diversity, and encourage students and educators from sexual minorities to come out.

The activist agency in such work has not yet seemed nearly as widespread in Canada. It may derive from the typical American optimism about the possibility of change, or the pragmatic willingness to translate discontent into concrete action in a country where public reliance on government is less valued. It also comes from the need for vigilance in the presence of conservative forces that have a completely transparent agenda for radical and regressive change.

# 10 Comparative Reflections on Public Recognition of Sexual Diversity

Across Canada, the public recognition of lesbian and gay family relationships took off in the mid-and late 1990s, not long after relationship and parenting issues moved to the front burner of the activist movement. Such changes were in the vanguard internationally, with only a small handful of countries in northwestern Europe keeping pace, and none of them doing so on parenting rights until the 2000s. Schooling was an exception, with only a late and slow start to urgently needed policy changes, though otherwise progressive countries in Europe and elsewhere could hardly claim to have done any better.

U.S. jurisdictions could be found in the vanguard of expanding conceptions of family. The frequency of same-sex couples having their own children increased rapidly from the 1980s on, and successful parenting claims proceeded steadily. Struggles over making schools more inclusive emerged earlier in the United States than elsewhere, and there too change spread steadily. This is more than can be said of most regions in Canada until much later.

There are many similarities in the agendas of Canadian and American activist challenge to existing family regimes, and in the way that claims for inclusiveness have been framed by proponents and opponents. The contexts in which they work also have important similarities. Social scientists are able to point to commonalities in belief systems on other issues across the international border; constitutional experts can point to growing similarities between American and Canadian rights frameworks; political economists highlight economic integration and U.S. corporate dominance; comparativists with a broad compass routinely place these two countries in the same categories.[1]

However, the contrasting patterns in the Canadian and American response to activist challenge on relational and parental issues give some credence to writers like Seymour Martin Lipset, who argues that differences are long-standing, and to more recent contributors like Michael Adam, who point to growing divergence on issues of morality.[2] When we broaden the comparative range to include other industrialized countries where struggles over family regimes have been prominent, there is evidence enough for the view that Canada is more like northwestern Europe, and that the United States is at the very least unusual – a view taken by Barry Adam, and perhaps more implicitly by Dennis Altman.[3] The power of conservative religiosity is one important source of distinctiveness, but so is the scale and energy of American activism favouring public recognition of sexual diversity.

Canada, too, has experienced a pattern of change that is distinctive, not only from the United States but also from all other industrialized countries, in large part because of the rapidity of change during the late 1990s, the extensive recognition given to de facto families, and the relatively uncontroversial inclusion of parenting in the systems of recognizing lesbian and gay couples. This is all during a period in which governments at the federal level and most provinces were shifting right, and in which few of them were to be proactive in their embrace of sexual diversity.

**An Overview of Change**

In Canada, the United States, most of Europe, Australia, New Zealand, Israel, and parts of South Africa and Latin America, the increased visibility of sexual minorities has resulted in a much greater public profile for same-sex couples, for lesbian and gay parents, and for openly LGBT youth. This profile in itself has generated pressure on existing family regimes, amplified by activist mobilizing on family-related issues. In a few countries, favourable legal and policy responses to this pressure first appeared in the late 1980s, since which time the spread and pace of change have quickened, most obviously on the public recognition of lesbian and gay relationships.

*Relationship Recognition*

The pressure for change on relational issues intensified as the space for same-sex couples to live together openly enlarged. The early rapid spread of AIDS among gay men also pushed partner rights to the fore in the late 1980s, particularly in respect to medical decision making and inheritance. The rising numbers of children raised by lesbian and gay couples particularly marked in the United States and Canada, also highlighted relational, parenting, and (eventually) schooling issues.

In 1984 Berkeley, California, extended its employees' benefits program to same-sex partners, at a time when the only other jurisdiction in the world to have taken any steps towards such recognition was the Netherlands. The late 1980s saw the creation of the first national civil union registry in Denmark, extending many rights and obligations to same-sex couples, and in that period the Swedish and Dutch governments were taking steps in the same direction. Hamilton, Ontario, in 1986 became the first major Canadian city to extend its employee benefits programs to same-sex couples. The end of the decade saw the first major American court ruling pushing the boundary of existing relationship regimes, in New York.

The early 1990s saw the rapid spread of inclusive employee benefits plans in Canada, with tribunals making clear that exclusion of same-sex partners would be found unconstitutional. In the United States, change was steady but slower, with the extension of public employees plans to gay and lesbian partners in several important American cities and a few states. The first major court victory on gay marriage in any country was won in Hawai'i in 1993, placing that issue irrevocably on the activist agendas of groups on both sides of the expanding battle line.

By the mid-1990s, favourable court rulings were multiplying on both sides of the border. In Canada, the extension of employment benefits was now routine in both the public and private sectors. In British Columbia's legislature, more radical change was occurring from 1992 on, through the incremental redefinition of spouse to include same-sex couples. In the United States, Hawai'i became the first American state to develop multi-policy recognition of same-sex relationships, even though it was far from marriage in scope, and meant as a consolation prize to accompany the refusal to recognize gay marriage. In addition, important court victories were being won on parental claims. Schools activism was intensifying, and supporting the launch of court challenges to school-based bullying.

In Europe, civil union regimes were spreading across Scandinavia in the late 1990s, and even more expansively in the Netherlands. Court-forced changes were starting in Israel, and Australia's capital region passed several statutes recognizing gay/lesbian relationships. Change in Canada was more radical, especially at the end of the 1990s with a monumental ruling by the Supreme Court effectively prohibiting the treatment of same-sex couples any differently from de facto heterosexual couples, which were already given most rights and obligations associated with marriage. A wave of measures at the provincial, territorial, and federal levels then followed. Marriage came in 2003, first to Ontario and then rapidly to other jurisdictions.

In 1999 Vermont's Supreme Court forced the state legislature to eliminate discrimination in state and local law, producing the first comprehensive civil union regime in the country. At about the same time, California took the first of a series of legislative steps to recognize same-sex couples. This, combined with the many policies adopted by local authorities and private employers, were part of a steady forward movement, though without the Canadian take-off. The comparatively early emergence of activist pressure on the specific question of marriage led to a second major court victory, in Massachusetts, this one not allowing the civil union escape route. Of course it could not extend rights and obligations under federal jurisdiction, and it was doomed to be relatively untransportable across state lines.

In the United States, the mid- and late 1990s saw important wins in court on schools issues, supporting student and teacher claims that ignoring homophobic harassment was unconstitutional. The religious right was of course opposed to any school recognition of homosexuality in anything other than condemnatory ways, and most schools were totally unresponsive to recognition claims from sexual minorities, but progressive change was still being more widely debated in the public arena than in any other country.

On all issues, the unevenness of gains in the United States is extraordinary. By 2004, when almost three-quarters of Canadian jurisdictions had extended significant recognition to gay and lesbian couples, and more than half allowed marriage, only 12 per cent of American federal or state governments had extended significant recognition to them, and only Massachusetts allowed marriage. Through to the present time, the march of change, short of marriage, continues steadily and with undiminished pace, but the gap with Canadian jurisdictions has remained dramatic (see table 10.1).

Figure 10.1 clearly shows the take-off pattern evident on relational issues in Canada, and the steady and slow spread of recognition across U.S. states even at a time when anti-gay-marriage measures were

Table 10.1    Federal/Provincial/Territorial/State Recognition of Same-Sex Relationships, Canada and the United States, 1999–2006* (%)

|  |  | United States | Canada |
|---|---|---|---|
| 1999 | partial recognition | 17 | 93 |
| 2002 | partial recognition | 23 | 100 |
|  | significant recognition | 6 | 64 |
| 2004 | partial recognition | 31 | 100 |
|  | significant recognition | 12 | 71 |
|  | marriage | 2 | 57 |
| 2006 | partial recognition | 41 | 100 |
|  | significant recognition | 18 | 86 |
|  | marriage | 2 | 100 |

* In Canada, 14 jurisdictions (10 provinces, 3 territories, federal government); in the United States, 52 jurisdictions (50 states, DC, federal government). Significant recognition in Canada refers to de facto couples, not requiring registration.

being enacted. Figure 10.2 illustrates the rapid development of comprehensive regimes recognizing gay and lesbian couples following the Supreme Court of Canada's 1999 *M. v. H.* ruling. Graphing the expansion of recognition for each Canadian province and territory would show a very tight clustering around the mean, with even the most distinctive provinces deviating only modestly. That is in stark contrast to the United States, where over half of the states remain continuously at the bottom of the graph, according no recognition to same-sex couples, and where only six states have extended broad recognition (again, only within state and local jurisdictions). Where change in the United States was most pronounced was in the corporate sector. The first large firm to extend benefits plans to same-sex partners of employees was in 1993, and by the end of the decade about 40 per cent of the country's largest companies had followed suit. Over half had done so by the end of 2006.

In Europe, as figure 10.3 shows, change was much more like that in Canada, with civil union registries for lesbian and gay couples spreading rapidly, and marriages being performed in the Netherlands (2000), Belgium (2003), and Spain (2003).[4] By the mid-2000s, most western Europeans had access to some form of registry, and over half of these regimes had very expansive rights and obligations associated with

Figure 10.1 Same-Sex Couple Recognition: Per Cent of Canadian Provinces/Territories and U.S. States Covered*

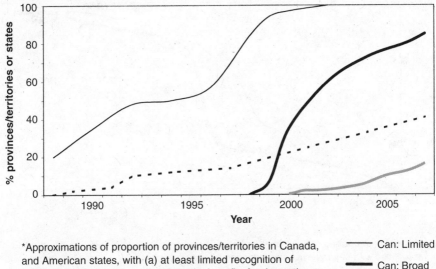

*Approximations of proportion of provinces/territories in Canada, and American states, with (a) at least limited recognition of lesbian/gay relationships – for example, benefits for domestic partners of state/provincial employees – and (b) broad or wide-ranging recognition of such relationships (as in those U.S. states with civil union regimes or equivalent).

——— Can: Limited

——— Can: Broad

- - - U.S.: Limited

——— U.S.: Broad

them. Change was also occurring in parts of central and eastern Europe (e.g., the Czech Republic, Hungary, Slovenia), even while activists were encountering fierce resistance to their claims for visibility in Russia, Poland, Latvia, and a few other eastern and central European countries.

European Union law was not moving nearly so quickly.[5] As recently as 1998, the European Court of Justice had ruled that the denial of same-sex benefits by a British employer did not constitute a form of discrimination covered by European law (*Grant v. South West Trains*). In 2001, the same court upheld the denial of benefits to the same-sex partner of a Swedish EU staff member, in part on the grounds that his registered partnership was not the same as marriage (*D and Sweden v. Council*). Only in 2004 was there some opening to the provision of such benefits for EU employees, providing the relationship was registered, that marriage was not available in the staff member's home country, and certain other criteria were met (*Karner v. Austria*).

Figure 10.2 Same-Sex Couple Recognition: Per Cent of Policy Areas Covered*

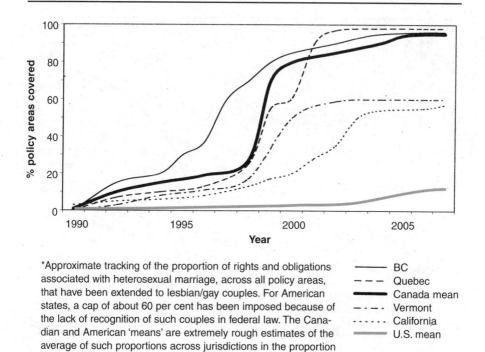

*Approximate tracking of the proportion of rights and obligations
associated with heterosexual marriage, across all policy areas,
that have been extended to lesbian/gay couples. For American
states, a cap of about 60 per cent has been imposed because of
the lack of recognition of such couples in federal law. The Canadian and American 'means' are extremely rough estimates of the
average of such proportions across jurisdictions in the proportion
of policy recognition.

——— BC
– – – Quebec
━━━ Canada mean
– · – · Vermont
······ California
▬▬▬ U.S. mean

Outside Europe and North America, public policy and law were
moving rapidly towards recognizing same-sex relationships in several
countries. New Zealand developed a wide-ranging civil union regime
in 2004, and at the same time significant recognition was accorded de
facto couples (as in Canada). Incremental change was occurring in
South Africa, Israel, Colombia, Honduras, Uruguay, and parts of Australia, Brazil, Argentina, Switzerland, Italy, and Mexico. In 2006, the
High Court of Israel ruled that same-sex couples married in Canada
(and presumably elsewhere) could register marriages in Israel. In that
same year, South Africa's parliament approved a bill allowing for
same-sex marriages, prompted by a favourable (and unanimous) Constitutional Court ruling.

Table 10.2   U.S. State and Canadian Provincial/Territorial Recognition of
Parenting Rights (%)

|  |  | United States | Canada |
|---|---|---|---|
| 1970s | early court wins | ✓ | ✓ |
| 1995 | partial recognition (adoption)[a] | 14 | 15 |
|  | major recognition (adoption) | 2 | 15 |
| 2000 | partial recognition | 20 | 100 |
|  | major recognition | 6 | 23 |
|  | prohibitions | 6 | 0 |
| 2004 | partial recognition | 30[b] | 100 |
|  | significant recognition | 12 | 77–85[c] |
|  | prohibitions | 10–18[d] | 0 |
| 2006 | partial recognition | 50 | 100 |
|  | significant recognition | 20 | 77–85 |
|  | prohibitions | 8–16 | 0 |

[a]These assessments are approximate, especially in light of the prominence of court
rulings in effecting change. 'Partial' refers to change in one policy area (e.g., custody),
or a court ruling in one jurisdiction. 'Major' refers to change across a wide range of parenting issues.

[b]Some estimates would increase this to about 50 per cent, based on the number of
states in which there had been at least some positive court rulings (at any level) on
parenting rights.

[c]There is no doubt that remaining inequalities in formal provincial or territorial policy on
parenting issues would not survive court scrutiny, so this figure represents only the
extent to which governments had taken steps to address change that would eventually
be forced upon them. The range reflects uncertainty about whether existing Yukon law
allows for same-sex adoption rights.

[d]The first figure represents explicit prohibitions on fostering or adoption; the second
adds in states where courts have ruled that existing law prevents adoption rights from
being extended.

## Parenting

Changes in parenting regimes, though related to broader shifts in relationship regulation, display patterns that resist easy generalization.
Despite considerable public unease among Canadians about allowing

Figure 10.3   Same-Sex Relationship Recognition outside Canada and the United States[a]

| 1979 | 1986–7 | 1989 | 1993 | 1994–5 | 1996–7 | 1998–9 | 2000 | 2001 | 2002 | 2003 | 2004 | 2005 | 2006 |
|---|---|---|---|---|---|---|---|---|---|---|---|---|---|
|  |  |  |  |  |  |  |  |  |  |  |  |  | Austral |
|  |  |  |  |  |  |  |  |  |  |  |  |  | AUSTRIA |
|  |  |  |  |  |  |  |  |  |  |  |  | Austral | SLOVEN |
|  |  |  |  |  |  |  |  |  |  | Austral | Austral | AUSTRIA | FR |
|  |  |  |  |  |  |  |  |  | Austral | S.Afr | S.Afr | PORT | PORT |
|  |  |  |  |  |  |  |  |  | S.Afr | U.K. | U.K. | HUNG | HUNG |
|  |  |  |  |  |  |  |  | Austral | U.K. | Spain | Spain | FR | CZECH |
|  |  |  |  |  |  |  |  | Israel | Spain | Israel | AUSTRIA | S.Afr | Israel |
|  |  |  |  |  |  |  | Austria | Spain | Israel | AUSTRIA | HUNG | Israel | Switz |
|  |  |  |  |  |  | Austral | Austral | AUSTRIA | AUSTRIA | N.ZEA | FR | Den | Ice |
|  |  |  |  |  | Fr | N.Zea | N.Zea | HUNG | HUNG | PORT | PORT | Ice | Den |
|  |  |  |  |  | N.Zea. | Israel | Israel | PORT | PORT | HUNG | Nor | Switz | Nor |
|  |  |  |  |  | Israel | Spain | Spain | FR | FR | FR | Den | Nor | Fin |
|  |  |  |  | Fr | Spain | HUNG | HUNG | N.ZEA | N.ZEA | Germ | Israel | Fin | U.K. |
|  |  |  |  | Israel | HUNG | FR | FR | Den | Den | Nor | Ice | U.K. | SWED |
|  |  |  |  | N.Zea | Fin | Fin | Fin | Fin | Fin | Fin | Fin | GERM | GERM |
|  |  |  |  | Spain | Neth | Neth | Swed | Swed | Nor | Ice | SWED | SWED | N.ZEA |
|  |  | Swed | Swed | Neth | Swed | Swed | Ice | Ice | Ice | Den | N.ZEA | N.ZEA | S.AFR* |
|  | Swed | Neth | Neth | Swed | Ice | Ice | Nor | Nor | Germ | SWED | GERM | SPAIN* | SPAIN* |
|  | Den | Nor | Nor | Nor | Nor | Nor | Den | Germ | SWED | BELG* | BELG* | BELG* | BELG* |
| Neth | Neth | Den | Den | Den | Den | Den | NETH* | NETH* | NETH* | NETH* | NETH* | NETH* | NETH* |

**Canadian and American Benchmarks[b]**

| | | | | | | | | | | | | |
|---|---|---|---|---|---|---|---|---|---|---|---|---|
| Canada A | | Can | Can | CAN | CAN | CAN | CAN | CAN | CAN | CAN | CAN* | CAN* | CAN* |
| Canada B | | Can | Can | Can | Can | CAN | CAN | CAN | CAN | CAN | CAN | CAN* | CAN* |
| U.S. A | u.s. | u.s | u.s. | U.S. | U.S. | U.S. | U.S. | U.S. | U.S. | U.S. | U.S. | U.S. | U.S. |
| U.S. B | | | u.s | u.s. | u.s. | u.s. | u.s. | u.s. | u.s. | u.s. | u.s. | u.s. | u.s. |

Note:

Light face lower case: recognition in 1–2 policy areas.

Light face caps: recognition across several policy areas.

Bold lower case: widespread recognition but with major exceptions (e.g., for adoption).

Bold caps: widespread recognition.

*Denotes marriage. The Belgian marriage regime excluded adoption until 2006; the Dutch excludes foreign adoptions.

[a]Australian states are not included, but a designation is given to the country as a whole to reflect widening state-level steps towards same-sex relationship recognition. Among major western European states, by 2006 only Italy, Ireland, and Greece had taken no significant steps towards same-sex relationship recognition, though there was some discussion of this in Ireland and Italy.

[b]In Canadian and U.S. lines, 'A' denotes patterns of recognition in pioneer provinces or states; 'B' indicates patterns in more than half of regions. In the U.S. case, 2000 marks Vermont's creation of civil unions, and is given a bold capital designation because all matters within state jurisdiction were made inclusive, even if the many areas under federal jurisdiction were left unaffected. The 'B' line is given a modest entry from about 2003 because of the number of employees (private and public sector) given same-sex benefits.

Source: Robert Wintemute and Mads Adenaes, eds., *Legal Recognition of Same-Sex Relationships* (Oxford: Hart, 2001); Kathleen Lahey and Kevin Alderson, *Same-Sex Marriage: The Personal and the Political* (Toronto: Insomniac Press, 2004); Yuval Merin, *Equality for Same-Sex Couples* (Chicago: University of Chicago Press, 2002); Kees Waalkujk, 'Levels of Legal Consequence of Marriage, Cohabitation and Registered Partnership for Different-Sex and Same-Sex Partners: Comparative Overview and Comparative Analysis,' in *Same-Sex Couples, Same-Sex Partnerships, and Homosexual Marriages: A Focus on Cross-National Differentials*, ed. Marie Digoix and Patrick Festy, Documents de travail, no. 124 (Paris: Institut national d'études démographiques, 2004), 47–92.

lesbians and gays to adopt or foster children, legal change on this front followed the take-off pattern evident in relationship issues, with formal acceptance of parental rights in place across most of the country in the early 2000s. British Columbia's legislature was the first any-where to take this step in the adoption area, in 1995, and an Ontario court ruling in the same year opened the door substantially to second-parent adoption and joint adoption. The 1999 Supreme Court ruling in *M. v. H.* was widely seen as prohibiting most discrimination in the par-enting domain.

Given how contentious parenting is, the American story is intrigu-ing. Change in the legal response to parenting claims has been if any-thing more widespread than the recognition of gay and lesbian rela-tionships, and it is more widespread than parenting rights in Europe.[6] Change began in the early 1990s, in custody and second-parent adop-tion. Near the end of that decade, two American states had widely extended parenting rights to lesbian/gay couples; by 2007 almost ten had done so. An additional dozen or so had seen major court rulings extending rights in one or another parenting domain, and one esti-mate has suggested that in about half of all U.S. states there was at least some court acceptance of second-parent adoption. There is no take-off here, but the spread of parenting rights is remarkable, especially in the face of mounting conservative pressure to bar such rights.

The northern European story, in other ways so similar to that of Canada, is a strikingly discriminatory one on parental issues. Adop-tion rights have been routinely excluded from or limited within the civil union and even marital systems developed for gays and lesbians in Europe, regimes that are otherwise far ahead of the American in eliminating discrimination based on sexual orientation. In 1999, Denmark became the first country in Europe to grant any parenting rights at all to same-sex couples, allowing a partner to adopt the child of a same-sex partner, but this excluded children adopted from a foreign country, and 'stranger' adoptions from anywhere.[7] The Dutch marriage legislation of 2000 effectively copied the Danish pattern, pointedly excluding the right to adopt foreign children (an exclusion the government seems now ready to remove). Belgian marriages for lesbian and gay couples, inaugurated in 2003, entirely excluded adop-tion rights, until additional legislative change in 2006.[8] Partial rights were extended by Iceland first in 2000, with provisions for joint custody and second-parent adoption in its civil unions, and then in

2006, with joint adoption added. By mid-decade Norway, Sweden, and Germany had taken similar steps.[9]

Same-sex marriages that were made legal in Canada in 2003, then, were the first anywhere that did not have glaring exceptions around parenting. The Spanish marriage regime that came into effect in 2005 was the second. Britain's civil union legislation was preceded by moves to extend adoption rights to gay/lesbian parents, and Scotland's legislature approved gay adoptions in 2006. That said, there was plenty of anecdotal evidence as to the hesitations and awkwardness surrounding adoption by British same-sex couples, some of whom (able to afford) it appeared to have an easier time in the United States, even in Florida![10]

The readiness to treat parenting as a controversial matter quite distinct from other relational issues is evident in the regulation of assisted reproduction. Civil union regimes in Europe have routinely left untouched a pattern of denying access to assisted reproduction clinics to all but married couples. The Netherlands and Denmark have been exceptions for some years; the United Kingdom and Belgium now have some clinics accessible to lesbian couples. Sweden recently legalized artificial insemination for lesbians, though in 2006, a Swedish court turned down a lesbian's request to formally adopt the child of her partner, conceived of through anonymous donor insemination in Denmark, on the grounds that children had a right to know their biological parents! In almost all other countries the exclusion of lesbians and gays (and single women) is explicit. The result of such restrictions, combined with the widespread limitations on adoption, means that far fewer European same-sex couples than North American have children. Even in the Netherlands, only 18 per cent of lesbians have children at home, and only 1 per cent of gay men, significantly fewer than the 33 per cent of lesbian and the 22 per cent of gay couples reporting having children in the last U.S. census.[11]

## Schooling

The schools issue further complicates our comparative portrait, for here we find a more effective challenge to exclusionary patterns in the United States than just about anywhere else. It is not that gains in American schools even approach an adequate response; rather, that schooling systems in almost all other countries, including Canada, show an even more appalling failure to respond.

In the United States more than anywhere, bullying in schools against sexual minority students became a wedge issue in the late 1980s, and even more widely in the late 1990s, opening the door gradually to discussion of other ways in which schools marginalized LGBT students and teachers. Advocacy has come from students, educators, parents, teacher unions, and advocacy groups, the latter bringing with them the considerable resources needed for court action. This has produced a few statewide policies enacted after much debate over specifically homophobic bullying and impressively high-profile court rulings against schools turning a blind eye to harassment and discrimination. Gay-Straight Alliances have been formed in both favourable and intimidating school environments to raise the profile of the inclusive agenda.

Reform has encountered inattention or resistance from religious and secular conservatives, from cautious educators, and from parents uneasy about the messages their children are receiving about gender and sexuality. Christian conservatives have created litigation groups ready to challenge reform, and in many states advocates of religiously shaped curricular programs have access to government funds supporting abstinence-only sex education. In the face of all this, however, equity-seeking advocates have produced real change in a large number of school districts.

A few school boards in Canada, and some individual schools, have taken steps to recognize sexual diversity among staff and students, the Toronto board being a pioneer. However, only in the 2000s has real and sustained pressure for change spread beyond a few isolated school boards. Canadian advocates of change do not face opposition on anything like the scale of their American counterparts, but they have also applied nothing like the activist pressure for change that has been mounted south of the border. They regularly encounter complacency or a form of Canadian smugness that assumes that things are so much better north of the international border.

Change on this front is scarce enough in Europe and in other countries that have seen important shifts in family regime. In the Netherlands, the long-established advocacy group COC has been sponsoring school talks since the 1970s, but Garda Schadee believes that the great majority of school authorities are still very cautious about broaching the question of sexual diversity.[12]

Britain's education ministry (with jurisdiction over England and Wales) established sex education guidelines in 2000 that included sexual orientation, but an additional note strikingly reminiscent of the notorious Section 28 (repealed that same year) warned against the promotion of any particular sexual orientation.[13] Only in 2004 were there signs of more significant change. Programs to combat homophobic bullying were spreading, the National Union of Teachers was issuing guidelines for teachers on supporting LGBT students, and the national group Stonewall was launching an 'Education for All' campaign. In 2007, a pilot program was developed for a selection of fourteen elementary schools across the country, introducing students to the idea of families headed by same-sex couples.[14]

In 2006, Irish authorities seemed prepared to address the question of homophobic bullying, after the publication of evidence on alarming rates in the country's school. That year, the Swedish parliament enacted a new anti-discrimination law for students, obliging schools to develop action plans to prevent discrimination on a variety of grounds, including sexual orientation. Until then, however, teacher unions had not taken proactive action on sexual diversity, and students in education faculties received almost nothing on the issue.[15] Also in 2006, the Spanish government unveiled plans to teach students about the variety of families – including those headed by same-sex couples – though this would cover only grades ten and over. Schools in some German states were addressing sexual diversity, though only in recent years.

## Explaining American 'Pioneering'

Early American movement towards recognizing new family forms and the need for change in schools arose in part because there was a critical mass of activists pressing for equity. By the 1970s, American activism was building on a scale far exceeding the political movements elsewhere.

This reflected in part the material conditions allowing for the emergence of identities based on sexual difference (though this would also be true in Canada). As John D'Emilio and others have argued, the ability to act on homosexual urges increases with capitalism, particularly with the kind of urbanization and dislocation that comes with advanced industrial and 'post-industrial' capitalism.[16] Large cities produce the kind of anonymity that creates spaces for homosexual activity, institutions catering to homosexual needs, and networks among them. American cities were hardly unique in providing such foundations for the development of a visible activist movement. What does seem to set the American case a little apart, though, is the extent of geographic mobility that has accompanied its economic growth, and the disconnection from extended family that can so often result by accident or on purpose.[17]

This provides opportunities not only for sexual diversity to become more visible, but also for political identities based on sexual difference to form. Here too the American case stands out, for the relative weakness of class as an identifier creates openings for identity formation on other grounds. Canada has also seen a long history of denying the relevance of class, but the pattern is more deeply set in the United States. And of course the greater population density of the United States creates more capacity for mobilization.

The growth of activist movements based on identities such as this had a model in the civil rights movement. Here was a movement that had worked outside and inside the existing political framework, and had marshalled the energies of both reformers and radicals. The environmental movement followed this pattern, as did the anti-war movement of the 1960s. The women's movement was the same, and American feminists were able to build a more sustained and resourced political movement than counterparts in most other countries.

The extent of progressive mobilization around sexual diversity issues is also, of course, a response to the power of conservative organizing and its leverage within the Republican Party. The American religious right poses a constant threat to every gain, and this fact requires a degree of vigilance that calls for considerable institutionalization of social movement groups. The threats posed by religious and secular conservatives on other policy fronts also helps secure support from civil rights groups, women's groups, and labour.

Institutional factors are at play in creating opportunities for activist pressure to make a difference. The complex fragmentation of the political system and its decentralization in areas relevant to families and schools create impediments to large-scale change, but also opportunities for 'innovation.' The decentralization of control in these policy areas has allowed a few states in progressive regions, and local authorities across all regions, to take important steps in responding to activists.

U.S. activists have additional openings through the court system. As Jason Pierceson points out, with Susan Mezey concurring on some issue fronts, the existence of distinct federal and state systems has frequently multiplied the windows of opportunity.[18] This was especially so because U.S. states have their own constitutions, with equity wording that has helped LGBT claimants in some states. This has often resulted in expansive rulings that have rivalled those in other countries where courts have ruled positively on sexual orientation cases. Across the country, litigants have also been able to rely on large and well-funded activist groups prepared to support litigation, groups like the American Civil Liberties Union and Lambda Legal Defense that have few parallels in other political systems.

Early recognition of sexual diversity in family law and schooling in some localities and states also benefited from prior victories on equality rights, and specifically on the rights of sexual minorities. I agree with both Kees Waaldijk and Robert Wintemute, writing of international comparisons, and Kenneth Wald writing about intra-state comparisons within the United States, in arguing that securing gains in relational, parenting, and schooling issues is much easier in areas where homosexuality has already been decriminalized and basic non-discrimination measures enacted.[19] A few American states decriminalized 'sodomy' in the 1970s, and included sexual orientation in human rights frameworks, as early as any jurisdictions in Canada or northern Europe. This created platforms on which family-related claims could be advanced.

*Relationship Issues*

On relationship issues especially, leverage for effecting change has been strengthened by earlier changes in family patterns. Relationships within marriage, and growth in divorce and cohabitation rates, changed some of the norms around conjugal relationships, even if legal change was slow in coming. True, real inequalities remained within heterosexual relationships, but formally marriage became more of a contract between equal parties, easier to enter into and exit from than it had been in the past.[20]

Claims that marriage was exclusively based in religious principles were still influential, but in some settings were harder to advance when divorce became more commonplace. Conflicts between separating spouses also confronted American judges with difficult dilemmas about property, income, and parenting. What many no doubt saw as dysfunctional heterosexual families helped provide a favourable context for the many claims made by relatively functional gay and lesbian families.

## Parenting Issues

There are additional reasons for the relatively early success of claims for parental recognition in the United States. Lesbian and gay couples had earlier access to assisted reproduction than same-sex couples almost everywhere else, even if at a high financial cost. Joint adoption may not have been available, and not even second-parent adoption, but with few exceptions across the United States there were no prohibitions on individuals applying to adopt children. This helped fuel a baby boom that pushed parenting issues towards the front of the activist agenda.

As Merin points out, too, securing parental responsibilities in the United States (and in Canada) routinely involves courts that have significant leeway (through common law) in arriving at judgments.[21] Judges have room to respond to the facts on the ground. The strength of neo-liberalism in the United States, and the fact that the state was never as expansive as in Canada and most of Europe, also provided a rhetorical vehicle for judges and policy makers to support recognition of same-sex relationship rights, and parenting rights especially. If the death of a biological mother meant that children became wards of the state rather than of a same-sex partner, even some right-wing politicians and judges could see that parental responsibilities should be extended to non-biological parents.

## Schooling Issues

The political fragmentation and decentralization that gave claims for recognition of sexual difference in family law a chance of early success also contributed to early gains in schooling. In those states with small school boards, unusually progressive suburbs or college towns often had their own boards, and were more open to innovation than the larger boards that prevail in Canada, or the more centralized educational regimes usually found elsewhere. As we have seen, the long experience of reformist educators in resisting religious conservative pressure has also broadened the alliance potential for those seeking recognition of sexual diversity. There is much less room for complacency here than in more uniformly 'progressive' countries.

Here, too, the courts have provided an avenue for activist intervention, supported by groups who recognize the high stakes involved in combatting religious conservatism. American courts have an uneven record in according constitutional rights protections to sexual minorities, but many gains in schooling have been secured on the basis of more firmly established principles like free speech and association, and the right to be free of harassment.

The incidence of violence in American schools has made the question of safety a wedge issue, reinforced by the considerable data made public from the late 1980s on about the risks facing sexual minority youth. This has prodded students and educators to take action, and at a comparatively early stage, in a surprising array of localities. Many advocates of change on this front, too, have used school safety as a framework for introducing a broad range of policy changes.

## Explaining the Absence of American Take-Off

But with all these advantages and openings, American activists have never achieved the point of take-off that their colleagues have on relationship issues, at least in Canada, northern Europe, and a few other settings. Why?

### Religion

Anyone writing comparatively about advances in the recognition of sexual diversity must give priority to the impediment represented by American religious conservatism.[22] Americans are highly religious, whether measured by frequency of church attendance or piety measured in other ways, and many of them are religiously conservative.[23] The sheer size of the religious right and of its constituency, and its eagerness to place sexual diversity at the centre of its agenda, makes it a powerful impediment to change.

Table 10.3 displays responses to a World Values Survey question about how important religion is in one's life, and it shows a remarkable 57 per cent of Americans saying 'very important' – higher than any country in western Europe. Even in the least 'religious' regions of the United States (for example, the Pacific Northwest), levels of religious practice and of conservatism among the religious are higher than anywhere in Canada, apart from quite specific pockets within such provinces as Alberta and British Columbia.

Table 10.3   Public Opinion on Religion, 1990–2000

| | Religion 'very important' in my life (% agreeing) | |
| --- | --- | --- |
| | 1990 | 2000 |
| North America: | | |
| United States | 53 | 57 |
| Canada | 31 | 30 |
| Europe | | |
| Netherlands | 19 | 17 |
| Sweden | 10 | 11 |
| Britain | 16 | 13 |
| Belgium | 15 | 18 |
| France | 14 | 11 |
| Spain | 21 | 19 |
| Italy | 34 | 33 |
| Elsewhere | | |
| Australia* | – | 23 |
| New Zealand* | – | 19 |
| South Africa | 66 | 70 |
| Brazil | 57 | 65 |

*Not asked in 1990.
Source: Ronald Inglehart, et al., *Human Beliefs and Values*,
tables F118, A006.
*A Cross-Cultural Sourcebook Based on the 1999–2002 Values
Survey* (Madrid: Siglo XXI Editores, 2004).

Religious conservative leverage over the Republican Party has help-ed cement a coalition between moral conservatism and anti-state neo-liberalism – a coalition that has been difficult to build in other liberal democratic political systems. Republican control of the executive or of any part of the legislative branch in any particular jurisdiction usually stymies attempts to extend policy recognition of sexual diversity, espe-cially in light of the party's high levels of cohesion on these issues. Even where Democrats are in formal control of all branches of government, they are often unable or reluctant to act because of persistent dissent within their own ranks – dissent born of principled opposition to gay rights or electoral fears of being associated with such issues.

There may be some weakening in the strength of Christian conser-vatism and the politicized religious right. An early 2007 survey by the

Pew Research Center showed a decline in the population reporting that prayer was an important part of daily life – down to 45 per cent from 55 per cent in 1999. The failure to secure a national constitutional amendment on marriage, and the reduced majorities that state referenda on the subject secured in the 2006 election, were also demoralizing to many conservatives. One early 2007 report in *U.S. News and World Report* was headlined 'Christian Right Feels Adrift.'[24] Nevertheless, religious conservatives continue to form a major constituency, and the religious right commands an impressive media profile that still plays on homosexuality as a sign of moral decay.

*Political Culture*

Some attitudinal indicators of political culture, for example those touching on deference to authority, criticism of government interference, and acceptance of diversity, do not as clearly differentiate Americans from Canadians as some comparative analysis would suggest. However, we have seen signs of growing divergence in attitudes towards moral questions, including those regarding homosexuality.

Americans also seem to fear social disintegration more than the populations of most industrialized countries. The strength of religious conservatism in the United States, the extent of geographic mobility that separates family members, and high crime levels fuel anxieties over 'family values' with few parallels in Canada or in other industrialized liberal democratic societies. Nowhere else does there seem to be so much support for radical individualism and at the same time anxiety about the inevitable atomization that results from it. As Michael Adams has put it, Americans 'seem inclined to latch on to traditional institutional practices, beliefs, and norms as anchors in a national environment that is more intensely competitive, chaotic, and even violent.'[25]

That anxiety may well be reinforced by the 'muscularity' of American nationalism, a characteristic associated with the country's imperial standing in world politics.[26] Concerns about the strength of American moral fibre have parallels with late-nineteenth-century Britain at the height of that country's imperial expansion, and it can be no coincidence that conservatives in the United States so often cite the 'decadence' of the late Roman Empire as prominent in their explanations of its decline. The superpower status of the United States also secures the social and political prominence of the military, and reinforces opposition to any moves that would weaken its masculine strength. The muscular nationalism that results builds on the historically rooted 'messianic vision' so prevalent in the United States, and easily embraces a belief that homosexuality is a perversion of core American values. It is not that other countries' nationalist traditions or contemporary military cultures are genuinely and equitably open to sexual minorities; it is that there is less fixation on the question of perversion and weakness. In any event, in other countries with highly visible LGBT populations, the military itself plays a less prominent role.

*Institutional and Legal Factors*

The forces of resistance to recognizing sexual diversity in the United States benefit from a political system deliberately designed to be cumbersome, just as proponents of change can sometimes profit from the system's multiple openings. Securing legislative victory would require a united Democratic Party to have firm control of both legislative houses and the governor's office in any particular state, and such a combination is rare.

Anti-gay opponents have taken advantage of referenda on issues related to sexual diversity, or have used the threat of referenda to intimidate politicians. The mobilizing capacity of the religious right has allowed it to gather large numbers of signatures required to place issues like gay marriage on state ballots, and to secure victories on many of them. There are many centrist and even progressive Democrats who fear the impact of having such measures on the ballot at the same time as they are up for election, and there is many a Republican strategist eager to take advantage of just that. In almost all other countries, referenda are unusual, and difficult or impossible to secure through popular initiative.

The absence of American take-off is also a product of the U.S Supreme Court's failure to prohibit discrimination against sexual minorities. This comes partly from a shift to more restrictive interpretations of equity rights over recent decades, as Ran Hirschl so tellingly chronicles, impelled in part by the resurgent power of neo-liberalism and the appointment of conservative justices by Republican presidents.[27] It also comes from the wide latitude provided by the very general equality rights provisions in the American constitution.

*Policy Context*

The fact that most states and countless localities have not yet established basic equality rights protections for sexual minorities is an obvious barrier to gains in policy areas that have typically built on such foundations. And the fact that consensual homosexual activity is still statutorily criminalized in some U.S. states (despite the U.S. Supreme Court's 2003 ruling in *Lawrence v. Texas*) has further slowed progress on other fronts.

The limited nature of U.S. legal recognition of de facto heterosexual couples has also been an impediment.[28] Advocates in Canada, New Zealand, the Netherlands, and Scandinavia could secure gains in family matters, for example, by first claiming equivalence to de facto straight couples. Americans have only limited access to that route, and only in the few states that have taken major steps towards recognition of de facto status. This circumstance tempted activists at an early stage to raise the highly emotive question of marriage, polarizing debate before much incremental advance on family policy had been achieved.

Another factor that has slowed the recognition of gay and lesbian relationships has been the high cost of health-care benefits in the United States, and the rhetorical wedge this provides to opponents. Sexual minorities are widely perceived (inaccurately) to be materially advantaged, so the prospect of them acquiring expensive benefits, and especially those that can be portrayed as a drain on the public treasury, hands opponents a useful weapon.

## Factors Explaining Take-Off in Family Regimes: Canada and Elsewhere

A number of the factors that have allowed for rapid change in Canada and elsewhere may be inferred from the discussion of barriers to change in the United States.

*Religion*

We have already seen that Canada has lower levels of religious practice than the United States, and of religious conservatism in particular. The contrasts to the American case are even stronger in most of Europe. Religious conservatism is an important current among Roman

Catholics in Canada, throughout Europe, and in Australia, but it is not nearly as widespread as in the upper reaches of the church hierarchy. Catholics as a whole in Canada, the United States, and Europe are not particularly adherent to conservative positions on issues like abortion and gay rights, and have years of practice sidestepping doctrinal guidelines in areas where their own beliefs do not coincide. In Quebec, Spain, Belgium, and other parts of Europe, anti-clericalism also remains a powerful force among many nominal Catholics, limiting the capacity of the church hierarchy to influence public policy.

Rejection of the Catholic Church, and resistance to its influence on public policy, has been an especially powerful ingredient in post-dictatorship Spanish politics, and particularly evident in recent years. In response to the 2000 World Values Survey, only 19 per cent of the population responded that religion was important in their lives. Once the Socialists took power, they secured high levels of popular support for one measure after another that was fiercely opposed by the Catholic hierarchy, including gay marriage.

An additional factor explaining the acceleration of change in family regimes in Canada and northwestern Europe is the progressivism of several major Protestant churches. Canada is especially distinctive on this front, with its largest Protestant denomination, the United Church, having long taken public stands in favour of LGBT rights, including civil marriage. It is proportionately larger than the United Church of Christ in the United States, with which it has many similarities, and it has gone further than Lutheran or other Protestant churches in northern Europe. There is also a strong progressive current within Canada's Anglican Church, a much smaller denomination but with unusually high visibility.

*Political Culture and Public Beliefs*

In Canada, most of northern Europe, and Spain, there is more acceptance of homosexuality than there is in the United States. The World Values Survey of 2000 indicated that American disapproval of homosexuality (32 per cent indicating that it was 'never justified') was significantly higher than most of northwestern Europe. Canada is only slightly behind on this survey, but there is much other evidence to suggest a wider 'disapproval' gap than this. Support for gay marriage is significantly higher in Canada and most of northwestern Europe than in the United States (see table 10.4). At the same time, Euro-

Table 10.4   European Attitudes on Same-Sex Marriage and Adoption, 2006, and on Homosexuality, 2000

|  | 2006 (% agreeing with) | | 2000 | |
| --- | --- | --- | --- | --- |
|  | Homosexual marriage[a] | Same-sex adoption[b] | % agreeing homosexuality never justified[c] | % not wanting homosexual neighbours[d] |
| Netherlands | 82 | 69 | 7 | 6 |
| Sweden | 71 | 51 | 9 | 8 |
| Denmark | 69 | 44 | 21 | 8 |
| Belgium | 62 | 43 | 27 | 18 |
| Spain | 56 | 43 | 17 | 16 |
| Germany | 52 | 42 | 19 | 14 |
| Czech Republic | 52 | 24 | 27 | – |
| France | 48 | 35 | 23 | 16 |
| Britain | 46 | 33 | 25 | 24 |
| Italy | 31 | 24 | 30 | 29 |

[a]Question: 'Do you agree with homosexual marriages being allowed throughout Europe?' (Approximate response for similar question about Canada and the United States: Canada, 62% U.S. 46%).
[b]Question: 'Do you agree with authorizing the adoption of children for homosexual couples throughout Europe?' (Approximate response for similar question about Canada and the United States: 51% both countries).
[c]'Please tell me for each of the following statements whether you think it can always be justified, never be justified, or something in between: Homosexuality' (never justified: Canada, 27%; U.S., 32%).
[d]'Would you like to have persons from this group as your neighbour?: Homosexual' (Negative response: Canada, 17%; U.S., 23%).
Source: Eurobarometer surveys, conducted by TNS Opinion and Social, of 29,000 respondents across all EU members, December 2006. World Values Survey, 2000.

barometer surveys show that support for same-sex adoption rights lags considerably behind support for marriage (on average by 12 per cent across the European Union). Only the Dutch and Swedes register majority support, and only the former at levels above recent polling levels in both Canada and the United States.

I agree with Miriam Smith that Canadian–American differences in policy development on issues related to sexual diversity cannot be straightforwardly predicted by contrasts in public opinion.[29] On relationship recognition, legal or policy change in South Africa and Latin America has not been accompanied by particularly favourable opinion shifts. Neither can the divergence on parenting or schooling in Canada and the United States be obviously explained by public attitudes. However, we do find an overall relationship between inclusive attitudes and progressive policies across North America and Europe, and favourable shifts in popular beliefs within and between countries have been important in creating ammunition for activists and room for policy makers.[30]

As Michael Adams shows, incremental changes in family regimes in Canada and northern Europe have been accompanied by shifts in public attitudes towards heterosexual marriage and cohabitation that are greater than in the United States.[31] Notions of formal equality within relationships are more widely accepted, as is the legitimacy of non-marital cohabitation.[32] This has helped open the door to greater acceptance of lesbian and gay relationships.

In Canada particularly, another contributor to the acceptance of sexual diversity is the extent to which acceptance of diversity in general has been incorporated into the country's self-image. Within most of the political class, and to some extent the population at large, the country is often seen positively as a social 'mosaic,' and contrasted to the American 'melting pot.'[33] The mosaic imagery is meant to suggest that there is less assimilationist pressure on ethnic and cultural minorities than in the United States, or for that matter in most European countries.

There is some mythology embedded in this imagery. Canada had a long history of discriminatory immigration policy and practice, and has experienced waves of anti-immigrant sentiment, much of it with strong racial undercurrents. The most lasting of the cultural differences in Canada – between the speakers of English and French – has often enough been a source of conflict rather than of mutual understanding.

But for most of Canada's recent history, the recognition of diversity has become a national identifier, and particularly for urbanites. Toronto and Vancouver are among the most ethnically and racially diverse cities in the world, and while prejudice remains widespread, the idea of ethnic and cultural diversity is accepted by many, and acquiesced to by more. Pew Research polling in 2002 found Canada the only country among forty-four surveyed in which a majority agreed with a statement that immigrants have a good influence on the country – and it was a strong majority of 77 per cent.[34] (In the United States 49 per cent agreed.)

How transferable such beliefs are to other forms of difference is unclear, but an argument can be made that they have helped sustain at least a 'toleration' of difference at both the official level and in the general population. They may also have helped create a degree of legitimacy for group rights, made still easier by the absence of an imperial past, and relatively low-key forms of nationalism in English Canada, and increasingly Quebec.

The prior recognition of other forms of difference has played a role in a few parts of Europe. The need to acknowledge minority religious and political interests emerged relatively early in the Dutch case, and may well have secured a pattern of accommodation that was then applied to sexual minorities.[35] The recognition of religious pluralism may well have had a particularly important role in diminishing the influence of any one religious current on public policy.

*Divisions on the Partisan Right*

The political right in Canada and much of Europe is not as influenced by religious conservatism as its counterpart is in the United States. This is partly due to the lower numbers of religious conservatives in the electorate, but also because moral conservatives and neo-liberals have not coalesced as effectively as in the United States. True, religious conservatives form an important core constituency in Canada's new Conservative Party. The party's leadership, though, has been scrambling to tone down that moral conservatism, knowing that it must do so to secure wide support outside the western provinces.

Several western European countries have Christian Democratic parties generally sympathetic to positions taken by the Roman Catholic Church, but their pursuit of anti-gay agendas cannot compare with the ferocity of such pursuit among American Republicans. They are also faced with the harsh reality of declining church attendance and increasing popular wariness of following the political dictates of the Vatican, especially on issues of gender and sexuality. Popular referenda held in Italy during the 1980s, for example, led to massive defeats for the positions taken by Christian Democrats and the Roman Catholic Church on questions of divorce and abortion. Spanish popular support for same-sex marriage in 2004 and 2005 remained very high despite angry denunciations by the Vatican, and the Popular Party was loath to attack the government too forcibly on gay marriage for fear of appearing homophobic and too conservative for the electorate.

In Canada and Europe, there are more right-wing politicians than in the United States who recognize the inconsistency between opposing government intervention in the economy and supporting government regulation of morality. In that sense, the natural tension between neo-liberalism and neo-conservatism is more widely recognized. At the provincial and federal levels in Canada, most parties on the right have been much more preoccupied by lower taxes and deregulation – the neo-liberal side of the right-wing agenda. They have campaigned and voted against major advances in the recognition of same-sex relationships, and especially marriage, but they have not sought to roll back advances already made. The federal Conservative Party was threatening to do just that in 2005 and 2006, but over time was soft-pedalling the issue.

In the United States the Republican Party's leadership at the federal level and in most state capitals prioritizes neo-liberalism over moral conservatism. As Clyde Wilcox points out, even the policy-making record of George W. Bush, the national leader most visibly shaped by religious conservatism, shows only modest success in rolling back or preventing gains by LGBT activists, compared to the considerable success in governing according to a pro-business agenda.[36] Nevertheless, there are many Republican voters and elected representatives who combine moral conservatism and neo-liberalism, and they are not likely soon to put aside the former.

In several countries centrist parties that have leaned to neo-liberalism on economic issues and government spending overall have taken moderately progressive positions on sexual diversity issues. Such stances are compatible with individualist ideals of equity and liberty, and promises on LGBT rights become a means of sustaining a reformist image. This has been evident in Canada's Liberal Party, Britain's Labour Party, and perhaps also the left coalition in Italy. In the Canadian case, Liberals have faced internal dissent but have come to the view that issues of sexual diversity give them an advantage over the Conservatives, and especially so because the courts have taken the lead on relationship and parenting issues. In the United States, Democrats have more widely embraced LGBT rights than ever, at the same time as they have shifted right on economic issues. They still retain great nervousness on some issues, like marriage, precisely because of Republican willingness to use such issues at election time.

Outside of the United States, progressive action has been facilitated by social democratic parties clearly advocating equality. This has not always been so, but more and more such parties in Canada, Europe, Australia, New Zealand, and parts of Latin America have developed firm positions on at least relationship issues.[37] Canada's New Democratic Party had awkward divisions and hesitations on such issues, but has almost always been readier to embrace sexual diversity than other parties. This is a better record than most European social democratic parties and the labour parties in Australia and New Zealand, though most of these also developed progressive stances over time.

*Institutional and Legal Contributors*

Once governments apart from the United States decided to act in these jurisdictions, the parliamentary systems in which they operate facilitated success. Governments are more able to control the policy agenda in parliamentary systems than in the U.S. political system, backed as they usually are by a disciplined party or coalition majority in the legislature. In Canada, and at times in Britain, issues related to homosexuality (and, for example, abortion, capital punishment, and euthanasia) are often exempted from the usual norms about strict party discipline. Nevertheless, the executive still gets to determine the timing of debate, and has considerable powers of persuasion over its own party members.

Constitutional frameworks have provided enormous boosts to equity-seeking advocates in a few systems, and have offered cover to cautious politicians. This has been a factor in South Africa, Israel, Hungary, and especially Canada. The Charter of Rights and Freedoms contains more elaborate and robust rights language than exists in the U.S. Constitution, and the Canadian judiciary was not particularly bound by literalist readings of the Charter or by doctrines of original intent. The exclusion of sexual orientation from the text itself, then, did not prevent courts from reading it into the Charter's open-ended language on discrimination.

Judicial appointments have also not been as politicized as in the United States. Cries of judicial activism have been leveled at courts when they ruled favourably on cases involving sexuality, but such charges have not been pursued as unrelentingly as in the United States. There have been calls for reform of the process of judicial appointment, but there are few Canadian admirers of the American system and the politicization that has flowed from it.

Courts in Israel and South Africa have also been delivering strong rulings on relationship recognition. Both have been influenced by the Canadian Charter, and in South Africa favourable rulings have been boosted by the explicit inclusion of sexual orientation in the country's post-apartheid constitution. Courts in Europe have a more uneven record, and the judicial institutions associated with the European Union and the European Convention of Human Rights have proceeded cautiously.[38]

## Policy Inheritance

As we have already seen, securing more inclusive family regimes has been facilitated by the earlier decriminalization of homosexuality and the enactment of basic prohibitions on anti-gay discrimination.[39] The first was largely secured across Canada in 1969. Several European countries decriminalized homosexuality in the nineteenth century, and most of the remainder in western Europe did so by the late 1970s.[40] European-level court rulings in the 1980s made clear that such measures would not pass muster, and in subsequent years new entrants to the EU would be obliged to decriminalize. Basic rights coverage was constitutionally recognized across most of Canada by the end of the 1980s. Non-discrimination language in European countries has not always explicitly included sexual orientation, but de facto coverage was secured across most of western Europe by the late-1990s, and within the European Union soon after.

In northwesten Europe, and to some extent in Canada, the expansiveness and coverage of the welfare state eased the extension of recognition to same-sex couples, since the additional costs associated with including them in state social insurance benefits would be negligible.[41] In Canada and parts of Scandinavia, most of the substantive rights and obligations traditionally associated with marriage were extended to all de facto couples before the issue of same-sex marriage came to the fore, in public policy and in the employee benefit programs of private employers, so the question of costs, however modest, was settled before marriage came to the front burner.

## Activism and Alliances

The point has already been made that advances outside the United States were not a result of better-resourced or more skilful activist movements. A more important factor is that activists in Canada and other countries have not faced anything like the opposition that can be mobilized by the American religious right. Another factor in several of these countries has been the strength of the labour movement, and the willingness of unions to take on issues of sexual diversity. Canadian unions have been in the lead internationally in taking up the cause of equity for lesbians, gays, bisexuals, and the transgendered, and they have applied themselves to bargaining for inclusive benefits, lobbying governments, and supporting litigation.[42] In most of Europe, Australia, and New Zealand, labour movements have been a little slower in taking up sexuality issues. But there have been individual unions, like Britain's Unison in the public sector, that have taken strong and influential leadership positions.[43]

Kelly Kollman argues that the development of transnational networks has significantly accelerated the spread of relationship recognition.[44] There is undoubtedly cross-national polination in agenda setting by activist groups, who are also able to cite advances in other countries deemed to be similar in broad cultural contexts to give their claims a rhetorical lever. But the density of transnational networks is high enough only among European Union countries – and even there, more so among the older members – to have had much concrete influence in policy making. This is especially so with the extremely slow path being taken by EU institutions themselves in recognizing lesbian and gay relationships. Transnational influence is evident in the 'learning' that takes place in senior appelate courts, in turn influential in those settings where courts have played important roles in provoking change in policy, though Europe's transnational courts seem not to have been very open to judicial trends outside of Europe.

### Explaining Parenting Anomalies

Why have parenting rights for same-sex couples spread so rapidly across Canada, and so slowly in Europe? And why has change on parenting issues been if anything more widespread in the United States than more basic individual or couple rights? In some ways, the willingness of European policy makers to exclude parenting from their civil union or marriage regimes is easy to explain. As the data in table 10.4 show, public ambivalence about gays and lesbians raising children persists in countries that have moved the furthest in recognizing gay/lesbian relationships. In most of Europe, and elsewhere, parenting by same-sex couples remains troubling to most people.

Polling results in Canada are on the favourable end of the spectrum, but still with a 50–50 split. So what explains the very different policy paths? One reason is the greater ease that Canadian lesbian and gay couples experience (compared to Europeans) in having children – in turn a product of access to assisted reproduction and adoption agencies earlier than most Europeans. Merin also makes the point that a large proportion of European adoptions are of foreign infants: in 1995, 69 per cent of Dutch adoptions were foreign, compared to 15 per cent in the United States.[45] The widespread prohibition on adoption by same-sex couples in countries where most adoptive children are located has provided a rationale for creating exceptions for adoption in otherwise inclusive regimes. However, about 50 per cent of Canadian adoptions are of foreign children, and this seems not to have led to the invocation of such a rationale.[46]

Another reason is that the courts have a prominent role in effecting change in Canada (and in the United States).[47] In Europe, family law is more exclusively dependent on legislative action, and governments have obviously been more intimidated by the prospect of public opposition. Most of the advances on parenting in Canada (BC and Quebec being important exceptions) have been made through court challenges, in which judges are usually confronting pre-existing parental relationships in well-functioning families. The same circumstances produce surprising levels of favourable rulings in the United States, especially because family court judges so often confront heterosexual families that are falling apart, or in which children are not being looked after adequately.

## Limits to Change

In no country has full equality been secured in the public recognition of sexual diversity. The most changed of formal regimes still retain elements of discrimination, whether in the registration of children on birth certificates or the willingness to give full standing to de facto parents. Where law has changed most radically, for example in parenting, there is no doubt that many agencies responsible for adoption and fostering retain a parenting hierarchy that accords higher standing to middle- or upper-class married heterosexuals.

Fear and unease about acknowledging sexual diversity remains especially intense when issues related to children are raised, and this is nowhere more evident than in public school systems. Here is where change is least evident in Canada, and in most other countries that have achieved take-off on relational issues. The resurrection of traditional approaches to schooling, and the underfunding of public education that has so widely accompanied the rise in neo-liberal politics, reinforces reluctance to press for or adopt new policies on equity that will cost money and create a fuss. All this applies to the United States, but there we find more activists to campaign for change whatever the odds.

In every setting, the reach of gains in recognition is uneven. The disadvantage experienced by some lesbians and gays because of class, race, regional location, and indeed gender are not eliminated by overall changes in family regime, even if the disadvantage is not exacerbated either. Parenting by same-sex couples in the United States is not less common among African Americans, for example, than Caucasians. Still, some parenting options are effectively unavailable to many prospective parents because of cost, particularly those options requiring assisted reproduction. The capacity to take advantage of legal remedies also remains unequal, and so is the response that real or prospective parents will get from parenting agencies.

The public face of the movement to change family regimes and public schooling inevitably will be one that emphasizes the most respectable face of the constituencies whose interests are at stake, and will cite examples that provoke the least discomfort in the public imagination. This does not necessarily limit the reach of the gains made, but it does potentially limit the range of constituencies that see themselves reflected in those campaigns. The safe and respectable face of activist pressure limits the visibility that such claims will have within already disadvantaged communities.

Bisexuals and the transgendered are among those who are most on the margins of campaigns for equity in the areas we are surveying here. It is not obviously the case that activism on relational and parenting issues has squeezed out their agendas. After all, the last decade has seen greatly increased mobilizing on transgendered issues in both Canada and the United States, at the same time that campaigning on marriage has been at its height. Bisexual activism has been far less visible, though it too has increased over the time that family-related issues have acquired prominence.

Still, there can be no doubt that the public recognition of sexual diversity chronicled here is far less extensive for those who cross and challenge gender boundaries than it is for those who are lesbian and gay. Prohibitions on discrimination based on gender identity, for example, are far less widespread than those based on sexual orientation, and institutional engagement with creating inclusive policy and practice for bisexuals and the transgendered lags far behind improvements for lesbians and gays. Public attitudes also reflect much less acceptance of gender ambiguity or gender change than of clear-cut homosexuality. This is undoubtedly more true when questions of youthful sexuality are introduced. Such lags, and the relative invisibility of bisexual and transgendered spokespeople in campaigns for shifting parental and schooling regimes, does not preclude their benefiting from the policy changes we have covered. But the reach of such benefits does have serious limits.

## Conclusion

The public recognition of sexual diversity has generally proceeded down very different paths in the United States and Canada, particularly with regard to relationship recognition and parenting. American localities and states often pioneered developments on issues like inheritence and child custody, as they had on the approval of basic human rights protections and anti-hate laws. Among these we also find pioneers in explicitly including gender identity within their human rights statutes, something still rare in Canada and almost unknown in Europe until the middle of the first decade of the twenty-first century.[48] Given the opposition of religious conservatives, and the complexity of the political process, these first steps never accelerated into a take-off pattern, though the steady expansion of recognition, especially in the Northeast and the West Coast, has not been slowed by the formidable campaigning against lesbian and gay marriage.

In Canada, the story is more national than regional, even if most accounts of Canadian politics highlight regional differences. The pacing and extent of change vary to some degree across provinces, with British Columbia a pioneer on some fronts, Ontario on others, Quebec on a few, but the contrasts are nothing like those we see across American states.

Schooling issues challenge the view that this national story and its equivalents in northern European countries are categorically more progressive than the American. No country has a record to be proud of in public education, especially when it comes to curricular recognition of diversity. Across Europe the skittishness we find on parenting issues is undoubtedly at play in ignoring the harm done by schools to all those who deviate from gender norms. Reluctance to act feeds stereotypes about the risk that homosexuality, and homosexuals, pose to children.

Both Canada and the United States are in many ways unusual cases. Canada is unusual for being one of the first countries in the world to experience a form of take-off in the recognition of families led by lesbian and gay couples, even before the question of marriage took centre stage. It was an international leader in the recognition of lesbian and gay parenting rights and the first to see fully equal marriage. All of this occurred in a setting where public opinion on these issues was hardly settled, where religious conservatism was able to mobilize noticeable opposition (even if not on an American scale), and where most governments were inclined to avoid the subject.

The United States may not be as exceptional as is widely believed. A great majority of Americans now believe in extending recognition to lesbian and gay couples, even if only a minority favour marriage. Most large corporations extend their family benefits coverage to the same-sex partners of employees. A steadily growing number of U.S. states and municipalities extend some form of recognition to the lesbian or gay partners of their own employees. Openly lesbian and gay characters make regular appearances on American television dramas, even if their portrayals have limitations. And across a wide range of regions and localities in the United States, countless lesbians, gays, bisexuals, and the transgendered are asserting the right to be visible.

In both Canada and the United States, religious conservatives are more organized than ever, and more intent than ever to resist the public recognition of sexual diversity. It would be foolhardy in either country, but especially the United States, to predict that such recognition will continue to spread in the way it has up to this point. The issue of marriage has shown the hazard of that view.

However, the steadily growing visibility of lesbians, gays, and, more slowly, bisexuals and the transgendered, does make it harder to imagine that the clock will be turned back, and that gains will simply stop being registered. Parents and their children will continue to challenge discrimination; policy makers and judges will find those claims incontrovertible; employers will increasingly recognize that their search for good employees demands equitable and respectful treatment. Educators may take a while, but more and more will realize that students, teachers, parents, and administrators are themselves members of sexual minorities, and that the denigration of sexual diversity harms everyone in the school system. Members of the public will increasingly recognize that the demands for public recognition are coming from their own children, their parents, their neighbours, their workmates, their closest friends.

# Notes

## 1. Publicly Recognizing Queer Families

1 Same-sex marriage was also legal at that time in the Netherlands and Belgium, but with restrictions on adoption.

2 Among the writers who emphasize the contrast in political institutions and its impact are Leslie Pal, in 'Between the Sights: Gun Control in Canada and the United States,' in *Canada and the United States: Differences that Count*, ed. David M. Thomas, 2nd ed. (Peterborough, ON: Broadview, 2002), 68–97; Raymond Tatalovitch, *The Politics of Abortion in the United States and Canada* (Armonk, NY: M.E. Sharp, 1997); and Miriam Smith, in 'The Politics of Same-Sex Marriage in Canada and the United States,' *PS: Political Science and Politics* 38 (April 2005): 225–8.

3 My colleague and friend Miriam Smith focuses on the impact of institutional factors in 'Social Movements and Judicial Empowerment: Courts, Public Policy and Lesbian and Gay Organizing in Canada,' *Politics and Society* 33, no. 2 (June 2005): 327–53, and elsewhere. Ray Tatalovitch and Michael MacMill focuses particularly on the importance of courts in 'Judicial Activism vs. Restraint: The Role of the Highest Courts in Official Language Policy in the United States and Canada,' *American Review of Canadian Studies* 33 (June 2003): 239–60. By implication, a similar analysis is developed by David Richards, in *The Case for Gay Rights: From Bowers to Lawrence and Beyond* (Lawrence: University of Kansas Press, 2005), and Jason Pierceson, in *Courts, Liberalism and Rights: Gay Law and Politics in the United States and Canada* (Philadelphia: Temple University Press, 2005).

4 There is a major strand of policy analysis that points to earlier policy developments as formative; among the most notable are Paul Pierson, *Politics in Time: History, Institutions, and Social Analysis* (Princeton, NJ:

Princeton University Press, 2004), and the much earlier Hugh Heclo, *Modern Social Politics in Britain and Sweden* (New Haven, CT: Yale University Press, 1974).

5  In the first group, Seymour Martin Lipset may be the most prominent of this school. His several versions of the argument include *Continental Divide: The Values and Institutions of the United States and Canada* (New York: Routledge, 1990). Other classic formulations, though different from one another, come from Kenneth McRae, 'The Structure of Canadian History,' in *The Founding of New Societies*, ed. Louis Hartz (New York: Harcourt, Brace and World, 1964), 219–75, and Gad Horowitz, 'Conservatism, Liberalism and Socialism in Canada: An Interpretation,' *Canadian Journal of Economics and Political Science* 32 (1966): 143–70. In the second group, among the notable contributors to this view are Neil Nevitte, in *The Decline of Deference: Canadian Value Change in Comparative Perspective, 1981–1990* (Peterborough, ON: Broadview, 1996).

6  See Debbie Epstein and James T. Sears, eds., *Dangerous Knowing: Sexuality, Pedagogy and Popular Culture* (London: Cassell, 1995); James Sears, ed., *Sexuality and the Curriculum: The Politics and Practices of Sexuality Education* (New York and London: Teachers College Press, 1992); J.M. Blount, *Fit to Teach: Same-Sex Desire, Gender, and School Work in the 20th Century* (Albany: State University of New York Press, 2005); Catherine Lugg, 'The Religious Right and Public Education: The Paranoid Politics of Homophobia,' *Educational Policy* 12, no. 3 (May 1998): 267–83; and C. Lugg, 'Thinking about Sodomy,' *Educational Policy* 20, no. 1 (January-March 2006): 35–58.

7  One thoughtful commentator on changes in family regime, though one who does not emphasize the internal contradictions as much as I do, is Margrit Eichler, *Family Shifts: Families, Policies, and Gender Equality* (Oxford: Oxford University Press, 1997).

8  See Kenneth Plummer, 'The Lesbian and Gay Movement in Britain,' in *The Global Emergence of Gay and Lesbian Politics*, ed. Barry Adam et al. (Philadelphia: Temple University Press, 1999), 133–57, and Dennis Altman,'What Changed in the Seventies?' in *Homosexuality: Power and Politics*, ed. Gay Left Collective (London: Allison and Busby, 1980), 52–63. See also Barry Adam's overview of the development of the activism movement, *The Rise of a Gay and Lesbian Movement*, rev. ed. (New York: Twayne, 1995). Early gay liberation and lesbian feminist writing includes much that echoes this view, often shaped by socialist analysis. Examples can be found in other writings in the New Left Collective volume; Gary Kinsman, *The Regulation of Desire: Homo and Hetero Sexualities*, 2nd ed.

(Montreal: Black Rose Books, 1996); and Ed Jackson and Stan Persky, eds., *Flaunting It! A Decade of Gay Journalism from the Body Politic* (Vancouver: New Star Books, 1982).

9 Michael Warner, *The Trouble with Normal: Sex, Politics and the Ethics of Queer Life* (New York: Free Press, 1999). Shane Phelan is somewhat more ambivalent on these questions. See *Sexual Strangers: Gays, Lesbians, and the Dilemmas of Citizenship* (Philadephia: Temple University Press, 2001). For an excellent distillation of such argumentation, see David Bell and Jon Binnie, *The Sexual Citizen, Queer Politics and Beyond* (Cambridge, UK: Polity, 2000). See also Steven Seidman, 'From Identity to Queer Politics: Shifts in Normative Heterosexuality and the Meaning of Citizenship,' *Citizenship Studies* 5, no. 3 (2001): 321–8.

10 Didi Herman and Carl Stychin, eds., *Legal Inversions: Lesbians, Gay Men, and the Politics of Law* (Philadelphia: Temple University Press, 1995); Didi Herman, *Rights of Passage: The Struggle for Lesbian and Gay Legal Equality* (Toronto: University of Toronto Press, 1994); Carl Stychin, *A Nation by Rights: National Cultures, Sexual Identity Politics, and the Discourse of Rights* (Philadephia: Temple University Press, 1998); Susan Boyd and Claire F.L. Young, '"From Same-Sex to No Sex?" Trends Towards Recognition of (Same-Sex) Relationships in Canada,' *Seattle Journal of Social Justice* 1, no. 3 (2002–3): 757–93; and Nancy Pokiloff, 'We Will Get What We Ask For: Why Legalizing Gay and Lesbian Marriage Will Not Dismantle the Legal Structure of Gender in Every Marriage,' *Virginia Law Review* 79, no. 7 (1993): 1535–50. Boyd and Young's analysis is particularly nuanced and comprehensive.

11 Alain Touraine, *The Voice and the Eye: An Analysis of Social Movements* (Cambridge: Cambridge University Press, 1981); Alberto Melucci, *Challenging Codes: Collective Action in the Information Age* (Cambridge: Cambridge University Press, 1996); and Claus Offe, 'New Social Movements: Challenging the Boundaries of Institutional Politics,' *Social Research* 52, no. 4 (1985): 817–68.

12 Sidney Tarrow, *Power in Movement: Social Movements: Collective Action and Politics*, 2nd ed. (Cambridge: Cambridge University Press, 1998); Doug McAdam, *Political Process and the Development of Black Insurgency, 1930–1970* (Chicago: University of Chicago Press, 1982); John D'Emilio, 'Cycles of Change, Questions of Strategy: The Gay and Lesbian Movement after Fifty Years,' in *The Politics of Gay Rights*, ed. Craig Rimmerman et al. (Chicago: University of Chicago Press, 2000), 31–53; Barry Adam, *The Rise of a Gay and Lesbian Movement*; Dennis Altman, *The Homosexualization of America* (New York: St Martin's Press, 1982).

13 This is a hallmark of various theoretical currents influenced by Marxism, and the more recent wave of writing influenced by Michel Foucault, himself partially shaped by socialist ideas. See *The History of Sexuality*, vol. 1, *An Introduction* (New York: Vintage, 1978). Much contemporary queer theory and major currents in critical legal study build on Foucault's ideas, and remain sceptical of campaigns for inclusion in or acceptance through existing political and legal institutions.

14 'From Identity to Queer Politics: Shifts in Normative Heterosexuality and the Meaning of Citizenship,' *Citizenship Studies* 5, no. 3 (2001), 321.

15 See, for example, Paula Ettelbrick, 'Since When Is Marriage a Path to Liberation,' *OUT/LOOK* 9:14–16; Valerie Lehr, 'Domestic Partnership, Civil Unions, or Marriage: One Size Does not Fit All,' *Albany Law Review* 64, no. 3 (2001): 905–14; Suzanne Danuta Walters, 'Take My Domestic Partner Please: Gays and Marriage in the Era of the Visible,' in *Queer Families, Queer Politics*, ed. Mary Bernstein (New York: Columbia University Press, 2001), 349–58; and barbara findlay, 'All in the Family Values,' *Canadian Journal of Family Law* 14, no. 2 (1997): 129–96.

16 For a portrayal of the conservative case for same-sex marriage, see Andrew Sullivan, 'The Conservative Case,' in *Same-Sex Marriage: Pro and Con*, rev. ed., ed. Andrew Sullivan (New York: Random House, 2004), 147–55.

17 Bell and Binnie, *The Sexual Citizen, Queer Politics and Beyond*.

18 Law Commission of Canada, *Beyond Conjugality: Recognizing and Supporting Close Adult Relationships* (Ottawa: Law Commission of Canada, 2001).

19 Not all critics of reformist politics are so sceptical of identity politics. Paula Ettelbrick, in her 1989 article 'Since When Is Marriage a Path to Liberation,' asserts that marriage is contradictory to the affirmation of gay identity, arguing that full justice will be attained when social acceptance comes despite lesbian and gay differences from dominant culture. Steven Seidman's version of queer politics rejects not identity politics, but rather the reliance on an identity that excludes and restrains and in other ways normalizes. 'From Identity to Queer Politics,' 326.

20 Judith Stacey and Timothy Biblarz make this point, and critically examine a number of the studies that have been conducted on the children of lesbian and gay parents. See '(How) Does the Sexual Orientation of Parents Matter?' *American Sociological Review* 66, no. 2 (2001): 159–84.

21 Valerie Lehr, *Queer Family Values: Debunking the Myth of the Nuclear Family* (Philadephia: Temple University Press, 1999). On parenting, see also Elizabeth A. Say and Mark R. Kowelewski, *Gays, Lesbians, and Family Values* (Cleveland: Pilgrim Press, 1998).

22  Cheshire Calhoun, *Feminism, the Family, and the Politics of the Closet: Lesbian and Gay Displacement* (Oxford: Oxford University Press, 2000).

23  This is a point made in the Canadian context by Winifred Holland, 'Intimate Relationships in the New Millennium: The Assimilation of Marriage and Cohabitation,' *Canadian Journal of Family Law* 17 (2000): 114–68. It is also made by Calhoun, *Feminism*, 113–14.

24  Jeffrey Weeks, Brian Heaphy, and Catherine Donovan, *Same-Sex Intimacies: Families of Choice and Other Life Experiments* (New York: Routledge, 2001), chap. 2.

25  Shelley Gavigan, 'A Parent(ly) Knot: Can Heather Have Two Mommies,' in *Legal Inversions,* ed. Herman and Stychin, 108.

26  Calhoun, *Feminism*, chap. 5.

27  Phelan, *Sexual Strangers.*

28  Weeks, Heaphy, and Donovan, *Same-Sex Intimacies*, chap. 2.

29  In September 1990, Queer Nation activists in San Francisco organized a marriage ceremony on the grand staircase inside City Hall in protest against California's purely heterosexual definition of marriage. They saw, and some of their ideological descendants today still see, the demand for marriage as a queer challenge to heteronormativity.

30  Eichler, *Family Shifts*, chap. 1.

31  Boyd and Young point to this and other conservatizing elements in the Canadian fight for marriage, in '"From Same-Sex to No Sex,"' 757–93.

## 2. Activist Contexts

1  For an overview of changes over the course of the last century or more, see Angus McLaren, *20th Century Sexuality: A History* (Oxford: Blackwell, 1999), and John D'Emilio, *Intimate Matters: A History of Sexuality in America* (NY: Harper and Row, 1988). See also Sean Cahill, 'Welfare Moms and the Two Grooms: The Concurrent Promotion and Restriction of Marriage in US Public Policy,' *Sexualities* 8, no. 2 (2005): 169–87.

2  In the United States, the removal of barriers to interracial marriage forms part of this overall trend. Statutory prohibitions were once widespread, and defended on the basis of both natural and religious principles. Those that remained in 1967 were ruled unconstitutional by the U.S. Supreme Court in *Loving v. Virginia.*

3  Jana B. Singer, 'The Privatization of Family Law,' *Wisconsin Law Review*, no. 5 (1992): 1443–567; repr. in William N. Eskridge Jr and Nan D. Hunter, eds., *Sexuality, Gender, and the Law* (Westbury, NY: Foundation Press, 1997).

4 Singer, 'The Privatization of Family Law.'
5 Kathleen Lahey, *Same-Sex Marriage: The Personal and the Political* (Toronto: Insomniac Press, 2004), 24–5.
6 Differential treatment persisted, though, as Winifred Holland points out, opposite sex cohabiting couples in the 1990s had more benefits and obligations than married couples did in the 1960s. 'Intimate Relationships in the New Millenium: The Assimilation of Marriage and Cohabitation,' *Canadian Journal of Family Law* 17 (2000): 114–50.
7 'Common law' is the term normally applied in Canada, but it has a somewhat different meaning in the United States, so is avoided here.
8 See Irene Demczuk et al., *Recognition of Lesbian Couples: An Inalienable Right* (Ottawa: Status of Women Canada, 2002), chap. 2.
9 William Eskridge wrote recently that 'American family law has been reconceived in the last generation, apparently accepting the liberal view of the self as autonomous and self-regarding, constructing patterns of intimacy on its own terms rather than the terms dictated by traditional institutions and roles.' This may be fair comment as a comparison to the American past, but it overstates the overall American change in comparison to a number of other countries, and most especially Canada. See *Gaylaw: Challenging the Apartheid of the Closet* (Cambridge, MA: Harvard University Press, 1999), 272.
10 The 1995 decision in *Connell v. Francisco* was the most definitive in holding that such property laws should be applied to all of what it oddly referred to as 'meretricious' relationships – stable marital-like relationships.
11 The Mississippi case is surprising, in light of the concentration of such changes in the west and northeast, though it derives in part from the high poverty rate and the large number of unmarried African-American families, and the state interest in reducing claims on the public purse (this point made by Robbie Morgan, in conversation, May 2007).
12 One of peculiarities of the American pattern is that in the nineteenth century most states accepted what was then (and still is) referred to as common-law marriage – a term now applied to cohabiting couples in Canada. According to its principles, a heterosexual couple living together and presenting themselves as married were treated in law as if they were indeed married. In the first half of the twentieth century, such state recognition was abolished. See J. Thomas Oldham, 'Unmarried Partners and the Legacy of *Marvin v. Marvin*,' *Notre Dame Law Review* 76 (October 2001): 1409–34. On the general legal response to cohabitation, see Grace Ganz Blumberg's insightful article, 'Unmarried Partners and the Legacy

of *Marvin v. Marvin*: The Regularization of Nonmarital Cohabition Rights and Responsibilities in the American Welfare State,' *Notre Dame Law Review* 76 (October 2001): 1265–310.

13  This is a different meaning than the term has in Canada, where it applies to all conjugal cohabitation.

14  See Anna Marie Smith, 'The Politicization of Marriage in Contemporary American Public Policy: The Defense of Marriage Act and the Personal Responsibility Act,' *Citizenship Studies* 5, no. 3 (2001): 303–20. This is also a point made by Catherine Lugg, personal correspondence, November 2006.

15  See Stephanie Cootnz, *The Way We Never Were: American Families and the Nostalgia Trap* (Jackson, TN: Perseus Books Group, 1991).

16  Among the overviews of American legal developments are William Eskridge, *Gaylaw*; Patricia A. Cain, *Rainbow Rights: The Role of Lawyers and Courts in the Lesbian and Gay Civil Rights Movement* (Boulder, CO: Routledge, 2000); Jason Pierceson, *Courts, Liberalism, and Rights: Gay Law and Politics in the United States and Canada* (Philadelphia: Temple University Press, 2005); David Richards, *The Case for Gay Rights: From Bowers to Lawrence and Beyond* (Lawrence: University of Kansas Press, 2005); Daniel R. Pinello, *Gay Rights and American Law* (Cambridge: Cambridge University Press, 2003); and Ellen Ann Anderson, *Out of the Closets and Into the Courts: Legal Opportunity Structure and Gay Rights Litigation* (Ann Arbor: University of Michigan Press, 2005).

17  This is an argument I share with Miriam Smith (e.g., in her 'The Politics of Same-Sex Marriage in Canada and the United States,' *PS: Political Science and Politics*, 38 [April 2005]: 225–8), though I am less heartily an institutionalist than she is.

18  Female homosexuality was never criminalized in Canada. The 1969 reforms retained some inequalities, for example, in the age of consent and in the interpretation given to acts of gross indecency. But sexual activity between two men aged twenty-one or over, in private, was no longer a criminal act.

19  Section 15(1) reads: 'Every individual is equal before and under the law and has the right to the equal protection and equal benefit of the law without discrimination and, in particular, without discrimination based on race, national or ethnic origin, colour, religion, sex, age, or mental or physical disability.'

20  Among the leading proponents of the activist thesis are Ted Morton and Rainer Knoppf, in *The Charter Revolution and the Court Party* (Peterborough, ON: Broadview, 2000). See also Ran Hirschl, *Towards Juristocracy:*

*The Origins and Consequences of the New Constitutionalism* (Cambridge, MA: Harvard University Press, 2004) for a highly perceptive comparative view.

21  'Dividing the Spoils: American and Canadian Federalism,' in *Canada and the United States: Differences that Count,* 2nd ed., ed. David M. Thomas (Peterborough, ON: Broadview, 2000), 274.

22  Alexander Smith and Raymond Tatalovich, *Cultures at War: Moral Conflicts in Western Democracies* (Peterborough, ON: Broadview, 2003), chap. 7.

23  These congressional score cards are available at http://www.hrc.org.

24  I have written on the congressional part of this story in *On the Fringe: Gays and Lesbians in Politics* (Ithaca, NY: Cornell University Press, 1998), chap. 7. See also Craig Rimmerman, ed., *Gay Rights, Military Wrongs: Political Perspectives on Lesbian and Gays in the Military* (New York: Garland, 1996).

25  On Canadian partisan polarization, see William Cross and Lisa Young, 'Policy Attitudes of Party Members in Canada: Evidence of Ideological Politics,' *Canadian Journal of Political Science* 35 (December 2002): 859–80.

26  Terms used to describe religious conservatives are varied, and often inappropriate. Some writers use 'evangelical,' but that homogenizes a spiritual orientation that includes many progressive voices. 'Fundamentalist' is widely used, but many Christian conservatives object, in part because the term refers to a specific set of religious beliefs that is distinct from those of Pentecostals, charismatics, Baptists, and others commonly associated with religious conservatism. The 'Christian right' or the 'religious right' seem the most appropriate terms. On the American religious right, see Clyde Wilcox, *Onward Christian Soldiers? The Religious Right in American Politics*, 3rd ed. (Boulder, CO: Westview, 2006); Kenneth Wald, *Religion and Politics in the United States*, 4th ed. (Lanham, MD: Rowman and Littlefield, 2003); Christian Smith, *Christian America? What Evangelicals Really Want* (Berkeley and Los Angeles: University of California Press, 2000); and articles by Didi Herman and John C. Green in *The Politics of Gay Rights*, ed. Craig Rimmerman, Kenneth Wald, and Clyde Wilcox (Chicago: University of Chicago Press, 2000).

27  On the role of religion in American politics, there are many worthy sources, including Clyde Wilcox, *Onward Christian Soldiers?* and Kenneth Wald, *Religion and Politics in the United States*.

28  Pew Research Center, *Religion and Politics: Contention and Consensus* (July 2003), http://pewforum.org/docs/.

29  Pew surveying in 2005 showed that 42 per cent of Americans accept the

creationist version of life's origins. David Masci and Gregory Smith, 'God is Alive and Well in America' (Pew Research Center, 4 April 2006).

30  Michael Adams, 'The Word, Unheeded,' *Globe and Mail*, 15 August 2003. In the mid-1990s, Dennis Hoover cited data showing that 25 per cent of Americans and 11 per cent of Canadians were 'evangelical.' 'Christian Right under Old Glory and the Maple Leaf,' in *Sojourners in the Wilderness: The Christian Right in Comparative Perspective*, ed. Corwin Smidt and James Penning (Lanham, MD: Rowman and Littlefield, 1997), 206.

31  Reginald Bibby, *The Future Families Project: A Survey of Canadian Hopes and Dreams* (Ottawa: Vanier Institute, 2004).

32  O'Toole, 'Religion in Canada: Its Development and Contemporary Situation,' *Social Compass* 43, no. 1 (1996): 119–34; Seymour Martin Lipset, *Revolution and Counter-Revolution: Change and Persistence in Social Structures*, rev. ed. (New Brunswick, NJ: Transaction, 1988).

33  Sam Reimer, 'Evangelical Subcultures in Canada and the United States,' in *Rethinking Church, State, and Modernity: Canada between Empire and the USA*, ed David Lyon and Marguerite Van Die (Toronto: University of Toronto Press, 2000), 228–49; and Reimer, *Evangelicals and the Contiential Divide: The Conservative Protestant Subculture in Canada and the United States* (Montreal and Kingston: McGill-Queen's University Press).

34  The same poll, however, showed virtually no differences between American and Canadian core evangelicals in response to the agree/disagree item 'Homosexuals should have the same rights as others.'

35  'Christian Right under Old Glory and the Maple Leaf,' in Smidt and Penning, *Sojourners in the Wilderness*, 193–215.

36  Dennis R. Hoover, Michael D. Martinez, Samuel Reimer, and Kenneth D. Wald, 'Evangelicalism Meets the Continental Divide: Moral and Economic Conservatism in the United States and Canada' (paper presented at the 2000 meetings of the Society for the Scientific Study of Religion).

37  See R. Scott Appleby, 'Catholics and the Christian Right: An Uneasy Alliance,' in Smidt and Penning, *Sojourners in the Wilderness*, 93–113.

38  Richard A. Lindsay and Jessica Stern, 'David v. Goliath: A Report on Faith Groups Working for Lesbian, Gay, Bisexual and Transgender Equality (and What They're Up Against)' (for the National Religious Leadership Roundtable of the National Gay and Lesbian Task Force, 2006), http://www.thetaskforce.org/downloads/reports.

39  As early as 1986, when I was heavily involved in a successful campaign to add sexual orientation as a prohibited grounds of discrimination in Ontario's Human Rights Code, we reproduced to great effect a pamphlet produced by REALWomen of Canada, an anti-feminist and anti-gay

group heavily informed by religious conservatism. Newspaper editorials and politicians picked up on its extremism as one of the rationales for the legislative change.

40  See National Gay and Lesbian Task Force, 'Anti-Gay Groups Active in Massachusetts' (March 2004), www.thetaskforce.org/reports_and _research/antigayMA, for an analysis of anti-gay-marriage forces, and the preoccupation of most conservative Christian national groups with homosexuality.

41  On the anti-gay agenda of the American religious right, see Didi Herman's *The Antigay Agenda: Orthodox Vision and the Christian Right* (Chicago: University of Chicago Press, 1997)

42  See Hans Hacker, *The Culture of Conservative Christian Litigation* (Lanham, MD: Rowman and Littlefield, 2005) for an overview of such legal activity in the United States.

43  In 1994, the Christian Coalition, at the time a major national presence, distributed 70 million such guides across the country (see www.religious-rightwatch.com).

44  See Reginald Stackhouse Jr, 'Bearing Witness: Christian Groups Engage Canadian Politics since the 1960s,' 113–28, in Lyon and Van Die, *Rethinking Church, State, and Modernity*. Dennis Hoover's interpretation of relative strength differs from this, arguing that Canadian Christian right organizing is substantial in comparison to the United States, factoring in population difference. See his 'Christian Right under Old Glory,' 193–215, in Smidt and Penning, *Sojourners in the Wilderness*.

45  A few of the leading opponents of gay marriage, for example in Focus on the Family (Canada) and its new institute, were either candidates for the Conservative Party or close to the leader. See Dreher, 'In Ottawa, Faith Makes a Leap to the Right,' *Globe and Mail*, 23 September 2006, and Marci MacDonald, 'Stephen Harper and the Theo-cons: The Rising Clout of Canada's Religious Right,' *Walrus*, 16 May 2007.

46  Polling by Alan Gregg in 2005 showed that 37 per cent of born-again Christians would vote for the Conservatives. See www.thestrategiccoun-sel.com. A 2006 poll indicated that 64 per cent of weekly Protestant church attendees voted Conservative (see Dennis Grvending, 'Getting Out the Religious Conservative Vote,' *Hill Times* 3 September, 2007).

47  This is a point made by Dennis Hoover, et al., 'Evangelicalism Meets the Continental Divide.'

48  Lipset, *Revolution and Counter-Revolution*.

49  Reported, for example, in Neil Nevitte, *The Decline of Deference: Canadian Value Change in Comparative Perspective, 1981–1990* (Peterborough, ON: Broadview, 1996).

50  George Perlin, 'The Constraints of Public Opinion: Diverging or Converging Paths?' in *Degrees of Freedom: Canada and the United States in a Changing World*, ed. Keith Banting, George Hoberg, and Richard Simeon (Montreal and Kingston: McGill-Queen's University Press, 1997), 71–150; and Smith and Tatalovich, *Cultures at War*.

51  Michael Adams, *Fire and Ice: The United States, Canada and the Myth of Converging Values* (Toronto: Penguin, 2004).

52  Ibid., 123–4.

53  Kenneth Wald and Allison Calhoun-Brown, *Religion and Politics in the United States*, 5th ed. (Lanham, MD: Rowman and Littlefield, 2006).

54  Morris Fiorina, *Culture War? The Myth of a Polarized America*, 2nd ed. (New York: Pearson Education, 2006).

55  See Michelangelo Signorile, 'Code Pink,' *New York Press*, 26 November 2002, http://www.nypress.com/15/48/news&columns/signorile.cfm.

56  For excellent analyses of public opinion in the United States, see Patrick Egan and Kenneth Sherrill, 'Neither an In-Law nor an Outlaw Be: Trends in Americans' Attitudes Toward Gay People' (Public Opinion Pros), www.publicopinionpros.com, accessed 2 February 2005; and Paul Brewer, 'The Shifting Foundations of Public Opinion and Gay Rights,' *Journal of Politics* 65 (November 2003): 1208–20. I co-authored (with Scott Bowler) an early analysis of public opinion in 'Public Opinion and Gay Rights,' *Canadian Review of Sociology and Anthropology* 25 (November 1988): 649–60.

57  Earlier U.S. poll numbers are drawn from American Enterprise Institute, 'Attitudes about Homosexuality and Gay Marriage,' AEI Studies in Public Opinion, updated 13 February 2004. In Canada, Gallup polling in 1975 showed that 62 per cent believed that homosexuality was always wrong; in 1990, the figure was 59 per cent. In 1999, an Environics poll gauging approval or disapproval of 'homosexuality' showed 34 per cent disapproval, a drastic decline from the results of a poll taken just three years earlier, showing 48 per cent disapproval.

58  'Gay Rights Attitudes a Mixed Bag,' *Gallup Poll Religion and Social Trends* (Princeton, NJ: Gallup Organization, May 2005).

59  'Neither an In-Law nor an Outlaw Be.'

60  See Patrick Egan and Nathaniel Persily, 'Gay Marriage, Public Opinion and the Courts,' paper presented at the Annual Meeting of the American Political Science Association, September 2005.

61  See Doug Ireland, 'Republicans Relaunch the Antigay Culture Wars,' *The Nation*, 2 October 2003. Support for gay marriage stood at 38 per cent in July 2003, and soon dropped to 30 per cent, rising to 39 per cent only in 2006. Pew Research Center Data, report released on 22 March 2006. Favourable responses to the Gallup question on whether homosexual

relations should be legal rebounded to the 2003 level of 59 per cent only in 2007. See Lydia Saad, 'Tolerance for Gay Rights at High Ebb,' 29 May 2007, http://www.gallup.com/nl/?27694.

62  Kaiser Family Foundation, 'National Study on Sex Education Reveals Gap in What Parents Want and What Schools Teach' (September 2000).

63  Brian C. Anderson, 'Amid the Ivy: Right on Campus,' *OpinionJournal* (14 January 2005), an online journal sponsored by the *Wall Street Journal*, www.opinionjournal.com.

64  Reported in 'High School Seniors Favor Gay Rights,' *Advocate*, 6 January 2006.

65  Reported in A.R. Augelli, 'Lesbian, Gay, and Bisexual Development during Adolescence and Young Adulthood,' in *Textbook of Homosexuality and Mental Health*, ed., R.P. Cabaj and S.S. Stein (Washington, DC: American Psychiatric Press, 1996), 267–88, and John Guiney, 'Gay and Out in Secondary School: One Youth's Story,' in *I Could Not Speak My Heart: Education and Social Justice for Gay and Lesbian Youth* (Regina: Canadian Plains Research Center, University of Regina, 2004), 29–42.

66  Poll conducted for Hamilton College, 'Hot Button Issues,' by Zogby International, http://www.hamilton.edu/news/more_newsZogby International press release, accessed 27 August 2001.

67  Quoted in Nara Schoenberg, 'I Have to Tell You Guys Something,' *Chicago Tribune*, 4 May 2003.

68  *The Future Families Project: A Survey of Canadian Hopes and Dreams* (Ottawa: Vanier Institute, 2004), 31, 56.

69  Poll conducted for People for the American Way, reported in 'Religious Beliefs Underpin Opposition to Homosexuality,' http://www.pfaw.org. 18 November 2003.

70  Gary Langer, 'Most Oppose Gay Marriage, Fewer Back an Amendment,' *ABC News*, 5 June 2006.

71  Pew Research report, 'Less Opposition to Gay Marriage, Adoption and Military Service,' released 22 March 2006. On gays in the military, southern respondents were 58 per cent in support, close to the national average of 60 per cent.

72  Results reported by Egan and Sherrill, 'Neither an In-Law nor an Outlaw Be.'

73  'The Political Foundations of Support for Same-Sex Marriage in Canada,' *Canadian Journal of Political Science* 38 (December 2005): 841–66.

74  Among the prominent writers on Canadian regionalism and federalism are Richard Simeon and David Elkins, eds., *Small Worlds: Provinces and*

*Parties in Canadian Political Life* (Toronto: Methuen, 1980), and the contributors to C. Dunn, ed., *Provinces* (Peterborough, ON: Broadview, 1996).

75 Nevitte, *Decline of Deference*, 64–73.

76 This classic portrayal, *The Nine Nations of North America* (Boston: Houghton Mifflin, 1981), divides the United States and Canada into New England, Quebec, the Foundry, the Breadbasket, Dixie, MexAmerica, Ecotopia, and the Empty Quarter. A more recent version can be found in Tom L. McNight, *Regional Geography of the United States and Canada* (Englewood Cliffs, NJ: Prentice Hall, 2001), 107, which includes the following cross-border regions: the Atlantic Northeast, the Heartland, the Boreal Forest, the Plains and Prairies, the Rocky Mountains, the North Pacific Coast, and the Arctic.

77 See http://www.strangemaps.wordpress.com/2006/09/10/3-united-states-of-canada-vs-jesusland.

78 Adams, *Fire and Ice*, 80–1. I am uneasy with the juxtaposition of 'modern' and 'post-modern' values, which is so widespread in the social sciences literature and is adopted by Adams. However, his placement of regions on these scales is still instructive.

79 Quoted in William G. Robbins, 'Complexity and Regional Narratives,' in *The Great Northwest*, ed. William G. Robbins (Corvallis: Oregon State University Press, 2001), 4. Ailsa Henderson points, for example, to findings that western Canada has within it an urban cluster containing cities like Winnipeg and Edmonton, a rural cluster, and a suburban Vancouver region that has more similarity to suburban Toronto than rural areas next door. 'Regional Political Cultures in Canada,' *Canadian Journal of Political Science* 37 (September 2004): 595–615.

80 Fiorina shows in his challenge to the 'culture war' thesis that in close to half of American states, the electoral results from the 2000 election were close enough to make their coloration as unambiguously red or blue debatable. More importantly, a mapping of presidential results at the county level, especially one that factored in size of majority, produced very substantial variations within most states. Democratic majorities appeared across urban areas in the South and Southwest, while Republican majorities appeared in areas outside the major cities in western and northeastern states. See *Culture War?*

81 See, for example, Micheline Dumont, 'The Origins of the Women's Movement in Quebec,' and Micheline De Sève, 'The Perspectives of Quebec Feminists,' in *Challenging Times: The Women's Movement in Canada and the United States*, ed. Constance Backhouse and David H. Flaherty, 72–89 and 110–16 (Montreal: McGill-Queen's University Press, 1992).

82  Lipset, *Continental Divide*, 86–7.
83  See 'Qui nous sommes: Portrait d'une société québécoise en plein boule-versement,' *l'Actualité*, 1 May 2007, 27–60. According to the CROP survey used for this analysis, only 62 per cent of Quebeckers thought marriage was important for them, and 16 per cent thought extra-conjugal affairs were 'not so serious' compared to 81 per cent and 7 per cent for the rest of Canada (p. 33). For an earlier report, see *Maclean's Magazine* (3 January 1994).
84  The classic formulation of such a view comes from C. Brough Macpherson, *Democracy in Alberta: The Theory and Practice of a Quasi-Party System* (Toronto: University of Toronto Press, 1953). See also Nelson Wiseman, *In Search of Canadian Political Culture* (Vancouver: UBC Press, 2007).
85  My own view, based on interviewing in Alberta soon after this episode, is that Klein never intended to take the step he mused over, but wanted to shore up his morally conservative base.
86  J.H. Paterson, *North America: A Geography of the United States and Canada*, 9th ed. (New York: Oxford University Press, 1994), 312.
87  On regional differences in religious conservatism, see Pew Research Centre, 'Religion and Politics.' On the strength of religious conservatives in the Republican Party, see Clyde Wilcox, *Onward Christian Soldiers*, 76.

## 3. Broadening Activist Agendas

1  See John D'Emilio's insightful article 'Cycles of Change, Questions of Strategy: The Gay and Lesbian Movement After Fifty Years,' in *The World Turned* (Durham, NC: Duke University Press, 2002, 78–98; and for overviews that apply to both countries, Barry Adam, *The Rise of a Gay and Lesbian Movement*, articles in Barry Adam, Jan Willem Duyvendak, and André Krouwel, eds., *The Global Emergence of Gay and Lesbian Politics* (Philadelphia: Temple University Press, 1999); Dennis Altman, *Global Sex* (Chicago: University of Chicago Press, 2001). On Canada specifically, see Tom Warner, *Never Going Back: A History of Queer Activism in Canada* (Toronto: University of Toronto Press, 2002), and Miriam Smith, *Lesbian and Gay Rights in Canada: Social Movements and Equality-Seeking, 1971–1995* (Toronto: University of Toronto Press, 1999).
2  See Ellen Anderson, *Out of the Closets and into the Courts* (Ann Arbor: University of Michigan Press, 2004), and Susan Mezey, *Queers in Court: Gay Rights Law and Public Policy* (Lanham, MD: Rowman and Littlefield, 2007).

3  *Continental Divide*, 37.
4  Private giving in some ways exacerbates the inequalities produced through the labour market, since they result in tax deductions that reduce the capacity of the state to remedy those inequalities.
5  There are professional groups, most notably within the Canadian Bar Association and its provincial counterparts, but these are not the kind of permanently staffed and continuously vigilant groups that populate the American landscape.
6  See Miriam Smith, 'Social Movements and Judicial Empowerment: Courts, Public Policy and Lesbian and Gay Organizing in Canada,' *Politics and Society* 33, no. 2 (June 2005): 327–53.
7  Social movement analysis has often pitted frameworks against one another in explaining mobilization and impact. I may seem to be siding here with 'resource mobilization' theory, and then later with those who lean towards explanations focusing on 'political opportunity structure.' I believe that relying entirely on one or the other approach is nonsensical, and I argue here that a variety of factors, resources, and opportunities, institutional and social, account for both activist growth and its success in shifting policy and law.
8  See Seymour Martin Lipset and Noah M. Meltz, *The Paradox of American Unionism: Why Americans Like Unions Much More Than Canadians, but Join Much Less* (Ithaca, NY: Cornell University Press, 2004), and Gerald Hunt and Jonathon Eaton, 'We Are Family? Labour's Response to Gay, Lesbian, Bisexual, and Transgendered Workers,' chap. 6 in *Equity, Diversity, and Canadian Labour*, ed. Gerald Hunt and David Rayside (Toronto: University of Toronto Press, 2007).
9  Even on an issue as basic as the addition of sexual orientation to Ontario's Human Rights Code, the CCLA offered only token support, resisting repeated requests for more substantial campaigning. This is based on personal experience as coordinator of the campaign urging the provincial government to amend the code, which it did in 1986.
10  I base this in part on personal interviews conducted in the late 1990s and early 2000s.
11  On this see John C. Millier, '"My Daddy Loves Your Daddy": A Gay Father Encounters a Social Movement,' in *Queer Families, Queer Politics: Challenging Culture and State*, ed. Mary Bernstein and Renate Reimann (New York: Columbia University Press, 2001), 221.
12  One survey of lesbians and gay men in major American cities, sponsored in 2000 by the Kaiser Foundation, revealed that 11 per cent of them had children in the home. Among those who were not parents, fully 49 per

cent said they would like to adopt children some day, and of the total sample 81 per cent thought that adoption rights were 'very important' (with an additional 15 per cent considering them somewhat important). 'Inside-OUT: A Report on the Experiences of Lesbians, Gays and Bisexuals in America and the Public's Views on Issues and Policies Related to Sexual Orientation' (Henry J. Kaiser Family Foundation, 2000), http://www.kff.org/kaiserpolls, accessed 12 May 2007. The sampling entailed random household phoning in fifteen major metropolitan areas, and including a question on whether there was any adult who was gay, lesbian, bisexual in that household. It therefore included only those prepared to so self-identify.

13 A 1980 *New York Times* article estimated that in that year 150 lesbians in the United States had conceived through anonymous donor insemination. Ten years later, the National Center for Lesbian Rights estimated that there were between five thousand and ten thousand lesbians who had done the same. See Anne Taylor Fleming, 'New Frontiers in Conception,' *New York Times Magazine*, 20 July 1980; and data supplied by Lambda Legal and the Colorado Lesbian and Gay Law Association in an amicus brief filed in the Colorado Appeals Court hearing on the adoption cases of TKJ and KAK (1995).

14 *21st Century Gay* (New York: M. Evans, 2000).

15 George Chauncey highlights the role of AIDS and parenting in pushing the marriage issue to the fore in the United States, in *Why Marriage? The History Shaping the Debate over Gay Equality* (New York: Basic Books, 2004).

16 See Gerald Hunt, ed., *Laboring for Rights: Unions and Sexual Diversity across Nations* (Philadelphia: Temple University Press, 1999).

17 This account and additional material in this section is drawn from Warner's book *Never Going Back*, chap. 10. The quote is drawn from page 231.

18 A 1999 survey of francophone lesbian activists, mostly in Quebec, revealed the extent of support for marriage even among those most likely to be critical of assimilating to existing institutions. Most of those interviewed placed 'great importance' on the legal recognition of lesbian couples, even though most felt they were not in a position to be fully enough out to be able to take advantage of such recognition. Only a small minority asserted that such recognition was not important. The prevailing opinion was that such recognition would have ramifications extending very widely, serving as a signal that would reduce prejudice and violence, increase visibility and public acceptance, and provide a lead for non-governmental institutions. This was based on interviews with

seventy-five activists in five lesbian organizations conducted by Irene Demczuk, et al., and reported in *Recognition of Lesbian Couples: An Inalienable Right*, chap. 4.

19 Leonard Link Blog, posted 30 October 2006, on http://newyorklawschool .typepad.com/leonardlink.

20 This is a point made by Mary Bernstein and Renate Reimann in an article that pays considerable respect to radical and queer critiques of the politics of respectability: 'Queer Families and the Politics of Visibility,' in *Queer Families*, 1–17. It was also a theme in the aftermath of the failed attempt to lift the American military's ban on gays and lesbians. See Craig Rimmerman, ed., *Gay Rights, Military Wrongs: Political Perspectives on Gays and Lesbians in the Military* (New York: Garland, 1996).

21 A subsequent referendum allowed the Hawai'i legislature to assert the heterosexuality of marriage in the state's constitution.

22 A Kaiser Foundation survey of lesbians, gays, and bisexuals in 2000 showed that 68 per cent saw marriage as very important, and an additional 25 per cent as somewhat important. Inheritance rights and employee benefits for partners were treated as very important by 90 per cent or more of the sample.

23 Gerald Unks, 'Thinking about the Gay Teen,' in *The Gay Teen: Educational Practice and Theory for Lesbian, Gay, and Bisexual Adolescents* (New York: Routledge, 1995), 4–5. For a first-rate overview of the need for school attention to sexual diversity, and many of the developments taken to address the challenge, see Arthur Lipkin, *Understanding Homosexuality, Changing Schools* (Boulder, CO: Westview, 1999).

24 'Thinking about Sodomy,' *Educational Policy* 20, no. 1 (January–March 2006): 37. For a historical overview of the gender and sexuality policing of American schools, see also Lugg, 'Sissies, Faggots, Lezzies, and Dykes,' *Educational Administration Quarterly* 39, no. 1 (February 2003): 95–134.

25 Arthur Lipkin, *Understanding Homosexuality*, provides an overview. See also Unks, *The Gay Teen*; Dan Woog, *School's Out: The Impact of Gay and Lesbian Issues on America's Schools* (Boston: Alyson, 1995); Jeff Perrotti and Kim Westheimer, *When the Drama Club Is Not Enough* (Boston: Beacon, 2001); and school climate surveys published on the web site of Gay, Lesbian and Straight Education Network, http://www.glsen.org. There is less in Canada, but an important study in BC was issued by the Auditor General, 'Fostering a Safe Learning Environment: How the British Columbia Public School System Is Doing' (2000), http://www.bcauditor.com/PUBS/subject/followup.htm, accessed

13 May 2007; and in Quebec, by Michel Dorais, *Mort ou fif: La face cachée du suicide chez les garçons* (Montreal: VLB Editeur, 2000).

26  See, for example, Rich Savin-Williams, *The New Gay Teenager* (Cambridge, MA: Harvard University Press, 2006).

27  Major school climate surveys have been conducted in 2001, 2003, and 2005, http://www.glsen.org. Many other studies have been undertaken, including Massachusetts Department of Education, School Nutrition, Safety, and Climate Unit, 'Massachusetts High School Studients and Sexual Orientation: Results of the 2003 Youth Risk Behavior Survey,' 2004.

28  *De l'égalité juridique à l'égalité sociale* (Quebec: Quebec Human Rights Commission, 2007), http://www.cdpdj.qc.ca/fr/communiques. See also G. Walton, 'Bullying and Homophobia in Canadian Schools,' in *Gay, Lesbian, and Transgender Issues in Education*, ed. James Sears (New York: Harrington Park, 2004), 89–102; and A. Grenier, 'Jeunes, homosexualité et écoles: Enquête exploratoire sur l'homophobie dans les milieux jeunesse de Québec' (GRIS-Quebec, Montreal, 2005).

29  Division of Adolescent Medicine, Children's Hospital Boston, March 2007.

30  The 2005 GLSEN survey showed that transgender students were significantly more likely to feel unsafe than gay and lesbian students.

31  See Michael Reynolds, 'The Abstinence Gluttons,' *The Nation*, 4 June 2007.

32  The American research is well summarized by Lipkin, *Understanding Homosexuality*, 151–4.

33  See, for example, Kevin Jennings, ed., *One Teacher in 10: Gay and Lesbian Educators Tell Their Stories* (Boston: Alyson, 1994); and Woog, *School's Out*.

34  In one American study, a sample of sexual minority youth reported that staff intervened about 60 per cent of the time, as compared to 87 per cent for sexist remarks and 90 per cent for racist remarks. This did represent a significant increase in 'intervention rate' for homophobic remarks over the previous two years. GLSEN, 'The 2001 National School Climate Survey' (New York, 2001), 11–12

35  The single best source on LGBT schools activism and its impact is Lipkin, *Understanding Homosexuality*.

36  For an excellent account of early teacher activism, see Jackie M. Blount, *Fit to Teach: Same-Sex Desire, Gender, and School Work in the Twentieth Century* (Albany: State University of New York Press, 2005), chap. 6.

37  Among GLSEN's initiatives was the preparation of *Just the Facts about Sexual Orientation and Youth* – a primer intended for all educators that was endorsed by the American Association of School Administrators, the

American Federation of Teachers, the National Education Association, and other groups.

38  See Lipkin, *Understanding Homosexuality*.

39  Peter Freiberg, 'Gay Issues in Schools Are Now a "Front-Burner" Issue,' *Washington Blade*, 19 January 1996.

40  This is a point made by Miriam Smith in comments on an earlier draft of this chapter.

41  On this and other early activism in Saskatchewan, see Valerie J. Korinek, 'Activism = Public Education: The History of Public Discourses of Homosexuality in Saskatchewan, 1971–93,' in *I Could Not Speak My Heart: Education and Social Justice for Gay and Lesbian Youth*, ed. James McNinch and Mary Cronin (Regina: Canadian Plains Research Center, University of Regina, 2004), 109–38.

42  For Toronto developments, see Tim McCaskell, *The Race to Equity: Disrupting Educational Inequality* (Toronto: Between the Lines, 2005)

43  On this, and other aspects of sexual diversity in BC schools, see Miriam Smith, 'Questioning Heteronormativity: Lesbian and Gay Challenges to Education Practice in British Columbia, Canada,' *Social Movement Studies* 3, no. 2 (October 2004): 131–45.

44  ETFO was formed from an amalgamation of the women's union and an elementary men's teacher union.

45  André P. Grace and Kristopher Wells, 'Engaging Sex-and-Gender Differences: Educational and Cultural Change Initiatives in Alberta,' in McNinch and Cronin, *I Could Not Speak My Heart*, 289–309.

46  On this, see Catherine A. Lugg, 'The Religious Right and Public Education,' *Educational Policy* 12, no. 3 (May 1998): 267–83.

47  On the larger issues at stake, see Lipkin, *Understanding Homosexuality*; Debbie Epstein and Richard Johnson, eds. *Schooling Sexualities* (Buckingham, UK: Open University Press, 1998); Debbie Epstein and James T. Sears, eds., *A Dangerous Knowing: Sexuality, Pedagogy and Popular Culture* (London: Cassell, 1999); James T. Sears, 'Crossing Boundaries and Becoming the Other: Voices across Borders,' in *Curriculum, Religion, and Public Education: Conversations for an Enlarging Public Square*, ed., Sears with James C. Carper (New York: Teacher's College Press, 1998), 36–58; and Bruce Macdougall, *Queer Judgements: Homosexuaity, Expression and the Courts in Canada* (Toronto: University of Toronto Press, 2000).

48  Ron Manzer, *Educational Regimes and Anglo-American Democracy* (Toronto: University of Toronto Press, 2003), chap. 4.

49  There has been debate among Quebeckers in recent years over whether policy towards immigrants should be assimilationist or 'multicultural.'

50 On this debate, see George Lakoff, *How Liberals and Conservatives Think* (Chicago: University of Chicago Press, 2002).

51 As Catherine Lugg points out, 'freedom of choice' school plans in the U.S. South would be mechanisms for securing racial segregation, even if in more recent times the same frame is more frequently used to support parents opting for religiously based schooling (personal correspondence, November 2006).

52 I have written on both of these episodes in 'Gay Rights and Family Values: The Passage of Bill 7 in Ontario,' *Studies in Political Economy* 26 (Summer 1988): 109–47, and *On the Fringe*, chap. 4.

53 In the early 1990s, Citizens United for Responsible Education (CURE) protested the Toronto school board's more substantial steps toward such recognition. (Several years later, when Toronto's school boards were being amalgamated, the Toronto District Muslim Educational Assembly warned that children were being taught that the homosexual 'lifestyle' was normal, and described this as 'moral corruption' and an 'abomination.' Presentation by Ibrahim El-Sayed, TDMEA President, at a seminar on Muslims Minorities' Challenges of a North American Environment, 21 October 2000, obtained on TDMEA web site: http://www.tdmea.com. See Nicola Luksic, 'Cultures Join to Fight Gay Rights,' *Now Magazine*, 5–11 October 2000; and Krishna Ran, 'Religion: Sticking Their Nose In,' *Capital Xtra*, 15 March 2007.

54 Quoted in Rusty Benson, 'Pro-Family Groups Multiply Effectiveness in Cooperative Effort: Leadership of AFA Founder Brings Together Major Pro-Family Groups,' *American Family Association Journal* (January 2005), http://www.afajournal.org/2005/january/1.05Arlington.asp.

55 'Republicans Relaunch the Antigay Culture Wars,' *The Nation*, 2 October 2003.

56 On this, see Keith Boykin, *Beyond the Down Low: Sex, Lies and Denial in Black America* (New York: Carroll and Graf, 2004), and Nicolas Ray, 'False Promises: How the Right Deploys Homophobia to Win Support from African-Americans' (Washington: National Gay and Lesbian Task Force, 2006), http://www.thetaskforce.org/press/releases/pr931_040406.

57 Richard A. Lindsay and Jessica Stern, 'David v. Goliath: A Report on Faith Groups Working for Lesbian, Gay, Bisexual and Transgender Equality (and What They're Up Against)' (for the National Religious Leadership Roundtable, the National Gay and Lesbian Task Force, 2006), http://www.thetaskforce.org/reports_and_research/david_v_goliath.

58 'Trop, c'est trop!' *La Presse*, 26 February 2006, and Michael Valpy, 'Catholic Group Takes Aim at Rome, Hierarchy on Social Issues,' *Globe and Mail*, 18 March 2006.

59  Reported in Steph Smith, 'Chicago Priests Revolt against Vatican Anti-Gay Stand,' http://www.365Gay.com, accessed 21 December 2003. See also Frank Bruni, 'Vatican Exhorts Legislators to Reject Same-Sex Unions,' *New York Times*, 1 August 2003.

## 4. Canadian Recognition of Same-Sex Relationships

1  Following British practice, only male homosexual activity had ever been criminalized. The 1969 legislation used twenty-one as the age of consent. The age of consent for most sexual activity was fourteen until 2007, when the Conservative government pushed for a change to sixteen. There remains on the statute books a provision that sets the age at eighteen for anal sex unless engaged in by husband and wife, though that provision has been ruled unconstitutional by courts in Ontario (1995) and Quebec (1998). See Gary Kinsman, *The Regulation of Desire: Homo and Hetero Sexualities*, 2nd ed. (Montreal: Black Rose Books, 1996).
2  For an account of such attacks, see Kinsman, *The Regulation of Desire*; and Tom Warner, *Never Going Back*.
3  The Metropolitan Toronto authorities, grouping representatives of several municipalities before 1998 amalgamation, were forced by tribunal ruling to accept same-sex benefits in 1997, following a challenge by its own employees.
4  For accounts of legal developments, see Miriam Smith, *Lesbian and Gay Rights in Canada*; Kathleen Lahey, *Are We 'Persons' Yet? Law and Sexuality in Canada* (Toronto: University of Toronto Press, 1989); Bruce MacDougall, *Queer Judgements: Homosexuality, Expression and the Courts in Canada* (Toronto: University of Toronto Press, 2000).
5  I have written more substantially on this in 'Social Democracy, Labour Unions, and Same-Sex Relationship Recognition in British Columbia' (paper presented at the Annual Meeting of the American Political Science Association, Boston, September 1998), and 'The Institutional and Partisan Context for Sexual Diversity Politics in Washington State and British Columbia' (paper presented at the Annual Meeting of the Western Political Science Association, Seattle, March 1999).
6  On which see my 'Gay Rights and Family Values,' *Studies in Political Economy*, no. 26 (Summer 1988): 109–47.
7  Daniel Gawthrop, *Highwire Act: Power, Pragmatism and the Harcourt Legacy* (Vancouver: New Star Books, 1996), 61.
8  I have written about this extensively in *On the Fringe*, chap. 5.
9  This was part of a systematic 'updating' of the Civil Code. In 1996, the

government eliminated a provision in the human rights charter that permitted continuing discrimination in social insurance policies, but then over the next two years it took only modest steps to actually change such policies.

10  There are many useful accounts of court developments; Petersen's is particularly helpful in its pointing to union-based grievances and labour tribunal decisions. 'Fighting It Out in Canadian Courts,' in *Laboring for Rights: Unions and Sexual Diversity across Nations*, ed. Gerald Hunt, 37–57 (Philadelphia: Temple University Press, 1999).

11  The Supreme Court of Canada read sexual orientation into Alberta's statute in the 1998 *Vriend v. Alberta* decision.

12  Claire Young has argued that the *Egan* ruling betrayed a systematic tendency to agree to benefits provided by the private sector and to resist favourable decisions that would constitute a drain on the public treasury, in 'Aging and Retirement Are Not Unique to Heterosexuals: *Rosenberg v. Canada*,' in *Sexuality in the Legal Arena*, ed. Didi Herman and Carl Stychin (London: Athlone Press, 2000), 151–63.

13  Decision in *Moore v. Canada*, quoted in Cynthia Petersen, 'Fighting It Out in Canadian Courts,' 51.

14  Universities were among the first large employers to extend benefits coverage to same-sex partners, several doing so in the 1980s and early 1990s. The University of Toronto was not a pioneer, but as the country's largest university its policy change in 1991 had particular significance. And when it did so, it included pension benefits despite the exclusionary definition of spouse in the federal Income Tax Act. Within a few years, virtually all major universities had made at least non-pension benefits inclusive.

15  See Gerald Hunt, 'No Longer Outsiders: Labor's Rsponse to Sexual Diversity in Canada,' in *Laboring for Rights*, 10–36.

16  The resistance to recognizing de facto heterosexual couples in earlier changes to the code had reflected in part the preferences of most organized feminists in Quebec. They had opposed automatic treatment as 'marriage-like,' since de facto relations were in reality highly varied, and since women did have the option of getting married. The difference in treatment of de facto relationships was striking in a province with many more such couples than other provinces: one in four cohabiting heterosexual couples are unmarried, as compared to one in ten elsewhere. See Irene Demczuk, et al., *Recognition of Lesbian Couples: An Inalienable Right* (Ottawa: Status of Women Canada, 2002).

17  Sylvain Larocque has written a comprehensive account of the development of the marriage challenges, and the legal and political responses to

them, in *Gay Marriage: The Story of a Canadian Social Revolution* (Toronto: Lorimer, 2006).

18  The Civil Code in Quebec, the only province where common law does not fully apply, did contain an explicitly heterosexual definition of marriage, which federal law acknowledged until the code's amendment.

19  I owe this analysis to Lorraine Weinrib of the Faculty of Law, University of Toronto.

20  The federal government is permitted to refer a question to the Supreme Court, even in the absence of an appeal from a lower court.

21  'Believe me, for someone of my generation, born and brought up [in] Catholic rural Quebec ... this is a very, very difficult issue. But I have learned over forty years in public life that society evolves, that the concept of human rights evolves even more quickly than some of us predicted, and sometimes even in ways that make people uncomfortable. At the end of the day, we have to live up to our responsibilities.' Quoted in Colin Nickerson, 'Gay Nuptials Causing Rift in Canada,' *Boston Globe*, 25 August 2003. I have written about the caution of the federal Liberals in *On the Fringe*, chap. 4.

22  Some non-Christian faith leaders – particularly Muslim – were also becoming outspoken. The Muslim Canadian Federation's chair described proposed legislation on marriage as reprehensible. Quoted in Jonathon Gatehouse, 'Backlash: Why Does Half of the Country Believe Same-Sex Marriages Shouldn't Be Legal?' *Maclean's*, 26 August 2003.

23  The motion was also supported by all Alliance members, three-quarters of the Conservative caucus, and a few members of the Bloc Québécois, but no NDP members.

24  Federal and provincial legislatures may do so, providing that they explicitly acknowledge they are doing so and that they re-enact the legislation in question every five years.

25  By this time, so many courts had ruled that an exclusively heterosexual definition of marriage was contrary to the Charter that a new statute encoding the exclusivity would never survive constitutional challenge. A letter sent publicly to Harper in January 2005, and signed by over 130 law professors from across the country, made this point clear, and accused him of not being honest with Canadians.

26  On 11 April a press conference supporting same-sex marriage included representatives of the United Church, the Muslim Canadian Congress, the World Sikh Organization, and others.

27  Canada, *House of Commons Debates*, 16 February 2005, http://www2.parl .gc.ca/HousePublications/Publication.aspx?DecDE1640291.

28  The 'sponsorship' scandal centred on misspent money designed to

counter sovereigntist sentiment in Quebec, following the near-victory of a pro-sovereignty referendum in that province.

29  Thirty-two Liberals voted against it; three Conservatives voted in favour (a fourth having earlier moved to the Liberals in part out of displeasure with the social conservatism of the Conservatives).

30  The party's web site did not mention the marriage issue, and none of its thirty issue backgrounders dealt with the issue.

31  Nicholas Ray, 'False Promises: How the Right Deploys Homophobia to Win Support from African-Americans' (National Gay and Lesbian Task Force, 2006), http://www.thetaskforce.org/reports_and_research/reports, accessed 10 May 2007.

32  Analysis of data from the 2004 election study suggests that same-sex marriage was not an important issue, and neither was abortion. If that was true in 2004, the argument would be even stronger for 2006. However, the marriage issue would seem to me to have acted as a symbollic marker of the Conservatives' willingness to defend 'traditional values,' and to have had a subtle influence on morally conservative voters even when they regarded issues like health as much more important. See Elisabeth Gidengil, et al., 'Back to the Future? Making Sense of the 2004 Canadian Election Outside Quebec,' *Canadian Journal of Political Science* 39 (March 2006): 1–25.

33  'Harper Victory Narrowed by Marriage Issue' (press release, 24 January 2006), http:// www.egale.ca.

34  An Environics poll in the spring of 2006 showed that 66 per cent did not want the issue raised again. 'Environics/CBC 2006 Federal Election Survey,' http://erg.environics.net/media_room/default.asp?aID=598, accessed 11 May 2007. On the substantive question, 59 per cent supported lesbian/gay marriage, and only 24 per cent strongly opposed. Environics Research Group, 'Canadians for Equal Marriage,' http://erg.environics.net/media_room/default.asp?aID=609, accessed 10 May 2007.

35  Bill Curry and Jill Mahoney, 'Legal Furor Erupts Over Same-Sex Proposal,' *Globe and Mail*, 5 October 2006.

36  Christopher Dreher, 'In Ottawa, Faith Makes a Leap to the Right,' *Globe and Mail*, 23 September 2006. Focus on the Family already had a foundation in Canada before the creation of its branch plant and Ottawa-based family institute. James Dobson's radio program, for example, is heard on 130 Canadian radio stations.

37  Gloria Galloway, 'Same-Sex Marriage File Closed for Good, PM Says,' *Globe and Mail*, 8 December 2006.

38 The caution of the Prime Minister's Office was evident when the RCMP marriage was announced in May 2006, with staff members instructing Conservative MPs not to comment on the story.

39 These steps, alongside those taken by American Episcopal dioceses, provoked intense opposition in other parts of the worldwide Anglican communion, and official rebuke put a brake on further developments for a time, though Canadian bishops resisted a full moratorium by agreeing only to not encourage or initiate such rites in the period of further deliberation. In most cases, parishes that had already received permission to bless such unions would be able to continue doing so.

40 Michael Valpy, 'Bishop Seeks "Better Theology" of Sex,' *Globe and Mail*, 10 March 2007.

41 When the provincial government enacted the first of two major bills extending rights to same-sex couples, the Quebec media routinely parroted the PQ government's distorted claim that such rights were unprecedented in Canada. In conversation with one cabinet representative at the time, I raised a question about British Columbia legislation, and received the inexplicable response that such legislation was not yet implemented!

42 Jean-François Breton (a PhD student at the Université de Montréal) points out the persistence of deference to the state in the decades since the 1960s, along with a widespread willingness to assume that politicians will do what is necessary. As in the rest of Canada (and other countries), political cynicism and apathy have undoubtedly increased in Quebec, though there remains a tendency to identify the state as an absolutely central institution in Quebec society. This was in a conversation during a conference on religion, sexuality, and politics held at the University of Toronto, in January 2007.

43 The 1999 poll was by Environics. A 2004 poll by Gallup showed 63 per cent support for civil unions, but an Ipsos-Reid poll in the same year, presenting a choice between civil unions, full marriage, and no recognition, showed that 71 per cent supported either civil unions or marriage.

44 Reginald Bibby, *The Future Families Project: A Survey of Canadian Hopes and Dreams* (Ottawa: Vanier Institute of the Family, 2004), 1.

45 Surveys that force a choice between marriage and civil unions show only minority support for full-fledged marriage (of around 40 per cent). In 2004, Ipsos-Reid asked: 'Many Canadian provinces have legalized same sex marriage and the Canadian federal government is waiting for advice from its Supreme Court before it acts. Which of the following statements is closer to your point of view on same sex marriage? It is wrong and it

should never be lawful; It should be fully recognized and equal to conventional heterosexual marriages; it should be allowed to exist in civil law but not have the same legal weight as a conventional marriage.' In response, 27 per cent favoured no recognition, 32 per cent favoured civil unions, and 39 per cent favoured full marriage. 'Canadians and Same Sex Marriage as the Supreme Court of Canada Makes Its Ruling,' 9 December 2004, http://www.ipsos-na.com/news/pressrelease.cfm?id=2491, accessed 11 May 2007.

46 Ted Morton and Rainer Knoppf are the most vocal proponents of this view, for example in *The Charter Revolution and the Court Party* (Peterborough, ON: Broadview Press, 2000).

47 The Supreme Court made explicit reference to this notion in the marriage reference. In this and many other cases, the Canadian judiciary had largely adopted a view of the constitutional rights framework as a 'living tree' – not a fixed doctrine for which original intent had to be divined.

48 This is an argument made by a few writers focussing on the U.S. case, as we shall see. Comparative studies have also made the point, e.g., Yuval Merin, *Equality for Same-Sex Couples: The Legal Recognition of Gay Partnerships in Europe and the United States* (Chicago: University of Chicago Press, 2002); and Robert Wintemute, *Legal Recognition of Same-Sex Partnerships: A Study of National, European, and International Law* (Oxford: Hart, 2001); C. Waaldijk, *Homosexuality, A European Community Issue: Essays on Lesbian and Gay rights in European Law and Policy* (Dordrecht and Boston: Martinus Nijhoff, 1993).

49 'The Political Foundations of Support for Same-Sex Marriage in Canada' (paper presented at the Annual Meeting of the Canadian Political Science Association, Winnipeg, June 2004).

## 5. American Recognition of Same-Sex Relationships

1 Important work exploring state and local developments includes James W. Button, Barbara A. Rienzo, and Kenneth D. Wald, *Private Lives, Public Conflicts: Battles over Gay Rights in American Communities* (Washington, DC: Congressional Quarterly Press, 1997); Button, Rienzo, and Wald, 'The Politics of Gay Rights at the Local and State Level,' in *The Politics of Gay Rights*, ed. Craig A. Rimmerman et al. (Chicago: University of Chicago Press, 2000), 269–290; Donald Haider-Markel and Kenneth J. Meier, 'The Politics of Gay and Lesbian Rights: Expanding the Scope of the Conflict,' *Journal of Politics* 58 (1996): 332–49; Haider-Markel, 'Lesbian and Gay Pol-

itics in the States: Interest Groups, Electoral Politics, and Policy,' in Rimmerman et al., *The Politics of Gay Rights*, 290–346 ; Steven Haeberle, 'Gay Men and Lesbians at City Hall,' *Social Science Quarterly* 77 (1996): 190–7; Robert Bailey, *Urban Politics, Gay Politics: Identity and Economics in the Urban Setting* (New York: Columbia University Press, 1999); and Elaine Sharp, ed., *Culture Wars and Local Politics* (Lawrence: University Press of Kansas, 1999).

2   Ohio's was undone in 1999.

3   This is established in work by Button, Rienzo, and Wald, *Private Lives*; and Haider-Markel, 'Lesbian and Gay Politics in the States.'

4   Patricia Cain, *Rainbow Rights: The Role of Lawyers and Courts in the Lesbian and Gay Civil Rights Movement* (Boulder, CO: Westview, 2000). This is also an important part of the argument made by Jason Pierceson, *Courts, Liberalism and Rights: Gay Law and Politics in the United States and Canada* (Philadelphia: Temple University Press, 2005)

5   Judgment available at: http://www.glbtq.com/social-sciences/kowalski _thompson.html.

6   On this, see You-Ta Chuang, Robin Church, and Ron Ophir, 'Tug of War: The Rise of Same-Sex Partner Health Benefits in Fortune 500 Corporations, 1990–2003' (unpublished ms., 2004).

7   Toronto had enacted a 'contract compliance' measure before this, but it had nothing like the impact of the San Francisco measure.

8   See Jonathon Goldberg-Hiller, '"Making A Mockery of Marriage": Domestic Partnership and Equal Rights in Hawai'i,' in Stychin and Herman, *Law and Sexuality*, 113–31 ; and *The Limits of Union: Same Sex Marriage and the Politics of Civil Rights* (Ann Arbor: University of Michigan Press, 2002).

9   Congressional legislation designed to toughen the resistance to illegal entry effectively closed off provisions that in the recent past had been interpreted in ways that allowed foreign partners of American lesbians and gay men into the country on compassionate grounds. There was now an inescapable obligation on officials to deport, and immigration authorities were estimating that tens of thousands of couples would be affected, some of them having lived together for years. See Andrew Jacobs, 'Gay Couples Split by Immigration Law,' *New York Times*, 23 March 1999. See also Susan Hazeldean and Heather Betz, 'Years Behind: What the United States Must Learn About Immigration Law and Same-Sex Couples,' *Human Rights Magazine* (2003), American Bar Association, http://www .abanet.org.

10   Charles W. Gossett, 'Dillon Goes to Court: Legal Challenges to Local

Ordinances Providing Domestic Partnership Benefits,' in *Gays and Lesbians in the Democratic Process: Public Policy, Public Opinion, and Political Representation*, ed. Ellen Riggles and Barry Tadlock (New York: Columbia University Press, 1999), 62–88.

11  Minneapolis was ruled to not have the power to enact domestic partnership legislation for its own employees in 1995. In 1999, Boston was prevented from extending insurance plan benefits in ways that contradicted the then-heterosexual definitions in the state pension plan. Some American states grant 'home rule' status to cities, but that has not always prevented relationship recognition ordinances being struck down. Localities cannot necessarily exceed the powers expressly granted to them, or enact measures that are not interpreted as indispensible to the objectives given over to localities. It has been the pattern of courts since the nineteenth century to rule against localities where there is a reasonable doubt about whether a particular measure properly falls within their jurisdiction. This is 'Dillon's Law,' enunciated by Iowa Supreme Court Justice John Dillon in 1868, on which see Charles Gossett, 'Dillon's Rule and Gay Rights.'

12  'The genius of Vermont's equity practice is that the state insisted that traditional family values give way to the recognition of lesbian and gay rights, but lesbian and gay family values give way to accommodation of tradionalist anxieties for the time being.' Eskridge, *Gaylaw*, 881.

13  Eskridge thinks the parallel with 'separate but equal' is not strong, in part because the Vermont Court insisted that the benefits and responsibilities be the same, and in part because the impulse behind the move was an essentially egalitarian one rather than one of containment. 'Equality Practice: Liberal Reflections on the Jurisprudence of Civil Unions,' *Albany Law Review* 64, no. 3 (2001): 853–85.

14  Ross Sneyd, 'Civil Unions Become Part of Vermont Fabric,' *Associated Press*, 8 January 2005.

15  Quoted in Linda Greenhouse, 'Supreme Court Paved Way for Marriage Ruling with Sodomy Decision,' *New York Times*, 19 November 2003.

16  Warren Richey, 'Gay Rights No Easy Sell in Courts,' *Christian Science Monitor*, 9 February 2006.

17  See Kai Wright, 'Unions May Retain Partner Benefits,' *Washington Blade*, 24 December 1999. On the uptake of sexual diversity issues by labour unions, see Hunt, *Laboring for Rights*.

18  Reform spread more slowly among smaller firms, though the total number of private employers with inclusive benefit plans more than doubled from 1999 to 2003. And while one 2003 survey found only 23 per cent of 578 companies offering same-sex benefits, two years later it was

32 per cent. Survey by the Society for Human Resource Management, reported in Amy Joyce, 'Sexuality an Overlooked Diversity Factor,' *Washington Post*, 25 April 2004. Results from 2005 reported in Leah Carlson Shepherd, 'Employers Continue Riding the Wave of Domestic Partner Benefits,' *Employee Benefit News*, May 2006.

19  This account is based largely on several stories in the *Washington Blade* by Peter Freiberg, 'Gay Policies Yanked,' 10 December 1999; 'Benefits Resolution Sustained,' 9 June 2000; 'Gay-Friendly Resolution Wins Support at ExxonMobil,' 1 June 2001; by Rhonda Smith, 'Call for Boycott Sparks Conflict,' 15 June 2001; 'Groups Still Undecided on ExxonMobil Boycott,' 29 June 2001; 'Equality Coalition Forms to Target ExxonMobil,' 19 October 2001; and by Kai Wright, 'Unions May Retain Partner Benefits,' 24 December 1999.

20  This section relies on several major newspaper reports, including Tho Emery, 'Lesbian Couple Wins Landmark Ruling by State's Highest Court,' *Associated Press*, 18 November 2003; Tim Harper, 'U.S. Court Lifts Gay-Marriage Ban,' *Toronto Star*, 19 November 2003; Yvonne Abraham, '10 Years' Work Led to Historic Win in Court,' *Boston Globe*, 23 November 2003; Michael Paulson, 'Black Clergy Rejection Stirs Gay Marriage Backers,' *Boston Globe*, 10 February 2004; William Symonds, 'Gay Marriage's Minefield for Businesses,' *Business Week*, 14 May 2004; Alan Cooperman, 'Massachusetts Clergy Are Divided on Eve of Historic Same-Sex Unions,' *Washington Post*, 16 May 2004; Carolyn Lochhead, 'Lawyer's Gay Rights Strategy,' *San Francisco Chronicle*, 24 May 2004.

21  Gallup polling showed a 12 per cent drop in the percentage of Americans who supported homosexual sex being legal, and other survey questions showed similar patterns. On this, as well as Republican uptake of marriage, see Doug Ireland, 'Republicans Relaunch the Antigay Culture Wars,' *The Nation*, 2 October 2003.

22  A summit meeting of conservative leaders in the spring of 2003 had come to precisely that view. See David Kirkpatrick, 'Conservatives Use Gay Union as Rallying Cry,' *New York Times*, 8 February 2004.

23  Only one Democratic senator (Ted Kennedy) actually spoke in favour of same-sex marriage

24  Brad Cain, 'Churches Key to Signature Campaign for Gay Marriage Ban,' *Associated Press*, 24 May 2004.

25  Alan Cooperman, 'Churchgoers Get Direction from Bush Campaign,' *Washington Post*, 1 July 2004.

26  Wilcox stated this claim during public presentations at the University of Toronto in January 2007.

27  Allan Abramowitz, 'Terrorism, Gay Marriage, and Incumbency: Explaining the Republican Victory in the 2004 Presidential Election,' *Forum* 2, no. 4 (2004), http://www.bepress.com/forum/vol2/iss4/art3.

28  Morris Fiorina, 'Postelection Perspectives,' *San Francisco Chronicle*, 21 November 2004, and *Culture War? The Myth of a Polarized America*, 2nd ed. (New York: Pearson Education, 2006); Ken Sherrill, '"Moral Values" Voters in the 2004 Presidential Election' (National Gay and Lesbian Task Force Policy Institute, 2004), http://www.thetaskforce.org.

29  In Ohio, for example, African American support for Republicans rose from 9 to 16 per cent, and in Florida from 7 to 13 per cent. Nicholas Ray, 'False Promises: The Courtship of the African-American Vote' (National Gay and Lesbian Task Force Policy Institute, 2006), 18.

30  Margaret Ebrahim, 'The Bible Bench,' *Mother Jones*, May/June 2006.

31  'Exit Polls Show Independents, Citing War, Favored Democrats,' *New York Times*, 7 November 2006.

32  See Patrick J. Egan and Kenneth Sherrill, 'Same-Sex Marriage Initiatives and Lesbian, Gay and Bisexual Voters in the 2006 Election' (National Gay and Lesbian Task Force, 2007), http://www.thetaskforce.org.

33  Joshua Lynsen, 'New Dems Mixed on Gay Issues,' *Washington Blade*, 17 November 2006.

34  Michigan's amendment read: 'To secure and preserve the benefits of marriage for our society and for future generations of children, the union of one man and one woman in marriage shall be the only agreement recognized as a marriage or similar union for any purpose.'

35  See Joanna Grossman, 'The State of the Nation on Same-Sex Marriage,' *Findlay Law*, 8 August 2006, http://www.findlaw.com.

36  The Arizona activist campaign included the AFL-CIO, the League of Women Voters, and other groups, and effectively highlighted the threat to benefits for unmarried couples, downplaying gay and lesbian claims. See Nathan Riley, 'In Arizona, Radicalism Rejected,' *Gay City News*, 16 November 2006.

37  See Joanna Grossman, 'The New Jersey Domestic Partnership Law,' *Findlay Law*, 13 January 2004, http://www.findlaw.com.

38  As Art Leonard argues, this was a case carefully pursued by Lambda Legal Defense, in a state ranked high by strategists (alongside Vermont and Massachusetts) as having the best chances of victory. See his 'Same-Sex Marriage and the Importance of Strategy,' and 'The New York Marriage Decision,' Leonard Link blog, comment posted October 25 and 30, 2006, http://newyorklawschool.typepad.com/lenoardlink/2006.

39  The measure also included unmarried heterosexual couples where one was over the age of sixty-two.

40  See Richard Florida, *The Rise of the Creative Class: And How It's Transforming Work, Leisure, and Everyday Life* (New York: Basic Books, 2002).

41  Christopher Swope, 'Chasing the Rainbow,' *Governing Magazine*, August 2003.

42  See Alan Murray, 'How Microsoft Tripped Over Gay Rights,' *Wall Street Journal*, 11 May 2005.

43  Marc Gunther, 'Queer Inc.,' *Fortune*, 30 November 2006.

44  There had been same-sex blessings in the Rochester, New York diocese for years, perhaps as early as the 1970s. There are also reports of widespread blessings at the local level in the Church of England.

45  See, e.g., Neela Banerjee and Katie Zezima, 'U.S. Catholics Are Divided over New Directive on Gays,' *New York Times*, 28 November 2005. In 2006, the Administrative Committee of the U.S. Conference of Catholic Bishops reaffirmed its support for an amendment to the U.S. constitution affirming a heterosexual definition of marriage.

46  Cited in Joseph Berger, 'Conservative Rabbies May Expel Colleague,' *New York Times*, 14 January 2005.

47  The Jewish Theological Seminary commissioned a national study of Conservative rabbis, cantors, educators, synagogue executives, and seminary students about gay ordination. The results showed strong majorities in all of these constituencies in favour of such ordination, majorities higher than those in Conservative circles in Canada, Israel, or elsewhere. See 'Survey Report on Gay Ordination' (The Jewish Theological Seminar, 31 January 2007), http://www.jtsa.edu/about/communication/press/20062007/20070131.shtml.

48  The University of Louisville and the University of Kentucky.

49  This argument is supported by Patrick Egan and Nathaniel Persily, 'Gay Marriage, Public Opinion and the Courts,' paper presented at the Annual Meeting of the American Political Science Association, September 2005.

50  According to Pew Research, in early 2004, 68 per cent of southerners opposed gay marriage and almost 40 per cent said they wouldn't vote for a candidate who disagreed with them. In the Northeast, the respective figures were 48 and 26 per cent. Cited in Lolita Baldor, 'Democrats Could Lose Southern Votes,' *Associated Press*, 9 July 2004.

51  Sheri Lunn, 'Bisexuals Overlooked in the Debate on Equal Marriage Rights,' *Out in America*, 24 September 2004, http://www.outinamerica.com.

52  Patrick Egan and Nathaniel Persily's analysis of public attitudes point, not surprisingly, to the influence of religiosity in general, and Protestant conservatism in particular, on negative attitudes towards homosexuality and such issues as gay marriage. They also strongly associate such reli-

giosity with measures of moral traditionalism used in American Election Studies. See 'Gay Marriage, Public Opinion and the Courts.'

53  See Hunt, *Laboring for Rights*.

54  Wald and his associates, and Haider-Markel, in *The Politics of Gay Rights*. In policy analysis more generally, policy legacies are often pointed to in explaining change. See, for example, Peter Hall, *Governing the Economy: The Politics of States Intervention in Britain and France* (Oxford: Oxford University Press, 1986).

55  Smith, 'The Politics of Same-Sex Marriage in Canada and the United States.'

56  T. Alexander Smith and Raymond Tatalovich, *Cultures at War: Moral Conflicts in Western Democracies* (Peterborough, ON: Broadview, 2003), chap. 7, point to the role of ballot measures in issue areas like abortion and gay rights.

57  Several writers have juxtaposed American and Canadian legal developments, including David A.J. Richards, *The Case for Gay Rights*; Pierceson, *Courts, Liberalism and Rights*; Ran Hirschl, *Towards Juristocracy*; Raymond Tatalovich, *The Politics of Abortion*; and Smith and Tatalovich, *Cultures at War*.

58  Craig Rimmerman, among others, has been critical of national group attention to state and local grassroots politics, though he acknowledged some years ago that there were encouraging signs of change. See 'Beyond Political Mainstreaming: Reflections on Lesbian and Gay Organizations and the Grassroots,' in Rimmerman et al., *The Politics of Gay Rights*, 54–78.

59  Donald Haider-Markel, 'Lesbian and Gay Politics in the States,' in Rimmerman et al., *The Politics of Gay Rights*, 298–9.

60  Haider-Markel, 'Lesbian and Gay Politics in the States,' in Rimmerman et al., *The Politics of Gay Rights*, 290–346; Button, Rienzo, and Wald, *Private Lives, Public Conflicts*.

61  This view accords with the substantial literature on political opportunity structure. See, for example, Sidney Tarrow, *Power in Movement: Social Movements: Collective Action and Politics*, 2nd ed. (Cambridge: Cambridge University Press, 1998).

62  Haider Markel makes this point, as do Chris Bull and John Gallagher, *Perfect Enemies: The Religious Right, the Gay Movement, and the Politics of the 1990s* (New York: Crown, 1996).

63  See, for example, Haider-Markel and Meier, 'The Politics of Gay Rights: Expanding the Scope of the Conflict'; Kenneth Wald, J.W. Button, and B.A. Rienzo, 'The Politics of Gay Rights in American Communities:

Explaining Antidiscrimination Ordinances and Policies,' *American Journal of Political Science* 40 (1996): 1152–78. There are also signs in this literature that state laws can sometimes reflect a backlash in the face of progressive local measures. An intriguing analysis of anti-marriage laws by Scott Barclay and Shauna Fisher, for example, shows that they are more likely in states where a significant number of localities have included sexual diversity in anti-discrimination ordinances. 'The States and the Differing Impetus for Divergent Paths on Same-Sex Marriage, 1990–2001,' *Policy Studies Journal* 31, no. 3 (2003): 331–52. Anti-marriage laws are also more likely in states with a relatively high number of same-sex couples declaring themselves as such in the U.S. census. They discount the role of variations in conservative religiosity across states, but do so with a deeply flawed measure.

64 Greg Lewis and Jonathon Edelson mine data on public opinion and congressional voting patterns, making just this point. 'DOMA and ENDA: Congress Votes on Gay Rights,' in Rimmer et al., *The Politics of Gay Rights*, 193–216.

65 Sharp, 'Introduction,' in *Culture Wars and Local Politics*, 1–20.

66 This is evident in the work of Kenneth Wald and his associates (*Private Lives, Public Conflicts*), as well as work by Bailey (*Gay Politics, Urban Politics*); and Haeberle, 'Gay Men and Lesbians at City Hall.'

67 See Roddrick A. Colvin, 'Agenda Setting, Innovation, and State Gay Rights Policy: An Event History Analysis,' *American Review of Politics* 25 (Fall 2004): 241–64; and Egan and Persily, 'Gay Marriage, Public Opinion and the Courts.' There is mixed evidence on whether regions with higher proportions of African Americans are more likely to see progressive legislation enacted on sexual diversity. See for example Button, Rienzo, and Wald, *Private Lives, Public Conflicts*, chap. 7.

68 Button, Rienzo, and Wald, *Private Lives, Public Conflicts*, chap. 7.

## 6. Parenting in Canada

1 For a general discussion of lesbian parenting, before major legal breakthroughs, see Katherine Arnup, ed., *Lesbian Parenting: Living with Pride and Prejudice* (Charlottetown, PEI: Gynergy Books, 1995), and Fiona Nelson, *Lesbian Motherhood: An Exploration of Canadian Lesbian Families* (Toronto: University of Toronto Press, 1996).

2 Carol Rogerson, 'The Child Support Obligation of Step-Parents,' *Canadian Journal of Family Law* 18 (2001): 9–158.

3  On this, see Susan Boyd, 'Lesbian (and Gay) Custody Claims: What Dif-
   ference Does Difference Make?' *Canadian Journal of Family Law* 15, no 1
   (1998): 131–52, and Bruce Ryder, 'Equality Rights and Sexual Orientation:
   Confronting Heterosexual Family Privilege,' *Canadian Journal of Family
   Law* 9, no. 1 (1990): 39–98. See also Martha McCarthy and Joanna
   Radford, 'Family Law for Same Sex Couples: Chart(er)ing the Courts,'
   *Canadian Journal of Family Law* 15, no. 2 (1998): 101–77.

4  Katherine Arnup, 'Finding Fathers: Artificial Insemination, Lesbians,
   and the Law,' *Canadian Journal of Women and the Law* 7, no. 1 (1994):
   97–115.

5  Canada, *Proceed with Care: The Royal Commission on New Reproductive Technologies* (Ottawa: Queen's Printer, 1993).

6  See Angela Campbell, 'Conceiving Parents through Law,' *International
   Journal of Law, Policy and the Family* (published online by Oxford University Press, 13 January 2007, http://lawfam.oxfordjournals.org/). In any
   event, most couples would use anonymous sperm donation. In Quebec,
   Newfoundland, and the Yukon territory, donors of sperm through clinics
   were barred from claiming parental rights, though in other provinces
   their chances of securing parental rights were minimal. For heterosexual
   couples resorting to surrogacy, formal agreements renouncing the surrogate's parental status are not always secure, and unenforceable in Quebec
   and Alberta in the face of conflict. (Recent federal legislation also prohibits payments for surrogacy or sperm donation.)

7  Interview conducted by author, 24 April 1998.

8  The Children's Law Reform Act essentially eliminated the distinction
   between cohabiting and married heterosexual couples, for example, in
   presuming the man to be the father of a child born during the relationship. At the same time, the legislation used gender-neutral language in
   its reference to parents, and therefore did not preclude the treatment of
   both partners in a same-sex relationship as 'natural' parents.

9  Quoted in Boyd, 'Lesbian (and Gay) Custody Claims,' 141.

10  A total of four Social Credit MLAs had switched to Reform in March
    1994.

11  There was still a presumption of parentage for married couples (even if
    the husband was uninvolved in conception) that did not extend to others.
    One anomaly that remained for all couples, whether married or not, was
    that the cohabiting partner of the parent of an adopted child was not able
    to also adopt that child.

12  Interview conducted by author, 28 April 1998.

13  Sarah Rose Werner, 'Lesbians and Donor Insemination,' *Family Pride*

*Parenting with Pride*, http://www.uwo.ca/pridelib/family/articles/insemination.html.

14  I have written about this in *On the Fringe: Gays and Lesbians in Politics* (Ithaca, NY: Cornell University Press, 1998), chap. 5.

15  Couples still had to go to court, with the associated expenses. And if there was any conflict – for example, a claim from a known sperm donor – the outcome might not be entirely predicatable. See Campbell, 'Conceiving Parents Through the Law.' Campbell also points out that a 1997 court ruling in *Buist v. Greaves* highlighted that the existing statute had language assuming only one mother, even if non-biological partners could adopt. But even if the court ruling denied custody to the non-biological parent (mostly on the grounds of the weakness of the parent-child bond), it did order child support payments. I would also argue that the limiting language in the statute would not, at the time, have survived constitutional challenge.

16  David Howell, 'Oberg to Uphold Ban on Gay Foster Parenting,' *Edmonton Journal*, 27 March 1997.

17  She had been given such leave only in regard to a particularly difficult case, but it was enough to convince Ms T. to drop her court case, and it did represent an important principled shift in policy.

18  Allyson Jeffs, 'Same-Sex Step-Parents May Be Allowed to Adopt,' *Edmonton Journal*, 22 April 1999.

19  Marilyn Shinyei, director of Adoption Options, quoted in *Alberta Report*, 5 May 1999.

20  Interview conducted by the author with Liberal MLA, 30 April 1999.

21  See Susan Boyd, 'Lesbian (and Gay) Custody Claims,' 131–52.

22  Personal correspondence with Mona Greenbaum, September 2006.

23  Werner, 'Lesbians and Donor Insemination.'

24  Carol Rogerson, 'The Child Support Obligation of Step-Parents,' *Canadian Journal of Family Law* 18, no. 1 (2001): 9–151.

25  In 2006, the group had about 700 families associated with it, with as many as two hundred attending meetings.

26  As Angela Campbell points, out, there are some ambiguities. The character of the 'parental project' is open to contestation, for example from a known sperm donor who contests a lesbian couple's portrayal of the understanding. In the case of fertilization as a result of intercourse, the Civil Code is in fact contradictory, apparently opening the door to a parental claim from the biological father. (See 'Conceiving Parents through Law,' 11–12.)

27  Http://www.justice.gouv.ca/english/publications/generale/union-civ-

a.htm, p. 3. This does not apply to a gay male couple, since the statute declares surrogacy contracts null and void.

28 There was greater flexibility introduced to parenthood rules in 1991 revisions to the Civil Code, though not as applicable to known biological partners now separated.

29 Amy Barratt, Mona Greenbaum, Brigitte Masella, and Nicole Paquette, *Access to Fertility Services for Lesbians: A Question of Health*, submitted by the Lesbian Mothers Association of Québec on draft legislation governing assisted human reproduction (available by request from info@aml-lma.org.). Cited in Sarah Rose Werner, 'Lesbians and Donor Insemination' (unpublished ms., 2002).

30 Interview conducted by author, 18 June 2002.

31 Quoted in Mikaëlle Monfort, 'Gaies et lesbiennes: Parents de plein droit!' *La Voix du Village* (January 2005), 35.

32 Monfort, 'Gaies et lesbiennes,' 35.

33 When the sperm donor was known, the non-biological mother had to go through formal second-parent adoption. However, this requirement could sometimes be circumvented because lesbian couples did not have to prove that they used anonymous donor sperm.

34 Campbell, 'Conceiving Parents through Law,' 8.

35 Under-the-table financial arrangements are apparently spreading rapidly, as of course is the use of American and other foreign surrogates. Still, this entails reduced availability and increased costs.

36 Data from ReproMed Ltd, Toronto. Screening for donor characteristics would add $250, and assessing a known donor would add a great deal more.

37 See Ian Austen, 'Canadian Court Rules Lesbian Partner Is a Parent,' *New York Times*, 12 January 2007.

38 Fiona Kelly has summarized evidence on this front, and the array of relationships that couples and their children retain with donors, in 'Nuclear Norms or Fluid Families? Incorporating Lesbian and Gay Parents and Their Children into Canadian Family Law,' *Canadian Journal of Family Law* 21 (2005–6): 133–78.

39 'Breaking the Link between Biology and Parental Rights in Planned Lesbian Families: When Semen Donors Are Not Fathers,' *Georgia Journal of Gender and Law* 2 (2000): 57. See also Katherine Arnup and Susan Boyd, 'Familial Disputes? Sperm Donors, Lesbian Mothers, and Legal Parenthood,' in *Legal Inversions*, ed. Didi Herman and Carl F. Stychin (Philadelphia: Temple University Press, 1995). This debate is also discussed in Kelly, 'Nuclear Norms or Fluid Families?'

40  Cited in Martha McCarthy and Joanna Radbord, 'Family Law for
    Same Sex Couples,' *Canadian Journal of Family Law* 15, no. 2 (1998): 101–
    77.

41  Maureen Sullivan points to the lesbianness of the American mothers she
    writes about being erased during informal or passing conversations with
    others. As in the United States, the very idea of a lesbian mother is
    beyond the ken of most Canadians. See 'Alma Matter: Family "Outings"
    and the Making of the Modern Other Mother (MOM),' in *Queer Families,
    Queer Politics: Challenging Culture and the State*, ed. M. Bernstein and R.
    Reimann (New York: Columbia University Press, 2001), 231–54.

42  This is a point eloquently made by Cheshire Calhoun, *Feminism, the
    Family, and the Politics of the Closet* (Oxford: Oxford University Press),
    96–100.

43  The Strategic Counsel poll, undertaken for the *Globe and Mail* and CTV,
    showed 55 per cent support for the position that the issue of same-sex
    marriage should not be revisited. See Brian Laghi, 'Same-Sex Marriage
    Bill Must Stand, Majority Say,' *Globe and Mail*, 18 July 2005.

44  Charlene Miall and Karen March, 'Social Support for Changes in Adop-
    tion Practice: Gay Adoption, Open Adoption, Birth Reunions, and the
    Release of Confidential Identifying Information,' *Families in Society* 86
    (January–March 2005): 83–92. The date of polling is not provided, but it
    can be surmised as about 1998.

45  Bibby, *A Survey of Canadian Hopes and Dreams* (Ottawa: Vanier Institute of
    the Family, 2004), 57.

## 7. Parenting in the United States

1  Valerie Lehr, *Queer Family Values*; and Sean Cahill, 'Welfare Moms and
   the Two Grooms,' *Sexualities* 8, no. 2 (2005): 169–87.

2  Renate Reimann, 'Lesbian Mothers at Work,' in *Queer Families, Queer Politics*, ed. Bernstein and Reimann, 254–72.

3  Yuval Merin, *Equality for Same-Sex Couples: The Legal Recognition of Gay
   Partnerships in Europe and the United States* (Chicago: University of
   Chicago Press, 2002), especially 253–62.

4  To varying degrees, this includes the American Academy of Pediatrics,
   the American Medical Association, the American Psychological Association, the American Psychiatric Association, and many child-focused
   social agencies. See Kevin Sack, 'Fathers in the Making,' *Los Angeles
   Times*, 30 October 2006.

5  This is underlined by Nancy Polikoff, 'Lesbian and Gay Couples Raising

Children: The Law in the United States,' in Wintemute and Andenaes, *Legal Recognition of Same-Sex Partnerships*, 153–67.

6  Sandra Barney, 'Accessing Medicalized Donor Sperm in the US and Britain: An Historical Narrative,' *Sexualities* 8, no. 2 (2005): 205–20.

7  I owe this point to Catherine Lugg, in personal correspondence and 'Sissies, Faggots, Lezzies and Dykes: Gender, Sexual Orientation and the New Politics of Education,' *Educational Administration Quarterly* 39 (February 2003): 95–134.

8  The Alaska ruling barred evidence of social stigma in reversing a lower court decision removing custody from a lesbian mother (*SNE v. RLB*). The California ruling removed a prohibition on the presence of a third person known to be a homosexual in granting visitation rights to a gay father (*In re the Marriage of Birdsall*).

9  See C.R. Leslie, 'Creating Criminals: The Injuries Inflicted by "Unenforced" Sodomy Laws,' *Harvard Civil Rights – Civil Liberties Law Review* 35 (Winter 2002): 102–18.

10  For a useful overview, see 'Adoption by Lesbians and Gay Men: An Overview of the Law in the 50 States,' Lambda Legal Defense and Education Fund, 1996. See also updates provided by Lambda through their web site, http://www.lambdalegal.org.

11  With somewhat different readings of the court record, see Nancy Polikoff, 'Lesbian and Gay Couples Raising Children,' and Susan Dalton, 'Protecting Our Parent-Child Relationships: Understanding the Strengths and Weaknesses of Second Parent Adoption,' in Bernstein and Reimann, *Queer Families, Queer Politics*, 201–20.

12  These data come from William Adams Jr, 'Whose Family Is It Anyway? The Continuing Struggle for Lesbians and Gay Men Seeking to Adopt Children,' *New England Law Review* 30 (Spring 1996), 579–624; and in a summary of state adoption provisions in a brief on adoption prepared in May 1994 by the Lesbian and Gay Rights Section of the BC Branch of the Canadian Bar Association.

13  State policy is clearest in the case of an individual gay or lesbian seeking to foster or adopt. The right of couples to formally foster or adopt, in other words the right of a same-sex partner to become second or stepparent, varies by county. In King and Pierce counties, such rights are secured, but they are not in most other counties.

14  Neil Modie, 'Ban on Gay Adoptions Threatened,' and 'Adoption by Gays Fuels Fierce Debate,' *Seattle Post-Intelligencer*, 5 October and 7 October 1993; and Ellis E. Conklin, 'Mother Fights Son's Adoption by Gay Couple,' *Seattle Post-Intelligencer*, 21 September 1993.

15  Chris Bull and John Gallagher, *Perfect Enemies: The Religious Right, the Gay Movement, and the Politics of the 1990s* (New York: Crown, 1996), 225–8.

16  Neil Modie, 'Court Ends Bid to Prevent Gay Adoption,' *Seattle Post-Intelligencer*, 13 September 1994.

17  Quote and some details taken from Patricia Cain, *Rainbow Rights: The Role of Lawyers and Courts in Lesbian and Gay Civil Rights* (Boulder, CO: Westview Press, 2000), 251.

18  Ginia Bellafante, 'Surrogate Mothers' New Niche: Bearing Babies for Gay Couples,' *New York Times*, 27 May 2005.

19  '7th Annual Listing of Gay-friendly Reproductive Tech Companies and More,' http://www.gayparentmag.com.

20  See Julian Murphy, 'Should Lesbians Count as Infertile Couples? Antilesbian Discrimination in Assisted Reproduction,' in Bernstein and Reimann, *Queer Families, Queer Politics*, 182–201.

21  Sandra Barney, 'Accessing Medicalized Donor Sperm,' 213.

22  John Bowe, 'Gay Donor or Gay Dad,' *New York Times Magazine*, 19 November 2006, 69.

23  Some states allow only married couples to enter into surrogacy agreements. See David Chambers, 'What If? The Legal Consequences of Marriage and the Legal Needs of Lesbian and Gay Male Couples,' in Bernstein and Reimann, *Queer Families, Queer Politics*, 306–37.

24  Kelly Griffith, 'Gay Parenting,' *Advocate*, 19 July 2005, 46.

25  'VA Court Sides with Adoptive Gay Couples on Birth Certificates,' *Associated Press*, 22 April 2005.

26  Kevin Sack, 'Fathers in the Making,' *Los Angeles Times*, 29 October 2006.

27  *Queer Family Values*, chaps 1–2.

28  'Missouri Judge Rules that Lesbian Can Be Foster Parent,' American Civil Liberties Union, 2 February 2006. The state decided not to appeal, in part because the state legislature had repealed statutory language criminalizing homosexual activity, though the state agency announced (ominously) that it would start asking prospective parents if they were homosexual. See Tim Hoover, 'State Eases Policy on Gay Parents,' *Kansas City Star*, 19 July 2006.

29  An appeal court's ruling in *Howard v. Child Welfare Agency Review Board* occurred in the same year as state voters approve an anti-gay-marriage amendment to the state constitution. That court ruling was affirmed by the state's supreme court in 2006

30  Lambda Legal Defense and Education Fund, 'Youth in the Margins: A Report on the Unmet Needs of Lesbian, Gay, Bisexual, and Transgender Adolescents in Foster Care,' Lambda Legal Defense and Education Fund

2001, http://www.nclrights.org/publications/lgbtqfostercare.htm.
Quoted in Sean Cahill, M. Ellen, and Sarah Tobias, *Family Policy: Issues Affecting Gay, Lesbian, Bisexual and Transgendered Families*, report prepared for the Policy Institute of the National Gay and Lesbian Task Force (22 January 2003), 127 (http://thetaskforce.org/reports_and_research/family_policy).

31 'Youth in the Margins.' They surveyed fourteen states (representing all regions, and including states like California, New York, and New Jersey – among the most likely to be progressive.

32 In 2000, lawmakers in Utah and Mississippi enacted laws that explicitly or effectively prohibited gay/lesbian adoptions, the former framed more broadly to apply to anyone cohabiting with another person outside of marriage, the later citing same-sex couples explicitly.

33 See Michael Kranish, 'Beliefs Drive Research Agenda of New Think Tanks,' *Boston Globe*, 31 July 2005.

34 'The Vatican Believes Gay Adoptions Are "Gravely Immoral,"' http://www.pinknews.co.uk, 3 March 2006.

35 Elizabeth Fernandez, 'Catholic Agency Finds Way Out of Adoption Ban,' *San Francisco Chronicle*, 27 August 2006.

36 A.J. Mistretta, 'Foreign Adoption Sometimes a Good Option for Gay Parents,' *Dallas Voice*, 13 July 2006.

37 Donaldson Adoption Institute, 'Adoption by Lesbians and Gays' (January 2007), 8, online at http://www.adoptioninstitute.org; and 'China Bars Massachusetts Gay Couples from Adopting,' *Associated Press*, 1 May 2006.

38 These data are available in map form at http://www.hrc.org. In 2007, Colorado law was changed to allow all unmarried partners (including gay and lesbian) to adopt at the same time, avoiding the two-step process normally required to ensure that both parents have a formally recognized parental role.

39 California, Connecticut, Illinois, Indiana, Massachusetts, New Jersey, New Mexico, New York, Oregon, Vermont, and Washington, DC.

40 Conducted by the Donaldson Adoption Institute, 'Adoption by Lesbians and Gays: A National Survey of Adoption Agency Policies, Practices, and Attitudes,' http://www.adoptioninstitute.org. Their results are probably skewed somewhat towards the positive, since a disproportionate number of agencies failing to respond to the survey were those that refused to accept or had never accepted homosexual applicants.

41 Lynn Waddell, 'Gays in Florida Seek Adoption Alternatives,' *New York Times*, 21 January 2005.

42  See the National Center for Lesbian Rights side, http://www.nclrights.org.

43  Cahill, Ellen, and Tobias, 'Family Policy Issues,' 14.

44  Adam Liptak, 'California Ruling Expands Same-Sex Parental Rights,' *New York Times*, 23 August 2005; and Rachel La Corte, 'State Supreme Court Rules Lesbian May Seek Parental Rights,' *Seattle Post-Intelligencer*, 3 November 2005. There were three cases settled by California's Supreme Court in 2005, covering various claims based on the rights and responsibilities of partners in same-sex relationships: *Elisa B. v. Superior Court*, *K.M v. E.G.*, and *Kristine H. v. Lisa R.*

45  The case involved Lisa and Janet Miller-Jenkins, and was working its way through Vermont and Virginia courts in 2004, 2005, and 2006.

46  *Wood v. Wood*. See http://www.nclrights.org.

47  Geoffrey Fattah, 'Utah Top Court Rules against Granting Same-Sex Parental Rights,' *Deseret Morning News*, 17 February 2007.

48  'Lesbian and Gay Parents in Child Custody and Visitation Disputes,' *Human Rights Magazine*, vol. 30 (Summer 2003), http://www.abanet.org/irr/hr/summer03/custody.html.

49  'Adoption by Lesbians and Gay Men: An Overview of the Law in the 50 States,' Lambda Legal Defense Fund, 1996, http://www.lambdalegal.org.

50  'What If? The Legal Consequences of Marriage and the Legal Needs of Lesbian and Gay Male Couples,' in Bernstein and Reimann, *Queer Politics, Queer Families*, 314. Similar treatment is often meted out to straight cohabiting couples – rarely given legal standing – though there are examples of courts granting standing to 'psychological' parents in heterosexual cases and denying it in same-sex cases (Colorado is an example).

51  Stephanie Armour, 'Gay Parents Cheer a Benefit Revolution,' *USA Today*, 10 January 2005.

52  Malone, *21st Century Gay*, 98.

53  Quoted in ibid., 99.

54  Quoted in an amicus brief from Lambda and the Colorado Lesbian and Gay Law Association, in the appeals court hearing of a case on the adoption of TKJ, 1995.

55  See Judith Stacey and Timothy Bilbarz, '(How) Does the Sexual Orientation of Parents Matter?' *American Sociological Review* 66 (2001): 159–83.

56  Paula Ettelbrick, a prominent lawyer, activist, and writer on these issues, argues for legal change to recognize more than just two-parent families, in 'Domestic Partnerships, Civil Unions, or Marriage: One Size Does Not Fit All,' *Albany Law Review*, vol. 64 (Spring 2001): 905–14. See also Kathleen Lahey, *Are We Persons Yet? Law and Sexuality in Canada* (Toronto: University of Toronto Press, 1999), preface.

57 The same survey found 21 per cent strongly in favour, 19 per cent somewhat in favour, 11 per cent somewhat opposed, 41 per cent strongly
   opposed.
58 PSRA/Newsweek polls for 1994 and 1998; Yankelovich/CNN/Time polls
   for 2002; Pew Research polls for 2004 and 2006; and ABC/Time poll for
   2006. A 2004 poll by Princeton Survey Research for Newsweek showed
   that 45 per cent supported 'adoption rights for gays and lesbians.'
59 *In re Adoption of Evan*, New York Supreme Court, 1992, quoted in Polikoff,
   'Lesbian and Gay Couples Raising Children,' 160.

## 8. Canadian School Lethargy

1 There are not many sources discussing the record of Canadian activism
   or its impact. Tom Warner, *Never Going Back*, provides useful information
   on activism. Various contributions to James McNinch and Mary Cronin,
   eds., *I Could Not Speak My Heart: Education and Social Justice for Gay and
   Lesbian Youth* (Regina: Canadian Plains Research Center, University of
   Regina, 2004) also address the current need for more schools attention.
2 On early developments, see John Campey, Tim McCaskell, John Miller,
   and Vanessa Russell, 'Opening the Classroom Closet: Dealing with
   Sexual Orientation at the Toronto Board of Education,' in *Sex in Schools:
   Canadian Education and Sexual Regulation*, ed. Susan Prentice (Toronto:
   Our Schools/Our Selves, 1994), 82–100, and Tim McCaskell, *Race to
   Equity: Disrupting Educational Inequality* (Toronto: Between the Lines,
   2005).
3 Vanek was reporting, in personal correspondence, on a survey of school
   policies undertaken for Egale Canada, 2007.
4 Insiders included Student Worker Tim McCaskell, trustee Olivia Chow,
   social worker Tony Gambini, and teacher John Campey.
5 See McCaskell, *Race to Equity*.
6 This section relies partly on McCaskell's account in *Race to Equity*, on
   news stories over many years in *Xtra!* magazine and other local media.
7 Miriam Smith discusses BC educator activism in 'Questioning Heteronormativity: Lesbian and Gay Challenges to Educational Practice in British
   Columbia, Canada,' *Social Movement Studies* 3 (October 2004): 131–45.
8 Kim Bolan, 'Surrey School Teachers Fight Ban on Books about Same-Sex
   Families,' *Vancouver Sun*, 25 April 1997. See also Michael Valpy, 'Gay
   Books in the Classroom,' *Globe and Mail*, 9 November 1997.
9 See Raj Takhar, 'Queer Kids Want Support,' *Angles*, April 1997; Ian
   Austin, 'Gays Recall Abuse in B.C. Schools,' *Vancouver Province*, 17 March

1997; and Kim Bolan, 'Demonstrators Face Off over Homosexuality Issue,' *Vancouver Sun*, 17 March 1997.

10  Simpson was also associated with the Christian Coalition of Canada. See Kim Bolan, 'Invitation to Anti-Gay Discussion Sparks Row,' *Vancouver Sun*, 9 April 1997.

11  At least one of the slate was linked to the Christian Heritage Party, and at least one other to the CRI. See Kim Bolan, 'Surrey School Teachers Fight Ban on Books about Same-Sex Families.'

12  He was also said in one media report to have been a member of Operation Rescue. Vaughn Palmer, 'In Surrey, They've Forgotten the Political Lesson about Intolerance,' *Vancouver Sun*, 10 May 1997.

13  Three days later, a meeting of Parent Advisory Groups from across the province approved resolutions proposed by a Surrey parents group opposing gay-positive materials in schools. One of the motions opposed curricular material dealing with same-sex couples or any material prepared by 'homomsexual lifestyle advocacy groups,' and it passed 165–158. Stewart Bell, 'Ban Urged on Teaching about Homosexuality,' *Vancouver Sun*, 28 April 1997.

14  'Minister Joins Rally to Battle Anti-Gays,' *Victoria Times-Colonist*, 4 May 1997.

15  Recall elections are highly unusual in Canada, but they are permitted in BC, although only if 40 per cent of the electorate in a constituency demands one.

16  Inteview conducted by author with BCTF staff, 11 May 1999.

17  'Being Out: Lesbian, Gay, Bisexual and Transgender Youth in BC: An Adolescent Health Survey' (Vancouver: McCreary Centre Society, 1999).

18  Interview conducted by author with Montreal activist, June 2002.

19  The 2000 Alberta Schools Act required boards to establish a safe and caring environment for all students, and sexual orientation was not explicitly named.

20  A highly publicized study on LGBT youth at risk was published in 2002 by Michel Dorais, *Mort ou Fif* (Montreal: Editions de l'homme, 2001).

21  'Incessant Teasing by Schoolmates Drove B.C. Teen to Suicide,' *National Post*, 16 March 2000.

22  Auditor General of British Columbia, 'Fostering a Safe Learning Environment: How the British Columbia Public School System Is Doing' (2000), 61–2.

23  Gary Mason, 'Safe Schools for All: Why Is B.C. Lagging?' *Globe and Mail*, 17 June 2006.

24  See Gary Mason, 'A Mother's Six-Year Saga of Sorrow,' *Globe and Mail*, 3 June 2006.

25  Equity and Women's Services, ETFO, Report to the Annual Meeting, August 2001. See also Noreen Shanahan, 'Safe at School: Gay and Lesbian Issues in the Classroom,' *Our Times* (February/March 2006): 30–5.

26  Declaine Finucane, 'Grade 4 Teacher Answers Lifestyle Questions,' *Toronto Star*, 19 June 2000; and letters to editor, *Toronto Star*, 27 June 2000.

27  This is a point made by Morgan Vanek on the basis of her cross-country survey of school policies. Personal correspondence July 2007.

28  Presentation to 'Hearts and Minds,' a conference organized by the Sexual Diversity Studies Program, University of Toronto, 2003.

29  Drawn from Jan Prout, 'Canada: Student Fights for Gay Prom Date,' *PlanetOut* News, 28 March 2002, http://www.plantout.com/news; and CAW website, http://www.caw.ca/whatwedo/pride.

30  Brian Hanslip, quoted in Gloria Galloway, 'Squaring Off Over Sexuality,' *National Post*, 15 April 1999.

31  *Gale Force* 15 (March-April 2005): 14.

32  *Chamberlain v. Board of Trustees of School District No. 36 (Surrey)*. For an analysis of the case, see Bruce MacDougall and Paul T. Clarke, 'Teaching Tolerance, Mirroring Diversity, Understanding Difference: The Effect and Implications of the Chamberlain Case,' in McNinch and Cronin, *I Could Not Speak My Heart*, 193–219.

33  Surrey trustees were still intent on discovering ways to secure the heterosexuality of school environments. In 2005, they cancelled a planned performance of the *Laramie Project* (based on Matthew Sheppard's 1998 murder in Wyoming). And then, in 2006, they turned down a request that the children's book *King and King* be used in its schools. In the meantime, however, they had acquiesced (in 2003) in the use of two books recognizing diversity in families.

34  Laval University Professor Michel Dorais was a key player in highlighting the risks of inattention to this issue, with work sponsored by Gai Écoute. As recently as 1998, sexual minorities were not identified as a risk group in a Health and Social Services report on suicide! 'Stratégie québécoise d'action face au suicide' (1998), cited in the Quebec Human Rights Commission Report, *De l'égalité juridique à l'égalité sociale*, 39.

35  Daniel Martin and Alexandre Beaulieu, 'Besoins des jeunes homosexuelles et homosexuels et interventions en milieu scolaire pour contre l'homophobie' (Commission scolaire de Montréal, Service des ressources éducatives, May 2002).

36  Union research reported in Quebec, Commission des droits de la per-

sonne et des droits de la jeunesse, *De l'Égalité juridique à l'égalité sociale*, March 2007, 25–6.

37  See, for example, Irène Demczuk, 'Démystifier l'homosexualité, ça commence à l'école' (GRIS, Montreal, 2003); Alain Grenier et al., 'Résultat de l'enquête exploratoire sur l'homophobie dans les milieux jeunesse' (GRIS, Montreal, 2005)

38  Commission des droit de la personne et des droits de la jeunesse, *De l'égalité juridique à l'égalité sociale*,' 27.

39  The resource guide is written by sociologist Irène Demczuk, 'Démystifier l'homosexualité.'

40  Interview conducted by author, June, 2004.

41  This is based on an interview with Bill Ryan (McGill University), 9 May 2006.

42  I say this on the basis of an annual questioning of my undergraduate students (in a large course dealing with sexual diversity) on their school experience. Jordan DeCoste came to similarly discouraging conclusions about implementation in an unpublished paper, 'The Problem of Leftist Tokenism for High School Anti-Homophobia Initiatives' (January 2005). See also Ronnalee Gorman, 'An Exploration of TDSB Anti-Homophobia Equity: The Roles and Responsibilities of an Intermediate School Principal' (MSW research paper, York University, 2004); and Noreen Shanahan, 'Safe at School: Gay and Lesbian Issues in the Classroom,' *Our Times* (February/March 2006): 30–5.

43  See http://www.campaignlifecoalition.com/press, accessed on 8 December 2004.

44  The content of this box is based on personal observation.

45  *Gale Force* 15, no. 2 (March-April 2005), 4.

46  Catholic school officials were concerned about anti-gay bullying in Calgary in the 1990s, at the same time or even earlier than officials in the public board. One of the GSAs formed in Edmonton high schools in the early 2000s was at a Catholic school. The Marc Hall school prom case revealed that some other Catholic high schools in the Greater Toronto Area had allowed same-sex partners to attend proms without incident. I also ask my own students (third-year undergraduate) about their schooling experience, and many who have come out of Catholic systems have reported positive experiences around sexual difference.

47  For a comparative treatment of Canadian public education, see Ron Manzer's excellent book *Educational Regimes and Anglo-American Democracy* (Toronto: University of Toronto Press, 2003).

48  Marc Hall was able to find help from the local CAW, but that kind of help is not yet routinized.

## 9. School Reform and the American Culture Wars

1  Among Catherine Lugg's articles documenting the long-standing pattern of policing gender and sexuality, and mobilizing the right to police even more restrictively, are 'Sissies, Faggots, Lezzies, and Dykes: Gender, Sexual Orientation, and a New Politics of Education?' *Educational Administration Quarterly* 39, no. 1 (February 2003): 95–134, and 'The Religious Right and Public Education: The Paranoid Politics of Homophobia,' *Educational Policy* 12, no. 3 (May 1998): 267–83. See also Jackie M. Blount, *Fit to Teach: Same-Sex Desire, Gender, and School Work in the Twentieth Century* (Albany: State University of New York Press, 2005) for an excellent overview of the regulation of and expectations of teachers, and their activist response to marginalization from the 1970s on.

2  'Sissies, Faggots, Lessies, and Dykes,' 109.

3  This is an argument I share with Catherine Lugg, in 'Thinking about Sodomy,' *Educational Policy* 20, no. 1 (January-March 2006): 35–58.

4  On Project 10%, see Dan Woog, *School's Out: The Impact of Gay and Lesbian Issues of America's Schools* (Boston: Alyson Books, 1995), 320–37.

5  Tracy Phariss, 'Public Schools: A Battleground in the Cultural War,' in *Gay Lesbian/Bisexual/Transgender Public Policy Issues*, ed. Wallace Swan (Binghamton, NY: Haworth Press, 1998); and N'Tanya Lee, 'Bridging Race, Class, and Sexuality for School Reform,' in *Creating Change: Sexuality, Public Policy, and Civil Rights*, ed. John D'Emilio (New York: St Martin's Press, 2000), 251–60.

6  In the next few years, this venture was emulated in the creation of the Eagles School in West Hollywood (Los Angeles) and the privately funded Walt Whitman School in Dallas.

7  U.S. Department of Health and Human Services, 'Report of the Secretary's Task Force on Youth Suicide' (1989), http://www.wonder.cdc.gov.

8  Catherine Lugg points out that the head of the department (Louis Sullivan) had links to the Christian right and particularly to Louis Sheldon of the Traditional Values Coalition. It was only with the new presidency of Bill Clinton that the report was publicly available. See 'The Religious Right and Public Education,' 273–4.

9  Reported by A. O'Connor, 'Who Gets Called Queer in School? Lesbian, Gay and Bisexual Teenagers, Homophobia, and High School,' *High School Journal* 77:7–12, cited in William McFarland and Martin Dupuis, 'The Legal Duty to Protect Gay and Lesbian Students from Violence in School,' *Professional School Counselling* 4 (3 February 2003), 172.

10  Some details taken from John Yoakam, 'Making the Invisible Visible:

Organizing Resources for Gay, Lesbian, Bisexual, and Transgender Youth in School and Communities,' in Swan, *GLBT Public Policy Issues*, 98–104.

11 *Alone No More: Developing a School Support System for Gay, Lesbian, and Bisexual Youth* (St Paul: Minnesota State Department of Education; Atlanta: Centers for Disease Control, 1994).

12 On this section, see Arthur Lipkin, *Understanding Homosexuality, Changing Schools* (Boulder, CO: Westview Press, 2001), chap. 12; Dan Woog, *School's Out*, and Jeff Perrotti and Kim Westheimer, *When the Drama Club Is Not Enough: Lessons from the Safe Schools Program for Gay and Lesbian Students* (Boston: Beacon Press, 2001) ; and Catherine A. Lugg, 'Safer Sexual Diversity Climates: Lessons Learned from an Evaluation of Massachusetts Safe Schools Program for Gay and Lesbian Students,' *American Journal of Education* 110 (November 2003): 58–88.

13 See Blount, *Fit to Teach*, chap. 8.

14 *Understanding Homosexuality*, 269. In 2002, state funding for the Safe Schools Program was eliminated, substantially weakening its capacity to induce change at the school and district levels.

15 The content of this box is drawn from David Bruton, 'Insisting on Ignorance: The Paradox of Withholding Knowledge in Our Schools,' in *One Teacher in Ten: Gay and Lesbian Eduators Tell Their Stories* (Boston: Alyson, 1994), 177–99.

16 This section draws on Tracy Phariss, 'Public Schools: A Battleground in the Cultural War,' in Swan, *G/L/B/T Public Policy Issues*, 76–9; and Lee, 'Bridging Race, Class, and Sexuality for School Reform'; and Lugg, 'The Religious Right and Public Education,' 274–6.

17 See Lyle Rossman, 'Sexual Orientation Issues Impact K–12 Education,' in Swan, *G/L/B/T Public Policy Issues*, 63–74.

18 Drawn from stories in the *Washington Blade:* Peter Freiberg, 'Utah's Community Comes Out,' 15 March 1996, and 'Utah Bans Student Groups,' 19 April 1996; Rhonda Smith, 'Officials Plan to Lift Club Ban,' 25 August 2000, and 'Utah Student Group Ban Rescinded,' 8 September 2000.

19 'School of Hard Knocks,' *Lambda News and Views*, June 2000.

20 From a variety of *Washington Blade* stories, and David Buckel, 'Legal Perspectives on Ensuring a Safe and Nondiscriminatory School Environment for Lesbian, Gay, Bisexual, and Transgendered Students,' *Education and Urban Society* 32 (May 2000): 390–8.

21 Title IX: ' No person shall, on the basis of sex, be excluded from participation in, be denied the benefits of or subject to discrimination under any education program or activity getting federal funds.'

22 David M. Horne, *Bruised Inside: What Our Children Say about Youth Vio-*

*lence, What Causes It, and What We Need to Do about It* (Washington, DC: Office of the Attorney General, April 2000), http://www.wa.gov/ago/pubs/bruised%5Finside041000.pdf.

23  Due process requirements mean that even with 'cause,' boards face high financial costs and long delays in undertaking a dismissal. This is a point made by Catherine Lugg, who points to the failure of a North Carolina board's attempt to dismiss a teacher because he was gay, and to the fact that in New Jersey dismissal with cause can still take three to five years (personal correspondence, November 2006).

24  Lisa Keen, 'Two Cases on Teachers' Rights Emerge Victorious,' *Washington Blade*, 22 October 1999.

25  Catherine Lugg points out, correctly, that the aura of criminality has not been removed, and that the states that still had anti-gay sodomy laws on the books at the time of *Lawrence* still did years later. Still, the court ruling contributed to a gradual shift in public perceptions towards more acceptance of sexual diversity in schools. See her 'Thinking about Sodomy.'

26  Quoted in Jon Ward, 'Montgomery Schools Revise Sex Ed Course after Backlash,' *Washington Times*, 23 April 2005.

27  Joshua Lynsen, 'Revised Sex-Ed Curriculum to Be Unveiled,' *Washington Blade*, 11 August 2006.

28  Stephanie Simon, 'Ex-Gays Seek a Say in Schools,' *Los Angeles Times*, 1 June 2006.

29  Ibid.

30  'Get the Facts: Feelings Change,' NEA Ex-Gay Educators Caucus pamphlet.

31  In April 2007, an evaluation of abstinence-only programs conducted by Mathematica Policy Research for the U.S. Department of Health and Human Services concluded that they failed to increase the rates of abstinence or raise the age of inititial sexual encounters, http://www.mathematica-mpr.com/welfare/abstinence.asp.

32  Jason Cianciotto and Sean Cahill, *Education Policy: Issues Affecting Lesbian, Gay, Bisexual and Transgender Youth* (Washington, DC: National Gay and Lesbian Task Force, 2003), 95.

33  J.M. Irvine, *Talk about Sex: The Battles over Sex Education in the United States* (Berkeley and Los Angeles: University of California Press, 2002).

34  P.J. Huffstutter, 'States Abstain from Federal Sex-Ed Funds,' *Los Angeles Times*, 8 April 2007; Lisa Wangsness, 'Patrick Seeks to Forgo Grant,' *Boston Globe*, 24 April 2007.

35  David Klepper, 'Kansas Revises Sex Education Standards,' *Kansas City Star*, 9 May 2007.

36  'Thinking about Sodomy,' 176–7.

37  See Michael Reynolds, 'The Abstinence Gluttons,' *The Nation*, 4 June 2007.

38  See Scott Gold, 'Texas' Textbook Changes Have a Wide Impact,' *Los Angeles Times*, 20 February 2005.

39  The language of SB 1437 prohibited the presentation of material that reflected adversely upon persons because of, for example, their sexual orientation. The governor also vetoed a bill proposing the establishment of a 'tolerance education pilot program,' with funding for ten schools.

40  Ben Feller, 'Education Secretary Condemns PBS Show,' *Associated Press*, 25 January 2005.

41  See a mid-1990s commentary by Berkeley teacher Alan Miller, cited in Woog, *School's Out*, 109–15.

42  GLSEN, 'The 2005 National School Climate Survey' (New York, 2005), 70. There are reasons to doubt the representivity of respondents to this survey, but it still provides a rough indication. Http://www.glsen.org/cgi-bin/iowa/all/library/record/1927.html.

43  GLSEN, 'The 2001 National School Climate Survey' (New York, 2001), 31. Http://www.glsen.org/cgi-bin/iowa/all/library/record/827.html. Most of such classroom references were at least partially positive. There are reasons to doubt the representiveness of respondents to this survey, but it still provides an indication of more widespread curricular attention than exists in Canadian schools.

44  California, Iowa, Maine, Minnesota, and New Jersey included both sexual orientation and gender identity; Connecticut, Massachusetts, Vermont, Washington, and Wisconsin only sexual orientation.

45  Drawn in part from Barbara Rienzo et al., 'Sexual Orientation Issues in the Schools,' in *Culture War*.

46  Miceli, *Standing Out, Standing Together: The Social and Political Impact of Gay-Straight Alliances* (New York: Routledge, 2005), chap. 7. GLSEN's estimate can be found in its 2005 school climate study. The disparity is in part a product of GLSEN's admittedly imperfect survey method, but also of the tendency of GSAs to be in relatively large schools.

47  'Safer Sexual Diversity Climates.'

48  This is still happening; in North Carolina, the Rowan Salisbury School Board was preventing students from establishing a GSA. See 'GlSEN Deeply Concerned by Local School board Decision in North Carolina' (13 April 2006), http://www.glsen.org.

49  'School Board Oks Students' Gay-Straight Alliance' (14 February 2002, GLSEN news clippings).

50  Arthur S. Leonard, 'Okeechobee – Another Lesson in School Board

Incompetence,' Leonard Link blog, comment posted 8 April 2007, http://newyorklawschool.typepad.com/lenoardlink/2007.

51  The religiously conservative Alliance Defense Fund, in response, organized a 'Day of Truth,' with 340 schools reportedly taking part in 2005. See Michael Janofsky, 'Gay Rights Battlefields Spread to Public Schools,' *New York Times*, 9 June 2005. See also Seema Mehta, 'Gay Teens Are Using the System,' *Los Angeles Times*, 12 March 2006.

52  Laura Pappano, 'Support No Certainty for Gay Teachers,' *Boston Globe*, 9 November 2003.

53  Dawn Murray's school district (Oceanside, California) settled for $140,000 and a commitment to provide training on sexual orientation issues to board employees, in response to a suit claiming harassment and failure to promote because she was a lesbian. Another California case in the same year affirmed a teacher's right to speak out against homophobia as well as racism (*Debro v. San Leandro School District*). In 2003, Robert Visconti was awarded close to one hundred thousand dollars by a U.S. district court after being forced out of a teaching job in Hicksville, New York, because of his sexual orientation. In 2005, award-winning basketball coach Merry Stephens negotiated a settlement with her Texas school board, following its attempt to terminate her contract, her case supported by the National Center for Lesbian Rights, the National Education Association, and the Texas State Teacher's Association.

54  The latest is Joseph G. Kosciw and Elizabeth M. Diaz, 'The 2005 National School Climate Survey: The Experiences of Lesbian, Gay, Bisexual and Transgender Youth in our Nation's Schools,' http://www.glsen.org.

55  Research by Harrison Interactive, 'From Teasing to Torment: School Climate in America–A Report on School Bullying' (GLSEN, 2005), http://www.glsen.org.

56  'The Extent of Public Education Nondiscrimination Policy Protections for Lesbian, Gay, Bisexual, and Transgender Students: A National Study,' *Urban Education* 41 (March 2006): 115–50. The criteria that he draws from GLSEN in 'scoring' states are (1) guarantees of equality based on sexual orientation in non-discrimination polices; (2) creation of a safe environment (through codes of conduct, complaint procedure for discrimination, and investigation procedures for harassment claims); (3) provision of students with freedom to meet or form student groups; (4) provision of training to school staff in violence and suicide prevention: (5) provision of gay/lesbian-related resources in school libraries; (6) inclusion of gay/lesbian issues in school curricula; (7) support for GSA-like groups; (8) provision of access to appropriate health education and care. As is

evident here, the article does not cover bisexuality or transgenderism systematically.

57  Cianciotto and Cahill, *Education Policy*, 56.

58  Harris Interactive, 'From Teasing to Torment.'

59  A successful Republican candidate, Tom Coburn, for the House of Representatives in the 2004 election warned of rampant lesbianism in southern Oklahoma. See Ron Jenkins, 'GOP Senate Candidate in Oklahoma Speaks of "Rampant" Lesbianism in Schools,' *Associated Press*, 11 October 2004.

60  This is a point made by Eric Rofes in 'Martyr-Target-Victim: Interrogating Narratives of Persecution and Suffering Among Queer Youth,' in *Youth and Sexualities*, ed. Mary Louise Rasmussen, Eric Rofes, and Susan Talburt (New York: Palgrave, 2004), 41–62.

61  The average age of coming out in the United States (obviously only among those now out) is declining, and now stands at about the age of high school graduation. Ritch Savin-Williams may well overstate conclusions about how ordinary and well-adjusted gay/lesbian teens are, on the basis of a sample that is probably skewed in educational, class, and racial terms, though the general point about how many such teens are well adjusted remains valid. See *The New Gay Teenager* (Cambridge, MA: Harvard University Press, 2005).

62  *Standing Out*, chap. 7. There are relatively high proportions of high schools covered by GSAs in California, Massachesetts, New York, and Connecticut, and (in 2005) none reported in such states as Arkansas and Wyoming. About 12 per cent of urban schools have them; about 2 per cent of rural and town schools.

63  Arthur Lipkin, *Understanding Homosexuality*, 203.

### 10. Comparative Reflections on Public Recognition of Sexual Diversity

1  On attitudes, see Neil Nevitte, *Decline of Deference: Canadian Value Change in a Cross-National Perspective* (Peterborough, ON: Broadview Press, 1996); on legal developments, see Ran Hirschl, *Towards Juristocracy: The Origins and Consequences of the New Constitutionalism* (Cambridge, MA: Harvard University Press, 2004); on economic integration, see Stephen Clarkson, *Governing under Stress: Middle Powers and the Challenge of Globalization* (London: Zed, 2004) and *Uncle Sam and Us: Globalism, Neoconservatism, and the Canadian State* (Toronto: University of Toronto Press, 2002).

2  Seymour Martin Lipset is the most notable writer in this current, *The Continental Divide: The Values and Institutions of the United States and Canada* (London: Routledge, 1990). See also Louis Hartz, *The Founding of New*

*Societies: Studies in the History of the United States, Latin America, South Africa, Canada and Australia* (Orlando, FL: Harcourt, Brace and World, 1964); Gad Horowitz, 'Conservatism, Liberalism, and Socialism in Canada: An Interpretation,' *Canadian Journal of Economics and Political Science* 32, no. 2 (1966): 143–71; and more recently, Michael Adams, *Fire and Ice* (Toronto: Penguin Group, 2004).

3 Barry Adam, 'The Defense of Marriage Act and American Exceptionalism: The "Gay Marriage" Panic in the United States,' *Journal of the History of Sexuality* 12 (April 2003): 259–76; Dennis Altman, *The Homosexualization of America* (Boston: Beacon Press, 1983).

4 On European developments, see Yuval Merin, *Equality for Same-Sex Couples: The Legal Recognition of Gay Partnerships in Europe and the United States* (Chicago: University of Chicago Press, 2002); Kees Waldijk and Andrew Clapham, eds., *Homosexuality: A European Community Issue* (Boston: Martinus Nijhoff, 1993); and Kees Waaldijk and Matteo Bonini-Baraldi, *Sexual Orientation Discrimination in the European Union: National Laws and the Employment Equality Directive* (The Hague: Asser Press, 2006).

5 Kees Waaldijk and Matteo Bonini-Baraldi, 'Introduction,' and Matteo Bonini-Baraldi, 'European Law,' in *Sexual Orientation Discrimination in the European Union.*

6 Yuval Merin has pointed this out in *Equality for Same-Sex Couples*, chap. 8.

7 See ibid., chap. 3; and Martin Dupuis, *Same-Sex Marriage: Legal Mobilization, and the Politics of Rights* (New York: Peter Lang, 2002), 129.

8 The vote approving adoption rights passed Belgium's Senate by only a one-vote margin.

9 Based on news stories, and on Kees Waaldijk, 'Eight Major Steps in the Legal Recognition of Homosexual Orientation' (unpublished information sheet, 2006).

10 See, for example, 'Gay Adoption: True Stories,' *The Independent*, 25 January 2007.

11 U.S. Census Bureau, 'Families and Living Arrangements,' in the 2006 U.S. Census Report (March 2006), http://www.census.gov/population/www/socdemo/hh-fam.html.

12 Presentation at the International Conference on LGBT Human Rights, Montreal, July 2006.

13 Daniel Monk (University of London), presentation at the International Conference on LGBT Human Rights, Montreal, July 2006.

14 This was met with protests from such groups as Christian Voice and the Muslim Council of Britain. Laura Clark, 'Four-Year Olds Will Get Gay

Fairytales at School,' *Daily Mail,* 11 March 2007; and 'Primary School Kids in Gay Book Scheme' (12 March 2007), http://www.gay.com.

15  This is an assessment of Love Nordenmark (Lärarhögskolan, Stockholm), interview, July 2006.

16  John D'Emilio, 'Capitalism and Gay Identity,' in *Making Trouble: Essays on Gay History, Politics, and the University* (New York: Routledge, 1992), 3–16.

17  One particularly important outgrowth of this pattern is the extent to which American young people attend post-secondary institutions that are at a considerable geographic remove from home.

18  Jason Pierceson, *Courts, Liberalism and Rights: Gay Law and Politics in the United States and Canada* (Philadelphia: Temple University Press, 2005). Mezey points to the caution of most state and federal courts on the question of marriage, and to the more general pattern of courts moving in tune with societal consensus, but acknowledges that in some areas of discrimination state and lower federal courts have been expansive. See Susan Mezey, *Queers in Court: Gay Rights Law and Public Policy* (Lanham, MD: Rowman and Littlefield, 2007).

19  Robert Wintemute and Mads Andenaes, eds., *Legal Recognition of Same Sex Partnerships: A Study of National, European and International Law* (Oxford: Hart Publishing, 2001); Waaldijk, *Homosexuality;* Kenneth Wald, James Button, and Barbara Rienzo, 'The Politics of Gay Rights in American Communities: Explaining Anti-discrimination Ordinances and Policies,' *American Journal of Political Science* 40 (November 1996): 1152–78.

20  Merin, *Equality for Same-Sex Couples,* chap. 2.

21  Ibid., 258–61.

22  See, for example, Barry Adam, 'The Defense of Marriage Act'; Lee Badgett, 'Variations on an Equitable Theme: Explaining International Same-Sex Partner Recognition Laws,' in *Same-Sex Couples, Same-Sex Partnerships, and Homosexual Marriages: A Focus on Cross-National Differentials,* ed. Marie Digoix and Patrick Festy (Documents de travail, no. 124, Ined, 2004), 95–114; and contributions by Kees Waaldijk, 'Towards the Recognition of Same-Sex Partners in European Union Law,' 635–42, and Robert Wintemute, 'Strasbourg to the Rescue?' 113–32, in *Legal Recognition of Same-Sex Relationships in Europe* (Oxford: Hart Publishing, 2001).

23  Several analysts of gains and setbacks on sexual orientation issues in the United States talk of this as a crucial factor explaining variations across localities and states, including Kenneth Wald, James Button, and Barbara Rienzo, 'The Politics of Gay Rights in American Communities'; Donald Haider-Markel and Kenneth Meier, 'The Politics of Gay and Lesbian

Rights: Expanding the Scope of the Conflict,' *Journal of Politics* 58 (May 1996): 332–49; and Barry Adam, 'The Defense of Marriage Act.' Scott Barclay and Shauna Fisher, 'The States and the Differing Impetus for Divergent Paths on Same-Sex Marriage, 1990–2001,' *Policy Studies Journal* 31, no. 3 (2003): 331–52 downplay the role of religious conservatism, but do so in part as a result of a deeply flawed indicator.

24   19 January 2007.

25   *Fire and Ice*, 52.

26   Barry Adam makes this point, characterizing superpower states as gendered male in 'The Defense of Marriage Act.' I make a similar point in *On the Fringe: Gays and Lesbians in Politics* (Ithaca, NY: Cornell University Press, 1998), chap. 7. See also my own and other chapters in Craig Rimmerman, ed., *Gay Rights, Military Wrongs: Political Perspectives on Lesbians and Gays in the Military* (New York: Routledge, 1996).

27   Hirschl chronicles and analyses this trend, and sets it in comparative context, in several publications, including *Towards Juristocracy*, and 'Constitutional Rights Jurisprudence in Canada and the United States: Significant Convergence or Enduring Divergence?' in *Constitutional Politics in Canada and the United States*, ed. Stephen L. Newman (Albany: State University of New York Press, 2004), 63–88. Though not confident about the Canadian Supreme Court's readiness to consider group rights in expansive terms in the face of neo-liberal pressure, he portrays its current jurisprudence in stark contrast to the dominant currents in U.S. Supreme Court rulings.

28   This is a point also made by Barry Adam, 'The Defense of Marriage Act,' though he is more inclined to treat the focus on marriage as a choice among activists rather than driven in substantial part by policy inheritance.

29   Smith, 'The Politics of Same-Sex Marriage in Canada and the United States,' *PS: Political Science and Politics* 38 (April 2005): 225–8.

30   Some analyses of variation across American states agree that favourable public opinion is a factor in shifting public policy. See Donald Haider-Markel and Kenneth Meier, 'The Politics of Gay and Lesbian Rights: Expanding the Scope of the Conflict,' *Journal of Politics* 58 (May 1996): 332–49; Scott Barclay and Shauna Fisher, 'The States and the Differing Impetus for Divergent Paths on Same-Sex Marriage, 1990–2001,' *Policy Studies Journal* 31 (2003): 331–52.

31   See Adams, *Fire and Ice*, on the Canadian–American relationship.

32   Lee Badget finds a statistical relationship between rates of cohabition and such policy change. See 'Variations on an Equitable Theme: Explaining

International Same-Sex Partner Recognition Laws,' paper presented to the annual meeting of the American Political Science Association, Chicago, September 2004.

33 This is a theme in many classic and contemporary commentaries. See, for example, Lipset, *The Continental Divide*.

34 Reported in Adams, *Fire and Ice*, 66–7.

35 The record of the Netherlands and of most continental European countries is not outstanding on the recognition of ethnic and racial difference, and explicitly xenophobic political mobilizing has been a recurrent feature of electoral politics across the continent.

36 Arguments made in public talks during a visit to the University of Toronto, January 2007.

37 This seems at odds with Lee Badgett's analysis, which finds no significant relationship between leftist control of government and the policy recognition of same-sex relationships. I persist in my view, in part because her analysis took insufficient account of the complexities of coalition government, the shifts that have occurred in centrist parties as well as left or social democratic parties, and the influence on the overall political climate of long-term centre-left government. See Badgett, 'Variations on an Equitable Theme.'

38 See Wintemute, *Legal Recognition of Same Sex Partnerships*, and Waaldijk, *Homosexuality: A European Community Issue*.

39 Several authors point to the importance of early removal of criminalization, including Barry Adam, 'The Defense of Marriage Act,' and Miriam Smith, 'The Politics of Same-Sex Marriage in Canada and the United States.'

40 See Waaldijk, 'Levels of Legal Consequences of Marriage, Cohabitation and Registered Partnership for Different-Sex and Same-Sex Partners,' 88.

41 This is compatible with Lee Badget's analysis in 'Variations on an Equitable Theme.'

42 I have pursued this question in detail in 'Equity and Solidarity in Comparative Perspective,' chap. 9 in *Diversity, Solidarity, and Canadian Labour*, ed. Gerald Hunt and David Rayside (Toronto: University of Toronto Press, 2007). See also Gerald Hunt, ed., *Laboring for Rights* (Philadelphia: Temple University Press, 1999). Barry Adam agrees that the relative weakness of American labour has been a factor in slowing progress in the United States, in 'The Defense of Marriage Act.'

43 Yuval Merin makes this case in *Equality for Same-Sex Couples*, 46–7.

44 'Same-Sex Unions: The Globalization of an Idea,' *International Studies Quarterly* 51, no. 2 (2007): 329–57.

45  Merin, *Equality for Same Sex Couples*, 256.
46  Information gleaned from the Adoption Council of Canada, http://www.adoption.ca.
47  This point is made about the United States in Merin, *Equality for Same Sex Couples*, chap. 8.
48  In 2007, the Spanish legislature approved a measure to allow transsexuals to change their name and gender on official documents without necessarily having surgical intervention. Iceland enacted a similar measure in late 2006.

# Index